T. H. Green

T. H. Green

*Ethics, Metaphysics,
and Political Philosophy*

EDITED BY

Maria Dimova-Cookson and W. J. Mander

CLARENDON PRESS · OXFORD

192
G79zt

OXFORD
UNIVERSITY PRESS

Great Clarendon Street, Oxford OX2 6DP

Oxford University Press is a department of the University of Oxford.
It furthers the University's objective of excellence in research, scholarship,
and education by publishing worldwide in

Oxford New York

Auckland Cape Town Dar es Salaam Hong Kong Karachi
Kuala Lumpur Madrid Melbourne Mexico City Nairobi
New Delhi Shanghai Taipei Toronto

With offices in

Argentina Austria Brazil Chile Czech Republic France Greece
Guatemala Hungary Italy Japan Poland Portugal Singapore
South Korea Switzerland Thailand Turkey Ukraine Vietnam

Oxford is a registered trademark of Oxford University Press
in the UK and in certain other countries

Published in the United States
by Oxford University Press Inc., New York

© The several contributors 2006

British Library Cataloguing in Publication Data

Data available

Library of Congress Cataloging in Publication Data

Data available

Typeset by Laserwords Private Limited, Chennai, India
Printed in Great Britain
on acid-free paper by
Biddles Ltd., King's Lynn, Norfolk

ISBN 0–19–927166–6   978–0–19–927166–5

10 9 8 7 6 5 4 3 2 1

Acknowledgements

An earlier version of Gerald Gaus's article 'The Rights Recognition Thesis: Defending and Extending Green' appeared in a special issue of the *British Journal for Politics and International Relations* (February 2005).

An earlier Avital Simhony's article, under the title 'T. H. Green's Community of Rights: An Essay on the Complexity of Liberalism' appeared in the *Journal of Political Ideologies* (October 2003).

In both cases we would like to thank the editors and publishers for permission to reproduce material here.

Contents

A Note on References

Prolegomena to Ethics = *PE* followed by section number.
Lectures on the Principles of Political Obligation = *LPPO* followed by section number.
All other Green references use *Collected Works*, ed. Nicholson = *CW* followed by volume and page numbers.

List of Contributors

LESLIE ARMOUR is Research Professor of Philosophy at the Dominican College of Philosophy and Theology in Ottawa.

DAVID O. BRINK is Professor of Philosophy at the University of California, San Diego.

MARIA DIMOVA-COOKSON is a lecturer in the School of Government and International Affairs at Durham University.

GERALD F. GAUS is a Professor of Philosophy at the University of Arizona.

T. H. IRWIN is Susan Linn Sage Professor of Philosophy at Cornell University.

W. J. MANDER is a Fellow of Harris Manchester College, Oxford.

PETER NICHOLSON was Reader in the Department of Politics at the University York until his retirement in 2001.

AVITAL SIMHONY is Associate Professor in the Department of Politics at Arizona State University.

JOHN SKORUPSKI is Professor of Moral Philosophy at the University of St Andrews.

COLIN TYLER is Senior Lecturer in Political Theory at the University of Hull.

ANDREW VINCENT is Professor of Political Theory at the University of Sheffield.

1

Introduction

MARIA DIMOVA-COOKSON AND W. J. MANDER

In recent years there has been a growth of interest in the philosophy of T. H. Green, which, despite its once pre-eminent status, was in twentieth-century philosophical thinking almost wholly neglected. It is the aim of this volume both to reflect and to stimulate that process of rehabilitation. Offering the largest collection of papers to date on Green, it represents a significant expansion in scholarship on this most important of British Idealists, substantially advancing our knowledge of his philosophy.[1]

I.

There has always been a place for Green in the heart of British political philosophy. Green is the British Idealist who enjoys the warmest reception by the predominantly non-Idealist Anglo-American philosophical public. Even during the period between the Second World War and the 1980s when the popularity of Idealism reached its lowest point, Green was taken into consideration by a leading liberal like Isaiah Berlin. Yet Melvin Richter's monograph on Green published in 1964 presents an image of a charismatic and

---

[1] Reflecting the growth of interest in his philosophy, a recent new edition of the *Prolegomena to Ethics*, edited with an introduction by David Brink (Oxford: Clarendon Press, 2003), has once again made Green's key philosophical text widely available.

The papers in this volume have been presented and discussed at three conferences. Most are based on presentations at the conference 'T. H. Green and Contemporary Philosophy', Oxford, 2002. Others were given at the Political Studies Association of the United Kingdom (PSA) conferences in Aberdeen and Lincoln, in 2000 and 2004 respectively. Some papers, given as plenary talks, were followed by discussion papers, which in their turn have been taken into consideration in the final drafts. Many good papers on Green have not been included in the volume as they have already found their way into academic journals.

influential thinker who belonged to the past.[2] Richter argued that the strength
of Green's philosophy resided in its ability to resolve the intellectual crisis
experienced by those who had lost their Christian faith: Green provided new
philosophical justifications for moral beliefs. When this book was written, it
seemed it was the last return to Green. The 1980s, however, brought a revival
of the interest in T. H. Green scholarship.

The return to Green in the 1980s was caused by an interest in his social
ontology: his specific way of explaining why individuals are social beings.[3]
This return was an attempt to counterbalance the dominant influence of
liberalism. Later, in the context of the liberal-communitarian debate, Green
was seen as someone who offered a better form of communitarianism. What
made him particularly interesting was that his 'communitarian' ideas had liberal
underpinning. In the 1990s, Green's liberal-communitarian reconciliation
model was well noted.[4]

Green was also popular among those who looked for alternatives to Marxist
socialism. Indeed, his philosophy was seen as the theoretical basis of the ideas
of 'the third way'.[5] Over the Eighties and Nineties Green's name started to
appear increasingly in the discussions of rights, freedom, political obligation,
property, and punishment.[6] Such engagement with the basic issues in political
theory made him more familiar to political theorists than to philosophers in
general; however, with revived interest in perfectionism, self-realization, the
common good, and Kantian ethics, soon Green's presence began to be felt
in the field of moral philosophy also.[7] In consequence of this new higher
profile Green's overall world-view and his detailed writings have now begun

---

[2] Melvin Richter, *The Politics of Conscience: T. H. Green and his Age* (1964; repr. Bristol: Thoemmes Press, 1996).

[3] Andrew Vincent and Raymond Plant, *Philosophy, Politics, and Citizenship: The Life and Thought of the British Idealists* (Oxford: Blackwell, 1984).

[4] Avital Simhony and David Weinstein (eds.), *The New Liberalism Reconciling Liberty and Community* (Cambridge: Cambridge University Press, 2001).

[5] Matthew Carter, *T. H. Green and the Development of Ethical Socialism* (Exeter: Imprint Academic, 2003).

[6] Peter Nicholson, *The Political Philosophy of the British Idealists* (Cambridge: Cambridge University Press, 1990); Avital Simhony, 'On Forcing Individuals to be Free: T. H. Green's Liberal Theory of Positive Freedom', *Political Studies*, 39:2 (1991), 303–20; Colin Tyler, *Thomas Hill Green and the Philosophical Foundations of Politics: An Internal Critique* (Lewiston, NY: Edward Mellen Press, 1997); Maria Dimova-Cookson, *T. H. Green's Moral and Political Philosophy: A Phenomenological Perspective* (Basingstoke: Palgrave Press, 2001); Thom Brooks, 'T. H. Green's Theory of Punishment', *History of Political Thought*, 24:4 (2003), 685–702.

[7] David O. Brink, *Perfectionism and the Common Good: Themes in the Philosophy of T. H. Green* (Oxford: Clarendon Press, 2003); Geoffrey Thomas, *The Moral Philosophy of T. H. Green* (Oxford: Clarendon Press, 1987); Timothy Hinton, 'The Perfectionist Liberalism of T. H. Green', *Social Theory and Practice*, 27:3 (2001), 473–500; David Weinstein, 'Between Kantianism and Consequentialism in T. H. Green's Moral Philosophy', *Political Studies*, 41 (1993), 618–35.

to capture the attention of scholars, with even such once heretical themes as his concept of the eternal consciousness coming back to the fore.[8] This collection reflects Green's increased influence in the fields of moral philosophy and metaphysics.

The papers offered here fall into the three general sections, dealing with ethics, metaphysics, and political philosophy. There are four unifying themes running through the eleven essays that follow: (1) issues of ethics; (2) assessment of the eternal consciousness; (3) rights and (4) links between Green's ideas and contemporary political theory.

The first of these, ethics, receives most attention since nearly all of the papers make reference to Green's moral philosophy, discussing such themes as the role of moral philosophy, the link between personal good and moral normativity, and the originality of Green's thought in relation to that of the eighteenth-century British moralists. Andrew Vincent's paper discusses the impact of Idealist metaphysics on ethics and the implications this carries about the extent to which a moral philosopher can influence the dynamics of moral practice. John Skorupski and David Brink address the link between the personal and the common good. While Skorupski argues that the personal good does not provide sufficient grounds for moral normativity, Brink contends that the concept of self-realization is the basis for justifying the idea of the common good, and for explaining moral impartiality. Terence Irwin demonstrates that Green's insufficient attention to Shaftesbury and Butler prevented him from appreciating the extent to which they also developed non-empiricist and non-naturalist moral philosophies. Some of the papers which deal with Green's political philosophy also touch on important aspects of his moral philosophy, such as the link between his and the moral internalist position, and his strategies for resolving moral conflict.

The three papers on Green's metaphysics in this volume share the premiss that if we are attracted to Green's ethical and political ideas, we have no reason to be embarrassed by his doctrine of the eternal consciousness. They unanimously dismiss attempts to defend Green's philosophy by distancing it from its strongest metaphysical claims, yet they support the eternal consciousness from three different perspectives: sociological, theological, and metaphysical. Peter Nicholson draws attention to Green's project of developing a moral philosophy which is rational in character yet manages to retain important religious and poetic insights about morality. The claim is that Green needs

---

[8] Colin Tyler, 'The Much-Maligned and Misunderstood Eternal Consciousness', *Bradley Studies*, 9:2 (2003), 126–38; Maria Dimova-Cookson, 'The Eternal Consciousness: What Roles it Can and Cannot Play. A Reply to Colin Tyler', *Bradley Studies*, 9:2 (2003), 139–48.

the eternal consciousness in order to explain the possibility of non-naturalist ethics. Leslie Armour pursues the link between metaphysics and ethics, and offers a theological interpretation of the eternal consciousness along the lines of McTaggart's community of timeless loving spirits. William Mander concentrates wholly on issues of metaphysics, and offers a thorough defence of Green's doctrine of the eternal consciousness, in part by logically completing those aspects of the position which Green left vague.

Green's theory of rights has already been for some time the focus of academic attention,[9] and this volume offers two more valuable contributions to that debate. Gerald Gaus defends Green's strategy of justifying rights on the basis of social recognition. Gaus demonstrates that Green's rights recognition thesis represents a form of moral internalism, and thus is more in tune with contemporary metaethics than many contemporary rights theories. Gaus's defence of Green's moral internalism contrasts with Skorupski's externalist critique of Green, based on the claim that moral ideals (as introduced by Green) are optional, while moral duties are not. Avital Simhony considers the main communitarian concerns over human rights, and explains how Green's theory accommodates these concerns, because it contains notions of both negative and positive rights. Like Marx and Raz, Green argues that the apparent opposition between personal good and social well-being is something which may be transcended.

The fourth unifying theme of the volume is Green in the context of contemporary political theory: parallels are drawn between Green and contemporary republicanism, and between Green's and contemporary liberal strategies for resolving moral conflict. While much has been said about the link between Green's philosophy and the contemporary liberal-communitarian debate, Colin Tyler points out that the connection between Green's ideas and contemporary republicanism has received little attention. Tyler argues that Green advocates a form of republicanism that straddles the divide between its protective and civic humanist variants and shares the respective strengths of both. Maria Dimova-Cookson explains the different strategies for resolving moral conflict offered by Green, on the one hand, and Rawls and Nagel, on the other. She points out that the two parties have different understandings of moral action: whereas the contemporary liberals base it on our capacity for impartial reasoning, Green links it to our ability to make sacrifice.

---

[9] Rex Martin, 'T. H. Green on Individual Rights and Common Good', in Simhony and Weinstein (eds.), *New Liberalism Reconciling Liberty and Community*; Darin Nesbitt, 'Recognising Rights: Social Recognition in T. H. Green's System of Rights', *Polity*, 33:3 (2001), 423–37; Maria Dimova-Cookson, 'T. H. Green and Justifying Human Rights', *Collingwood and British Idealism Studies*, 7 (2000), 98–115.

II.

Despite the recent growth of interest in Green, he remains a figure largely unfamiliar to contemporary philosophers, and in the remainder of this introduction we offer a general account of his thought to serve as both foundation and context for the papers that follow.

Thomas Hill Green was born on 7 April 1836 in Birkin, not far from Pontefract in Yorkshire. Son of the local rector, his mother died when he was only a year old. His father subsequently remarried, and Thomas was brought up in a large family of seven children. He was educated at Rugby (1850–5) and Balliol College, Oxford (1855–9), where he studied classics, philosophy, law, and modern history. After graduating, he was appointed as a temporary lecturer at Balliol, teaching ancient and modern history until, in November 1860, he was elected to a College Fellowship, after which time he taught philosophy. In 1871 he married Charlotte Symonds, the sister of one of his undergraduate friends. They had no children. His influence in Balliol was great, not simply as a teacher, but also in his role of Senior Dean, where the high moral tone which he set served as an inspiration and stimulus to a whole generation of students. Nor was his influence felt in Balliol alone. It extended to the wider university, for example, in his support for Nonconformist colleges and women's colleges. And, most unusually for a don at that time, it was felt in the city itself as well. Noted for his involvement in the temperance movement (his brother was an alcoholic), in 1875 he set up a coffee tavern in the town, while in 1876 he was elected to the city council for the Liberals. In that capacity he was one of the leading figures behind the founding, in 1881, of the City of Oxford High School for Boys. In 1878 Green was appointed to the White's Chair in Moral Philosophy. He occupied this post until his sudden death from blood poisoning on 26 March 1882, aged only 45.

He published little in his lifetime: a handful of articles and a substantial introduction to an edition of Hume's *Philosophical Works* (1874) which he edited together with Thomas Grose, a contemporary tutor at Queen's College. All of his other major works—*Prolegomena to Ethics* (1883), *Principles of Political Obligation, Lectures on Logic and Lectures on Kant* (1885)—were published posthumously.

Green lived in the middle of the Victorian age—an era, not simply understood by historians, but genuinely felt by those who lived in it, as a period of great stress and change. Socially, the worst excesses of industrialization, urbanization, and Britain's largely unreformed class and political system were becoming only too apparent to anyone with a conscience; while intellectually, the discoveries of geology, Darwin's evolutionary theory, the higher criticism of the Bible, and the general prospect of a purely scientific study of man all combined together to worry and challenge once-settled religious and moral conceptions. As exercised by these problems as anyone in his age, Green was in the progressive movement with regards to how best they might be dealt with. He was, moreover, committed to the belief that only through reason could a solution be found; pushing further on, rational thought alone had the power to heal the wounds it had first opened up. In this respect Green was neither a theologian nor a classicist, but arguably the first professional philosopher.[10]

The philosophy of T. H. Green had an immense influence. He gave the lead to a generation of philosophers, and was the principal inspiration behind the British Idealist movement, which dominated philosophy until the turn of the century and remained active up to the 1920s. Much of his impact was personal, through his students, such as F. H. Bradley, A. C. Bradley, Bernard Bosanquet, and D. G. Ritchie, who went on to make important philosophical contributions of their own, but his books became required reading, the starting-point for everyone else. The influence of Green's philosophy was not confined to philosophical circles. It extended into social and political fields. Collingwood, in his *Autobiography*, wrote that Green sent out 'a stream of ex-pupils who carried with them the conviction that philosophy, and in particular the philosophy they had learned in Oxford, was an important thing and that their vocation was to put it into practice'.[11] This impact extended from such specific and practical matters as the setting up of University Settlements to more general and abstract spheres as the development in Britain of socialism itself. Green's philosophy was influential also in religious spheres. In professional circles, theologians such as Scott Holland and J. R. Illingworth were much inspired; while at a more popular level, the novel *Robert Elsemere*, essentially a fictionalized account of an ordinary person's crisis of faith as he engages with Green's religious view, was a runaway success precisely because its theme expressed the feelings of a generation. Nor was his influence limited to purely intellectual circles. The city of Oxford itself took Green to its heart as it has no other member of its university, and when he died, the Mayor and Corporation, together with 2,000 people, processed (through torrential rain) from the council chambers to Balliol and thence to the St Sepulchre's Cemetery, where he was buried.

---

[10] That is to say, he conceived his subject as quite autonomous, and one requiring specialist training on the part of those who taught it (Richter, *Politics of Conscience*, 140).

[11] R. G. Collingwood, *An Autobiography* (Oxford: Oxford University Press, 1939), 17.

III.

The ideas of such figures as Darwin, Mill, or Comte, which in their various different ways posed such intellectual challenges to conventional thinking about moral, political, and religious matters, share in common the belief that there can be a purely scientific study of man. But this very starting-point, thought Green, is where they go wrong; the methods of the natural sciences are wholly different from those of the moral sciences. In order to establish this, in order to make room to develop his own theory by clearing the ground of rivals, Green focuses on one specific aspect of human life—knowledge—and attempts to demonstrate that our knowledge of nature could never itself be a part or product of nature.

Green's argument is simple. Knowledge involves relations: that is to say, system or structure. For what is the difference between those experiences we deem knowledge and those we classify as merely dream, error, or illusion other than that the former may be fitted into a system of unalterable relations? Yet all relation, Green argues, is the work of the mind. Particulars may be given, but the connections between them must be made. Indeed, we could not even grasp particular sensations without relations to individuate them—the latter are the key which make possible our experience of the former, and in that sense even produce them. The point holds generally, but Green best illustrates it with respect to the relation of succession. Succession is not given, for no sequence of experiences can yield experience of sequence; rather, the relation must be one added to the sequence by a conscious agent itself outside the time series. Green concludes that the empiricist model of knowledge is inadequate, that there is more to our experience of the world than simply what we can sense. Thought too is required. But if the world we experience exists only for our thought, the same can hardly be said for the world as a whole—for it is something far wider than anything any finite being will or even might experience. Green concludes that, as we stand to our world, so there must exist some conscious principle analogous to our thought which grounds and unifies the world itself. A kind of world-consciousness in which resides everything that there is, this principle he terms the 'eternal consciousness'. In so far as human knowledge grows, it may be thought of as gradually reproducing itself in us; or, to look at the same movement from the other side, we may be thought of as coming gradually to participate in it.

With respect to this argument it is clear that Green's greatest debt is to Kant. It represents his understanding of Kant's argument in the Transcendental Deduction that experience is not a chaotic manifold, but something ordered and related by an enduring transcendental subject. But for Green, unlike Kant, there exists nothing outside the phenomenology of this analysis; no separate world of things-in-themselves causing the manifold, and no separate noumenal self adding or imposing the relational structures. For Green, Kant's unity of apperception *is* the self.

Green's general argument for the eternal consciousness occasioned many puzzles and objections—several of which are considered in the papers of this volume—for the claim that knowledge cannot be dealt with empirically is a strange one. How, we might ask, can it be squared with the fact that we manifestly can conduct empirical investigation into, say, sight or hearing? Since Green never denies that knowledge takes place through the medium of physical stimulus, there would be no need for him to outlaw such studies, but he would have to hold that they were not studies of perception or experience *per se*, but simply of the physiological phenomena associated with them. This answer is perhaps consistent, but renders most pressing the puzzle of how these two realms—the physical and the cognitive—stand one to another. This problem becomes even more acute as Green's overall argument advances to its next stage: that is, to the theory of freedom which he builds upon the doctrine of the eternal consciousness.

The result so far is one about knowledge, and has no immediate significance for action. But Green goes on to argue that just as naturalism is unable to explain knowledge, so it is also unable to explain conscious purposive action. For in so far as we are conscious, we are free. '[I]n respect of that principle through which [a person] at once is a self and distinguishes himself as such, he exerts a free activity,—an activity which is not in time, not a link in the natural chain of becoming, which has no antecedents other than itself but is self-originated' (*PE* §82). Actions which are free in this sense are not undetermined *per se*, but they are undetermined by prior natural forces such as desire. For desire in so far as it is conceived in consciousness becomes motive, as the self posits some object which would satisfy the desire, but to explain something by motive or reason is to understand it teleologically, in terms of its final as opposed to its efficient cause. Yet, as before with respect to knowledge, a deep puzzle remains as to how this world of 'free' actions relates to the causal world which underlies and indeed expresses it.

IV.

Human agency then, is to be explained in terms of motive rather than desire. Unlike the mere animal pushed from behind by some want, desire, or impulse, human beings, because they are self-conscious, have the capacity in thought to transcend both the present and the actual and to look forward to possible future states, thereby creating for themselves ends which they then endeavour to bring about.

Green goes on to argue that the motive determining an agent's will is always an idealized future state of his own self, a conception of himself as satisfied—whatever it may be that he seeks. For this reason, argues Green, moral action is 'the process of self-realisation, i.e. of making a possible self real'.[12] In historical terms, Green's arrival at the formula of self-realization represents an important shift in ethical thinking. Instead of asking with the utilitarian, intuitionist, and even the Kantian philosophers of the day, 'What ought I to do?', Green and the many Idealists who followed him re-construed ethical inquiry in the mould of an older question, 'What kind of person ought I to be?'.

But what leads Green to this formula? The answer is not wholly clear. At times the derivation seems a trivial one, amounting to no more than the claim that, whatever we want, in wanting it we necessarily want also a state in which our own wanting is satisfied. In this sense it amounts to more than the claim that the act is a self-conscious or deliberate one. At other times, however, Green seems to be asserting a stronger thesis equivalent to some type of psychological egoism. He says that self-reflection reveals to us that the only desire possible is for our own personal good in some form or other (PE §§91, 95): that unless an act was for the agent's own good (however we may go on to construe that notion), he would simply have no reason to perform it.

There are, of course, a great many things which we might desire for ourselves. But it is notorious that not everything we want is really in our own best interests. And what we want today, we may grow out of tomorrow. Green introduces the notion of what he calls the true good, which he describes as 'an end in which the effort of a moral agent can really find rest' (PE §171), 'an abiding satisfaction of an abiding self' (PE §234). The true or unconditional good is thus that which fulfils the agent's desire for long-term satisfaction on the whole. Linking with Green's theme of moral and cognitive growth, it is what would satisfy us in our fullest development.

But what would such a good be? One of the most interesting aspects of Green's moral philosophy is his claim that this cannot be known. The moral ideal amounts to the complete realization or perfection of human capacities, but since these have never yet been perfectly realized, we cannot now properly say what this would amount to. Green's moral theory is a species of ideal or perfectionist ethics, but since our moral understanding stands in need of

---

[12] 'The World is Nigh Thee' (CW iii. 224).

development just as much as our moral nature itself, a measure of ignorance is, he concludes, unavoidable.

But fortunately we are able to venture a few pointers towards the nature of true good. Some of these Green thought we could learn by looking at actual historical moral developments, such as—less than twenty years before he wrote—the abolition of slavery. Others he thought self-evidently the case: for instance, that it consists in the intrinsic development of human capacities and not the external receipt of good fortune (*PE* §246), or that it gives to human beings an intrinsic value not absorbed in anything else (*PE* §189).

V.

Most importantly of all, Green holds that the true good is a common or social good. Transforming his earlier egoism into something almost directly its opposite, Green argues that while it is indeed true that the moral ideal is one of personal development and that the only possible motive for action is the attainment of personal good, it needs to be recognized that people are fundamentally social creatures, and hence that our true personal good properly understood turns out to be social good. To pursue a selfish life is to misunderstand one's own true nature, and hence where one's own true happiness lies. 'The perfection of human character—a perfection of individuals which is also that of society, and of society which is also that of individuals—is for man the only object of absolute or intrinsic value .... this perfection consisting in a fulfilment of man's capabilities according to the divine idea or plan of them' (*PE* §247). The theory of the common good thus gives a distinctive twist to Green's account. According to it, in the same way as we carry a vision and a will for a better self, we carry also interests in the good of other persons, 'interests which cannot be satisfied without the consciousness that those other persons are satisfied' (*PE* §199). Green calls this a 'distinctive social interest' (*PE* §200), and he views it as a permanent feature of human nature, not simply enlightened self-interest or the result of some process of evolution from earlier stages in which men were less civilized. The common good helps Green to define the moral ideal substantively, providing content to what would otherwise remain a merely formal notion.

The notion that the true good for each one of us is something social, and thus that there is ultimately no conflict between self-directed and other-directed concern has, not surprisingly, been a focus of much discussion. Several of the papers in this volume consider it. For while there can be no doubt about

Green's position on this matter—'society is the condition of the development of personality', he insists—his own argument for, and development of, this theme leave much to be desired. Indeed, the near universal acceptance by subsequent Idealists of Green's thesis of the fundamentally social nature of the self certainly owes more to F. H. Bradley's carefully argued case for it in his *Ethical Studies* (1876) than to Green's own sketch of the idea in the *Prolegomena*.

Green's common good has been widely read as expressing the idea that social well-being overrides personal freedom, and, as such, the doctrine did not enjoy much popularity throughout the greater part of the twentieth century. However, since the 1980s, communitarian and republican theories have revived interest in the common good, and some recent attempts to reconcile liberalism and communitarianism have worked to restore its credibility and its position as a key concept in political theory.

One of the reasons why Green's theory of the common good has always been a focus of attention (and contention) is that it delivers a number of different messages: for example, the ideas that human nature is social, that the true good is to be found in some form of social activity, and that we should seek the good in objects that do not allow of being competed for. Each of these messages is important in its own right, but each of them can be, and often has been, contested.

The theory of the common good is about the priority of the social good over the private good, and this can be contested from a liberal point of view. But when it is made clear that the purpose of the common good is to explain moral agency, and moral agency is displayed in one's capacity for 'distinctive social interest'—the message becomes less controversial. In the context of moral behaviour, exclusively personal interests give way to interests in joint well-being. In the same way as 'distinctive social interest' is fundamentally different from self-interest, so moral behaviour is different from general behaviour. In its proper context—Green's moral theory—the concept of the common good conveys a universal message.

VI.

Moving from moral to political philosophy, Green's central concept is that of the State, which he holds needs to be understood in terms of its goal, or *telos*, rather than its origin or form. He regards the state as an instrument for the moralization of man—it 'is an institution for the promotion of the common good' (*LPPO* §124)—and all of its powers and legitimate functions as well as its success or failure need to be understood in these terms. The State, of course, cannot *make* us good, since an act is only good when done for the sake of its own goodness. Thus the State, for all its moral ambitions, is limited to setting the right conditions for, and removing hindrances to, moral growth. With respect to its legitimacy or warrant, Green rejects the view that this is the result of a *social contract* (*LPPO* §55), locating its foundation rather in the general will: that is, the wills of individuals as directed by reason to the true or common good. It is in the context of a State thus understood that what Green has to say about obligation, rights, and freedom all needs to be read.

Green argued that citizens have a duty to the State, but the basis of this obligation to obey the laws of the State is neither fear nor mere expediency, but man's moral obligation to avoid those actions which are incompatible with the attainment of his moral end. For Green political obligation is owed to any State which embodies (through a system of publicly promulgated laws) and promotes the common good of the society. But the duty of good citizenship is not 'an obligation under all conditions to conform to the law of his state, since those laws may be inconsistent with the true end of the state, as the sustainer and harmoniser of social relations' (*LPPO* §143). Green thus allows to individuals the duty to resist a bad State.

The State also provides the basis of our rights. These attach to individuals, but only in so far as they are members of a society (*LPPO* §138). Green attacks the natural rights tradition of Hobbes, Locke, and Spinoza, arguing that it neglects the fact that human identity (including its values and meanings) is itself derived from society. Rights concern what is required for moral development—'the claim or right of the individual to have certain powers secured to him by society, and the counter-claim of society to exercise certain powers over the individual, alike rest on the fact that these powers are necessary to the fulfilment of man's vocation as a moral being' (*LPPO* §21). The vocation in question is, of course, a common and not just an individual good, which in turn means that the right, to be real, must be recognized by society (although not necessarily by the state). 'There can be no right without a consciousness of common interest on the part of members of a society', insists Green (*LPPO* §31). It is precisely the recognition (which can be either implicit or explicit) that a particular activity contributes to or is essential for the good in which they all share, that makes it a right.

The state too is essential for freedom. In *On the Different Senses of 'Freedom'* he distinguishes between three distinct senses of freedom: (1) freedom of the will, (2) 'the juristic sense of the power to "do what one wills"' or the 'exemption from compulsion by others', and (3) what he calls 'real freedom' (*CW* ii. 315, 309, 308) or 'freedom in the positive sense'. This last, which he describes as 'the positive power or capacity of doing or enjoying something worth doing or enjoying' (*CW* iii. 372, 370–1), Green regards as a condition in which the will is determined by an object adequate to itself, and as such it necessarily involves the common good. For this reason, it is not a freedom which may be enjoyed by one person in isolation from or at the expense of others, although the State may be entitled to limit some lesser freedoms of individuals in order to help bring it about. In this way Green champions the claims of the destitute and oppressed to 'such positive help ... as is needed to make their freedom real' (*PE* §270). Going beyond the classical liberal notion of freedom into realms of possible interference, positive freedom is one of Green's most controversial legacies to the field of political theory, but it too has seen something of a revival in recent years.

Green's philosophy will certainly never enjoy the popularity and unquestioning dominance it once enjoyed, for it is very much a product of the late Victorian era from which it emerged, and thought never goes backwards. But as we move out of the long period of almost total rejection which was the lot of British Idealism in the twentieth century—perhaps the inevitable fate of all once-popular doctrines—it is becoming possible again to assign to Green a position in our intellectual heritage which recognizes his permanent value and contribution to philosophical thought.

PART I
Ethics

2

Self-Realization and the Common Good: Themes in T. H. Green

DAVID O. BRINK

T. H. Green's *Prolegomena to Ethics* develops a perfectionist ethical theory that aims to bring together the best elements in the ancient and modern traditions.[1] Green was heavily influenced by the Greek eudaimonist tradition in ethics, especially by the views of Plato and Aristotle. He thought the Greeks were right to ground an agent's duties in a conception of his own good whose principal ingredient is the exercise of his rational or deliberative capacities. Green interprets this aspect of eudaimonism in terms of self-realization. Like Aristotle, he thinks that the proper conception of the agent's own good requires a concern with the good of others, especially the common good. However, Green thought that the Greeks had too narrow a conception of the common good. It is only with Christianity and Enlightenment philosophical views, especially Kantian and utilitarian traditions in ethics, Green thinks, that we have recognition of the universal scope of the common good. This leads Green to claim that full self-realization can take place only when each rational agent regards all other rational agents as ends in themselves on whom his own

Earlier versions of this paper were presented at the universities of Michigan, Southern California, and Wisconsin, at the 2000 International Society for Utilitarian Studies at Wake Forest University, and at the 2002 conference on 'T. H. Green and Contemporary Philosophy' at Harris Manchester College, Oxford University. I would like to thank audiences on those occasions for helpful discussion. This material was subsequently incorporated into a larger study of Green's ethical thought: David O. Brink, *Perfectionism and the Common Good: Themes in the Philosophy of T. H. Green* (Oxford: Clarendon Press, 2003).

[1] All parenthetical references to the *Prolegomena* are to section numbers in T. H. Green, *Prolegomena to Ethics* (originally published in 1883), ed. D. O. Brink (Oxford: Clarendon Press, 2003). Parenthetical references to the *Collected Works of T. H. Green*, ed. P. Nicholson (Bristol: Thoemmes Press, 1997) will be by volume and page number.

happiness depends; in such a state, there can be no conflict or competition among the interests of different rational agents (*PE* §§191, 200, 232, 244, 376).

However inspiring, these claims about self-realization and the common good are rather extraordinary. To assess them, we must understand Green's perfectionism, the role of the common good in self-realization, and the way in which Green's idealism supports his reconciliation of the agent's own good and the good of others. My reconstruction of these issues will appeal in part to Aristotle's claims about *eudaimonia*, friendship, and the common good, on which Green's own views about self-realization and the common good draw.

I. Self-Consciousness and Responsibility

Green's ethics of self-realization depends on his understanding of the role of self-consciousness in responsible action.[2] Though it is common to think that moral responsibility is threatened by determinism and requires indeterminism, Green denies this. Indeed, he thinks that indeterminism is a greater threat to responsibility, inasmuch as it is unclear why we should hold a person accountable for actions that are not produced by his character (*PE* §110; *CW* ii. 108–9). Responsibility neither is threatened by determinism nor requires indeterminism; it requires self-consciousness (*PE* §§87, 90, 106, 109–10). Moral responsibility requires capacities for practical deliberation, and practical deliberation requires self-consciousness. Non-responsible agents, such as brutes and small children, appear to act on their strongest desires, or, if they deliberate, to deliberate only about the instrumental means to the satisfaction of their desires (*PE* §§86, 92, 96, 122, 125). By contrast, responsible agents must be able to distinguish between the *intensity* and the *authority* of their desires, to deliberate about the appropriateness of their desires and aims, and to regulate their actions in accord with these deliberations (*PE* §§92, 96, 103, 107, 220). Here, as elsewhere, Green shows the influence of a long tradition of thinking about agency that extends back to the Greeks and is given forceful articulation by moderns, such as Butler, Reid, and Kant.[3] This requires that one be able

---

[2] My own account of these matters is indebted to Terence Irwin, 'Morality and Personality: Kant and Green', in A. Wood (ed.), *Self and Nature in Kant's Philosophy* (Ithaca, NY: Cornell University Press, 1984).

[3] Cf. Plato, *Republic* 437e–442c; Aristotle, *De Anima*, book ii, ch. 2, and *Nicomachean Ethics* 1102^{b}13–1103^{a}3, 1111^{b}5–1113^{a}14; Cicero, *De Officiis*, book i, §11; Bishop Joseph Butler, *Fifteen Sermons Preached at the Rolls Chapel*, Sermon I, para. 8; Sermon II. paras. 12–15; Thomas Reid, *Essays on the Active Powers of the Human Mind*, essay ii, ch. 2; and Immanuel Kant, *Groundwork for the Metaphysics of Morals*, 396, 437, 448; *Critique of Pure Reason*, A534/B562, A553–4/B581–2, A802/B830; *Critique of Practical Reason*, 61–2, 87 (Prussian Academy pagination).

to distinguish oneself from particular desires and impulses—to distance oneself from them—and to be able to frame the question about what it would be best for one on the whole to do (*PE* §§85– 6).

Green thinks that the process of forming and acting on a conception of what it is best for me on the whole to do is for me to form and act from a conception of my own overall good (*PE* §§91–2, 96, 128).

A man, we will suppose, is acted on at once by an impulse to revenge an affront, by a bodily want, by a call of duty, and by fear of certain results incidental to his avenging the affront or obeying the call of duty. We will suppose further that each passion ... suggests a different line of action. So long as he is undecided how to act, all are, in a way, external to him. He presents them to himself as influences by which he is consciously affected but which are not he, and with none of which he yet identifies himself .... So long as this state of things continues, no moral effect ensues. It ensues when the man's relation to these influences is altered by his identifying himself with one of them, by his taking the object of one of them as for the time his good. This is to *will*, and is in itself moral action. (*PE* §146)

In claiming that a moral effect ensues just in case the agent reflectively endorses his appetites, Green is not saying that reflective endorsement is sufficient for morally good action; rather, that it is sufficient for morally assessable or responsible action (*PE* §§95, 115). In fact, it is not clear that he means to say that action is responsible only when it is the product of reflective endorsement. Presumably, we want to hold people responsible for those actions for which they had the capacity for reflective endorsement (cf. *PE* §154).

So responsibility or moral agency requires deliberative self-government, and this requires self-consciousness, where self-consciousness involves the ability to represent these different impulses as parts of a single psychological system and recognition of the self as extended in time and endowed with deliberative capacities (*PE* §220). And because Green believes that what is not itself an element of consciousness is non-natural (*PE* §§32, 51–4, 65), he appears to agree with Kant that responsibility presupposes non-naturalism, even if his reasons for accepting non-naturalism are somewhat different (*PE* §§87, 90; cf. *CW* ii. 110–11). It is in this way that responsibility presupposes deliberative self-government, self-consciousness, and non-naturalism, rather than indeterminism.[4]

Green considers the apparent threat to responsibility resulting from the claim that agents necessarily act on their strongest desires (*PE* §§103–6, 139–42).

---

[4] Green does discuss the relationship between the self and its desires, and seems to claim that the self is distinct from, but not independent of, its desires (*PE* §§100–1). This might be true if the desires were parts of the self, but the self also includes deliberative faculties that assess and select desires.

He thinks that the threat is specious, because it rests on an ambiguity. The intensity of some desires is stronger than that of others; their force is stronger. The action of non-responsible animals is just the vector sum of these forces; they do act on their strongest desires, in this sense. But responsible agents, who can distinguish between the strength or intensity of a desire and its authority and act on these judgements, need not act on their strongest desire. Green associates regulation of one's actions by such deliberations with strength of character, and claims that strength of character can overcome strength of desire. But strength of character, Green thinks, is no threat to responsibility; rather, it is a pre-condition of it. It is only by failing to distinguish between these two different kinds of strength, Green thinks, that one could see a threat to responsibility here. Another way to put Green's point is this. The claim that one must act according to one's strongest desire either (a) associates strength of desire with its felt intensity or (b) associates it with whatever desires move one to act after due deliberation. On the (a) reading, the alleged necessity of acting on one's strongest desires would threaten responsibility, but is false; whereas on the (b) reading, the alleged necessity is trivially true, but no threat to responsibility.

II. Against Hedonism

Green claims that the responsible agent acts not simply on appetites or passions but as the result of 'ought' judgements or in light of a conception of goods. But he also says that the deliberating agent takes the object of reflectively endorsed desire as his own good (*PE* §§91–2)—indeed, his own greatest good (*PE* §§96, 128)—and that he aims at 'self-satisfaction' (*PE* §§89, 104).

We may wonder why pursuit of goods or the good has to be understood as pursuit of the agent's own good. My responsible actions may express my choices, commitments, and conception of the good. But why should I think that pursuing or achieving my conception of the good promotes my own interests? Isn't this a confusion of the *ownership* and the *content* of my aims? Green thinks of pre-deliberative desires as 'alien' or 'other', and he regards deliberative endorsement as a process of 'identification' (*PE* §146). The objects of deliberative endorsement reflect my sometimes deeply held convictions about what is worthwhile, which will reflect how I think of myself and how I value myself. He seems to believe that I cannot separate thinking that a course of action is worthwhile for me to do and thinking that it is better for me to act that way. There is some force to this line of reasoning, but we may wonder if it doesn't make the pursuit of a good or the good prior in explanation to pursuit of a personal good.

Book II offers us an account of responsibility—common to both a good will and a bad will—in terms of the deliberative capacities of a self-conscious mind. But, as Green recognizes, this does not provide an account of the good will or of what distinguishes the good and bad wills (*PE* §154). The quality of a person's will depends upon the *content* of her will, the objects in which she seeks self-satisfaction (*PE* §154).

Green spends considerable time explaining what the good is *not*. In particular, he is very concerned to reject the hedonism that he finds in the utilitarian tradition and that he associates with a naturalistic approach to ethics (*PE* §§2, 8). Green interprets Mill as a hedonist, and focuses his criticism of hedonism on Mill's claims in *Utilitarianism*. Green's criticisms of Mill are quite interesting, and often quite subtle and probative, defying easy summary.[5] One of Green's main complaints is that the plausibility of evaluative hedonism rests on a commitment (perhaps implicit) to psychological hedonism, which rests on the fallacy, which Butler exposed, of inferring that pleasure is the object of desire from the fact that it is expected that pleasure will attend the satisfaction of desire.

Green thinks that psychological hedonism is prima facie implausible; it seems that we pursue many things other than our own pleasure, and often at the expense of our own pleasure (*PE* §159). But, on reflection, this apparent evidence against psychological hedonism may not seem compelling. After all, it seems that we always expect pleasure from the satisfaction of our desires, and that the anticipation of this pleasure can make us desire it (*PE* §157). Butler thought that this defence of psychological hedonism was fallacious.

That all particular appetites and passions are toward *external things themselves*, distinct from the *pleasure arising from them*, is manifested from hence—that there could not be this pleasure were it not for that prior suitableness between the object and the passion; there could be no enjoyment or delight from one thing more than another, from eating food more than swallowing a stone, if there were not an affection or appetite to one thing more than another.[6]

---

[5] Green's critical discussion of Mill focuses on the doctrine of higher pleasures (*Utilitarianism* (Indianapolis: Bobbs-Merrill, 1957), ch. 2) and the 'proof' of the principle of utility (*Utilitarianism*, ch. iv). In both cases, Green identifies things Mill says about value (e.g. the higher pleasures doctrine) or desire (the claim that we desire virtue for its own sake) that appear to be incompatible with hedonism and explains Mill's failure to see the inconsistency by appeal to the hypothesis that Mill fallaciously inferred that pleasure is the object of desire from the fact that pleasure is expected to attend the satisfaction of desire. Whatever the interest and merits of Green's criticisms of Mill's (alleged) hedonism, it is unfortunate that Green does not do justice to the perfectionist elements in Mill's ethical and political views or acknowledge the similarities between these aspects of Mill's thought and his own perfectionist ethical and political views.

[6] Butler, *Fifteen Sermons*, xi. 6.

Butler's point is that it is a fallacy to suppose that we aim at the pleasure that we expect to accompany the satisfaction of our desires (*PE* §158). The pleasure in getting x (P1) is predicated on the prior desire for x (D1); the desire is not predicated on that pleasure. And even if the anticipation of P1 produces a new desire for x (D2), that gives no reason to think that the original desire for x (D1) is predicated on the expectation of pleasure.

As I think Butler recognizes, and as Green clearly does, exposure of this fallacy does not imply that psychological hedonism is false; rather, it undermines one common source of support for that doctrine (*PE* §§158, 169). Butler's point is that pleasure depends upon the satisfaction of desires for various things. But this point does not show that we do not desire these things on account of their (expected) pleasurableness. If we distinguish between *ultimate* and *proximate* objects of desire, we can admit Butler's point and still claim that pleasure is the only ultimate object of desire or, in Green's terms, the only thing desired intrinsically or for its own sake. However, Green thinks that when this claim is clearly identified and stripped of fallacious defences, it will seem implausible. Life is replete with examples of people choosing worthy courses despite the expectation of securing the lesser pleasure (*PE* §159).[7]

So Green thinks that Mill's evaluative hedonism rests on a fallacious defence of psychological hedonism (*PE* §221). But he also wants to reject evaluative hedonism outright. One argument he makes is that evaluative hedonism is actually inconsistent with psychological hedonism. Evaluative hedonism says that our ultimate aim ought to be to maximize net pleasure or to seek the largest sum of pleasures, whereas psychological hedonism claims that pleasurable experience is the ultimate object of desire. But a sum of pleasures is not itself a pleasure, and so, according to psychological hedonism, we could not act on the requirements of evaluative hedonism (*PE* §221). This is a problem for someone who combines both evaluative and psychological hedonisms.[8]

III. Self-Realization as the Good

Green wants to argue not only against hedonism but also for self-realization. He suggests that it is the very capacities that make moral responsibility possible in the first place that determine the proper end of deliberation (*PE* §176).

---

[7] This is one of many points on which Green's view bears comparison with Bradley's. While both are critical of psychological egoism, and, in particular, psychological hedonism, Green's discussion is clearer, more sympathetic, and more trenchant than Bradley's. See F. H. Bradley, *Ethical Studies* (originally published 1876) 2nd edn. (Oxford: Clarendon Press, 1927), 252–62.

[8] However, this is not a problem for the sort of evaluative hedonist, such as Sidgwick, who eschews psychological hedonism (*PE* §222). Green must offer some other argument against the person who thinks that a self-conscious agent would identify his personal good with pleasure.

Responsible action involves self-consciousness and is expressive of the self. The self is not to be identified with any desire or any series or set of desires; moral personality consists in the ability to subject appetites and desires to a process of deliberative endorsement and to form new desires as the result of such deliberations. So the self essentially includes deliberative capacities, and if responsible action expresses the self, it must exercise these deliberative capacities that are essential to the self. This explains why Green thinks that the proper aim of deliberation is a life of activities that embody rational or deliberative control of thought and action (*PE* §§175, 180, 199, 234, 238–9, 247, 283).

One can ask about any conception of the good why one should care about the good, so conceived. Why should the good, so conceived, be normative? Green's defence of self-realization makes the content of the good consist in the exercise of the very same capacities that make one a rational agent in the first place. This promises to explain why a rational agent should care about the good conceived in terms of self-realization.

This justification of self-realization also explains why Green treats the imperative of self-realization as a categorical imperative. Like Kant, Green seeks an account of the agent's duties that is grounded in her agency and does not depend upon contingent and variable inclinations. The goal of self-realization, Green thinks, meets this demand.

At the same time, because it [self-realization] is the fulfilment of himself, of that which he has in him to be, it will excite an interest in him like no other interest, different in kind from any of his desires and aversions except such as are derived from it. It will be an interest as in an object conceived to be of unconditional value; one of which the value does not depend on any desire that the individual may at any time feel for it or for anything else, or on any pleasure that ... he may experience. On the contrary, the desire for the object will be founded on a conception of its desirableness as a fulfilment of the capabilities of which a man is conscious in being conscious of himself. ... Self-realization will express itself in [the] imposition ... of rules requiring something to be done irrespectively of any inclination to do it, irrespectively of any desired end to which it is a means, *other than this end, which is desired because conceived as absolutely desirable.* (*PE* §193)

Because the demands of self-realization depend only on those very deliberative capacities that make one a responsible agent, they are categorical imperatives.

Green recognizes that his conception of the good in terms of self-realization, perfection, or the exercise of deliberative capacities is abstract and perhaps vague in comparison with the apparent definiteness of the hedonist's conception of the good (*PE* §193). Moreover, he thinks that one is unable to specify fully the content of self-realization independently of its embodiment (*PE* §193).

This claim may reflect Hegelian themes about the form of an individual's good being historically conditioned. It may also reflect the more familiar ideas that the perfection of one's capacities is an ideal that one can at most hope to approximate and that any conception of perfection by imperfect beings must be defeasible. None the less, Green's conception of the good in terms of self-realization or the exercise of deliberative capacities is not empty.

IV. Self-Realization and the Common Good

In particular, Green links self-realization and a common good. He believes that full self-realization can take place only in a community of ends (*PE* §§183–4, 190–1, 199, 232) in which each cares about others for their own sakes (*PE* §199). I must view others as my 'alter egos' (*PE* §§191, 200) and aim at a common good (*PE* §§202, 236). But why?

At one point, Green suggests that this concern for others, at least for those within one's immediate circle, is given or natural.

Now the self of which a man thus forecasts the fulfilment, is not an abstract or empty self. It is a self already affected in the most primitive forms of human life by manifold interests, among which are interests in other persons. These are not merely interests dependent on other persons for the means to their gratification, but interests in the good of those other persons, interests which cannot be satisfied without the consciousness that those other persons are satisfied. The man cannot contemplate himself as in a better state, or on the way to the best, without contemplating others, not merely as a means to that better state, but as sharing it with him. (*PE* §199)

Green might simply be invoking this familiar concern that one has for one's intimate associates. But this would not justify the claim that another's good is part of my own. Green might be appealing to his account of the personal good. If I do care about the welfare of my associates, and these desires survive deliberative endorsement, then, according to Green, I make their welfare part of my own personal good (*PE* §§91–2).

But this won't do. It would be fallacious to draw conclusions about the agent's own good from claims about the goods she pursues. This seems to conflate the *content* with the *ownership* of desires. Moreover, it makes an agent's interest in others dependent on her contingent desires; it does not explain why an agent who does not have such desires is making a mistake or why one who does have these desires should retain them. To explain how the demands of the common good are categorical imperatives, we need to explain how pursuit of a common good is an ingredient in self-realization.

We would do well to attend to Green's claims that a rational agent's interest in others is rooted in her search for a 'permanent' good (*PE* §§223, 229–32, 234). Rational action must be responsible action, ripe for assessment. This requires impulse control, which requires the ability to distinguish myself from my appetites and to frame the question what it would be best for me—a temporally extended agent—on the whole to do. This will involve endorsing some goals as good and as worth making short-term sacrifices or investments for. This is to value goals and projects in which I am involved that have some degree of permanence. Green seems to think that the right sort of association with others extends this permanence in a natural way—indeed, that it provides a kind of counterbalance to mortality or surrogate for immortality.

That determination of an animal organism by a self-conscious principle, which makes a man and is presupposed by the interest in permanent good, carries with it a certain appropriation by the man to himself of the beings with whom he is connected by natural ties, so that they become to him as himself and in providing for himself he provides for them. Projecting himself into the future as a permanent subject of possible well-being or ill-being—and he must so project himself in seeking for a permanent good—he associates his kindred with himself. It is this association that neutralises the effect which the anticipation of death must otherwise have on the demand for a permanent good. (*PE* §231)

But whereas intrapersonal permanence is clearly in the agent's interest, it is less clear that interpersonal permanence is.

We are more likely to be sympathetic to Green's claims if we attend to his ideas about *self*-realization. As we've seen, Green insists that the self is not exhausted by any set of beliefs and desires. A responsible self exercises deliberative capacities that assess beliefs and desires and regulate action in accord with these deliberations. On this view, the persistence of the self ought to involve the continuity of deliberative capacities to regulate beliefs, desires, and actions. In the intrapersonal case, I preserve myself when the actions and intentional states of a future self depend in the right deliberative way on the actions and intentional states of my present and past selves. But interpersonal association involves deliberative connections between associates, in which the intentional states and actions of each depend on those of the other. This might explain why Green thinks that I realize my capacities more fully in association with others and why I should treat the good of my associates as part of my own good.

V. Aristotelian Friendship

To better understand and assess Green's claims about self-realization and the common good, it might be helpful to compare them with Aristotle's claims about friendship and the way in which friendship contributes to the agent's own eudaimonia. This is an appropriate interpretive aid in so far as Green thinks that Aristotle was right to ground an agent's duties in an account of *eudaimonia* whose principal ingredient is a conception of practical virtue regulated by the common good (*PE* §§253, 256, 263, 271, 279), and Aristotle's account of the common good rests on his account of friendship.[9]

Aristotle discusses friendship (*philia*) in books viii–ix of the *Nicomachean Ethics*.[10] Initially, he suggests that all forms of friendship involve reciprocal concern for the other's own sake (1155^b28-33). He then identifies three different kinds of friendship: (1) friendship for *advantage*, found in associations for mutual advantage; (2) friendship for *pleasure*, found in associations in which each takes pleasure in the qualities and company of the other; and (3) friendship for *virtue*, found in associations between virtuous people, which he regards as the best or most complete kind of friendship (viii. 3–8). Both advantage friendship and pleasure friendship, Aristotle claims, involve something *less* than concern for the other's own sake (1156^a11-13). Both kinds of friendship are to be contrasted with virtue friendship. This is friendship among people similarly virtuous in which each cares about the other for the other's own sake. Despite these and other differences between virtue friendship, on the one hand, and pleasure friendship and advantage friendship, on the other hand, Aristotle insists that virtue friendship supplies the 'focal meaning' of friendship. In calling it the best or most complete kind of friendship, he signals that it is friendship to the fullest extent, and that other associations are friendship by virtue of their approximation to it (1157^a26-32).

Virtue friendship cannot be widespread, inasmuch as virtuous people are rare (1156^b25), and that sort of friendship requires a degree of intensity that cannot

---

[9] The legitimacy of this interpretive aid is also suggested by Green's 'Notes on Moral Philosophy' (*CW* v. 188–90) and by his marginalia in his two copies of the Greek text of Aristotle's *Nicomachean Ethics*, especially Aristotle's discussion of friendship in books viii–ix, in which he comments favourably on how Aristotle's conception of friendship allows for the reconciliation of self-love and altruism (*Nicomachean Ethics* ix. 8) and relates Aristotle's concerns to his own. Green's copies of the *Nicomachean Ethics* are contained in the Green Papers in Balliol College, Oxford. For extracts from Green's marginalia I am indebted to Peter Nicholson and the Master and Fellows of Balliol College.

[10] Translations of passages from the *Nicomachean Ethics* are from *Nicomachean Ethics*, trans. T. Irwin, 2nd edn. (Indianapolis: Hackett, 1999); translations of passages from other works by Aristotle are from the Revised Oxford Translation in *The Complete Works of Aristotle*, ed. J. Barnes (Princeton: Princeton University Press, 1984).

be maintained on a large scale (1158^a11-17, 1171^a1-20). Complete friends share similar psychological states, such as aims and goals (1170^b16-17) and live together, sharing thought and discussion (1157^b8-19, 1159^b25-33, 1166^a1-12, $1171^b30-1172^a6$). Virtue friends care about each other for the other's own sake. If complete friendship is a virtue, then, as a eudaimonist, Aristotle must think that it contributes to the lover's, as well as the beloved's, *eudaimonia*.

Aristotle anticipates some of his claims about the justification of virtue friendship (which begins at ix. 4) in viii. 12, where he suggests that we should take parental friendship as our model of friendship. The parent is concerned with the child's welfare for the child's own sake. This concern is appropriate on eudaimonist grounds, because the parent can regard the child as 'another self' (1161^b19, 28). The child can be regarded as another self of the parent, presumably because the child owes its existence and physical and psychological nature in significant measure to the parent. This both echoes and helps explain the common view that a parent's interests are *extended* by the life of the child.[11] Aristotle suggests that similar claims can be made about friendship between siblings. In virtue of living together, siblings causally interact in important ways and share many things in common, and so can regard each other as other selves (1161^b30-5).

Despite important differences between familial friendship and virtue friendship, Aristotle's account of familial friendship brings out clearly what is crucial to his justification of virtue friendship. He explains the justification of virtue friendship in terms of proper *self*-love (1166^a1-2, 10, 1166^a30-2, $1168^b1-1169^a12$; *Eudemian Ethics* $1240^a22-b13$).

> The excellent person is related to his friend in the same way as he is related to himself, since a friend is another self; and therefore, just as his own being is choiceworthy for him, the friend's being is choiceworthy for him in the same or a similar way. (1170^b6-9)

Aristotle believes that proper self-love requires a proper conception of the self and what is beneficial for the self.

> However, it is this [the virtuous person] more than any other sort of person who seems to be a self-lover. At any rate, he awards himself what is finest and best of all, and gratifies the most controlling part of himself, obeying it in everything. And just as a city and every other composite system seems to be above all its most controlling part, the same is true of a human being; hence someone loves himself most if he likes and gratifies this part. (1168^b28-34; see also 1166^a15-23)

---

[11] In so far as this is true, Aristotle can provide further justification for his assumption that there are posthumous benefits and harms and that the welfare of one's loved ones and the success of one's projects, after one is dead, are part of a complete good (1100^a10-31, 1101^a23-30).

Here Aristotle identifies a person with the controlling part of his soul or his understanding. He thinks that a human is essentially a psycho-physical compound in which reason can regulate thought and action ($1097^{b}24-1098^{a}16$, $1102^{b}13-1103^{a}3$). This would explain why Aristotle thinks that proper love for oneself involves a concern for one's practical reason and its virtuous exercise.

This account of proper intrapersonal love suggests a plausible interpretation of Aristotle's claims about the relation between interpersonal friendship and self-love. I preserve or extend myself by exercising my practical reason—forming beliefs and desires, deliberating about them, and acting as the result of deliberate choice. But the same sort of psychological interaction and interdependence can be found, presumably to a lesser extent, between two different persons. On Aristotle's view, friends share similar psychological states, such as aims and goals ($1170^{b}16-17$), and live together ($1157^{b}8-19$, $1159^{b}25-33$, $1166^{a}1-12$, $1171^{b}30-1172^{a}6$). Even if psychological similarity is necessary for friendship, it is clearly insufficient; it should be produced and sustained by living together and sharing thought and discussion ($1157^{b}5-12$, $18-21$, $1170^{b}10-14$).[12] This account of interpersonal psychological dependence among friends allows us to see how Aristotle thinks we can view a friend as another self and so how he can view the justification of friendship in terms of self-love. But then we can see how Aristotle can think that friendship involves concern for the friend's own sake and yet admits of eudaimonist justification. If B extends A's interests, then B's interests are a part of A's. This is true both when A and B are the same person and when they are different people. My friend's good is a part of my own overall good in just the way that the well-being of my future self is part of my overall good.

This provides a eudaimonist account of why one should care about those with whom one is already friends. But it doesn't explain why one should cultivate friendships in the first place. Aristotle argues that it is in my interest to exercise those capacities that are central to the sort of being I essentially am. Because I am essentially a rational animal, the principal ingredient in

---

[12] Though Aristotle sometimes writes as if the relevant relationships among friends must involve similar beliefs and values ($1159^{b}3-5$, $1161^{b}35$, $1162^{a}13$, $1165^{b}17$, $1166^{a}7$, $1167^{a}23-^{b}10$, $1170^{b}16$), it is not clear that this is an essential feature of his position. Within my own life, I exercise deliberative control and establish psychological connections with my future self when I intentionally modify beliefs, desires, or values, as well as when I maintain them unchanged. It may be that my successive selves will typically be fairly similar; perhaps wholesale and instantaneous psychological change is impossible, or at least would involve a substantial change, which I would not survive. But intrapersonal psychological dependence is compatible with significant qualitative change. Our own persistence requires only continuous deliberative control, not fixity of character. If so, in the interpersonal case Aristotle can allow friends to be psychologically dissimilar provided the mental states and actions of each exert significant influence on those of the other. Indeed, much of the value of having friends depends upon them being no mere clones of oneself.

my *eudaimonia* is the exercise of my deliberative capacities. Interpersonal psychological interaction of the right sort promotes my *eudaimonia* by making possible the fuller realization of my deliberative capacities. The central premiss of Aristotle's argument is that I am not self-sufficient at producing a complete deliberative good (1162^a20-4, 1170^a5-7; *Eudemian Ethics* 1244^b1-12; *Magna Moralia* $1212^b24-1213^b2$; *Politics* 1253^a25-7, 1261^b10-15).

> For it is said that the blessedly happy and self-sufficient people have no need of friends. For they already have [all] the goods, and hence, being self-sufficient, need nothing added. But your friend, since he is another yourself, supplies what your own efforts cannot supply. (1169^b4-6)

Aristotle focuses on the sharing of thought and discussion, especially about how best to live, as well as co-operative interaction. Sharing thought and discussion with another diversifies my experiences by providing me with additional perspectives on the world. By enlarging my perspective, it gives me a more objective picture of the world, its possibilities, and my place in it. Aristotle echoes Plato's claim in the *Phaedrus* that part of the value of intimates, with whom one shares thought and conversation, consists in their providing a 'mirror' on the self (*Phaedrus* 255d5; *Nicomachean Ethics* 1169^b34-5).

> Since then it is … a most difficult thing … to attain a knowledge of oneself … we are not able to see what we are from ourselves (and that we cannot do so is plain from the way in which we blame others without being aware that we do the same things ourselves; and this is the effect of favour or passion, and there are many of us who are blinded by these things so that we judge not aright); … when we wish to see our own face, we do by looking into the mirror, in the same way when we wish to know ourselves we can obtain that knowledge by looking at our friend. For the friend is, as we assert, a second self. (*Magna Moralia* 1213^a13-24; cf. *Eudemian Ethics* 1245^a29-36)

In so far as my friend is like me, I can appreciate my own qualities from a different perspective; this promotes my self-understanding. Here Aristotle articulates an idea about the role of others in self-consciousness that will figure prominently in Hegel and influence Green.[13] But there are limits to the value of mirrors; interaction with another just like me does not itself contribute to self-criticism. This is why there is deliberative value in interaction with diverse sorts of people many of whom are not mirror images of myself. Different perspectives can correct for limitations in my own perspective. This suggests another way in which I am not self-sufficient deliberatively. Sharing thought and discussion with others, especially about how to live, improves my own

---

[13] See, e.g. Hegel's famous discussion in the master–slave passage: G. W. F. Hegel, *Phenomenology of Spirit*, trans. A. Miller (Oxford: Clarendon Press, 1977), §§178–96.

practical deliberations; it enlarges my menu of options, by identifying new options, and helps me better to assess the merits of these options, by forcing on my attention new considerations and arguments about the comparative merits of the options. Here Aristotle might appeal to Socratic claims about the deliberative value of open and vigorous discussion with diverse interlocutors. Moreover, co-operative interaction with others allows me to participate in larger, more complex projects, and so extend the scope of my deliberative control over my environment. In this way, I spread my interests more widely than I could acting on my own. Here too diversity can be helpful; co-operation is improved and extends each further when it draws on diverse talents and skills. In these ways, interpersonal psychological relationships arguably make for fuller realization of my deliberative capacities. This may be part of what Aristotle has in mind in claiming that we are essentially political animals (*Nicomachean Ethics* 1097^{b}9–12; *Politics* 1253^{a}2) and that, as a result, the complete good for an individual can be realized only in a political community.

VI. Intrinsic Concern for Others

Both Aristotle and Green justify concern for the common good on individualist grounds. They argue that concern for others is justified, because associational bonds make the interests of one's associates part of one's own interests. This justifies other-regarding concern in terms of self-love; I should be concerned for others because this contributes to my own good. But if justified concern for another is, as Aristotle and Green claim, a special case of self-love, then mustn't such concern be at bottom instrumental? If so, this is objectionable, because it fails to justify concern for others for their own sakes and because it threatens to make the justification of other-regarding concern insufficiently stable.

We might begin assessing this complaint as applied to Aristotle. On Aristotle's view, a good is complete if it is chosen for its own sake, and a good is unconditionally complete if other things are chosen for its sake and it is not chosen for the sake of something else (1094^{a}18–19, 1097^{a}27–^{b}6). Aristotle believes that *eudaimonia* is the only unconditionally complete good; all other goods are chosen for its sake. Some goods chosen for the sake of *eudaimonia*, though not choiceworthy in themselves, are choiceworthy as causal means to some ingredient of *eudaimonia*; these goods are incomplete, instrumental goods. But other goods—such as the virtues—that are chosen for the sake of *eudaimonia* are also choiceworthy in themselves. They are chosen for the sake of *eudaimonia* in the sense that they are constituent parts of *eudaimonia*; they are valuable in their own right and for their constitutive contribution to a valuable life. Such goods are complete or intrinsic goods, not mere instrumental goods, though they are not unconditionally complete goods. If the lover treats the good of his beloved as a complete good that is also choiceworthy for the sake of his own *eudaimonia*, the lover is concerned for the other's own sake while valuing his beloved's well-being for the constitutive contribution this makes to his own *eudaimonia*.

Similarly, in suggesting that interpersonal permanence is an extension of intrapersonal permanence, Green seems to be saying that the right sort of association makes the good of one's associate part of one's own good, much as one's own future good is part of one's overall good. When I undergo a present sacrifice for a future benefit, I do so because the interests of my future self are interests of mine. The on-balance rationality of the sacrifice depends upon its promoting my overall good. But because the good of my future self is part of this overall good, concern for my overall good requires, as a constituent part, a concern for the good of my future self. In this way, concern for my future self for its own sake seems compatible with and, indeed, essential to self-love. If psychological relations extend an agent's interests, then the good of others can be part of my overall good just as my own future good can be. Though the on-balance rationality of other-regarding action depends upon its promoting my overall good, concern for my overall good requires, as a constituent part, concern for the welfare of those to whom I am appropriately psychologically related.

So both Aristotle and Green have the analytic resources to provide a eudaimonist justification of interpersonal concern that is derivative but not instrumental. This is why Green views interpersonal love as the next best thing to immortality (*PE* §231) and why Aristotle and Green both claim that a proper conception of how others figure in self-love undermines the popular contrast between self-love and altruism (*Nicomachean Ethics* ix. 8; *PE* §232).

VII. The Scope of the Common Good

Green accepts Aristotle's claims about the importance of the common good in self-realization; it is Aristotle's conception of friendship that justifies his claims; and Green's own justification parallels Aristotle's in important respects. But Green does not accept Aristotle's account of the *scope* of the common good. Whereas Aristotle recognizes significant restrictions on the scope of the common good, Green thinks that its scope should be universal (*PE* §§205–17, 249, 253, 271, 285).

Though there are important differences between virtue friendship, which serves as Aristotle's principal model for friendship, and political association,

Aristotle can extend the central elements of his eudaimonist defence of friendship to political association, because political communities that are just have to a significant degree the two features that are crucial to the justification of virtue friendship and familial friendship: there is commonality of aims among members of the political association, and this commonality is produced by members of the association living together in the right way—in particular, by defining their aims and goals consensually (1167^a25-8, 1155^a24-8). This establishes a common good among citizens, each of whom has a share in judging and ruling (*Politics* 1275^a22-33). Justice aims at a common good (1129^b15-18), and this is how Aristotle can construct a eudaimonist defence of justice. But this conception of the common good is still quite limited. Restricted as it is to those whom Aristotle thinks are fit for citizenship, it excludes women, barbarians, slaves, and manual labourers (1278^a3-9). It is these restrictions on the common good that Green finds unacceptable.

> The idea of a society of free and law-abiding persons, each his own master yet each his brother's keeper, was first definitely formed among the Greeks, and its formation was the condition of all subsequent progress in the direction described; but with them ... it was limited in its application to select groups of men surrounded by populations of aliens and slaves. In its universality, as capable of application to the whole human race, an attempt has first been made to act upon it in modern Christendom. (*PE* §271)

As the last part of this passage suggests, Green's own conception of the common good is universal; full self-realization and the securing of a really permanent good occurs only when each respects the claims made by other members of a maximally inclusive community of ends (*PE* §§214, 216, 244, 332). It is only with the advent of Christianity and Enlightenment conceptions, such as Kantianism and utilitarianism, Green thinks, that the universal scope of the common good has been widely recognized (*PE* §§213–14).[14]

There are good eudaimonist reasons for recognizing a more inclusive common good than Aristotle does. For one thing, there are already significant forms of personal, social, and economic interaction and interdependence between Aristotle's citizens, on the one hand, and women, slaves, manual labourers, and resident aliens, on the other. The arguments for recognizing a common good based on interpersonal association require including them in the common good. If they are part of the common good, it seems as

---

[14] In so far as he conceives of the common good universally, Green's view is perhaps closer to the Stoic than the Aristotelian view. See Cicero, *De Finibus* iii. 63. This aspect of the Stoic view is emphasized in Julia Annas, *The Morality of Happiness* (New York: Oxford University Press, 1993), ch. 12.

though they ought to be given a share in ruling, inasmuch as Aristotle believes that political activity is part of the good of rational animals (*Politics* vii. 8–9, esp. 1329^{a}35–8).

So there appears to be no good reason for Aristotle not to recognize the claims to citizenship that existing patterns of interaction justify.[15] This provides a backward-looking justification for recognizing a more inclusive conception of the common good. Moreover, as we have seen, interaction with others contributes to the full realization of my deliberative powers by diversifying my experiences, by providing me with resources for self-criticism as well as self-understanding, by broadening my deliberative menu and improving my deliberations, and by allowing me to engage in more complex and varied activities. Moreover, the deliberative value of this interaction is enhanced when others have diverse perspectives and talents. This provides a forward-looking justification for recognizing a more inclusive conception of the common good.

In so far as this push toward a more inclusive conception of the common good is motivated by Aristotelian considerations, it could be viewed as just the sort of friendly amendment to Aristotle that Green offers elsewhere in his sympathetic reconstruction of the contributions of his predecessors. But can the common good be genuinely universal in scope, as Green wants it to be, if it is the result of interpersonal interaction? For then there must be someone—the proverbial remotest Mysian (Plato, *Theaetetus* 209b8)—with whom one has no previous relation, however indirect.[16] Should it somehow come within my

[15] Perhaps Aristotle's view is that they are part of a common good, but not of a political common good, because they are unfit for sharing in political rule. He thinks that some—such as slaves and, to a lesser extent, women—are naturally inferior (*Politics* ii. 4–7, 12–13). They are, he thinks, like the non-rational part of the soul; they can apprehend and follow the reason of another, but they are incapable of the sort of deliberation involved in ruling and necessary for human happiness (1254^{b}20–4, 1260^{a}12–22). If so, these natural inferiors, even if part of a common good, are better suited to manual labour than citizenship.

This argument rests on the assumption of natural inferiority. Aristotle might think that he has empirical support for his position. His observations about women and slaves might lead him to suppose not simply that they had achieved less by way of individual and civic accomplishments than full-fledged citizens, but also that they were, in one sense, capable of less. But this sort of incapacity is presumably the *product*, rather than the cause, of being denied citizenship. Aristotle realizes that capacities must be cultivated and stimulated in order to develop properly. If I have not been given a proper education and training or suitable deliberative opportunities and responsibilities at various points in my development, I won't be prepared for proper deliberation about the management of my own affairs or those of the community. So even if everyone had equal innate capacities, we should expect the unequal development of deliberative capacities in systems where education and deliberative opportunities and responsibilities are distributed unequally. But then the unequal capacities that discriminatory practices and institutions produce cannot be appealed to as justification for those practices and institutions.

[16] The introduction of the proverbial remotest Mysian into discussions of the scope of ethical concern is discussed by Annas, *Morality of Happiness*, ch. 12.

power to help the remotest Mysian, at little or no cost to myself, it might seem that the eudaimonist cannot explain justified concern for him.

If the remotest Mysian and I stand in no relationship of psychological connection, then his good is not already part of mine. So I can have no backward-looking eudaimonist reason to be concerned about him. But I can have forward-looking reasons. For it is now within my power to interact with him, and all the reasons for cultivating interpersonal self-extension apply and provide a forward-looking rationale for concern. Even when the remotest Mysian and I have no prospect of further interaction, my assistance will enable or facilitate his pursuit of his own projects, and this will make his subsequent actions and mental states dependent upon my assistance. Indeed, other things being equal, the greater the assistance I provide, the greater is my involvement in his life. To the extent that another's actions and mental states are dependent upon my assistance, I can view the assistance as making his good a part of my own. Assistance to the remotest Mysian earns me a share, however small, of his happiness, much the way in which care and nurture of my children grounds posthumous interests I have in their continued well-being. This is why Green thinks that self-realization involves contributing to a larger, more permanent and comprehensive good (*PE* §§229–32). If so, it explains how a eudaimonist can legitimately seek a universal common good, of the sort Green contemplates.

VIII.   Impartiality and the Common Good

Green's conception of the common good is impartial in so far as it is universal in scope; it includes all rational agents. Is it impartial in the further sense that it demands an *equal weighting* of everyone's good? Some such conception of impartiality is plausible in special contexts; for instance, we expect governments to be impartial in the sense of treating all their citizens with equal concern and respect, and we expect parents to be impartial in the treatment of their children, not favouring Dick over Jane. But, of course, it is common to think that parents can and should be partial to their own children, in relation to the children of others, and that governments can and should give higher priority to their own citizens than to citizens of other countries.

C. D. Broad provides one intuitive conception of moral impartiality in which moral concern has universal scope but variable weight. In 'Self and Others' he argues that common-sense morality recognizes both impartiality and partiality; this is the view he calls *self-referential altruism*.

On the other hand, the altruism which common sense approves is always *limited in scope*. It holds that each of us has specially urgent obligations to benefit certain individuals and groups which stand in certain special relations to *himself*, e.g. his parents, his children, his fellow-countrymen, etc. And it holds that these special relationships are the ultimate and sufficient ground for these specially urgent claims on one's beneficence.[17]

Broad seems here to conflate issues of scope and weight. I think that what he means to say is that the altruism that common sense approves of is of variable weight, rather than limited scope. On this reading, self-referential altruism is impartial in one sense—in so far as it recognizes non-derivative reason to benefit others—but it is partial in another sense—in so far as the weight or strength of the agent's reasons is a function of the relationship in which she stands to potential beneficiaries.

Green's attitude toward this familiar and attractive kind of partiality is ambivalent. On the one hand, he sometimes appears hostile toward this kind of partiality. He regards the philosophical and political influence of utilitarian and Kantian conceptions of impartiality as progressive influences (*PE* §§213–14). According to the utilitarian conception, everyone should count for one, and no one for more than one (*PE* §213); according to the second main formula of Kant's categorical imperative, one must treat humanity, whether in one's own person or in others, always as an end in itself and never merely as a means (*PE* §214).

Does this sympathy for utilitarian and Kantian conceptions of impartiality force Green to deny partiality? While acknowledging the progressive influence of the utilitarian conception, Green argues in favour of the Kantian conception, chiefly on the ground that the latter is distributively sensitive in ways that the former is not (*PE* §§215, 217). This preference for Kantian impartiality may seem significant in so far as only the utilitarian conception is clearly hostile to partiality. Whereas the utilitarian can justify some forms of partiality as the most reliable way of promoting total happiness, it seems that she cannot attach intrinsic significance to special relationships.[18] By contrast, Kant may be able to accommodate partiality, as he hopes to in the *Metaphysics of Morals* (451–2). The formula of humanity requires only that rational agents treat one another as ends, and not merely as means. So long as one has intrinsic and not merely instrumental concern for all rational agents, it may be permissible for one to have greater concern for those to whom one stands in special relationships.

---

[17] C. D. Broad, 'Self and Others', in D. Cheney (ed.), *Broad's Critical Essays in Moral Philosophy* (London: George Allen and Unwin, 1971), 280.

[18] See David O. Brink, 'Impartiality and Associative Duties', *Utilitas*, 13 (2001), 152–72.

However, this appears not to be how Green understands the implications of Kantian impartiality.

> The essential thing is that he [the just man] applies no other standard in judging of the well-being of others than in judging of his own, and that he will not promote his own well-being or that of one whom he loves or likes, from whom he has received service or expects it, at the cost of impeding in any way the well-being of one who is nothing to him but a man. (*PE* §212)

Here Green apparently claims that I should not discriminate between my self, my intimate associates, and the remotest Mysian.[19]

This apparent denial of partiality is not only counter-intuitive but is also in tension with some of Green's other commitments. For one thing, Green appears to think that the common good does not demand disinterested benevolence but can and should be pursued by focusing on one's own circle of associates and one's own station and its duties (*PE* §183).[20] Provided that this kind of partiality is not merely instrumental to advancing impersonal values, it requires moral concern with variable weight.

Moreover, Green's account of the agent's interest in the common good, like the Aristotelian account on which it is modelled, seems committed to a form of partiality of the sort contained in self-referential altruism. The Aristotelian argument, with which Green is sympathetic, claims that the agent is justified in caring for others in so far as they stand to him in the same relationship of psychological interdependence that he stands to himself. But the strength of associational ties varies. It might be useful to distinguish between psychological *connectedness* and *continuity*. Connectedness obtains between people who influence each other psychologically; continuity obtains between people who are linked by chains of connected people. Both connectedness and continuity are matters of degree. Normally, there are more numerous and direct psychological connections among successive stages within a single life than between lives. And where the connections among links in a

---

[19] There are at least two ways of interpreting this passage so that it is consistent with partiality. (1) It may be significant that Green characterizes the just man impartially. Perhaps justice requires impartiality, but other virtues do not. However, this way of saving partiality may require a kind of separation of the virtues that may be hard to square with Green's sympathy for an Aristotelian account of the virtues that unifies them by the way in which they are all regulated by the common good. (2) It might be claimed that Green here condemns only those forms of partiality that 'impede' the good of others. In order for this to help, Green would apparently have to be marking some important distinction between doing and allowing harm to another's good. Of course, there are doubts about how to draw this sort of distinction and about whether partiality should operate only when there is no prospect of harming another.

[20] Here Green seems to echo an important theme in Bradley's version of idealist ethics. See Bradley, *Ethical Studies*, esp. essay V.

chain are all weaker, continuity between any points in the chain will also be weaker. If so, we can see how I am more weakly continuous with my intimates than I am with myself. We can also see how I might be continuous with others, besides my intimates. I interact directly with others, such as colleagues and neighbours, and this interaction shapes my mental life in certain ways, even if the interaction in such cases is less regular than is my interaction with intimates and even if the effect of such interactions on my mental life is less profound than is the effect produced by interaction with my intimates. Moreover, I interact with a much larger net of people indirectly, when our psychological influence on each other is mediated by other people and complex social institutions. We can think of the degrees of connectedness and continuity in terms of a set of concentric circles with myself occupying the inner circle and the remotest Mysian occupying the outer circle. As we extend the scope of psychological interdependence, the strength of the relevant psychological relationships appears to weaken, and the weight of one's reasons to give aid and refrain from harm presumably weakens proportionately. Despite the wide scope of justified concern, it must apparently have variable weight. This *interpersonal discount rate* justifies partiality at a fundamental level.[21]

Partiality of variable weight is consistent with impartiality of universal scope. Moreover, it fits the common view that, even if morality has universal scope, the demands that it imposes are a function not simply of the amount of benefit that one can confer, but also of the nature of the relationship in which one stands to potential beneficiaries. If we fill in the details of Green's claims about the role of the common good in self-realization with the help of Aristotle's eudaimonist justification of virtues that aim at the common good, then it's hard to see how Green can avoid endorsing this sort of partiality.[22]

---

[21] The degree of partiality depends, in part, on the precise shape of the interpersonal discount rate. As long as psychological connectedness is itself one of the psychological relationships that matter, then there will be an interpersonal discount rate, because an agent will be differentially psychologically connected to others. But as long as psychological continuity is also one of the relationships that matter, a significant level of concern can be justified for anyone with whom one is psychologically continuous. Suppose A is friends only with B, whereas B is also friends with C. All else being equal, A is as continuous with his friend's friend, C, as he is with his friend, B. So in so far as continuity is one of the relationships that matter, A has as much reason to be concerned about his friend's friend as about his friend. He will have reason to give greater weight to the interests of his friend in so far as connectedness also matters. These points generalize beyond friendship. So the importance of psychological continuity ensures that a significant threshold of concern can be justified well out into outer circles. There will none the less be significant differences in the degree of concern that can be justified, above this threshold, in different circles if connectedness has independent significance.

[22] Aristotle clearly accepts this sort of partiality; he thinks that, all else being equal, it is better to help and worse to harm those to whom one stands in special relationship than it is to do these things to others (*Nicomachean Ethics* 1160^{a}1–6, 1169^{b}12; *Politics* 1262^{a}27–30).

IX. Moderate and Extreme Harmony of Interests

On Green's view, proper self-realization implies that the good of each includes in part the good of others. This conclusion, he thinks, undermines the popular contrast between self-love and benevolence (*PE* §232). We should view those with whom we participate in such associations as 'alter egos', for whom we care as we care about ourselves (*PE* §§191, 200). We should weight their interests with our own, and see ourselves as compensated when we make what would otherwise be sacrifices for them and for our common projects (*PE* §376). Indeed, Green goes so far as to claim that when each is engaged in proper self-realization, there can be no conflict or competition of interests (*PE* §244).

How can this be? Green treats this claim as true by definition if he simply defines the common good as that set of goods for individuals in which the size of one individual's share in no way diminishes the size of others' shares and in which all must participate equally.[23] But this approach to the common good would raise two worries. First, is there actually a common good? Are there goods that are non-competitive? Moreover, if there are such goods, why or how much should we care about them? If it is only some special class of goods that are common in this way, why should we be especially concerned to promote them, rather than familiar potentially competitive goods? Non-competitive goods might be easier to secure, more stable, and less subject to loss. But these pragmatic virtues of non-competitive goods do not show that potentially competitive goods are not worth wanting, and Green shows no signs of valuing a common good for these pragmatic reasons.

By contrast, my interpretation of Green's conception of the common good does not define it as non-competitive; rather, it seeks to explain how it is that the goods of distinct individuals, when conceived in perfectionist terms, can be shown to be substantially interdependent. Only if he argues in this way is Green entitled to claim that a common good, which includes the good of others, is part of self-realization. This interpretation of Green's account of the role of the common good in self-realization models interpersonal relations and concern on intrapersonal relations and concern, and thereby extends the boundaries of self-interest and self-love so as to include the good of others. This view implies a conception of interpersonal relationships that should lead us to see people's interests as metaphysically, and not just instrumentally, interdependent. This allows Green to claim that there is a substantial harmony between the agent's own interests and those of others. Call this *moderate harmony*. Important as these

---

[23]   I think that Nicholson favours this interpretation of the common good. See Peter Nicholson, *The Political Philosophy of the British Idealists* (Cambridge: Cambridge University Press, 1990), 58–9, 80.

claims are, they do not yet establish the strong thesis, which Green sometimes embraces, that there can be no conflict or competition of interests among people (*PE* §244). Call this *extreme harmony*.

Even if, as moderate harmony insists, the good of others is a necessary and distinctively valuable part of an agent's overall good, it can only be a proper part of the agent's good and cannot exhaust his good. For if the good of each consisted only in the good of others, there would be nothing to ground anyone's good. A's good would refer to the good of B–D, B's good would refer to the good of A and C–D, and so on. To make sense of the good of each being part of the good of each, there must be some part of the good of each that can be characterized independently of the good of others. But then even if the good of others is part of an agent's overall good, it is one aspect of an agent's overall good that must interact and may compete with more self-confined aspects. When I expend intellectual, emotional, and financial resources on meeting the legitimate claims of others, this contributes to my overall good in distinctive ways; but it also consumes resources that might have been spent on my own education, vocation, or avocations. There are opportunity costs to every commitment, especially to important commitments, and sometimes the opportunity costs of important commitments are themselves important.[24]

X. Liberalism and Extreme Harmony

One prospect that Green sees for accommodating partial and impartial demands lies in his *liberal* political commitments. For present purposes, we might note the Green's brand of liberalism mixes egalitarian social and economic reforms with a commitment to democratic institutions and a system of personal and civic liberties and opportunities.[25] Egalitarian reforms establishing a decent minimum standard of living and a system of state-sponsored education provide each citizen with resources with which to pursue his own self-realization; democratic procedures allow for individual participation in collective decision making; and individual liberties create space for individual self-determination.

---

[24] Bradley is perhaps clearer than Green in recognizing personal or non-social components of self-realization that have the potential for conflicting with the demands of a common good. See Bradley, *Ethical Studies*, 219, 222. But Green faces this potential conflict as well. This worry about extreme harmony underlies Sidgwick's worries that Green (a) conflates moral and non-moral forms of perfection and (b) fails to recognize the conflict between the agent's own perfection and perfection generally. See Henry Sidgwick, *Lectures on the Ethics of T. H. Green, Mr. Herbert Spencer, and J. Martineau* (London: Macmillan, 1902), 65–72, 106. For discussion of Sidgwick's concerns, see Brink, *Perfectionism and the Common Good*, §XXVII.

[25] A good discussion of Green's perfectionist liberalism is contained in Nicholson, *Political Philosophy of the British Idealists*, chs. 2–5. Also see Brink, *Perfectionism and the Common Good*, §XXII.

This kind of liberal regime would effect a division of moral and political labour that might accommodate the potentially conflicting demands of partiality and impartiality. For individuals would be free to express partial commitments to themselves, their intimates, and their immediate associates provided the political community they live in ensures to each the resources, education, and opportunities necessary to pursue his own self-realization effectively. Partiality would be legitimate in a liberal political system, once an individual had met his responsibilities of democratic citizenship.

But notice two things. First, harmony or accommodation is possible only in suitable liberal regimes. Just as Hegel thought that an individual's reconciliation to the social world was possible only in the modern social world that he found in nineteenth-century Germany, so too Green would have to regard the sort of non-competitive common good he seeks as a political good and achievement, not fully within any one individual's control. In fact, Green would have to view a perfectly harmonious common good as an unrealized ideal. One reason for this is the simple fact that some of the requisite liberal reforms had yet to take place in Britain, the United States, and other Western democracies. But another reason for the failure of extreme harmony is the universal character of the common good. Even if extreme harmony would (otherwise) obtain among the members of a suitable liberal regime, it would not obtain for members of non-liberal regimes. But Green believes that the common good is maximally inclusive of all rational agents, and that a good cannot be common in which some do not share. Of course, members of liberal regimes may be closer to securing a share of the common good than others, but as long as there are non-liberal regimes, no one—including members of a suitable liberal regime—can enjoy the common good.[26] Requiring, as it would, the universal establishment of liberal institutions, Green's political defence of extreme harmony must be a precarious and as yet unrealized ideal.

XI. Absolute Idealism and Extreme Harmony

But Green has available a metaphysical, as well as a political, defence of extreme harmony. Scepticism about extreme harmony is plausible as long as we rely on *individualist* assumptions about an agent's interests. But on some versions of the sort of social *organicism* to which Green is attracted, the prospects for

---

[26] In 'Liberal Legislation' Green claims that even aristocrats in ancient Greece lacked true freedom inasmuch as their position depended on the slavery of others (*CW* iii. 371–2). Cf. President John F. Kennedy's speech in West Berlin about the Berlin Wall in which he said, 'Freedom is indivisible, and when one man is enslaved, all are not free' (quoted in Nicholson, *Political Philosophy of the British Idealists*, 272).

extreme harmony might look brighter. If there were a corporate agent of which individual persons were organic parts and the good of the parts had to be understood in terms of the contribution those parts make to the good of the whole, then it would be harder to see how there could be any genuine sacrifices that individuals might have to make for the sake of the common good.

To appreciate this defence of extreme harmony, it might be helpful to return to the intrapersonal–interpersonal analogy. The common good certainly requires some kinds of impartiality that demand what we would pre-theoretically describe as interpersonal balancing of interests and individual sacrifice. Even self-referential altruism would require one to bear a small cost so that others might receive a significant benefit. This sort of interpersonal balancing is parallel to the sort of intrapersonal balancing that prudence demands within a single life. But intrapersonal and interpersonal balancing may seem, on reflection, importantly disanalogous.[27] Diachronic, intrapersonal balancing (now-for-then sacrifice) is acceptable, because the person who makes the sacrifice is later compensated; benefactor and beneficiary are the same. So, in one sense, prudence demands no genuine intrapersonal sacrifice. By contrast, interpersonal balancing may seem problematic, because interpersonal compensation is not automatic; benefactor and beneficiary are distinct. Unless interpersonal sacrifice is reciprocated, it would seem to be genuine, uncompensated sacrifice.

But some interpretations of Absolute Idealism might make the intrapersonal–interpersonal analogy more robust. If there is a single corporate agent of whom individual agents are organic parts, then there is a corporate agent in the interpersonal case that is both benefactor and beneficiary, much as we take the individual to be both benefactor and beneficiary in the normal diachronic intrapersonal case. This would apparently show that the common good demands no genuine sacrifice of the corporate agent. By itself, it would not show that the common good demands no genuine sacrifice of individual agents. They are distinct parts of the whole; their sacrifices are not automatically compensated.

But parallel claims can be made about the intrapersonal case. The temporal parts of a single life are distinct. Whereas I am compensated later for sacrifices I make now, me-now is not compensated for its sacrifices for me-later. We can reject this challenge to prudence if we can argue either that temporal parts are

[27] Worries about the lack of compensation in interpersonal balancing are connected with the separateness of persons and forcefully articulated by John Rawls, *A Theory of Justice* (Cambridge, Mass.: Harvard University Press, 1971), 23–4, 26–7, 29, 187–8, 191, and Robert Nozick, *Anarchy, State, and Utopia* (New York: Basic Books, 1974), 31–4.

normatively less important entities than whole persons or that their interests must be understood in terms of the interests of the whole of which they are parts.[28] But the Absolute Idealist might offer a similar response to the challenge to extreme harmony, arguing either that individual persons are normatively less important entities than the corporate agent or that the interests of individual persons must be understood in terms of the interests of the corporate whole of which they are parts.

We know that Green accepts some of the premises of this Idealist defence of extreme harmony. We know that in the first book of the *Prolegomena* he claims that empiricist and Kantian dualisms between things as they appear and as they are in themselves are untenable (*PE* §41). He thinks that realism is untenable, because it cannot explain how the order of appearances comes to correspond to the order of nature (*PE* §31). He thinks that realism is unnecessary, because the idealist can account for fallibility (and hence objectivity) by finding local anomalies within a larger pattern of an individual's appearances (*PE* §§12–13, 64). In order to account for common empirical content among different cognizers and to explain the possibility of systematic individual error, Green argues that we require the idea of a single trans-historical consciousness of which individual consciousnesses are proper parts (*PE* §§26, 67, 69). This gives us the notion of a corporate agent, of which individual agents are proper parts. Sometimes Green claims that this corporate agent has no existence over and above that of the individual agents that exist at different places and times (*PE* §184), as someone might claim that an individual agent is nothing over and above the temporally dispersed selves that compose her life. But this is hard to square with Green's insistence that the corporate agent is eternal (*PE* §§67, 69). Unless Green is willing to assume that there have always been and always will be individual agents, he cannot recognize an eternal corporate agent who is nothing over and above individual agents. However that tension is best resolved, Green recognizes a corporate agent that is distinct from particular individual agents.

But how credible is Absolute Idealism and its commitment to corporate agency? Many will remain unpersuaded by these metaphysical and epistemological arguments. If relations are given in experience, as Moore and Russell believed, then they are not the workmanship of the understanding, and so the relational character of experience, on which Green insists, does not support Idealism.[29]

---

[28] For some discussion, see my 'Rational Egoism and the Separateness of Persons', in J. Dancy (ed.), *Reading Parfit* (Oxford: Blackwell, 1997).

[29] Moore's and Russell's reactions to Green's relational arguments for Idealism are usefully discussed in Peter Hylton, *Russell, Idealism, and the Emergence of Analytic Philosophy* (Oxford: Clarendon Press, 1990), 110–12.

Moreover, some might find the arguments against realist explanations of cognitive success unpersuasive. And even if Absolute Idealism was a pre-condition of the possibility of knowledge, without some independent evidence of the existence of such a corporate agent, readers might find scepticism easier to accept than Absolute Idealism.

These issues are complicated and cannot be adequately addressed here. However, I want to suggest that it is Green's theory of moral personality and his claims about the role of the common good in self-realization, rather than his views about objectivity or epistemology, that provide the resources for his best defence of the sort of corporate agency required to maintain extreme harmony. Green's argument for thinking that the common good is part of self-realization appeals to the fact that the relations of psychological—especially deliberative—interdependence that unify the temporal parts of a single life also obtain to a significant degree in interpersonal associations. But then Green might argue that just as there is an individual agent that spans temporally dispersed selves in the intrapersonal case, so too there is a single corporate agent that spans spatially and temporally dispersed selves in the interpersonal case.

We can flesh out this argument with the help of ideas about personal identity. In Locke's *Essay Concerning Human Understanding*, he insists that the concept of a person is a forensic or (as we might say) normative concept.[30] In morality and law, persons are the bearers of rights and responsibilities. What makes persons responsible, Green insists, is their possession of deliberative capacities—their ability to distinguish between the intensity and authority of their desires and the ability to regulate their appetites, emotions, and ultimately their actions in accordance with their deliberations.

It is natural to combine this deliberative conception of personhood with a suitable mentalistic view about personal identity over time. On one such mentalistic view, what makes persons at different times the same person and, hence, what unites different parts of a single life is psychological continuity.[31] A series of persons is psychologically *continuous* in so far as contiguous members in the series are psychologically well connected. A pair of persons are psycho-logically *connected* in so far as the intentional states (e.g. beliefs, desires, and intentions) and actions of one are causally dependent upon those of the other. Of particular importance—if persons are essentially responsible agents—are *deliberative* connections that hold among actions, intentions, and prior delib-erations in the deliberate maintenance and modification of intentional states

---

[30] Locke, *Essay Concerning Human Understanding* II. xxvii. 8, 15, 17–21, 23, 26.

[31] Similar mentalistic views are defended by Derek Parfit, *Reasons and Persons* (Oxford: Clarendon Press, 1984), part III, and Sydney Shoemaker, 'Personal Identity: A Materialist's Account', in S. Shoemaker and R. Swinburne, *Personal Identity* (Oxford: Blackwell, 1984).

and in the performance of actions that reflect these prior deliberations. On this view, personal identity consists in maximal (non-branching) psychological continuity.[32]

Normally, we find maximal continuity within single lives. But, as Aristotle's account of friendship and Green's account of the common good show, there are significant forms of continuity *across* individual lives. Interpersonal, as well as intrapersonal, psychological continuity is quite common. Interpersonal connections and continuity can be found among intimates who interact on a regular basis and help shape each other's mental life. In such relationships, the experiences, beliefs, desires, ideals, and actions of each depend in significant part upon those of the other. We can see this in the familial friendships that Aristotle and Green take as their model. Similar relations hold among spouses and friends who share experiences, conversation, and plans. They can also be found, to a lesser extent, among partners in co-operative ventures where the deliberations, desires, plans, and expectations of each are formed together and conditioned by each other. More generally, membership in various sorts of associations will affect the beliefs, desires, expectations, and plans of members so as to establish significant interpersonal psychological continuity among the association's members. In these ways, interpersonal psychological connectedness and continuity can extend broadly, even if the degree of connectedness (and sometimes continuity) often weakens as these relations extend further.

This argument for corporate agency relies on familiar ideas about agency and personal identity, not on Idealist metaphysics.[33] It may be sufficient to deliver moderate harmony, which would be no small feat. However, it does not justify extreme harmony. To do that, it would not only have to recognize a maximally inclusive corporate agent but also to privilege this agent in relation to all other agents, corporate or individual, in just the way that Absolute Idealism does. But the argument for corporate agency does not establish this. It establishes a great many corporate agents, corresponding to every interpersonal association. There will be a maximally inclusive association, perhaps one that includes everyone as a member, but that association will not be the most normatively significant association to which each belongs. For the normative significance of membership in an association varies directly with the strength of the interpersonal bonds among members. We said that we can think of the degrees of connectedness and continuity in terms of a set of concentric circles

---

[32] Because personal identity is a one–one relation and psychological continuity can be one–many, personal identity must consist in non-branching maximal psychological continuity.

[33] For further discussion of corporate agency, within a mentalistic conception of personal identity, see Carol Rovane, *The Bounds of Agency* (Princeton: Princeton University Press, 1996).

with myself occupying the inner circle and the remotest Mysian occupying the outer circle. As we extend the scope of psychological interdependence, the strength of the relevant psychological relations appears to weaken, and the weight of one's reasons to give aid and refrain from harm presumably weakens proportionately. Despite the wide scope of justified concern, it must apparently have variable weight. This sort of partiality ensures that there can be genuine conflicts of interest between different people. This means that Green's most interesting and plausible arguments for corporate agency do not support the demands of extreme harmony.

XII. The Importance of Green's Claims

Green's claims about self-realization and the common good have an important bearing on traditional debates about the normative authority of other-regarding moral demands. As modern moral traditions recognize, moral demands are impartial; they impose categorical duties to respect and aid others, independently of the agent's own aims and interests. But heeding these other-regarding duties often appears to constrain the agent's pursuit of her own aims and interests. This creates a tension between living right and living well. In the *Methods of Ethics* Sidgwick, who interpreted the elements of this tension hedonistically, treated it as a fundamental dualism of practical reason.[34] Those who hold a broadly prudential conception of practical reason see this tension as raising doubts about the rational authority of other-regarding moral requirements. Indeed, these doubts can arise even if practical reason can itself be impartial—recognizing non-derivative reason to promote the welfare of others. For as long as prudence is one part of practical reason, conflict between impartial and prudential reason remains possible. Without some reason to treat impartial reason as superior, the supremacy of other-regarding morality must remain doubtful.

Green's arguments about the role of the common good in self-realization address these doubts by drawing into question the sharp contrast between self and others that they presuppose. He argues that the right sort of interpersonal association extends the agent's own good so that the good of others is a part of his own good in much the same way as his own future good is. On this view, people's interests are metaphysically, and not just strategically, interdependent. Moreover, this justification of other-regarding concern is

---

[34] Henry Sidgwick, *The Methods of Ethics* (originally published 1874), 7th edn. (London: Macmillan, 1907), esp. pp. xv–xxi, 162–75, 496–509.

robust. It explains how each should regard this interdependence as good; the right form of interpersonal association makes possible the fuller realization of the very deliberative powers that make each an agent in the first place. Green's argument makes the justification of other-regarding concern prudential but non-instrumental, and it provides an inclusive conception of the common good that justifies other-regarding concern with wide scope. Moreover, the associational relations that justify concern on this view are commonly regarded as morally significant relations as well.

These claims imply that acting on other-regarding moral demands is a counterfactually reliable way of advancing the agent's own interests. This is not enough to deliver the strong rationalist thesis that the authority of other-regarding morality is always supreme or overriding. To establish that would require the truth of Green's assumptions about the extreme harmony of interests. Extreme harmony, I have argued, is implausible (§§IX–XI). Self-confined and other-regarding aspects of a person's welfare can conflict, and there is no a priori reason to suppose that other-regarding aspects must dominate. But Green's failure to vindicate the supremacy of other-regarding morality does not leave us where we started in thinking about the authority of morality. He makes a plausible case for rejecting the simple contrast between prudence and altruism, and for thinking that the good of others forms a distinctive and valuable part of a person's good, whose importance must be reckoned in the balance of reasons. If practical reason is purely prudential, this vindicates the weak rationalist thesis that there is always reason to act on other-regarding demands, such that failure to do so is *pro tanto* irrational, even if it leaves the supremacy of other-regarding demands in doubt. If practical reason has impartial elements as well, then Green's claims help to defend an even stronger rationalist thesis. For then both impartial reason and prudence, in one voice, speak in favour of other-regarding morality, and only prudence, in another voice, might speak against it. This does not settle how often the balance of reasons will tip in favour of other-regarding morality, but it suggests a reasonably robust defence of the rational authority of other-regarding morality. Green may not be able to avoid entirely some version of Sidgwick's dualism, but his attempts to overcome that dualism provide a distinctive and valuable contribution to debates about the authority of morality.[35]

---

[35] For further discussion, see David O. Brink, 'Self-Love and Altruism', *Social Philosophy & Policy*, 14 (1997), 122–57.

3

Green and the Idealist Conception of a Person's Good

JOHN SKORUPSKI

I. Introduction

Idealist philosophers of the nineteenth century shared a certain conception of a person's good. It can be found in Fichte and Hegel, and then later in Britain in Bradley and Green. In Green, as in these other Idealists, it fits into a philosophical scheme that has far-reaching metaphysical as well as moral dimensions. Each philosopher presents a distinctive picture: Green's picture is arguably more like Fichte's than Hegel's, and is quite different from Bradley's. None the less, all of them belong to a single album, so to speak, a series of connected efforts to picture how individuals in modern societies can live reconciled or unalienated, and spiritually fulfilling, lives. This series is one of the important products of ethical thought in the nineteenth century; it is a resource that can still greatly benefit present-day ethical and political reflection.

I am not assuming, in saying this, that we can or cannot, should or should not, attempt to renew this vision. It is not obvious that there *is* a way in which modern individuals can live 'spiritually fulfilling' lives, or find the reconciliation with each other that Idealists hoped for, or even that this is something to be aimed for. On the contrary, these issues are pressing and unresolved, perhaps not finally resolvable. When one considers Idealism's influence in its time, and then its aftermath, it is easy to see it as a vision that failed. It played virtually no role, political or philosophical, in the 'short' twentieth century. Philosophically, it was followed by plenty of twentieth-century theorizing about the absurdity and meaninglessness of life; practically, by plenty of evidence of the way life is atomized and commodified in stable modern democracies. One inevitably wonders, in the light of that experience, how to respond to Green's perfectibilist faith in human potentialities.

All the same, Idealism is attractive. It places self-realization, understood as the moral development of the individual, at the centre of liberal ethics, but is sufficiently rooted in an analysis of modernity, and in particular of the politics of modern societies, not to seem merely anachronistic, or of purely personal interest.[1] It is a social as well as a personal moral philosophy. When contrasted to it, the many contemporary varieties of 'ethically neutral' liberalism can easily seem evasive and tinny. They give no account of how people in present-day liberal democracies can and should lead fulfilling lives, or of how a liberal civic framework should provide sustaining conditions for that. Immediately, of course, one can respond by asking, is that bad? Is it sensible to look for the kind of ethical and civic vision that Idealism tried and mostly (though by no mean wholly) failed to make into a public ideal? Would it have been a good thing if it had succeeded more? Should liberal political practice tie itself to a positive conception of individual good? Must not hard twentieth-century experience make one a pessimist about people, and a sceptic about how thick or substantial the public ethos of a modern State should be? Liberalism, we may remind ourselves, is first and foremost about resisting tyranny from wherever it comes—the State, an oligarchy, or the people. A robust combination of ethical neutrality, rule of law, and the free market may be the only safe liberal way.

These continuing dilemmas about the ethical basis of liberal politics arouse my own interest in the Idealist conception of a person's good. Not that Idealism is the only liberal legacy to be explored; the choice is certainly not neutrality or Idealism. The Idealist tradition-cum-critique is important, but other proponents of a comprehensive liberal ethic, and other critics, are as important. I am convinced that a general rethinking of *all* these late-modern ethical ideas is timely, and that such rethinking (which is already going on) can be fruitful for politics in present-day liberal democracies.

In comparison to this rather vast agenda, however, my aim here is very limited. I will re-examine the main themes of Green's version of the Idealist conception of individual good and ask how well they stand up. My focus will be ethical, not metaphysical or political, and more contemporary than historical. I do want to end by asking what influence on us Green's conception of a person's good should have and to indicate a response (though I certainly won't give a full one). But I shall mainly be concerned to set some of it out as

---

[1] It has evident affinities with the classical eudaimonist tradition. But there are important differences which give it a 'modern' feel—its historicist conception of self-development, its individualist concern with ideals of inward conscience, on the one hand, and active citizenship, community, and reconciliation, on the other, its account of the modern State and, of course, not least its preoccupation with the problems of Christian faith in science-based societies.

defensibly as possible and then to explain, rather more critically, its structural role in his moral philosophy and its influence on his liberal outlook.[2]

Let's begin by noting some of its main features.

1. The Idealist conception, in Green's account, as in others, takes it that the good of a person consists in self-realization, and that self-realization is freedom. Neither of these claims has an immediately evident meaning. Both give rise to scepticism and suspicion. What is it to realize oneself anyway? And what is so good about it? What if I'm not interested in realizing myself? And why should this rather obscure thing, whatever it is, be called 'freedom'? Doesn't it introduce a notion of freedom which is quite unclear in comparison to what we all know and feel personal freedom to be—and one that is all too open to manipulation by well-intentioned interventionists, and convinced political or religious dogmatists?

2. According to Green, one's true good is the realization of what one 'truly' or 'really' desires—so self-realization is realization of one's true desires. Here too suspicion is easily aroused. What is a true desire, and is all and only that which I truly desire a part of my good?

3. There is, in Green's view as in that of other Idealists, no need to posit, as an underived principle in practical reason, a postulate of impartiality which says that the good of any one individual has no inherently greater reason-giving force than the good of any other—not even in the shape of an 'impartial point of view' that is both indispensable for ethics and yet also irreducible to the true interests of an individual moral agent. Green's ethics rests firmly on a basis of formal egoism. What the self has reason to do, according to the formal egoist, is to pursue its own good. This is the only *ultimate* practical reason-giving consideration.

4. But then a particularly strong theme in Green is that the good of other persons and things can become a part of one's own good. One finds this also in Hegel, and indeed in Mill, who was no Idealist. Once again suspicion is

---

[2] I am indebted, as must all writers on Green's ethics be, to Peter Nicholson's *The Political Philosophy of the British Idealists* (Cambridge: Cambridge University Press, 1990). I have also benefited from David O. Brink's recent work on Green: *Perfectionism and the Common Good: Themes in the Philosophy of T. H. Green* (Oxford: Clarendon Press, 2003), and the introduction to his edition of Green's *Prolegomena* (Oxford: Clarendon Press, 2003). I give a very brief account of how Green's philosophy fitted into the culture of his time in my *English-Language Philosophy 1750–1945* (Oxford: Oxford University Press, 1993), and I sketch the more general European development of some of these nineteenth-century themes in 'Ethics and the Social Good,' forthcoming in Allen Wood (ed.), *The Cambridge History of 19th Century Philosophy* (Cambridge: Cambridge University Press). I have discussed Sidgwick's criticisms of Green in 'Desire and Will in Sidgwick and Green', *Utilitas*, 12 (2000), 307–28. The present discussion focuses more directly on Green's views.

aroused. How can another's good be a part of mine? Isn't this a metaphor that cries out for explanation?

5.   Green thinks that virtue is best for the individual—thus far following the eudaimonist tradition. But he insists, in a way unknown to classical thought, that virtuous action consists in contributing to a good which is *common* to all individual persons—a good for which there can be *no competition*. This means that the notion that others' good can become one's own has a systematic or structural importance for Green which it does not have for Mill. It is an essential part of the reconciliationist project that is central to Green's moral philosophy. The truer my understanding of my own self and my own good, Green thinks, the more I understand its identity-in-difference (metaphysically speaking) or differentiated at-one-ness (ethically speaking) with other selves and their good. My own true good *is* 'the common good'. I achieve it by being and doing good—this not because of the rewards offered in an afterlife, but in virtue of an identity-in-community with others which can be seen to hold through purely metaphysical and ethical reflection.

It is a strange, and characteristically idealist, feature of this vision that in pursuing one's own realization, one seems eventually to leave one's own self behind. Self-realization, it turns out, is self-transcendence. No doubt Idealism takes itself to have the means to preserve individuals in their particularity, even as it transcends their distinctness. Identity-in-community is differentiated identity. None the less, it provides a philosophical vocabulary for an ideal of self-renunciation which is (in one sense of that confusing word, 'individualism') anti-individualistic; this is fundamental to its spiritual appeal. Green, like Fichte, belongs to its activist division, as against the contemplative or mystical division to which Bradley belongs. By means of social activism, and personal struggle towards the moral ideal, individuals break the chrysalis of their particularity and fly towards a common home. This yearning for a common home, for at-one-ness, comes across as strongly in Green as it does in Marx's occasional rhapsodizing about Communist society—in fact, Green is more single-minded in his conception of it and works it through in his philosophy with more moral fervour. The yearning for reconciliation is in general one of the most striking (and momentous) *leitmotifs* of nineteenth-century ethics.[3] Which is not to say that it is coherent. Like many other critics, I don't think that Green's

[3] See Skorupski, 'Ethics and the Social Good'. There has been a justified reaction against the Berlin/Popper thought that nineteenth-century Idealism's concept of 'positive freedom' was a high road to totalitarianism. But this other side of Idealism, the quest for total social reconciliation, is a more plausible candidate. No one could dream of seeing Green as a totalitarian. Yet this quest, found in Green and before him in Comtean positivism and Marxism, was a nineteenth-century obsession that eventually opened up intellectual space for totalitarianisms of the Left and Right to seize. Importantly, however,

conception of the common good ultimately makes sense. However this very important reconciliationist theme will occupy us only tangentially here.

Nor do I think that ethics can be founded on formal egoism; contrary to Green, I think a fundamental—i.e. underived—principle of impartiality is indispensable in our ethical thought. There are reasons for acting that are in no sense whatever grounded in formal egoism. So I don't want to defend point (3) above, and in fact I will try to indicate how it distorts Green's ethics. But again, such a very fundamental issue is too big to be treated in its own right here. I am going to restrict myself to providing some defence, though not a full defence, of points (1), (2), and (4). I begin with point (2).

II. Solicitation, Desire, and Will

My true good consists in the realization of my true or real desires—but what are true or real desires? Let us start by considering Green's conception of desire.

He thinks that it is to be understood as an action of the self rather than a passion which the self merely receives or undergoes. Passions or impulses I can adopt, reject, or for the moment ignore. Desire in the full sense, however, is not just impulse or passion, or in Green's good word, mere 'solicitation'—an invitation that I passively encounter or experience. It is a 'solicitation' with which I identify; as one might say, I *make* it mine. For Green, this action of identifying oneself with a solicitation consists in resolving to satisfy it:

> though we cannot fix the usage of words, it is clear that the important real distinction is that between the direction of the self-conscious self to the realisation of an object, its identification of itself with that object, on the one side ... and, on the other side, the mere solicitations of which a man is conscious, but with none of which he so identifies himself as to make the soliciting object his object—the object of his self-seeking—or to direct himself to its realisation.[4]

This, as Sidgwick noted, appears to conflate desire and volition.[5] It is one thing to desire something, it is another thing to resolve to satisfy that desire—even

---

none of these nineteenth-century thinkers had the totalitarian's faith in revolutionary voluntarism. That was a distinctively twentieth-century addition to the mix.

[4] *PE* §143.

[5] 'There seems to me no doubt that I can recognize a distinction in kind between (*a*) the psychical fact of desire as an impulse to which I do not necessarily yield ... and (*b*) the psychical fact of volition, resolution, determination, making up one's mind to aim at something ... And it seems to me more convenient and more in accordance with usage to restrict "desire" to (*a*). Hence to say (*e.g.*) that "*every* desire implies an *effort* on the part of the desiring subject" seems to me misleading—when a desire is checked the "effort" is the other way ...

To say that every desire implies effort on the part of the desiring subject seems to me to mix up things so diverse as *feeling an impulse to do a thing* and *trying to do it*' (Sidgwick, *Lectures on the Ethics of T. H. Green, Herbert Spencer, J. Martineau* (London: Macmillan, 1902), 27, 30).

by way of a conditional decision to satisfy it if an appropriate occasion turns up. But, according to Green:

in the act of will [a] man does not cease to desire. Rather he, the man, for the first time desires, having not done so while divided between the conflicting influences. His willing is ... a desire in which the man enacts himself, as distinct from one which acts upon him. Whether its object—the object to which the moral action is directed—be the attainment of revenge, or the satisfaction of a bodily want, or the fulfillment of a call of duty, it has equally this characteristic. The object is one which for the time being the man identifies with himself, so that in being determined by it he is consciously determined by himself.[6]

The disagreement may seem a verbal dispute about the use of the word 'desire'. Both Sidgwick and Green consider choice, volition, resolution, the adoption of an end or a policy as something to pursue, as actions of the will imputable to the self. Green sets this conception of choice as self-activity against a mechanical (and he says Humean[7]) desire/aversion model which he rejects: on this model, behaviour flows from the overall balance, or vector sum, of desire, while the self seems to drop out of the picture other than as a locus of passions and impressions.[8] Sidgwick agrees with Green. Equally, both recognize that passion—the passive experience of solicitation or inclination—has a role in motivation. So far, so good. For ethical purposes we need to recognize (whatever more theoretical account we may want to give of it) an imputable activity of choosing whether or not to act on a solicitation, which may or may not be the one that is antecedently the strongest. And Sidgwick's way of making this distinction does seem closer to common usage.

Still, how Green uses the word 'desire' is not just a matter of terminology. For he holds that one's good is the realization of one's desires. I interpret this to mean the satisfaction of those solicitations *with which I identify*. Furthermore, I think there is force in Green's distinction between mere 'solicitation' and desire. In fact we need a three-way, not a two-way, distinction: between (i) solicitation, (ii) desire (solicitation with which one identifies, chooses to take into account), and (iii) decision or resolution to satisfy the desire. This is to depart from Green's account, but not, I think, essentially. For the important thing for Green is not so much identifying will and desire as showing them to be equally *activity of one and the same unified self*.

---

[6] *PE* §146. In fact Green uses 'desire' in both ways, to refer to solicitations as such as well as to solicitations which the self identifies with. For example, 'the Ego identifies itself with some desire, and sets itself to bring into real existence the ideal object, of which the consciousness is involved in the desire' (*PE* §102). In the section from which this is quoted he uses the word 'motive' to signify the state in which a self identifies with a solicitation.

[7] *PE* §115 n. 1.   [8] See e.g. *PE* §116.

It is part of the Idealist story, as set out, for example, by Green in *Prolegomena* §§118–29, that the self is active in shaping and particularizing the raw material of affect. Desire, understood in these terms, arises whenever a solicitation is, we can say, *fixed* and *taken up* by the self. Even at the level of 'solicitation', desire presents its object as desirable, as something that it would be non-instrumentally reasonable to pursue. It solicits endorsement. To 'identify' with the solicitation is then to take up or accept that presentation—it is to acknowledge realization of the object as a non-instrumental reason for action. Acknowledging it in this way is recognizing it as an apt candidate for consideration in one's decisions. This does not mean that one has decided to act on it, or even that one decides to consider it actively in a particular episode of decision making that one is engaged in. Reading the travel pages, for example, I feel an impulse to visit Central Asia. Reading further, I fix the object: I come to feel that Bukhara would be the place to go. I recognize this as a perfectly reasonable desire: to be accepted not dismissed. This fixing and endorsing of a solicitation is a work of 'self-consciousness', which is thus effective in determining a desire. It is still true, however, that it takes another decision (another bit of self-activity) to put that desire on my agenda as something under active consideration on a particular occasion when I'm deciding where to go on holiday.[9] Contrast an impulse of resentment at another's success. The action that it solicits is something detrimental to the other. It presents that as reasonable (he deserves a bit of bad fortune)—I might try to fix or specify a desirable, satisfying, way of doing it, I might fantasize about it quite a bit. But I cannot endorse it as reasonable. I try to shrug it off, put it to one side, 'silence' it. In contrast, I don't put aside my desire to visit Central Asia. But I may decide that it can't come into consideration until I've carried out some other project, or fulfilled some obligation, or I may simply never get round to thinking about it.

Green does not have to identify these processes with an action of the will, in the sense of resolving to do this or that or to adopt this or that aim or plan. The 'reaction of the man's self' to a solicitation consists rather, at this point, not in volition but in endorsement of the solicitation as *legitimate*, that is, in his affirmation of its object as one that it's *reasonable* for him to desire. Allowing this distinction marks a further step away from the mechanical model of motivation towards a moral psychology suitable for ethics. It makes desire something that is at least in part imputable—that is, for which the person is at least in part accountable. Furthermore, given that Green thinks that individual good is the satisfaction of individual desire, and given that he means by that a

---

[9] I can also of course be impelled to act and even resolve to act on a solicitation which I do not acknowledge as rational.

solicitation which the individual has endorsed, it makes the good of individuals something that they themselves at least in part construct. And it does not force him into the implausible thesis that satisfaction of a desire would contribute to my good only if I have resolved to act on it. There can be desires I fail to act on, goods consciously or unconsciously forgone.

Now we can ask what true desire and thus true good are. According to Green, to think of an object as good is to think of it as 'such as will satisfy desire'.[10] Given Green's special use of the word 'desire', this means: to think of it as satisfying a solicitation I have identified with, or in other words—according to the suggestion just made—to accept its object as one that there is a non-instrumental reason for me to desire, that it is reasonable for me to desire 'for its own sake'. So an object *is* a part of my good if there *is* reason for me to desire it for its own sake. Inclination, or 'solicitation', presents the object as contributing to one's good, as 'good to have'—identifying oneself with the inclination is thus *endorsing* that presentation, whether or not the endorsement ever gives rise to any resolution of the will.

Satisfying my desire is satisfying what I take (at the time of desiring) to be my good. But this does not show that it actually *is* satisfying my good. Now Green would not, I think, accept this distinction between my conception of what is good for me and what *is* good for me as philosophically fundamental. His picture is, rather, that in endorsing some solicitations as ones whose realization would be part of my good, I *make* their realization part of my good. Constructivism, in this further sense, is a feature of the Idealist account of a person's good; self-conscious self-activity generates normativity. Even so, he still has to make some room for the distinction, since it is clearly a critical resource we apply in thinking about our own or another's good. He does so by distinguishing between truer and less true conceptions of my good, or alternatively, between determinately potential, immanent desires of my truest self, the self towards whose realization it is my *telos* to progress, and desires of less true, more transient selves. And he has a criterion for deciding which desires are those of my truest self:

regarding the good generically as that which satisfies desire ... we shall naturally distinguish the moral good as that which satisfies the desire of a moral agent, or that in which a moral agent can find the satisfaction of himself which he necessarily seeks. The true good we shall understand in the same way. It is an end in which the effort of a moral agent can really find rest.[11]

So far we've been using 'satisfaction' and 'realization' in the sense that your desire that *p* is satisfied or realized if it's the case that *p*. But when Green

---

[10]   *PE* §171.   [11]   ibid. §171.

in this passage talks about a desire as one in which 'a moral agent can find the satisfaction of himself which he necessarily seeks', he uses 'satisfaction' in another, more familiar way. He means not just that you get what you want, but that you are satisfied with it. You don't regret trying to get it, it doesn't turn out to be Dead Sea fruit; you want it not just *ex ante*, before you've got it, but also *ex post*, after you've got it.

The assumption is that human beings have determinate natures which shape, both actually and potentially, the ends they seek, and in virtue of which some activities and achievements bring fuller satisfaction than others. That thesis is needed for any developmental, progressivist notion of an individual's good, Idealist or other. Friedrich Schiller, Marx, or Mill need it as much as Green or Hegel do. And in itself it does not seem unrealistic. But of course, as we see in this passage and more explicitly elsewhere, Green is making a more heroic teleological assumption, which is that lasting satisfaction is provided for all human beings by, and only by, virtuous pursuit of the common good, and that it is this fuller satisfaction that they 'necessarily' seek, and only this in which they 'can really find rest'. We shall come back to this.

There is something of a tension between this criterion of lasting satisfaction and the constructivist element in Green's conception of the good. How can my lasting satisfaction, in the sense of my being satisfied with the object, content with it, when I get it, be the criterion of my good, if my endorsement of a solicitation already determines that its satisfaction, in the formal sense of its object being realized, is part of my good? Should we say that my good consists not in the realization of my desires but in whatever it is in which I would find lasting satisfaction? Actually, it seems to me that neither account is correct, because both are reductive. The fact that I identify with or endorse a solicitation does not make it true that realizing it would contribute to my good. But neither does the fact that realizing its object would give me lasting satisfaction make it true that it would contribute to my good. On the one hand, it can turn out that what I desire gives me no lasting satisfaction when I get it. In other words, when I get it, I find that I *don't* want it, or perhaps don't want it as much as I thought I would. In that case, the test of antecedent desire is defeated by the test of posterior desire.[12] What I desired, and what I believed I had reason to desire, there was in fact no reason for me to desire. On the other hand, the fact that something gives me lasting satisfaction equally does not entail that achieving it contributed to my

---

[12] I'm ignoring important complications to do with whether I know that I've got it. And of course I may not want it when I've got it for incidental reasons, such as illness, etc., which do not defeat the reasonableness of wanting it in the first place.

good. Achieving it may have been deleterious to my personality, reduced my capacities for enjoyment, made me an addict, affected my capacity to take in relevant information, etc.

This is not the place for a careful investigation of all the pitfalls of this kind that attend reductive models of a person's good. The general point (I would want to argue) is that no facts about what a person does or would desire, either *ex ante* or *ex post, entail* a conclusion about that person's good. The connection is criterial. Facts about what a person does and would desire can be better or worse a priori evidence for conclusions about the person's good, about what is desirable for that person, and nothing other than facts of this kind can be a priori evidence. But the evidence is always in principle defeasible, however good it is in practice. So the correct account of a person's good must be in explicitly and irreducibly normative terms: it is what *there is reason* for him or her to desire.

However, let's waive this general point, about the difference between criteria and truth conditions for propositions about a person's good. I want to go on describing Green's view in terms of the notion of a 'true desire'. So I shall use this phrase in such a way that those same sets of facts about a person's actual or potential desires that would constitute good criterial evidence, to varying degrees of goodness, that there's reason for him to desire that p (that its being the case that p would be part of his good, desirable for *him*) will constitute equally good criterial evidence, to the same varying degrees, that this person 'truly' desires that p. Green takes it that such true desires have a genuine though potential existence in me, presumably as solicitations, in a way that gives them power to determine the course of my development. So my true desires are, roughly, the desires that my most fully realized self would come to endorse in a conscious way.

Anything that's desired is desired under some idea of one's good. What is truly desired is desired under a true idea of one's good. But it is misleading to say, with Green, that all desire is the desire for self-satisfaction. In the formal sense of 'satisfy', it is trivially true that a desire is always a desire for that which would satisfy it. But if satisfaction, and in particular, *self*-satisfaction, are used substantively, to refer to the state of being satisfied with the achievement of one's desire, then it is false that all desire is desire for self-satisfaction. One can desire something which one will never know one has achieved, such as posthumous fame, to take Sidgwick's example,[13] or the happiness of one's children after one's death. And this is important in highlighting the expansive nature of Green's conception of a person's good.

[13] Sidgwick, *Lectures*, 31.

We'll consider in the next section the objection that it is *too* expansive. But before turning to that important question, I end this section by tying Green's formal egoism to his theory of motivation. Green thinks that *all* my actions, in the full imputable sense of intentional action from a motive, are motivated by desires, and hence by some idea of my good:

> To every action morally imputable, or of which a man can recognise himself as the author, the motive is always some idea of the man's personal good.[14]

> [I]n all conduct to which moral predicates are applicable a man is an object to himself ... such conduct, whether virtuous or vicious, expresses a motive consisting in the idea of personal good, which the man seeks to realise by action.[15]

In terms of the German philosophical debate that Green was trying to bring to Britain, one can say that he takes sides on this matter with Hegel rather than Kant. On the Kantian view there can be reason to pursue an end irrespective of whether one desires it, or indeed whether it is reasonable to desire it: there can be reason to pursue it just because it is right to pursue it. The recognition that the end is right can itself be a motive. Such a motive involves no process of self-identification with any solicitation or impulse *presented* to the will. In Kant's understanding, which identifies the will (*Wille*) with practical reason, it is wholly *internal* to the will. Practical reason itself judges reasons for action and determines action in light of that.

We thus note three steps away from the mechanical model of motivation, involving three distinctions. The first step distinguishes between solicitation and desire, in the way we have examined. Desire involves taking up a solicitation, acknowledging it as reason-giving. This is a good, indispensable distinction. The second step distinguishes between desire and the activity of practical decision. Acknowledging a solicitation as reason-giving is one thing, resolving to act on it, even if only conditionally (placing it on the agenda), is another. The third step distinguishes between motive and desire. This step allows that there can be a source of practical reasons irrespective of solicitation, and thus of desire.

Green refuses to go beyond the first step. But this is not enough to give the self autonomy (which he wants to give it, as we shall see in section IV). Autonomy presupposes all three distinctions just mentioned. It requires all the abilities involved in assessing the reasonableness of solicitations, deciding whether to take desires into account in some process of decision making or to rule them off that decision-making agenda, and, no less importantly, deciding whether there is reason to bring about an outcome irrespective of whether I

---

[14] *PE* §95.   [15] ibid. §115.

desire that outcome—even if I do not desire it—and acting accordingly if one so decides.[16] Green does not give himself the philosophical room to deal with all this. As he says, the mechanical model of motivation makes the will 'merely a designation for any desire that happens for the time to be strong enough to determine action'[17]—Green's model does not do that, but it still makes the will a servant of solicitations or passions, a servant whose only discretion lies in picking which passion to serve, instead of mechanically identifying with the one that's most peremptory. Autonomy, however, lies in being able to recognize that there is reason to bring about an outcome irrespective of whether I desire that outcome—even if I do not desire it—and in being able to act on that recognition.

It is not 'empiricist' preconceptions that prevent Green from taking the Kantian direction.[18] His motive, like Hegel's, is to avoid dividing the self. At one level the Absolute Idealist striving for unity doesn't stop until everything has been incorporated in the self—even if that self is hard to recognize as oneself. At this level there's a question about where 'solicitations' come from, just as there's a question about where the sensations involved in perception come from. Once we're on the Absolute Idealist train, we have to conclude that they themselves somehow come from the self. But a more modest unifying view is more tenable: the unifying fact is the play of self-consciousness, in the form of rational assessment, in the three spheres of belief, feeling, and action. My passions are mine both in the sense that they are spontaneous to me, not products of indoctrination, and in the sense that they are shaped and acknowledged by my own reflection. They don't have to be mine in the sense of somehow being produced by me. Indeed, if they were, it would be a mystery why different individual people have different passions. This is one of the ways in which Idealism (rather than utilitarianism) has difficulty in coping with the separateness of people.

But there's also a very good question underlying the Hegelian direction: on the Kantian model of conscientious action, there seems to be no room for the self to find satisfaction in doing its duty. How can duty be at the same time absolute irrespective of one's desires and at the same time satisfying, liberating? How can it give meaning to one's life? To this question we shall return.

---

[16] I can recognize that there is reason for me to desire an outcome without actually desiring it, and still be motivated just by that recognition. I can also recognize that there is reason for me to bring about an outcome even though there is no reason for me to *desire* it—even though it is for *me* entirely undesirable—and still be motivated by that recognition.

[17] *PE* §116. Here too Green uses 'desire' to mean 'solicitation'.

[18] Mill, the arch-empiricist, does distinguish desire and will, and allows that action may proceed from the will. (Which is not to say that he has a satisfactory explanation of how this comes about.)

For the moment, we conclude that Green's psychological egoism is the product of two things: a model of motivation in which desire is the only motive and a definition of personal good in terms of desire. This in turn underpins his normative egoism. By removing the model of motivation to which Green adheres, we remove this underpinning, even if we still maintain a definition of personal good in terms of desire.

We also make it easier to defend the Idealist conception of individual good. If we use *desire* widely, as in effect equivalent to *motive*, it becomes implausible to identify individual good with realization of the individual's desires. If we use it narrowly, it becomes at least more plausible. One's good is the satisfaction of what one has reason to desire: of those solicitations which one has reason to take up, endorse. This is no longer a formally egoistic view: there can be good reason to pursue objectives that are distinct from one's own good. Nevertheless, isn't this conception of a person's good still too expansive? Don't people have desires, and reasonable desires, that have nothing to do with their own good?

III. Self-Enlargement

In response to this question, one can ask another.[19] If some desires have nothing to do with one's good, what is the difference between those that do and those that do not? If it's too broad to characterize a person's good as that which there is reason for that person to desire, how should one characterize it more narrowly? And furthermore, once we've acknowledged that not all motivation is desire-based, what motivates the posited further distinction between desires for my own good and desires for other things? What is its ethical point?

For many practical purposes we have a working notion of well-being couched in terms of a person's physical and psychological flourishing. 'Flourishing' in this sense is an empirical quality of a person that doctors and psychologists can help define. Obviously Green could and should accept that working notion as such, and he could accept that, other things equal, a person's physical and mental well-being is likely to be an important part of his good. It's difficult to imagine self-constructions of one's good in which it wouldn't feature at all. This is also the part of a person's good that is often easiest to focus on for policy purposes—though that already merits critical scrutiny, especially from the Idealist's ethical standpoint. At any rate, it's not in question

---

[19] In this section I restate and expand points made on Green's behalf in my 'Desire and Will in Sidgwick and Green'.

that this working notion is what we often have in mind when we ask after a person's well-being. But this does not yield much philosophical leverage in criticizing Green's conception. For it is not just possible, but quite plausible, that a person may sometimes further his true good at the expense of his physical and psychological flourishing. There must therefore be elements in a person's good that go beyond flourishing in this sense.

Another approach is through a substantive characterization, or 'objective list', of what contributes to my good. Such a list would give us an independent criterion for judging whether a desire is for my own good or for something else. Clearly, however, Green's approach is inconsistent with objective-list intuitionism. This intuitionism assumes that we have at our disposal a pre-given notion of individual good, rather than having to construct it from actual and potential human desire. Green wouldn't concede that we have that. If we find it plausible that the concept of individual good must be rooted epistemologically, in the way explained above, in what is desired *ex ante* and *ex post*, we will agree with him.

A third approach is to contrast desires that have one's own good, or at least something about oneself that's intuitively related to one's good, in their content, with desires that don't, and to suggest that only satisfaction of reasonable desires of the first kind contributes to one's good.

But self-reference can appear in the content of a desire in a variety of ways, more and less salient, and the difficulty is to know where and why, in this shading off of self-reference, to draw the line. Suppose, as a first example, that you have joined a group of car-owners who ferry home-bound people to hospital in their cars. You have joined because you want to help others; you get satisfaction from doing so. If someone asked you why you joined, you could truly say 'because I enjoy making myself useful'. You could equally well answer by explaining why it's useful to have an organizing group providing ferry services to the hospital with their cars. Do you yourself enter into the content of your desire? The desire that causes you to act is that these people should have somewhat less inconvenient, more comfortable lives. You don't enter into the content of that desire. None the less, you have fixed on that object because you want to make yourself useful. You do enter into the content of that one.

This is the kind of case in which Mill's distinction between doing something as a part of your good and as a means to it is relevant. We must not ignore the fact that you're helping out *because* you enjoy making yourself useful. That enjoyment does enter into the explanation of why you act. But it is misleading to say that you act *in order to get* the enjoyment of making yourself useful. The correct account of your motives is not that you have a desire for your own enjoyment that combines with a belief that helping others will prove to be enjoyable. The correct account is that you simply have a desire to make yourself useful to these people, a desire that expresses itself in the conception of that task as an enjoyable one. However, it is the *task* that features in the content of the desire, not the thought of it as enjoyable.[20] Helping others is a part of your good, not a means to it. Green should certainly acknowledge this distinction; he needs it as much as Mill does in order to show why his formal egoism does not collapse down to the doctrine that people are always selfish.[21]

In the above example, no general desire for the agent's own enjoyment plays a motivating role. The agent desires the *particular object*, under the idea of it as enjoyable; that is not to say that he acts from a desire for his own enjoyment. Still, in thinking of the object as enjoyable, he is of course thinking of it as enjoyable to *him*. But why shouldn't we also accept that people make all sorts of self-transcending ends a part of their good with no thought at any level of their own enjoyment? Suppose an art collector caught in his burning house shouts out to us through the window, 'Don't worry about me, save my art collection.' One could describe him as caring more about his art collection than his own well-being—where well-being refers to his personal flourishing in the physical and mental sense. But one could also say that the fate of his art collection has become a part of his good, and a more important part than his personal flourishing. The art collector may quite reasonably care more about his art collection than about his personal flourishing. He rightly thinks the collection is valuable and wants to save it. That is his immediate desire. Self-reference still comes into the underlying desires: he wants to save it because he has spent a lifetime on it, he has put most of himself into it, he wants to pass this thing that *he* has done on to others. And it may be that in this desperate situation, where either he burns or his art collection does, saving his art collection matters more to him than saving his own life. Why, then, shouldn't we say that it contributes more to his good, though not to his physical and mental flourishing?

We can say, it is true, that the art collector sacrifices himself. But that does not show, it seems to me, that his action does not on the whole contribute to his

---

[20] In a similar way, when a person acts from duty, it can be misleading to say that he acts *in order to bring it about that* he has done his duty, even though it *is* because he thinks this is his duty that he acts. The formulation may suggest a moral narcissism that isn't there, or a wish to get the duty out of the way. The doctor who tends you is doing it because that's his duty—not because, for example, you're a personal friend he wants to help. But to say that he's doing it in order to discharge his duty suggests, for example, that he's accumulating moral points, or in a hurry to get home.

[21] Which makes it disappointing that in his critique of hedonism he does not allow Mill its benefit. Compare Nicholson, *Political Philosophy of the British Idealists*, 70, for the criticism that Green's theory of motivation makes all action self-interested (i.e. selfish, not benevolent). I agree with Nicholson that Green's theory does not have this consequence, but my interpretation and defence of Green as regards this point differs from his.

good. Someone may go to civic meetings which he has no desire at all to go to, out of pure conscientiousness. He may be said to 'sacrifice himself', or at least to sacrifice his effort and time, for the common good. What, then, of someone who has become thoroughly identified with the town, wants to make himself useful, and goes for that reason? Does he sacrifice himself? He wants to go, and his desire to go is reasonable, even if he's going to find this particular meeting boring. He wouldn't say he was sacrificing himself. Contributing to the good of the town has become a part of his good. All the same, at the end of his civic career, he deserves thanks for the sacrifices of time and energy that he's made. There was a sacrifice in the sense that he was giving up, for the good of the town, something rightly considered as precious—his time and energy—and which he was *entitled to use as he thought fit*. It would be a low-minded response to say, 'Well, he only did it because he felt like doing it'. Pursuing something as a part of your good is not necessarily acting selfishly or self-interestedly in any normal sense. On the contrary, making the good of the town a part of your own good is in itself admirable, and something that deserves thanks.

In all these cases, when the background desires are fully characterized, they still have self-reference in their content. Granted, this does not make the desire a selfish one. None the less, it may be suggested, it is this element of self-reference that gives point to saying, in these cases, that you desire something as part of your good. What about desires that have no self-reference of this kind? Suppose Mary desires the happiness of her grandchildren. She desires, reasonably and non-instrumentally, that they should be happy. This desire is not the same as the desire that *she* should contribute to their happiness. Of course, if she acts on the former desire, *she* is pursuing its object, but that applies to any of her desires.

Still, Mary wants the happiness of *her* grandchildren. But there need be no self-involvement in the content of a desire, at any level. Rahul desires the success of an athlete he greatly admires; Jane desires the long-term regeneration of the Caledonian forest.[22] These are objects with which, in Green's terms, they identify themselves.

Can these objects be regarded as a part of their good? What makes your success, but not the success of your grandchildren, a part of your good? What makes the success of your grandchildren, but not the regeneration of the Caledonian forest, a part of your good? You might leave money in your will for regeneration work on the forest as well as for your grandchildren. You might ask a close friend to continue, for *your* sake, the forest work you've been doing. Similarly, your friend, even if you have said nothing, might take a benevolent

---

[22] I am waiving deeper questions about whether *all* mental content involves indexical self-reference.

interest after your death in the fortunes of your grandchildren—not exactly for their sake but for *your* sake, because he knew how much they mattered to *you*.[23]

Against that, one might ask: when the good of others—or outcomes which can be characterized without any reference to me at all, such as the long-term regeneration of the Caledonian forest—becomes 'a part of my good', is this not a dilution of the notion of personal good, a fading of its boundaries, in that the notion of self fades from the content of the desire? Can it be plausible to see it instead as an *expansion* of the notion of the self, an enlargement of its objectification in the world through self-identification with others, or with outcomes beyond my stream of experience? Green could argue that there is both dilution and expansion: the psychological process involved is the fading of a lower, because narrower, conception of the limits of one's self (or more accurately one's good) in favour of a more expansive one. And this seems to me a notable, ethically insightful aspect of the Idealist conception of a person's good. It is a deep feature of the good of human beings that they are able to achieve this kind of self-enlargement by identifying with other objects, people, causes, and assimilating the good of those 'significant others' into their own good. Human beings are existentially a kind of being whose good can transcend its own physical and mental flourishing. None the less, this insightful feature of Idealism is also potentially dangerous. The point about dilution is not to be ignored: at some point, identification with others can become a kind of abnegation or submission that is bad for oneself and open to exploitation by others. This difference between self-expansion and self-abnegation can undoubtedly be very hard to make out—both are real phenomena—but from a liberal point of view it is vital. It's hard to feel that in his accounts of the common good Green is sufficiently aware of the danger. At points like this one feels like reaching for one's copy of Nietzsche.

IV. Self-Realization and Freedom

I turn finally to the theses of which I said at the beginning that I wanted to give a partial defence: that the good of a person consists in self-realization, and that self-realization is freedom, so that the good of a person consists in freedom.

---

[23] It would make no sense to promote, for *your* sake, the satisfaction of a desire of yours which one believed to be irrational. Nor would it make sense to promote for your sake a desire you no longer had. What this means is that the desire must be one that you still have, if you are alive, or that you still had when you died. If you had long ago lost your interest in the Caledonian forest, it would be bizarre to make a posthumous contribution to its regeneration for *your* sake. Your self-identifications are, so to speak, frozen at death.

At a formal level, 'self-realization' can simply mean the realization of what I truly desire. It is then a trivial corollary of what has already been said that the good of the self consists in self-realization. However, Green has a substantive, far from trivial, perfectionist conception of self-realization in mind. To realize oneself is to perfect one's capacities; specifically, it is to perfect one's capacity of *moral* agency, or at any rate to work towards that perfection. Furthermore, moral agency is freedom, so self-realization is freedom.

Some obvious questions arise. Why should it be thought that self-realization in this stronger, substantive sense—the perfecting of one's capacities—is what human beings truly desire, as Green must hold? Even granting that we truly desire to perfect ourselves, is this all we truly desire? And why should the focus of this desire for self-perfection be on perfecting oneself as a *morally virtuous agent*? And what has this to do with freedom?

The link with freedom goes through rationality. Green upholds the Kantian theses that freedom in the positive sense is rational agency, which is moral agency.[24] He calls freedom in this positive sense moral freedom, or autonomy:

The determination of will by reason ... which constitutes moral freedom or autonomy, must mean its determination by an object which a person willing, in virtue of his reason, presents to himself.[25]

We are free in this sense, autonomous or morally free, when we do what we have most reason to do, from recognition that it *is* what we have most reason to do. I agree that we have this notion, and that it is in play when we assess responsibility. To impute an action to an agent, to hold the *agent* fully responsible, answerable, for what he did, is to hold him capable (on that specific occasion) of acting autonomously, whether or not he did. And as Green also notes, again following Kant, this concept of autonomy is stronger than mere self-determination, since I also determine myself when I act badly. Since this concept of autonomy and its connection with responsibility and blame have been much discussed, strongly attacked, and well defended, I won't say more about the concept here than that its exploration and reinstatement seem to me to be among the valuable legacies of Idealism.[26] But two things are required

---

[24] Kant's references to the 'positive' sense of freedom: *Practical Philosophy*, in *The Cambridge Edition of the Works of Immanuel Kant*, trans. and ed. Mary J. Gregor (Cambridge: Cambridge University Press, 1996), 95, 166. And of course Green's 'Liberal Legislation and Freedom of Contract', in Paul Harris and John Morrow (eds.), *T. H. Green, Lectures on the Principles of Political Obligation and Other Writings* (Cambridge: Cambridge University Press, 1986), 199–200.

[25] 'On the Different Senses of "Freedom" as Applied to Will and to the Moral Progress of Man', *CW* ii. 332.

[26] See John Skorupski, 'Freedom, Morality and Recognition: Some Theses of Kant and Hegel', in *Ethical Explorations* (Oxford: Oxford University Press, 1999). I discuss some of Sidgwick's criticisms of

to show, via this conception of positive freedom, that one's good consists in perfecting one's moral agency. First, it must be shown that my good consists in perfecting my freedom—that is, my rational agency. Second, it must be shown that rational agency consists in moral agency.

Why, then, should I believe that my good consists in perfecting my own positive freedom? We have most reason to do what we have most reason to do. So we have most reason to do what we would do if we were acting from rational autonomy. These are tautologies—but it is *not* tautologous either that we truly desire or that we have reason to desire the perfection of our rational autonomy: that is, the power of coming to accurate conclusions about what we have reasons to do and acting from those conclusions. It may be that improving your rational autonomy is justified on instrumental grounds: you're more likely to do what you've got most reason to do if you are good at knowing what that is and acting on the knowledge. But in that case we must also compute the opportunity cost of developing that capacity. What if it increases your stress levels and decreases your spontaneous relish for life? In any case, Green's claim is not instrumental. He thinks that autonomy is desirable for its own sake.

He does not try to present this as a supposedly formal truth about practical rationality, or as a self-evident intuition about the content of practical reason. It is a strength of the Idealist tradition that it does not do so. As we have seen, his criterion for an individual's good is historicist or developmental. Your true good is what you truly desire: what you want more clearly, the more you develop, and what gives enduring satisfaction. I've argued above that these are the right criteria—but do they produce Green's result? The claim must be that *positive freedom* is what you come to want more clearly as you develop, and what gives you enduring satisfaction.

Before pursuing this point, we must bring in the second step, that rational agency is moral agency. Here again Green's argument is distinctive.

One way to identify moral agency with autonomy would be to derive morality from practical reason. If practical reason consists in impartial concern for all, for example, then the fully free, because fully rational, agent is one who acts out of impartial concern for all. This could be the view of someone who accepted a utilitarian theory of practical reason and a positive conception of freedom as rationality.[27] Or if morality is simply the total set of categorical

---

Kant's and Green's account of freedom in Skorupski, 'Desire and will in Sidgwick and Green'. Green thinks that the conception of freedom as rationality has older roots in the Stoics and St Paul (*CW* ii. 310). But it's still German Idealism that worked it out most fully, gave it a starring role in ethics and more generally in its account of modernity, and left an unavoidable set of challenges about it for later philosophy.

[27] Some themes in Mill play strongly in this direction.

principles of practical reason, then even more directly the fully free agent is the moral agent. That is Kant's view. And the conclusion would continue to hold even on the weaker claim that moral duties are at least a subset of the categorical principles of practical reason.

Green does not take these lines. It would be inconsistent on his part to do so, because he is committed to the view that the only underived principle of practical reason is formal egoism. Hence, if reason is to require virtue, it must require it as constituting one's good. And that is what he argues:

Why ... it may be asked, should the moralizing influence in man, the faculty through which the paths of virtue are marked out, whether followed or no, be specially called reason? We answer: because it is through the operative consciousness in man of a possible state of himself better than the actual, though that consciousness is the condition of the possibility of all that is morally wrong, that the divine self-realising principle in him gradually fulfils its capability in the production of a higher life. With this consciousness, directed in the right path, *i.e.* the path in which it tends to become what according to the immanent divine law of its being it has to be—and it is as so directed that we call it 'practical reason'—rests the initiative of all virtuous habit and action.[28]

In reflective self-determined action, as against merely animal action, the 'operative consciousness in man' forms a conception of a possible state of the self better than the actual, and determines action in its light. This applies in all such action, so in the case of wrong as well as right doing. None the less, this consciousness has an immanent—as Green thinks, divine—principle: a *telos* that determines certain among its conceptions of a better state of the self as those which tend naturally to prevail. And these conceptions, whose true content, Green thinks, emerges gradually in human history, are conceptions of perfect virtue as the perfect state of the self. When the operative consciousness works according to this principle, we call it practical reason, because it is these states of the self that constitute our true good, and practical reason consist in the pursuit of our true good, that which we truly desire.

Notice how Green talks in this passage of better states *of* me, rather than better states *for* me. He is thinking about ideals, the admirable, rather than ends, the desirable. He takes it as immanent in our nature to respond to an ideal of ourselves as virtuous beings: what he calls the 'moral ideal'. But to respond in what way? I might admire virtue, see it as a great excellence, without desiring to achieve it in myself, just as I might admire high mathematical ability, or brilliant skiing, see it as a great excellence, without desiring to achieve it in myself. If realizing the 'moral ideal' in myself is to be even a part of my good, it

---

[28] *PE* §178.

must be because it answers to some true desire in me to achieve this excellence in particular. Only then will it better *for* me to be in this better state *of* me; only if achieving this admirable state of myself is truly desirable to *me*. Allow me now to quote another, rather long, passage from the *Prolegomena*:

Supposing such an idea [viz. the moral ideal] to be operative in man, what must be the manner of its operation? It will keep before him an object, which he presents to himself as absolutely desirable, but which is other than any particular object of desire ... because it is the fulfilment of himself, of that which he has in him to be, it will excite an interest in him like no other interest, different in kind from any of his desires and aversions except such as are derived from it. It will be an interest as in an object conceived to be of unconditional value; one of which the value does not depend on any desire that the individual may at any time feel for it or for anything else, or on any pleasure that, either in its pursuit or in its attainment or as its result, he may experience. The conception of its desirableness will not arise, like the conception of the desirableness of any pleasure, from previous enjoyment of it or from reflection on the desire for it. On the contrary, the desire for the object will be founded on a conception of its desirableness as a fulfilment of the capabilities of which a man is conscious in being conscious of himself.

  In such men and at such times as a desire for it does actually arise—a desire in that sense which implies that the man puts himself forth for the realisation of the desired object—it will express itself in their imposition on themselves of rules requiring something to be done irrespectively of any inclination to do it, irrespectively of any desired end to which it is a means, *other than this end, which is desired because conceived as absolutely desirable.* With the men in whom, and at the times when, there is no such desire, the consciousness of there being something absolutely desirable will still be a qualifying element in life. It will yield a recognition of those unconditional rules of conduct to which, from the prevalence of unconformable passions, it fails to produce actual obedience. It will give meaning to the demand, without which there is no morality and in which all morality is virtually involved, that 'something be done merely for the sake of its being done,'[29] because it is a consciousness of the possibility of an action in which no desire shall be gratified but the desire excited by the idea of the act itself, as of something absolutely desirable in the sense that in it the man does the best that he has in him to do.[30]

The difficulties Green faces in this passage arise from his wish to uphold the unconditional status of the moral law while rejecting the moral psychology on which Kant bases this unconditionality—according to which there is a sharp distinction between the noumenal domain of reason and duty and the phenomena of desire. For Green there can be reason for me to do something only in virtue of it bringing about something desirable for me.

---

[29] Green's footnote to this quotation cites a passage from Fichte.   [30] *PE* §193.

And 'desirable for me' must mean, if Green is consistent, something I truly desire. So Green cannot mean what Kant means by saying that moral rules are unconditional, because on Green's own account there can be reason to follow moral rules only inasmuch as following them brings about an end that I truly desire. In what sense, then, does Green think that moral rules are unconditional?

We impose them on ourselves, he says, irrespective of any end '*other than this end, which is desired because conceived as absolutely desirable*'. And this end is the 'fulfilment of the capabilities of which a man is conscious in being conscious of himself'. In what sense is it, as against other ends, absolutely desirable? How does the desire for this end stand out as special, in comparison, say, to the desire for pleasure? Why is pleasure not absolutely desirable? In the first paragraph of the quoted passage Green noticeably gives the difference a Kantian spin: the conception of the 'desirableness' of the moral ideal does not arise from 'previous enjoyment of it or from reflection on the desire for it'. And certainly he can point out, as I have suggested, that the desire for virtue, as against the desire for pleasure, arises because a virtuous life—unlike a life of pleasure—is experienced as admirable in itself, an ideal. Virtue comes to be desired because it is admired. All the same, given his moral psychology, if he thinks that the good of the individual consists *wholly* in moral virtue, as it seems he does, then he must hold that the desire for pleasure is in all or at least most individuals not 'as true' as the desire to fulfil the moral ideal.

This is surely fervour for morality carried to excess. I will come back to this, but let us first explore a bit further the persuasive way in which Green draws on the moral psychology of ideals. The moral ideal in a man, Green says, 'will excite an interest in him like no other interest, different in kind from any of his desires and aversions except such as are derived from it'. That is because 'it is the fulfilment of himself, of that which he has in him to be'. Likewise, 'the desire for the object will be founded on a conception of its desirableness as a fulfilment of the capabilities of which a man is conscious in being conscious of himself'.

In these passages Green appeals to the place we give, in our conception of how to live, not just to ends but to ideals, and on how it feels when ideals motivate us. As just noted, one may or may not desire what one admires. However, an ideal can *come* to be something that one desires. I can come to see it as a capacity or way of living that is right for *me*—a way for me to make the best of myself. When a person comes to see some admirable way of being and doing as in this way right for *him*, he sees it, in Green's words, 'as the fulfilment of himself, of that which he has in him to be'.

A fundamental aspect of the psychology of ideals is that ideals of being and doing can *grip* you. An ideal that has gripped you is experienced as compulsory; it has what Bernard Williams called 'practical necessity'. 'I must go to those starving in this famine and try to bring comfort and aid.' 'I must preserve and rebuild this great house and estate.' 'I must rescue the nation and make it great again.' 'I must throw away my worldly property and live a life of contemplation among animals and birds.' This psychology, the psychology of vocation, has normative significance: we make due allowance for someone gripped by an ideal we regard as worthy. For example, we may excuse them, if we're sufficiently persuaded of their sincerity and rationality, from obligations we might otherwise think they had. We are also prone to feel a certain lack of respect for those with no ideals at all, for whom making something worthwhile of their life has little or no importance—though such responses take us on to dangerous and delicate territory.

To live by an ideal is one form of positive freedom, because it is one form of self-imposed necessity. Unfreedom is constraint by something that is not me. Negative freedom is the mere removal of that constraint. But, if the constraint is something I give or 'legislate' to myself, or again, if it takes the shape of an 'other', a not-me that I can at the same time find myself in, be 'with myself in' (in Hegel's phrase), then instead of removing unfreedom and replacing it by arbitrariness, I have transcended unfreedom and replaced it by the positive freedom of self-enlargement. By free extension of boundaries on myself, I 'differentiate' and 'actualize' myself. I can do this through long-term commitment to worthwhile achievement, voluntary service, changing the world, ethical union with particular others, ascetic spirituality, etc.

These are different and admirable ideals, and there are many more from the very great to the very small. It is important, and well brought out by Green, that the experience and acceptance of duty can be for most people something that is personally worthwhile, in the way that living by a great ideal can be worthwhile; in other words, in a way that is more worthwhile—contributes more to the satisfying personal forging of a character or identity—than just going around enjoying yourself (or staying on the couch enjoying yourself).

All the same, even when all this is fully understood and properly estimated, Green's presentation of the role of morality in life remains both too weak and too strong. It is too weak, in that the *only* categoricity he can give it is the experienced liberation-through-compulsion, or 'practical necessity', of ideals. But although ideals can grip one, and although someone who responds to no worthy ideal at all may be a poor sort of character, ideals are none the less optional in a way that moral obligations are not. If someone makes a life of moral excellence his ideal, one can say, 'Well, yours is the moral ideal, and I admire you for it, but it's not mine. Mine is to be a great musician, or mine is to preserve and enrich the family estate.' In the sense in which one can truly say that, one is not giving oneself an exemption from morality. One is simply not making it the ideal of one's life. Morality retains its claim, because that claim does not *depend* on whether one has made the life of virtue the ideal that shapes one's life. In contrast, I may admire the sacrifices you make for your music without having any obligation to engage in musical activity at all—even if I too have great musical capabilities which I could fulfil. My lack of interest in following that path may be very sad, but it would be absurd and, specifically, illiberal to regard it as *blameworthy*. The point is that moral obligation has a reason-giving force that does not depend on whether it is desirable to you to lead a life of moral excellence, whether that is what you decide to 'commit to'. It is not generated from the fact that complying with moral obligations would fulfil your moral capabilities. Suppose that you would fulfil your musical capabilities by doing music. That would be generally accepted, certainly, as a reason to commit to doing it. If you do so, you may become gripped by it; it may become one of your vital routes to self-realization. But it's still up to you. It is not like that with morality. You don't have the option of staying out.

At the same time, the role which Green gives to the 'moral ideal' is too strong. Being the sort of person whose focus is on civic service, or improving the world, or exemplary personal standards of virtue, is certainly *one* fulfilling ideal of being and doing, but it is not the only great ideal. These two weaknesses are connected. It is the logic of Green's position that forces him to hold that the moral ideal is the only true ideal and the only 'absolutely desirable' end. For he rejects Kant's conception of the categoricity of morality, yet still (rightly) wants morality to be categorical in some basic way in which nothing else is: the exclusive dominance of the moral ideal is then the only basis for morality's non-optional standing that he can provide. It's not enough, on this approach, that the moral ideal occupies a very high place among ideals, one of the highest. It has to be incommensurably, absolutely, higher. In contrast, if we grant that moral duties are categorical irrespective of any desire, including the desire to pursue some great ideal, we can give the desire to pursue a moral ideal its place among other equally ultimate desires. We can say to someone, 'OK, you're not interested in working for the community, don't care about changing the world or being a paragon of moral virtue—get on with what matters to you, but don't think that lets you off the duties that you, along with everyone else, none the less still have.'[31]

---

[31] Though, as I noted above, if someone pursues a non-moral ideal with sufficient commitment and chance of success, we may be willing to waive *some* obligations we might otherwise think they had.

In these ways Green's—as it seems to me, mistaken—attempt to ground morality on an Idealist conception of personal good has systemically distorting effects on his moral and political outlook as a whole. But we should not forget that this mistaken argument is only part of the story. Green was making a direct and substantive contribution to a crucial debate among nineteenth-century liberals about what ideals to place at the heart of liberalism. His case for the surpassing importance, especially in his time, of the moral ideal was influential partly through his abstract metaphysics—his thoroughgoing re-analysis of self-identity and reason—and partly through the circumstances of the time, but at least as much through truly impressive personal force, inspiration, and example. I want to end by turning to this question of liberal ideals.

V. Ideals of Positive Freedom

Idealism was not the only nineteenth-century outlook that emphasized the importance of self-development in a full, personally worthwhile life. This was a very broadly shared conviction. Liberals of that century understood their view not as a merely negative doctrine about resisting tyranny from wherever it comes, but as a positive doctrine about the good of human beings. Human good is, or includes, a positive freedom achieved through self-development; civil and political institutions of liberty are the social conditions needed to achieve and maintain it. Whatever their philosophical persuasion, these comprehensive liberals (to use Rawls's term) typically saw themselves as going beyond, or deepening, the shallowly grounded political constructions of the Enlightenment. Most of them would have endorsed the ethical ideas that we have been discussing, of self-realization through self-enlargement, and freedom as liberation through self-imposed necessity, even though it was Idealism that provided the moral vocabulary to express them.

Inasmuch as the ideology of our contemporary liberalism sidelines the conceptions of human life thereby expressed, or cramps and flattens them to 'matters of private preference', it loses vital formulations and diminishes our notions of individual good.[32] That can be recognized as a decline in the scope and depth of comprehensive liberal discussion—whatever one thinks about how neutral the liberal State should be. There is, certainly, some degree of separateness between these two issues. One could accept the importance, for the *ethos* of liberal cultures, of recovering and reassessing such ideals, but still

---

[32] I discuss aspects of this in 'The Future of Ideals', in *Philosophy at the New Millenium*, Royal Institute of Philosophy Supplement (Cambridge: Cambridge University Press, 2001).

hold that the *State*, and even the 'public reason' of democracies, should refrain from promoting, maintaining, or facilitating this or that conception of the good, including those propounded by classical liberals. It falls outside the scope of this paper to consider whether such neutralism is sensible. To me it seems that a healthy liberal State requires an *ethos*, at least in the form of a hinterland of active ideals of life that are congruent with it. How strictly these should remain a hinterland strikes me as a matter of political tactics, rather than political principle, but this is a view that would have to be defended against those who think otherwise. What I want to do here by way of conclusion is simply to highlight an important difference among two great nineteenth-century liberal ideals, and to contrast both of them with our own sceptical or disenchanted attitude towards all great ideals.

Allowing for interesting divergences on each side, we have a broad contrast between, on the one hand, the various emphases on conscience, reconciliation, and mutual recognition to be found in Fichte, Hegel, and Green, and on the other, the liberal tradition of Schiller and Humboldt, Mill and Arnold. The latter tradition sees freedom as consisting not only or mainly in duty and service in a community, but also or mainly in the growth of individual, divergent emotional spontaneity. Its fundamental theme is that our picture of human good must take full account of the aesthetic educability of feeling. Philosophies that subjectivize emotional spontaneity, deny its immanent rationality, and thereby impose a crude opposition between reason and feeling are its *bête noire*. All human value, it holds, is founded on this immanent rationality of the feelings, and can be founded in no other way. That the education of the feelings consists in developing this immanent rationality, is inherently dialogical and exploratory, and can therefore take place fully only under conditions of freedom, is the master theme of its liberalism.

Underlying both approaches there is much extensively developed philosophy. Both sides base their conception of human good on a developmental account of what human beings 'truly' desire (admire, love, etc.). Each approach can be presented as an account of positive freedom, and of what sort of positive freedom contributes to the individual's good. Neither forsakes the conception of freedom as reason. According to the one tradition, what human beings truly desire, or find lasting self-satisfaction in, is virtue as pursuit of common good; whereas according to the other, it is work in its true nature of free and creative play. Since both focus on self-realizing activity in the world, one can attempt to combine them, as Marx did in his vision of communism.

In one of his letters Sidgwick called them the 'Christian' and the 'Goethean' ideal. One might call them more neutrally the ideal of conscience and service, and the ideal of individuality. In the English context, Mill stood for the latter. But by the time Green wrote, that ideal of individuality was on the wane, whereas the Christian ideal, infused by German Idealism, was achieving extraordinary, if temporary, influence. Sidgwick's apologetic preference for the Goethean ideal testifies to the change of feeling:

The effort to attain the Christian ideal may be a life-long painful struggle; and therefore, though I may believe this ideal when realised productive of greater happiness, yet individually (if it is not a question of life or death) my laxness would induce me to prefer a lower, more attainable Goethean ideal.[33]

Could any true believer in the ideal of individuality regard it as lower, or more attainable? Or accept that the Christian ideal is, 'when realised, productive of greater happiness'?

Partly through his extraordinary personal qualities and partly through the particular anxieties and needs of his time, Green was able to give real power to these convictions about the Christian ideal. But, as I noted at the beginning, the underlying yearning for reconciliation and transcendence of the private self were by no means peculiar to English Christian idealism alone. They are a pervasive nineteenth-century theme, starting with reactions such as those of Comte and Hegel to the Enlightenment and the French Revolution. Mill had already replied to Comte's version of this ideal of self-transcending service:

The golden rule of morality, in M. Comte's religion, is to live for others, 'vivre pour autrui' ... Novalis said of Spinoza that he was a God-intoxicated man: M. Comte is a morality-intoxicated man. Every question with him is one of morality, and no motive but that of morality is permitted.

May it not be the fact that mankind, who after all are made up of single human beings, obtain a greater sum of happiness when each pursues his own, under the rules and conditions required by the good of the rest, than when each makes the good of the rest his only object, and allows himself no personal pleasures not indispensable to the preservation of his faculties? The regimen of a blockaded town should be cheerfully submitted to when high purposes require it, but is it the ideal perfection of human existence? M. Comte sees none of these difficulties.[34]

Green was also a morality-intoxicated man—and indeed, a 'God-intoxicated' man. His aspirations for liberal society are, in truth, too reconciliationist, too moralistic, too focused on service. What are we to do when we're *not*

---

[33] In A. S. [Arthur Sidgwick] and E. M. S. [Eleanor Mildred Sidgwick], *Henry Sidgwick: A Memoir* (London: Macmillan, 1906), 90. Quoted by Bart Schultz in *Henry Sidgwick: Eye of the Universe* (Cambridge: Cambridge University Press, 2004), 142. (I'm not sure how serious Sidgwick was being about his laxness.)

[34] J. S. Mill, *Auguste Comte and Positivism*, in *Collected Works of John Stuart Mill*, gen. ed. J. M. Robson (London: Routledge; Toronto: University of Toronto Press), x. 335– 6, 337.

serving each other? (Marx, just because of his Schillerian side, caters for this un-Christian thought a little, though not much, better.) Is there not something positively perverse in making these aspirations the focal ideal of *liberalism*?

However, it is rather too easy nowadays to criticize Green's moralism and affirm Mill's Goetheanism, without really thinking either of them through. I have two things in mind. One is that we operate with coarsened versions of the ideal of individuality, which leave out the crucial idea of the educability of feelings, taking the expression of feeling to be valuable in its own right. This ideal is not so easily attainable. Cultivating the feelings doesn't mean uncritically encouraging them to let rip; on the contrary, it is the process of criticizing them by their own internal standards. Self-expression minus self-criticism is not self-development. It is not through being laxer about standards that the ideal of self-development differs from the 'Platonic and Christian ideal of self-government'[35]—it differs because it does not see those standards as set by some criterion of the reasonable that is outside them, belonging to a different part of the soul, an agency external to them and set over them. It sees the standards as immanent to the development of the feelings themselves. This is a deep difference, but not in the direction of personal relaxation. It still endorses unpopular standards of responsibility, self-criticism, and high-minded striving. Thus its criticism of the feelings is felt as outrageous, diminishing, and elitist. And quite apart from that—even when this ideal is generously acknowledged as noble, rather than merely resented as exclusive—it remains of first-rate importance that no great ideal offers a way for everyone. The ideal of individuality appeals neither to the longing for at-oneness with others nor to the wish to give true service. Yet these motives are admirable and deserve respect. To those who feel them, the ideal of individuality can seem self-absorbed and hard-edged. For them Green gives an account which promises to show how their ideal can receive that respect in a comprehensively liberal outlook.

Once we've seen this, discussion could turn to how far Green succeeds in his recasting of underlying liberal ideals, whether, or in what ways, a liberal outlook should attach itself to either or both of these great ideals, encourage them to understand each other, rethink them in the light of yet others, etc. But there is a stumbling-block. It's not clear that contemporary liberal attitudes even make serious room for them (as against paying lip service). Our current culture is unreceptive or even hostile to *any* serious and demanding ideal—not so much out of eighteenth-century fear of 'enthusiasm' as out of sheer exhaustion. In this respect Nietzsche's prognoses about European nihilism have a depressingly

---

[35] See Mill in *On Liberty*, in *Collected Works of John Stuart Mill*, xviii. 265–6.

more accurate look than the optimism about human beings of either Schiller, Humboldt, and Mill, on the one hand, or Fichte, Hegel, and Green, on the other. To note this is to raise a wholly new issue, of course. But it would be foolish to regard the issue as one that optimistic liberals, who want to think afresh about the ethical bases of their outlook, can afford to ignore. The audience for their efforts is very different from the audience that existed for a Mill or a Green. How to engage that new audience is no easy question.

4

Metaphysics and Ethics in the Philosophy of T. H. Green

ANDREW VINCENT

In her book the *Sovereignty of the Good* Iris Murdoch remarked that moral philosophy often presupposes a philosophy of mind and a metaphysical doctrine.[1] Certainly this is the case with T. H. Green. But in what way do Green's philosophy of mind and metaphysics enable a deeper grasp of his moral philosophy? They do, I believe, but the question is what kind of conception of moral philosophy do they give rise to? Although my focus is on the writings of T. H. Green, many of the points made in this essay are also of relevance (with some qualifications) to other Idealist thinkers.

The chapter initially sketches (very briefly) a distinction between philosophical ethics and ethical practice. It then explores two arguments which appear within Green's ethical and metaphysical writings: I call these the 'grey on grey' and 'injunctive' arguments. These terms will be explained more fully in subsequent sections. Basically, the injunctive argument is premissed on the idea that there are clear substantive ethical injunctions present in Green's moral philosophy. In this case, the individual moral philosopher has a positive role to play in arguing for certain kinds of moral action over others. Prima facie, the 'grey on grey' argument can be interpreted as a metaethical thesis which explains the nature of moral language. However, I contend that the 'grey on grey' argument is much more complex than at first appears. There are a number of different ways to interpret the argument. As indicated, one cruder way is to understand it simply as a metaethical thesis; I argue against this. Another path of argument reads it as containing strong, if indirect, implications

[1] Iris Murdoch, *The Sovereignty of the Good* (London: Routledge & Kegan Paul, 1970). I would like to thank Peter Nicholson, Ben Wempe, and Maria Dimova-Cookson for helpful critical commentary on the first draft of this chapter. I am certain I have not met their careful criticisms, but they have helped me to focus my argument more precisely.

for ethical practice. It is this latter body of argument which will occupy the bulk of this chapter.

It is important to realize immediately that I am arguing that one can unearth quite legitimate philosophical reasons for *both* sets of argument in Green's *oeuvre*. Although it might look as if I am examining an overt philosophical contradiction in Green's work, I contend that it is more likely to be a problem concerning the fact that Green—in dying comparatively young and never being able to complete his work systematically—was never able to develop his arguments adequately in this area.[2] We can then only speculate as to how Green might have resolved this issue. But I still contend that there is a philosophical issue here, in the interpretation of Green's work, which needs to be explored. Having laid out the above two arguments, the discussion elucidates the crucial metaphysical underpinnings of the 'grey on grey' thesis and its relation to Green's central doctrines of thought and the eternal consciousness. It then turns to the philosophical repercussions of Green's articulation of the 'injunctive' argument. One of the key metaphysical anxieties embedded within the injunctive argument is then illustrated through one of Green's last writings. The central philosophical problem of the chapter is then briefly restated. The final section sketches an alternative way of articulating Green's understanding of ethics. This alternative view, in effect, makes another case for the 'grey on grey' argument, whilst downplaying the metaphysical role of the eternal consciousness. This latter section, though, is a purely speculative sketch which minimizes the role of direct moral injunction in Green's philosophy. This point alone would unsettle many contemporary interpreters of Green. The chapter concludes on a sceptical note with regard to how Green viewed the issues.[3]

I. The Status of Ethical Concepts

There is an initial distinction to note here between a philosophical ethics implying some form of meta-level analysis concerning the status of moral

---

[2] As is well known, Green's key systematic philosophical work, the *Prolegomena to Ethics* (1883), was compiled posthumously by A. C. Bradley. It was based upon lectures that Green gave as White's Professor of Moral Philosophy from approximately 1877 until his death in 1882, although some of the first quarter of the volume had been printed in the philosophical journal *Mind* in 1882.

[3] I would suggest that aspects of the problem, at the heart of this chapter, also underpin (in quite different formats) a number of excellent studies of Green: e.g. Ben Wempe, *Beyond Equality: A Study of T. H. Green's Theory of Positive Freedom* (Leiden: Eburon Delft, 1986); Colin Tyler, *Thomas Hill Green (1836–1882) and the Philosophical Foundations of Politics* (Lewiston, NY: Edwin Mellen Press, 1997); Maria Dimova-Cookson, *T. H. Green's Moral and Political Philosophy: A Phenomenological Perspective* (Basingstoke: Palgrave, 2001). None phrases or addresses the problem in the form of this article, but some very similar basic issues arise in all these studies.

concepts, which has no necessary bearing on moral practice, and an ethics which is intimately and practically focused on motivating and initiating moral conduct. On the first count, one can conceive of philosophical ethics as simply an explanation of the nature of moral language. In one sense, a great deal of twentieth-century ethical argument has been focused on this. Doctrines such as naturalism, emotivism, descriptivism, prescriptivism, contractualism, or rational choice have often had strong metaethical connotations. The other broad dimension of ethical argument is that which is concerned directly with the kind of moral injunctions which ought to govern moral conduct.[4] In other words, the real content of an ethics should be 'how we ought to live or conduct our lives'. Modern utilitarianism and much neo-Kantianism have been particularly active in this field—in what I call here the *injunctive argument*. A philosophical ethics worth its salt should, according to the injunctive argument, provide rigorous justificatory reasons for specific kinds of conduct.

The metaethical role of ethics is not necessarily totally precluded from the more engaged practical reading. It has been a standard practice in much justificatory ethical argument over the last century to first explain moral language at a metaethical level and then recommend or try to persuade the audience, with 'good reasons', why one ethical approach is superior to another for governing or guiding moral conduct. Admittedly, some arguments would not be terribly helpful on this point. For example, if, having convinced one's audience that ethical propositions are just emotional effusions, it is difficult to see how one could offer any clear concrete reasons as to why one might morally effuse one way or another.

However, it is important to lay stress on the point that there are different philosophical accounts of the relationship between philosophical ethics and ethical practice. Idealism has its own unique reading of this relationship. Further, not all such Idealist arguments should necessarily be characterized as metaethical. This point is crucial to the argument of this chapter. In the case of emotivism, the point is that meaningful propositions can really only be found in the spheres of logic, science, or mathematics. Ethical propositions, in practice, being emotive, are seen as unenlightening (except in so far as they tell us about the psychological state of the utterer). In the case of prescriptivism, there are reasons as to why we act morally, but these are not empirical reasons.

Idealism, as indicated, has its own reading of the relationship between philosophical ethics and ethical practice—which I link in this chapter with

---

[4] There is, though, something odd about abstractly configuring a moral language which we 'ought' to adopt. The statement seems to invite an interrogative: viz. why 'ought' we to adopt it?

the 'grey on grey' argument. This latter argument forms part of the core conundrum of this essay. I would not associate this argument with metaethics, the fundamental reason being that one important interpretation of the 'grey on grey' argument *still* embodies a practical articulation of ethics. However, it is not the expected understanding of the terminology that one encounters in, for example, the more common *direct* injunctive form of moral argument. It is a more *indirect* understanding. This point contains the core problem of Green's ethics. Put very crudely, the 'grey on grey' argument gives a substantive, if indirect, philosophical priority to ethical practice (over and against direct injunctive ethical argument). The 'grey on grey' thesis thus articulates an ethics which is embedded in ordinary established moral practices. It is an ethics which is understood only indirectly, usually *ex post facto*, by the individual moral agent. But it is still fully active in the world. One important rendition of this 'grey on grey' argument—which forms a central theme in this chapter—is also closely linked to the metaphysical arguments about the eternal consciousness and the epistemological doctrine of thought. I call this the *stronger* rendition of the 'grey on grey' argument. The *softer* rendition (which is linked to a social practice argument) is something I pursue mainly in the more speculative final section of the chapter.

Despite the above 'grey on grey' perspective (and its strong philosophical underpinning in Green's metaphysics), Idealism has an overt reputation—particularly in a writer such as T. H. Green—for being overly forthright about what we 'ought to do', and seeing a very positive injunctive role for moral philosophy. British Idealists particularly have often been seen by posterity as almost overly moralistic in this injunctive sense. Thus, my interpretation of the 'grey on grey' argument might appear oddly out of kilter with one more popular image of Idealist ethics: namely, as embodying necessarily a robust injunctive moral philosophy.

II. The 'Grey on Grey' Argument in Outline

What I wish to do in this section is: first, to very briefly situate the 'grey on grey' argument; second, to examine Green's application of it; and finally, to explains its nature and usage in the present chapter.

First, the 'grey on grey' argument can, of course, be sourced in Hegel. The argument embodies a more general thesis about the nature of philosophy itself (which I will not go into directly), the basic gist being that one must be beyond something in order to *know* it. In the case of ethics, its substance can therefore only be known philosophically *ex post facto*. In the context of British Idealism,

F. H. Bradley formulates the argument thus: 'All philosophy has to do is "to understand what is", and moral philosophy has to understand what exists, not to make them or give directions for making them. Philosophy in general has not to anticipate the discoveries of the particular sciences nor the evolution of history; the philosophy of religion has not to make a new religion ... political philosophy has not to play tricks with the state, but to understand it; and ethics has not to make the world moral.'[5] In philosophical ethics we thus look at the world as cut and dried, and critically reflect upon it. Moral practice is *not* something which flows from the philosopher's premises. The alternative view Bradley caricatures as the 'moral almanac' view of the world (a view which he thinks plagues utilitarians and other such injunctive perspectives).[6]

Second, Green articulates a very similar argument to both Bradley and Hegel.[7] He admits, for example, that most of us suffer moral perplexity, yet philosophical theories of the good are generally 'superfluous'.[8] The concrete, lived process is crucial for morality, not any overt philosophical arguments. As Green notes, 'Any value which a true moral theory may have ... depends on its being applied and interpreted by a mind which the ideal, as a practical principle, already actuates.'[9] Consequently, Green contends that moral ideas 'are not abstract conceptions'. Rather, they 'actuate men independently of the operations of the discursive intellect'.[10] Such ideas are deeply at work in human practice long before they are understood philosophically.[11] They 'not only give rise to institutions and modes of life, but also express themselves in forms of

---

[5] F. H. Bradley, *Ethical Studies*, 2nd edn. (Oxford: Clarendon Press, 1970), 193. For Hegel's usage, see G. W. F. Hegel, *The Philosophy of Right*, trans. T. M. Knox (Oxford: Clarendon Press, 1971), preface, 10–11. Hegel probably found the terminology of the 'greyness of theory' in Goethe. The nice irony of Green appearing as Professor Grey in Mary Ward's *Robert Elsmere* (London, 1888) is doubly appropriate here.

[6] Bosanquet, in his ethical writings, also states the point well, fleshing out Bradley's remark. Moral values are to be realized in and through lived experience. One *must* live and become aware of the problems and intricacies of living before making any full sense of ethics. As he comments, if you 'cut yourself loose' from the lived process, 'you would be nothing'. The process of living is one of self-moulding 'whose being shall incorporate what it can of value'. To work with values and to mould oneself is not a deductive process from ethical first principles. A moral life, if anything, is inductive. No rules pre-condition one's actions. The more precise analogy for ethics, for Bosanquet, is with art, which sounds mysteriously like Foucault's 'care of the self'. The self-moulding and the role of ethics are thus conceived as 'artistic creation *ex nihilo*'; see Bernard Bosanquet, *Some Suggestions in Ethics* (London: Macmillan, 1918), 158.

[7] W. D. Lamont, in articulating Green's conception of the role of moral philosophy, makes the point quite precisely: for Green, the moral philosopher 'is not to create—not even to advocate—moral ideals, but simply to understand them, analysing their nature and demonstrating their implications' (W. D. Lamont, *Introduction to Green's Moral Philosophy* (London: George Allen & Unwin, 1934), 20). Green does, I think, give a stronger emphasis to the 'guiding' role of philosophy than Bradley.

[8] Green, *PE* §310.   [9] Ibid. §311.   [10] Ibid. §317.

[11] This idea is also central to Green's historical writing: e.g. his 'Four Lectures on the English Commonwealth', *CW* iii. 277–364.

the imagination'—that is, in poetry and the arts generally.[12] To get anything from philosophy, one needs to have already had moral discipline, a discipline which 'cannot be derived from philosophy'.[13] He therefore suggests that moral philosophy 'is only needed to remedy the evils which it has itself caused'.[14]

Philosophy, in general, and moral philosophy in particular, can also foster moral difficulty and indeed *even* immorality.[15] Philosophical engagement alone, although intelligently executed, can in the end be just self-serving egoism. Philosophical perplexity can therefore be intelligently manipulated for immoral ends. Philosophy may simply encourage insincere philosophical dalliance (under the guise of seeking adequate or rigorous justificatory reasons) over different formulae of the good. It thus assists in fostering what Green refers to as self-deluding 'self-sophistications'. Moral philosophy essentially becomes casuistry.[16] In actual moments of real moral decision, philosophy is usually of little or no significance. If sincerely pursued, it can, at one level, help to counter scepticism, but it is unreliable even here. At the moment of really difficult moral choice, intuitive judgements (representing a long course of habit and imagination) are the crucial element.[17] As Green notes, certain habits and intuitions implicitly embody authorities. They have 'become part of the "*a priori* furniture" of men's minds—injunctions to family duty, obedience to the state, honour'.[18] There is definitely something quite Humean, and more explicitly Burkean, in these arguments, specifically where moral intuitions are linked to long-term social habits and traditions.[19] This is an interpretation of Green's moral thought which I will develop more systematically in the final more speculative section, although I would not interpret Green in any 'conservative light'.

The core of Green's rendition of the 'grey on grey' argument is therefore, *in nuce*, that individual moral philosophizing does not embody *any* direct injunctive moral dynamic. Individual moral philosophizing is not there to overtly recommend or initiate moral conduct in any direct injunctive sense. This also appears, in part, to be a rejection of what Bradley referred to as the 'moral almanac' view of ethics. Any pretension to provide such a moral almanac (or what might be seen as an injunctive moral argument), Green describes as a 'great impertinence'.[20] The moral philosopher is not there to

---

[12] Green, PE §317.   [13] Ibid. §328.   [14] Ibid. §311.

[15] Philosophers are generally the last people from whom one would necessarily expect moral integrity.

[16] Green, PE §314.   [17] Ibid. §320.   [18] Ibid. §322.

[19] John MacCunn reports that Green often advised his students to read Burke on the question of traditions and the development of institutions (*Six Radical Thinkers* (London: Edward Arnold, 1910), 229). There is, in part, an inductive dimension to Green's conception of morality and custom here, which has some odd unexpected parallels with Hume.

[20] Green, PE §327.

foster moral beliefs by offering strong justificatory reasons for a particular view. This is a misunderstanding of the role of moral philosophy, and, if you want to guide conduct really substantively in some way, you would do far better, Green comments, to ask for an orthodox preacher. The basic point, therefore, of the 'grey on grey' argument, in the ethical sphere, is that philosophy has no *direct* injunctive dimension. It is more often an *ex post facto* form of human understanding. This, as I will argue more fully, does not entail that the 'grey on grey' argument contains no substantive moral content. On the contrary, the 'grey on grey' argument embodies a deep, substantively rich understanding of morality, but it is an *indirect*, not a *direct*, understanding. As Green puts it, the philosopher always serves 'a purpose subordinate to the "moral dynamic"'.[21] The rich moral dynamic is embedded in the agency of the eternal consciousness.

Third, there is obviously a philosophical dilemma here in this portrayal of the 'grey on grey' argument (with the important proviso, mentioned earlier, that this may well be more a problem of an argument which has not been fully developed). The core of the dilemma is that one very common understanding of Green's ethics is that it embodies a rigorous set of direct injunctive arguments, setting out how we 'ought' to conduct our private and public lives. However, the 'grey on grey' view, as outlined above, embodies an argument in which the role of ethics is more *indirect* and also temporally prior to individual philosophical understanding. Further, in this latter understanding it is not the role of moral philosophy to engage in any *direct* injunctive arguments. Direct moral argument is usually casuistry.

One crude way to resolve the above dilemma would be to argue that the 'grey on grey' argument is simply a metaethical thesis. If this is the case, then it does not necessarily contradict the injunctive argument. Both can be held in tandem. The 'grey on grey' argument would be 'commenting on' moral language, from a metaethical standpoint, and the injunctive argument would be offering rigorous justificatory reasons for certain types of conduct on a more practical level. Thus, the central argument of this chapter would be undermined. There are two insuperable problems with this solution. First, the manner in which Green articulates the 'grey on grey' argument appears to rule out, *tout court*, the more direct injunctive dimension of ethics. As Green puts it, if you want moral injunctions, you should go to an orthodox preacher, not a moral philosopher. Thus, one strong reading of the 'grey on grey' thesis explicitly contradicts the direct injunctive argument. Second, the more complex and paradoxical point, which I want to explore here, is that

---

[21] Green, *PE* §327.

the 'grey on grey' perspective itself embodies certain more indirect substantive arguments about ethics—although they are not configured in the injunctive sense. In this sense, I would deny that the 'grey on grey' argument is simply a metaethical claim. My contention is that to grasp this latter point, one has to understand the *relationship* between the 'grey on grey' argument and the metaphysics of the eternal consciousness.

III. The Injunctive Sense of Ethics

Before moving on to discuss the metaphysical character of the 'grey on grey' thesis, I wish to outline briefly Green's alternative commitment, to a more standard normative or direct injunctive form of argument. The more general anxiety (outlined in the previous section) about the ambivalence of Green's moral philosophy is well articulated by David Brink. He remarks that Green, at various points, 'seems to think that the precepts of conventional morality and one's own conscience are adequate guides to conduct and the goal of moral philosophy should be not so much to reform or to resolve perplexity but to provide understanding of familiar moral precepts'. Brink describes this thesis as 'troubling'. He continues that 'It displays a disappointing form of moral complacency that is hard to square with his [Green's] ... own calls for liberal reform'.[22] As any serious reader of Green knows very quickly, he was, despite the implications of the above 'grey on grey' thesis, deeply interested in the practical injunctive dimension of both ethics and liberal reform. In fact, my own (and many others') earlier work on Green and Idealism placed considerable emphasis upon this dimension of his work.[23]

It is worth reminding ourselves, briefly, though, of one immediate philo-sophical response to this injunctive view within Green's writings. It is a response which made Green a puzzle even for his contemporaries. Thus, as indicated earlier, Green argues that moral philosophy can really serve only an

---

[22] David O. Brink, *Perfectionism and the Common Good: Themes in the Philosophy of T. H. Green* (Oxford: Clarendon Press, 2003), 73. Brink disagrees with this aspect of Green, and bases his whole case on Green as an (in my terminology) 'injunctive' moral philosopher—premised on an innovative use of perfectionist argumentation.

[23] Andrew Vincent and Raymond Plant, *Philosophy, Politics and Citizenship: The Life and Thought of the British Idealists* (Oxford: Blackwell, 1984), and Andrew Vincent (ed.), *The Philosophy of T. H. Green*. Avebury Series in Philosophy (Aldershot: Gower Publishing, 1986). The more recent work of e.g. Geoffrey Thomas, *The Moral Philosophy of T. H. Green* (Oxford: Clarendon Press, 1987); David Weinstein, 'Between Kantianism and Consequentialism in T. H. Green's Moral Philosophy', *Political Studies*, 41:4 (1993), 618–35; Dimova-Cookson, *T. H. Green's Moral and Political Philosophy*; and Avital Simhony, 'Was Green a Utilitarian?,' *Utilitas* 7:1 (1995), 121–44, and Brink, *Perfectionism*, all focus on this dimension of Green's work.

'indirect role' in human affairs. As Green comments, the philosopher 'under certain conditions can render a "practical service". But he will render it simply by fulfilling with the utmost possible completeness his proper work of analysis. The philosopher needs to be detached. As a moral philosopher he analyses human conduct; the motives which it expresses, the spiritual endowments implied in it, the history of thought, habits and institutions through which it has come to be what it is.'[24] In other words, the moral philosopher can, in certain situations, clarify the conditions within which an agent makes moral decisions. This is particularly the case for Green in times of social or moral upheaval; as he puts it, 'whenever a sufficient liberation of the intellectual faculties has been attained, there is needed a further pursuit of the … speculative processes'. Once the good will is present historically, then philosophy can make it 'independent of the conflicting, because inadequate, formulae in which duties are presented to it'.[25] Philosophical ethics acts, therefore, as an 'enabler' of ideas of moral perfection to be more adequately realized; this reconfigures slightly the 'grey on grey' argument. We might call this the *enabling thesis* on moral philosophy. But it is not an argument which Green develops extensively. By contrast, my own view is that this enabling argument, in the final analysis, embodies the seeds of a more defensible conception of Green's ethics, even if it provides a much more restricted role for moral philosophy.[26] This is something I wish to return to in the final section of the chapter.

However, the above view is manifestly not the popular image of Green. The more popular image contends that Green's moral philosophy does have a very direct, substantive, and injunctive role to play, which goes well beyond simply enabling and clarifying moral beliefs. Moral philosophy provides the motivational content of what we 'ought to do', and indicates precisely where we will find that substantive moral content. The standard approaches to Green usually associate his moral views with variants of a readjusted neo-Kantianism, a qualified utilitarianism (or consequentialism), or a form of perfectionism.[27] But it is not necessary to illustrate this 'direct moral substantive point' too extensively. All that is being argued (at present) is that, in one important *popular* assessment of Green, he had a direct substantive injunctive view of moral philosophy. I am not therefore arguing about whether or not Green had

---

[24] Green, *PE* §327.   [25] Ibid. §311.

[26] Given Green's early death, this issue though remains speculative.

[27] Others, more recently, such as Avital Simhony or Dimova-Cookson, see Green's substantive moral perspective as quite unique and distinctive. Dimova-Cookson, in *T. H. Green's Moral and Political Philosophy*, analyses Green's moral philosophy in the context of a qualified Husserlian phenomenology. Simhony, in 'Was Green a Utilitarian?', sees Green in the context of what she calls a distinctive 'relational approach'.

a substantive injunctive moral philosophy; I believe he did. I assume this to be a well-established pattern of analysis of Green's moral philosophy going back to early critics such as E. F. Carritt and H. A. Pritchard.[28]

My own personal reading of the substance of Green's moral thought is that, whatever specific philosophical shape it might take, its inner substance is none the less embedded in a very particular conception of a 'Christian society'. It is thus, in essence, a 'Christian moral code' which provides the substance of moral conduct for Green. As Nettleship noted, Green's *Prolegomena to Ethics* must be read in connection on the one side with the addresses on "The Witness of God" and "Faith", on the other side with the *Lectures on Political Obligation'*.[29] The substance of ethics can be identified—even if it appears in the outward shape of, for example, perfectionism, neo-Kantianism, or a variant of consequentialism. The ideas of moral perfection, residing within our reason, society, and conscience, are derived from the substantive beliefs of an undogmatic, non-miraculous, liberal Protestant Christianity, which is in turn identified with an underlying historical teleology.[30] What we experience now—or what we experience in terms of Christian sensibilities—is the fruition of certain ideas which have been developing, minimally, for the last three to four centuries, certainly since the Reformation. These substantive ideas are also embedded within the conventions and institutions of Christian societies. Such ideas become a substantive source of moral action and direction when they are activated in the human conscience 'working under a felt necessity of seeking the best'.[31]

Much of Green's impact on a generation of thinkers, civil servants, journalists, churchmen, and politicians, in many ways derived from this injunctive moral dimension. It would indeed be quite difficult to make much sense of Green's impact—to name but a few areas—on the university settlement movement, the development of social work theory, the growth of ethical societies, the considerable rethinking of the role of the State and law in human affairs at the close of the nineteenth century, without noting Green's substantive injunctive

---

[28] E. F. Carritt, *The Theory of Morals* (Oxford: Oxford University Press, 1928); *idem, Morals and Politics* (Oxford: Oxford University Press, 1935); H. A. Pritchard, *Moral Obligation* (Oxford: Clarendon Press, 1949).

[29] Richard Lewis Nettleship, 'Memoir', in *CW* iii. p. cxlii.

[30] I have dealt with this issue at greater length, more recently, in 'T. H. Green: Citizenship as Political and Metaphysical', in David Boucher and Andrew Vincent (eds.), *British Idealism and Political Theory* (Edinburgh: Edinburgh University Press, 2001), 27–54. Some of these ideas go back to my earlier work with Plant, *Philosophy, Politics and Citizenship* in 1984. This is obviously a contentious point. However, I would add here that it is *not* contentious in terms of the argument I am constructing. The only point I wish to establish here is that Green does have (from one important perspective) an injunctive account of moral philosophy. If that is accepted, then my point has been made, regardless of how the moral content is interpreted.

[31] Green, *PE* §308.

moral beliefs and their influence.[32] Specific renderings of his views on the common good, self-realization, and forms of perfection were significantly inspiring motifs for a generation up to 1914. Suffice it to say that man's best moral state, for Green, was clearly the 'full realisation of his capabilities'.[33] However, this was not the realization of *any* capabilities; it was, rather, the capabilities which link to the 'eternal and perfect'. Man's capabilities imply a 'living for the ends of which the divine principle that forms his self alone renders him capable'.[34] As Green noted, a man's capabilities are part of what Green calls his 'heaven born' nature, which he is trying to actualize.[35] This substantive teleology underpins important notions such as the common good, human perfection, and self-realization.

IV. The Metaphysical Underpinning for 'Grey on Grey'

What I have outlined briefly in the previous section is Green's overt philosophical commitment to a direct injunctive ethical argument. Given the discussion to date, it might be contended that Green's philosophical ethics appears to be self-contradictory. However, the issue is not straightforward. The word 'contradictory' is not fair, since I also believe that part of the problem derives from the fact that Green's arguments remain underdeveloped. It is my belief that had Green lived to complete his own version of the *Prolegomena*, he would have dealt with this problem. None the less, there are still deeper reasons within Green's system of philosophy which give rise to this problem. These deeper reasons underpin basic aspects of his philosophical thinking. Considerations of space permit me only to skim across some of these. The key issue, though, relates to the doctrine of the eternal consciousness, which will be pursued at greater length.

First, for Green, nothing lies behind or beyond experience. It is all there is. Philosophy basically disentangles the implications of experience. But the crucial question is: what is experience? Green notes: 'It was in effect to answer this question that Locke and Hume wrote.' However, as he continues, with evident relish, we should also be very wary of those who declaim the loudest about their focus on 'experience'. The materialists, empiricists, and naturalists who declaim loudly about their empirical credentials are all deeply suspect. As Green continues, 'It is not those, we know, who cry "Lord, Lord!" the loudest, that enter into the kingdom of heaven, nor does the strongest assertion of our dependence

---

[32] See the general discussion in Vincent and Plant, *Philosophy, Politics and Citizenship*.
[33] Green, *PE* §173.   [34] Ibid. §176.   [35] Ibid. § 177.

on experience imply a true insight into nature.'[36] This is the cue for Green's qualified Kantianism. Essentially, for Green, Kant's major contribution was to indicate that experience always implies a thinking subject. Experience is not prior to thought, it is coincidental with thought. Thus, a pure sensationalism, in Green's terms, would be 'speechless'.[37] Consequently, 'there is no perception without an intellectual interpretation of sensation'.[38] Every perception involves a judgement, and judgement brings something into a relationship with something else. Everything we perceive, we automatically bring into a relationship. Therefore, anything that is real is 'an inexhaustible complex of relations'.[39]

It is important to grasp here that, for Green, the notion of an objective or external order (to thought) is still philosophically credible. Yet, as he comments, 'The fact that there is a real external world of which through feeling we have a determinate experience, and that in this experience all our knowledge of nature is implicit, is one which no philosophy disputes. The idealist merely asks for a further analysis of a fact which he finds so far from simple.'[40] This further questioning reveals that thought 'by the relations which it "invents" constitutes both the inner and outer'. The real philosophical problem arises when human thought 'is treated as itself the inner "substratum" '. Thought then 'becomes the creature of its own suppositions'.[41] This latter problem is the essence of Kant's predicament for Green. Kant's error is trying to identify a purely 'objective possibility' (Green's terminology): that is, a phenomenon taken as given, *apart* from the 'complex of relations'. In effect, he rejects Kant's dualism. For Green, Kant failed to go on from his creative and imaginative premiss (concerning the role of thought) to the conclusion that ' "the cosmos of our experience" is only possible in relation to a thinking subject'.[42] Thought itself is the source of the distinction between subject and object, and for Green it cannot be conscious of itself 'except in distinction from an object'.[43] When we think, we self-objectify or self-distinguish. We posit the subject and object relation in thinking. Experience, *per se*, presupposes the self-conscious or self-distinguishing agent. Thus, reality and objectivity have no meaning 'save as expressing a relation which without thought could not be'.[44] Matter 'is a state of some relation or other'.[45] I will call this argument in Green 'the doctrine of thought'.

---

[36] Green, *CW* i. 291.   [37] Ibid. 36.   [38] Green, *CW* ii. 176.
[39] Green, *CW* i. 36.   [40] Ibid. 337.   [41] Ibid. 110.
[42] Green, *CW* ii. 74.   [43] Ibid. 182.

[44] Ibid. 180. Green notes: 'The conceived object, the thing individualised by relations which does not come and go with sensation, is the only thing. There is no real thing other than it' (Ibid. 188).

[45] Ibid. 178. Green comments that 'the very proposition, that reality is nothing but a succession of feelings, is self-contradictory, for, in the absence of everything but such succession, the succession itself could not be. A system like Hume's which started from such a proposition—a proposition, we must

In addition to the 'doctrine of thought' argument, Green, as is well known, also employs, quite extensively, a form of transcendental argument when speaking about this relational conception of knowledge. The gist of the argument is that no event, in any series of events, can be a consciousness of a series of events.[46] Consciousness, *per se*, cannot itself be a product of a series of events. It is, rather, the transcendental condition of any series of events (including time). This argument keeps recurring throughout Green's philosophical *œuvre*. In effect, a 'world which is a system of relations implies a unity self-distinguished from all the things related, yet determining all as the equal presence through relation to which they are related to each other; and such a unity is a conscious subject'.[47] Yet, it is also very important to note that the full and complete read-out of this transcendental argument on the conditional character of the self-distinguishing consciousness implies eventually, for Green, something much more cosmically exalted: namely, the eternal subject (or eternal consciousness). The eternal consciousness is the ultimate transcendental condition for the unity of all human knowledge. This idea, as mentioned, appears throughout Green's philosophical *œuvre*. Although there is a slightly more systematic attempt at an exposition in Book I of the *Prolegomena to Ethics*, it is an idea which appears in some of Green's earliest writings. Yet, as many commentators suggest, even in the *Prolegomena*, it still remains frustratingly undeveloped.[48] I concur with this judgement. However, even if it remains undeveloped, we should not thereby conclude that it is unimportant to Green. It also raises additional, quite fundamental problems in the field of ethics.

A similar point concerning the role of the eternal consciousness also underpinned Green's conception of history.[49] History was definitely not just 'one damn event after another'. There was (as in Hegel), conversely, a deep process of teleological development, basically from the Greeks to the present. For Green, something formed the cement of this historical process, giving it meaning, purpose, and direction. Thus, the Greeks, for Green, embodied,

---

not forget, to which philosophy has been brought in the attempt to work out consistently a conception of reality still current among us—was foredoomed to failure' (*CW* i. 381–2).

[46] Green, *PE* §§ 15–18.   [47] Green, *CW* i. 498.

[48] Although not all agree on this; Colin Tyler, e.g., in his 'The Much-Maligned and Misunderstood Eternal Consciousness', *Bradley Studies*, 9 (2003), 126–38, argues that Green was not building a complete epistemology, but was only developing the first stage of a linked argument on the will. Tyler thus vigorously disagrees with those who try to dismiss the first book of the *Prolegomena* as failing to provide an adequate account of knowledge; see pp. 129–30.

[49] As Brink comments, 'much of Green's ethics, political philosophy, and theology, seems to treat the corporate spiritual principle as a transhistorical agent that is immanent in the lives of individual agents and progressive institutions' (*Perfectionism*, 19). Brink contends, though, that Green must make up his mind here and settle for either an immanent or a transcendent reading of this eternal subject.

for example, significant moral ideas, but they remained undeveloped. But it was not a question for Green of these being better or worse moral ideas. However, it was still important to reveal, as Green put it, ' "some increasing purpose through the ages", of which the gradual fulfilment elicits fuller exertion of the moral capabilities of individuals'.[50] Green therefore saw history holding together, the 'holding together' being via an intrinsic teleology. In the same way that diverse particles of experience presuppose a unifying self-consciousness, so, equally, history presupposes a consciousness which is itself not an event in the diverse series of historical events.[51] There is a teleology which undergirds both individual and collective actions in historical terms. As I have argued elsewhere, this teleology firmly underpins, for example, Green's historical writings, such as his *Four Lectures on the English Commonwealth*, and his assessment of the Reformation.[52]

In summary, the deeper reasons which underpin the issue of the 'grey on grey' argument are tied logically to his whole theory of knowledge, his conception of consciousness, human experience, religious belief, and indeed human history. The central metaphysical and epistemological issue is this: the reason why individual philosophizing understands rather than recommends is that the underlying dynamic behind *all* morality, history, religion, and knowledge is the metaphysical agency of the eternal consciousness. Individual philosophizing does not initiate. Rather, it tries to take hold of what is already the case within human practice. It is important to note, though, that this is Green's philosophical claim about the nature of human practice.[53] It is crucial, therefore, for my argument to grasp the point that the deeper reasons which explain the character of the 'grey on grey' argument relate to the whole dynamics of Green's system of philosophy, particularly to the crucial argument on the eternal consciousness, to which I now turn.

V. 'Grey on Grey' and the Eternal Consciousness

I want to focus in this section on the role of the eternal consciousness, in order to tease out the problem of the problematic character of Green's moral philosophy. This section therefore explores the manner in which the eternal consciousness

---

[50] Green, *PE* §271.

[51] This also forms the core of Green's judgement on the 'historical' significance of Christ in Western thought. In a nutshell, Christ's life is not important as a *historical* event.

[52] See discussion in Vincent, 'T. H. Green: Citizenship as Political and Metaphysical', 31 ff.

[53] This argument, which prioritizes human practice, is a metaphysical argument which is a crucial factor in Green's philosophy.

argument affects the way in which moral philosophy is conceived. In order to reveal this, I examine the question: what is the relationship between the eternal consciousness and individual human person, particularly as regards morality? One philosophical premiss here—which I have developed at length in previous writings and will not therefore expand on now—is that there is a genuine problem in Idealism (particularly Absolute Idealism) of how one relates the finite human agent to the eternal consciousness.[54] Although there are sophisticated counter-arguments within Absolute Idealism from the late 1890s, none the less there is still a philosophical problem concerning the nature of finite human agency in British Idealist thinking, which relates back directly to Green's arguments.[55]

I have no doubt at all that Green places great value on the individual human person and frequently sees moral progress being initiated within this domain. Yet, at the same time, the theory of the eternal consciousness is also metaphysically, transcendentally, and historically crucial for his whole system of philosophy. In one sense, the previous two sentences contain the *core* of his philosophical dilemma. Metaphysically, what makes sense not only of our ordinary human knowing, but also of our historical development as a species, as well as our everyday attempts at moral action, is ultimately the *agency* of the eternal consciousness. This same thesis underpins the 'grey on grey' argument. Thus, in one crucial reading, there is no sign of a break in the philosophical system between metaphysics, human knowledge, and everyday moral action. I am therefore insisting on the *unity of the system of thought* within Green's philosophy. This unity is embedded in the agency of the eternal consciousness. The argument here—in terms of the unity of the philosophical system—is that there is a fundamental connection between the eternal consciousness, the doctrine of thought, and the whole issue concerning the character of moral philosophy. The agency of the eternal consciousness (which underpins the stronger reading of the 'grey on grey' argument) cannot be viewed as a metaethical argument, for the starkly obvious reason that the eternal consciousness is the *core of morality* itself, and *moral conduct* in particular. Any human action which could be considered moral must manifest the agency of the eternal consciousness.

[54] For a full discussion of this debate about the individual and the absolute in British Idealist thought, see Andrew Vincent, 'The Individual in Hegelian Thought', *Idealistic Studies*, 12:2 (1982), 156–68; also David Boucher and Andrew Vincent, *A Radical Hegelian: The Social and Political Philosophy of Henry Jones* (Cardiff: University of Wales Press, 1993), ch. 2.

[55] I should stress here that I am definitely not saying that Green was an Absolute Idealist. However, certain knotty issues relating to the character of the finite individual person, which plagued some of the later Absolute Idealist writings, can, I believe, be traced back to certain discussions in Green's work.

However, this still leaves the nagging question: what is the relation between my personal moral conduct and the agency of the eternal consciousness? In one Greenian interpretation, the individual person is only an isolated particular. What makes a person perfect or morally complete is the eternal consciousness. Put in other terms: if our morally significant thoughts and actions are the eternal consciousness working through us, then moral philosophy (and philosophy in general) has to be seen as a strong 'grey on grey' exercise. We, as moral philosophers or moral actors, are *not* the primary dynamic moral agents. We cannot initiate—unless something initiates through our actions. As Brink, for example, notes—with a slight hint of alarm—Green does quite definitely at points indicate that there is a corporate agent 'over and above individual agents'.[56] Yet, this corporate agent appears to be acting through individuals. If one thinks of Green's discussions of figures such as Christ and St Paul, or Vane and Cromwell in the *English Commonwealth Lectures*, or Martin Luther, one gets an overwhelmingly strong sense of a deep purposive agency driving human individuals through historical events, events which make sense only *ex post facto*. The 'force of circumstance' (as Green put it) therefore underpins all our actions. Morality remains embedded in the agency of the eternal consciousness (or the force of circumstance). Our own individual attempts at moral philosophy only 'see through a glass darkly'. The most we can do is try to clarify and sharpen the *telos* of the eternal agency.

In stressing the strong sense of agency of the eternal consciousness, Green is therefore certain that we do *not* create morality. Our moral powers are limited and finite, unless we will ourselves to be a vehicle of the agency of the eternal consciousness (or in Green's often asserted Pauline theological terms, 'we die to ourselves in order to live'). We do not create our character or our moral conscience. We neither make the moral ideas or ideals of perfection which mould our moral lives, nor have much role in constituting our social or political values.[57] Green thus notes that 'No individual can make a conscience for himself'.[58] In one sense, we are in part at the mercy of circumstance. But, as indicated above, this circumstance is not contingent for Green. It is teleologically underpinned, and the source of that teleology is the *agency of the eternal consciousness*. Ultimately, that which brings historical circumstance, societies, knowledge, and individuals into a realizable frame is the logically necessary transcendental condition of the eternal consciousness.

---

[56] Brink, *Perfectionism*, 66.

[57] As mentioned earlier, Brink sees this as a troubling 'moral complacency' on Green's part (Brink, *Perfectionism*, 73). I am not sure, though, that Brink quite sees the deep metaphysical roots to Green's arguments here or the linkages within his overall philosophical system.

[58] Green, *PE* §321.

As Green puts it, 'Philosophy does but interpret, with full consciousness and in system, the powers already working in the spiritual life of mankind, and as these powers at every stage gather strength which they never finally lose, so the philosophical expression which they have found in one age, is not lost however it may be qualified, in the ages that follow.'[59] Our idea of perfection—which we place before ourselves in moral action—derives wholly from the 'complete perfection' of the eternal consciousness. The eternal consciousness is therefore the essence of moral conduct. This metaphysically based conception of morality (and philosophy in general) is present throughout Green's philosophical work. However, as argued, it does not sit easily with the direct injunctive understanding of moral philosophy, and it was also, I contend, an argument that periodically made Green uneasy. It was this background unease that Sidgwick referred to when he reported Green as saying (in conversation) that Hegel's whole philosophy was a 'strange *Wirrwarr*', in effect 'chaos', and had to be worked over again.[60]

The eternal consciousness thus fulfils a powerful systematic integrating role right across the board in Green's whole structure of philosophy. It makes sense of history and human knowledge. Its relationship with the natural human organism is analogous to an infinite rider upon a timed finite vehicle. As Green comments unequivocally, 'this eternal mind uses the animal organism in man as its vehicle so as to constitute a being self-conscious, yet limited by the conditions of the organism ... thus the human mind, qua mind, has not a beginning in time'.[61] Completeness and perfection always lie in the agency of the eternal consciousness. The eternal consciousness thus renders possible not only nature, but also morality.[62] The eternal consciousness is thus the real core of morality.[63] As indicated, I take this latter contention to reinforce the philosophical point that the 'grey on grey' argument is quite clearly not

---

[59] Green, *CW* iii. 93.

[60] See Henry Sidgwick, 'The Philosophy of T. H. Green', *Mind*, 10 (1901), 19.

[61] Green continues: 'That which exists in time is the organism fitted to be a vehicle for self-conscious thought, and of this the beginning is not properly to be fixed at birth or at "conception in that womb"; it has had a history of which we seek the beginning in vain. But this history itself,—the connected series of events, determined by the constant system of nature, which forms it,—as it exists only to an eternal and self-conscious mind, is knowable by us only because this mind constitutes the "me" in each of us; only because it so uses the animal organism of man as to form a being formally self-conscious, and thus capable of knowledge, able to conceive a world of which each element is determined by relation to the whole' (*CW* ii. 182).

[62] As Green comments, 'if we speak of the eternal subject as God, we must not suppose, because God renders nature possible, that this is the full account of God. He must at least render morality possible too' (ibid. 74).

[63] I concur with Ben Wempe when he comments, 'It would seem, indeed, that if any conclusion can be derived from the inclusion of two books on metaphysics in a treatise of moral philosophy, it is as to the central position metaphysics occupied in Green's thinking' (*Beyond Equality*, 80).

a metaethical issue. Rather, it is directly related to the agency of the eternal consciousness, which, in turn, provides the only rich groundwork for moral action. This leaves individual moral philosophizing in a much more residual, indirect position.

VI. Repercussions of the Injunctive Thesis

Yet, on the other count, if one emphasizes the initiating role of the individual person or agent struggling to realize him or herself and striving to act morally, then moral philosophy can appear to have a predominantly injunctive role. Green, on many occasions, clearly viewed his own actions and those of his contemporaries in this light. Indeed, in countering one reading of the strong 'grey on grey' view, outlined above, if we viewed our best actions as really a 'cosmic' agent working through us, this might well diminish our efforts. We might have little choice here; we might indeed welcome this 'cosmic agent' absorbing us and slough off our individual sense of self (in something like Buddhism), or we might well just give up and say, 'well it will all happen anyway with or without me'. Alternatively, Green's injunctive argument envisages us as finite centres of moral struggle, striving, on an everyday basis, to realize the best life and possible self in an undogmatic Christian sense.[64]

However, if one accepts this individual agent-centred injunctive reading, then certain metaphysical consequences follow. One important consequence affects the 'doctrine of thought' and the 'doctrine of eternal consciousness'. Thus, the counter question to the 'injunctive agency' reading becomes: if I fully and freely initiate and direct my moral activity, and argue persuasively that others ought to adopt a pattern of moral action, then what is the relation between my moral thought and the thoughts of others (that is, what accounts for the 'thought-relatedness' of an incredibly diverse range of individuals)? Further, what happens to the teleological unity underpinning human history? Another way of putting this is that pressing the 'individual injunctive agency' argument too hard cuts away at the base of the stronger metaphysical and teleological arguments concerning the eternal consciousness. More significantly, what is the relationship between my individual (moral or otherwise) thought and the logically necessary transcendental existence of the eternal consciousness? The consequences and philosophical dilemma, put simply, are that adhering strongly to the individual injunctive agency thesis

---

[64] One must die to one's present or actual self and live within the rules of the Christed 'possible' self.

undercuts the conceptual and practical relationship between my thought and that of the eternal consciousness.

In one sense, this argument is obliquely reflected in Dimova-Cookson's contention that the really significant (and correct) aspect of Green's philosophy appears in Book II of the *Prolegomena*, where he lays out a philosophy of will and practice. Yet, the attempt by Green, in Book I, to construct a metaphysics of knowledge and a deep account of nature and its spiritual grounding is regarded as wrong-headed and incorrect. The only significance of Book I, therefore, is where it points to the philosophy of the will and human practice in Book II.[65] This argument, in giving priority to the will of the individual agent, does not deny any role for the eternal consciousness. However, it is a reconfigured role; it is considered a supportive adjunct to the theory of the will. The eternal consciousness basically encourages the individual agent to look beyond common sense and the ordinary. It serves 'as a guarantee that certain qualities of human spirit ... have somewhere a permanent existence'.[66] The eternal consciousness thus becomes a sympathetic addendum to the primacy of the individual agent.

However, if one adheres to the stronger rendition of the eternal consciousness, then one obvious answer to the latter dilemma would be to abandon the 'injunctive argument' altogether. This alleviates the problem of the eternal subject immediately, and explains my consciousness and the role of moral philosophy. Green was obviously not prepared to do this. Another position would be to retain the 'grey on grey' argument, but then to throw the emphasis on my thought, and that of the moral philosopher, as having an indirect 'facilitating' role, but *not* an initiating one. This is what I referred to earlier as the 'enabling thesis'. There is still no moral almanac here, other than what we are directed to see in history and society. The moral philosopher understands, but still does not seek to convert or persuade. Yet, contrary to this latter view, Green at times does clearly want to talk about the substance of morality and politics, and to persuade his audience, for example, not to accept utility or naturalistic-based ethics but to adopt a more positive rendering of human liberty over the more negative perspective, and so forth. He wants individuals to initiate substantive changes to reflect moral beliefs more adequately. In other words, he sees a direct, injunctive, practical and initiating role for moral and political philosophy. Green, indeed, often appears to be a great deal more comfortable with this latter argument.

---

[65] She even suggests that it would have been more helpful if Book II had been the first book of the *Prolegomena*; see Maria Dimova-Cookson, 'The Eternal Consciousness: What Role it Can and Cannot Play. A Reply to Colin Tyler', *Bradley Studies*, 9 (2003), 143.

[66] Ibid. 144–5.

If I am correct about Green, that both he, and particularly many of his admirers, often appear to feel much more comfortable with the injunctive view, then it follows that there would have to be some definite textual evidence of Green's anxiety and doubt about the stronger metaphysical 'doctrine of thought' and its strong 'grey on grey' concomitant (despite the fact that he articulates that argument in many places). I turn now to this evidence.

VII. Green's Anxiety

Given Green's early death and the fact that many of his philosophical arguments were still in a process of subtle formation, the evidence for any anxiety remains inevitably somewhat sketchy. However, one particular piece does address this anxiety in a quite illuminating manner. It was written shortly before his death in March 1882, and provides an insight into this metaphysical anxiety. In many ways it is a slightly less guarded reflective piece: namely, a long book review in 1880 of Principal John Caird's *Introduction to the Philosophy of Religion*. It is also worth noting that the review coincides with Green's growing and serious interest in Herman Lotze's neo-Kantian philosophy and his growing unease with Absolute Idealism, in this case in Caird's work.[67]

Caird's book is what might be described as an undiluted, enthused attempt at a rendition of Hegel's philosophy of religion. Green comments—which is odd, given the rise of interest in Idealism from the 1880s—that Caird's ideas are unlikely to carry much weight with a contemporaneous readership obsessed with positivism and materialist thinking. He notes, that

Hegel's doctrine has been before the world now for half a century ... yet as a doctrine it has not made way. It may be doubted whether it has thoroughly satisfied even those among us who regard it as the last word of philosophy. When we think out the problem left by previous inquirers, we find ourselves led to it by an intellectual necessity; but on reflection we become aware that we are Hegelians, so to speak, with only a fraction of our thoughts—on the Sunday's of "speculation", not on the weekdays of "ordinary thought".

[67] This view of Green also ties in with Wempe's judgement that 'Green was heavily influenced by Hegel in his younger years, an influence gradually replaced by an orientation towards Kant ... In this sense Green in my view occupied a position essentially similar to the revival of Kant Studies which was seen in Germany' (Wempe, *Beyond Equality*, 63). Wempe also notes here the significance of Green's review of John Caird. Green's later anxiety over Hegel was also pointed out by Henry Sidgwick; see Sidgwick, 'Philosophy of T. H. Green', 19. Green's arguments here on Caird would be equally applicable to the writings of F. H. Bradley and Bernard Bosanquet.

This comment in many ways encapsulates Green's philosophical anxiety. The great virtue of Caird's work, for Green, is that it forces those who admire Hegel to reconsider 'certain points in Hegel's doctrine, which are a stumbling block'.[68]

The key stumbling-block is Hegel's 'doctrine of thought'. For Green, there is a strong implication in Hegel that thought and reality are being identified. Philosophizing appears then to be the Absolute (or eternal consciousness) thinking through individuals. This, in many ways, is the key problem. Green calls this the 'one essential aberration of his [Hegel's] doctrine', commenting that, 'if thought and reality are to be identified ... thought must be other than the discursive activity exhibited in our inferences and analyses, other than a particular mode of consciousness which excludes from itself feeling and will'. Until the doctrine of thought is properly sorted out, 'a suspicion will attach to his doctrine'.[69] On my interpretation, this would entail that Green must be suspicious of his *own* doctrine of the eternal consciousness.

Green takes this 'suspicion' to be the crux of Caird's and Hegel's predicament, commenting: 'As a follower of Hegel [Caird] ... must and does hold that the objective world, in its actual totality, is thought, and that the processes of our intelligence are but reflections of that real thought under the conditions of a limited animal nature'. Readers, continues Green, will naturally ask about what 'this thought is which seems to be and to do anything and everything. ... And he will rightly refuse to believe that an examination of his own abilities or infirmities of conception can help him to understand what God is or what the world is as it is for God.' The core of the Caird/Hegel problem for Green is therefore the idea ' "that it is not we that think, but the universal reason that thinks in us" '.[70] Again, this idea is one important reading of Green's own argument about the eternal consciousness. None the less, he sees the idea as 'repugnant'! It also strikes Green that an 'unwarrantable inference is being drawn from the power of conceiving to the reality of that which is conceived'. In effect, the core of the philosophical dilemma is that there is an unsubstantiated conflation between two dissimilar propositions: namely, 'the proposition that a thing is only conceivable by thought ... with the proposition that the thing only exists for thought'.[71] For Green, the fact that, in thought, we can rise above and conceive our own individuality 'is no proof ... of the reality of a universal intelligence, nor would a universal intelligence,

---

[68] All quotations from Green, *CW* iii. 141–2.   [69] Ibid. 142–3.   [70] Ibid. 143.

[71] Ibid. 144. Green also comments critically on the identification of 'the proposition, again, that no object can be *conceived as existing* except in relation to a thinking subject, with the proposition that it cannot exist except in that relation. He will think that he traces this fallacy through the whole passage' (ibid.).

if it existed, be at the same time the reality of things, any more than our own intelligence, from which this existence is inferred, carries with it the reality of the objects about which it thinks'.[72] This comment by Green again strikes me as in large part a rejection of his own arguments for the eternal consciousness.

For Green, this subtle conflation of propositions runs through the core of Hegel's and Caird's work and contains the crux of the problem (or 'stumbling-block') concerning the 'doctrine of thought'. Anxiety over the doctrine will keep 'reoccurring', says Green, 'until it is made more clear that the nature of that thought, which Hegel declares to be the reality of things, is to be ascertained, if at all, from the analyses of the objective world, not from reflection on those processes of our intelligence which really presuppose that world'. In short, the central issue is that thought is 'the *prius* of things is, after all, only relatively true. It is true as a correction of the assertion that things are the *prius* of thought, but may in turn become as misleading as the assertion of which it is a corrective.' For Green, Caird had, in effect, been overpowered by the 'doctrine of thought'. It is clear from this that there is some evidence, in 1880 at least, that Green was anxious about the 'doctrine of thought' and its concomitant relationship with the eternal consciousness.[73]

VIII. The Problem Restated

At this stage, in 1880, Green, in distancing himself from a *stronger* reading of the doctrine of thought (which is directly linked to the stronger eternal consciousness thesis), does clearly make room for ordinary, imperfect human moral struggle. The human self is, in a way, disengaged from the eternal consciousness and made 'self-responsible'. The self stands out from the world. As Green comments, 'The unifying principle of the world is indeed in us; it is our self.' He warns us that this self is 'conditioned by a particular animal nature', and that 'our actual knowledge remains a piecemeal process'. He has, in an important sense, made room for the 'injunctive agency' view of moral philosophy. He also makes room for human failing, immorality, and particularly evil (something with which the more severe renditions of the

---

[72] Ibid.

[73] Quotations, ibid. 144–5. Yet, still, we should not forget that, for Green, if we examine the objective world around us, even within the natural sciences, 'we find that they all imply some synthetic action which we only know as exercised by our own spirit'. The objective world, therefore, only has a 'being in relations', and thus, 'what other medium do we know of but a thinking consciousness in and through which the separate can be united in that way which constitute relation?' (ibid. 145).

Absolute Idealism had severe philosophical difficulties).[74] Individual persons are viewed as passing 'from condition to condition, from effect to effect; but, as one fragment of truth is grasped, another has escaped us, and we never reach that totality of apprehension through which alone we could know the world as it is'.[75] I view this statement as consistent with his critique of Caird's doctrine of thought.

One upshot of this interpretation is that we need, in effect, to slough off aspects of the metaphysical argumentation to make sense of the injunctive thesis. There is also a deeper critical argument here for some votaries of Green (and indeed Hegel): namely, that Idealist metaphysics is a 'non-starter', particularly in the present philosophical environment. Thus, we should embrace Green's own more hesitant anxieties about the 'doctrine of thought' and the 'eternal consciousness'.[76] We need to retain the valuable components of Green's philosophy and jettison the bulk of the metaphysics. More charitably, the metaphysics of knowledge (particularly Book I of the *Prolegomena to Ethics*) can be safely put to one side as a kind of overreaction to empiricism.[77] The astute reader of Green's moral philosophy should therefore move straight to Book II on the will, where one can begin to explore the valuable 'injunctive' possibilities of Green, without the nagging problems of the Idealist metaphysics of knowledge.[78] The metaphysics is viewed as either redundant or just inadequately worked out. Green might have worked it up in later years, but dying as he did comparatively young, the metaphysics of knowledge

---

[74] For the Absolute Idealist circuitous perambulations around the problem of evil, see Andrew Vincent, 'Divine Immanence and Transcendence: Henry Jones and the Philosophy of Religion', *Idealistic Studies*, 23:2/3 (1993), 161–77, and Boucher and Vincent, *Radical Hegelian*, ch. 3.

[75] Green, *CW* iii. 145.

[76] Dimova-Cookson carries the critical analysis of the metaphysics to Green's 'doctrine of thought' and the theory of relational consciousness. She notes that 'Green's concept of relation is too closely linked with "thought", the ambiguities about the nature and function of thought make this concept untenable. No wonder it has no important use in Green's theories of general and moral practice. Unfortunately, it holds a central position in his epistemology and in his extensive criticism of Hume's philosophy' (Dimova-Cookson, *T. H. Green's Moral and Political Philosophy*, 32; for a more general and comprehensive discussion of the issues here, see ibid. ch. 1). I am not convinced, though, that the relational theory has no 'use' in his moral philosophy. In my own reading, minimally, it links (as a social epistemology) with the relational view of the self which is crucial for Green.

[77] See Dimova-Cookson, 'Eternal Consciousness', 142.

[78] As Wempe comments, 'Perhaps the most unfortunate omission of his account of first principles in [the] *Prolegomena* is that Green failed to make clear the intrinsic link he construed between metaphysics and ethical philosophy' (*Beyond Equality*, 80). This was also one of Sidgwick's main criticisms of Green; see Henry Sidgwick, *The Ethics of T. H. Green, Herbert Spencer and J. Martineau* (London: Macmillan, 1902). Another way of accommodating this critical argument is to distinguish between the metaphysics of knowledge and the metaphysics of morals. One can then retain a metaphysical perspective (with a mere glimmering of the eternal consciousness), but only via the prior role of human will and practice. I would take this as the direction of Dimova-Cookson's interpretation.

remains more mute. For many modern critics, Green therefore needs a sympathetic revisionist appraisal. I would suggest that much of the recent revived interest in Green's moral and political philosophy is premised on this general assumption.

However, this view (as I have already argued) does create a more general problem about knowledge and history within Green's system of philosophy. The metaphysics of the eternal consciousness (in one format) serves a logically validating and binding role. Green was also obviously attached, at points, to the idea that individual philosophizing does not necessarily reveal much about moral conduct. Rich substantive moral conventions pre-exist philosophy. The philosophical reasons which Green adduces for this are, first, that philosophy, in general, has a role to understand; second, that there is an underlying teleology which underpins, initiates, and constitutes moral and political beliefs; and third, that there is a set of transcendental claims which uphold the knowledge claims, so, unless the eternal consciousness were present (via a transcendental unity of apperception), then, ordinary knowledge claims by individuals (and subsequently moral claims) would simply not be present in any adequate or understandable form.[79]

IX. A Sketch of an Alternative

I want now to sketch, in speculative outline, an alternative view, whereby Green's 'grey on grey' argument might be upheld without the rich metaphysical diet of the eternal consciousness.[80] Yet, if one were to slough off the metaphysics of the eternal consciousness argument, what happens to the 'grey on grey' argument? In tackling this issue, I would emphasize a distinction (drawn at earlier stages of this chapter) between *harder* and *softer* renditions of the 'grey or grey' argument.[81] The *harder* rendition insists upon the initiating agency of the eternal consciousness, and consequently allows little or no space for direct individual injunctive argument. The eternal consciousness works through individuals. The *softer* rendition overlaps with what I called earlier the 'enabling thesis' in Green. It suggests the philosopher can try to grasp what is and can discuss the relative merits of the various moral formulae (as Green puts it) as a way of enabling the moral agent, but it still remains sceptical of

---

[79] The eternal consciousness (in tandem with the doctrine of thought) thus forms the actual *substance* of moral conduct, knowledge, and history.

[80] In one sense, this might even be considered a more Humean perspective, with a twist.

[81] For resonant, if different, ways of looking at this distinction, see Dimova-Cookson, *T. H. Green's Moral and Political Philosophy*, 27 ff., and Tyler, *Thomas Hill Green*, 33.

any full-blown injunctive arguments. This argument strikes me as a defensible view of the role of Green's philosophical ethics, which still integrates aspects of the 'grey on grey' argument.

In developing this softer rendition of the 'grey on grey' argument, I am, to a degree, close to one aspect of Dimova-Cookson's reformulation of Green's moral argument, particularly her emphasis on social practices. However, there is a crucial difference: namely, that I utilize the notion of social practice, ironically, to reinvigorate the softer 'grey on grey' thesis. This latter thesis, on my reading, still plays down the initiating role of both the individual agent and, more particularly, moral philosophy. In my own interpretation, this softer rendition makes sense of Green's quite obvious hesitancy about the role and character of both moral philosophy and moral action. In this context, I also disagree with David Brink's view that Green's position here necessarily invokes a 'moral complacency'. None the less, I still concur with Brink that Green's overall position here is 'troubling'.[82]

This softer rendition can be built up from certain suppositions implicit in many of Green's arguments. The first supposition is that we should not draw a hard distinction between reasons and conventions. In effect, ordinary moral practice is not governed by any external imperative of reason. The idea of historical traditions and conventions being prior to philosophical reason is not to suggest that such conventions and traditions are unreasonable or irrational. Many philosophers detach reason from conventional practice, partly because reason is seen as a universal, neutral, and impartial standard of judgement. Thus, if something is not directed or guided by the external imperatives of reason, then it is unreasonable, almost by default. However, this latter view presupposes that reason is distinct from convention, traditions, and everyday human experience. As Green notes, on many occasions, conventions, institutions, and tradition embody an implicit reason which 'actuate[s] men independently of the operations of the discursive intellect'.[83]

The second supposition is that Green implicitly acknowledges *two* senses of both knowing and reason. There is an abstract *ex post facto* philosophical knowing, and there is a concrete knowing from within the complex worlds of social practice, institutions, and ordinary existence. Morality is not primarily an abstraction; it is integral to human institutions and practices. We can make it an abstraction in philosophical reflection, but the latter has quite a limited role in human affairs. Greater knowledge of morality cannot be gained by moving away from practices and impersonalizing or abstracting them. We learn morality continuously *in* concrete contexts. As Iris Murdoch put it: 'We

<hr>

[82] See Brink, *Perfectionism*, 73.   [83] Green, *PE* §317.

ordinarily conceive of and apprehend goodness in terms of virtues which belong to a continuous fabric of being. And it is just the historical, individual, nature of the virtues as actually exemplified which makes it difficult to learn goodness from another person.' Consequently, 'Where virtue is concerned we often apprehend more than we clearly understand and *grow by looking.*' Goodness is related to knowledge, but not to impersonal, detached, abstract, neutral, quasi-scientific knowledge, but to a 'refined and honest perception of what is really the case, a patient and just discernment and exploration of what confronts one'.[84]

There is, oddly, the merest hint, in the softer 'grey on grey' argument, of G. E. Moore's later moral intuitionism. However, *contra* Moore, for Green, we can define the 'good', but to do so effectively, we need to examine social conventions and practices. We need an analysis of the occasions in which the word 'good' is conventionally used. If the good still remains difficult to define, this is not for G. E. Moore's non-naturalistic reasons, but rather 'because of the infinite difficulty of the task of apprehending a magnetic but inexhaustible [moral] reality'.[85] Murdoch's account here catches, for me, an important aspect of Green's potential, softer 'grey on grey' argument.

The third supposition is that we should not draw a hard distinction between morality and convention, or even between morality and prudence. Moral norms are embedded within conventions and institutions. Green shows, for example, how conventional institutions, such as the family and the neighbourhood, can 'enable' individuals to develop morally. In other words, such processes facilitate individuals in seeing themselves as both involving and relating to other selves. Responding morally to the needs of a family or a neighbourhood becomes virtually naturalized. It does not require moral philosophy, or a choosing moral self prior to the experience, to prescribe this moral conduct.

Outside the family or the neighbourhood, moral concern for others becomes trickier. It is not always so immediate. Yet, for Green, it can become more natural and more immediate as the person's 'character' develops. This is the fourth supposition: moral development is not about increasing adeptness with moral philosophy or a facility with reason. It is not about any developed intelligence—although it might imply an emotional intelligence. As Green notes, great intelligence and philosophical adeptness can just as well go hand in hand with greater immorality, insensitivity, and moral self-delusion. Moral progress is about an increasing sensitivity in practice to a wider range of things and persons. In other words, it becomes more natural

---

[84] Murdoch, *Sovereignty of the Good*, 30–1, 38.   [85] Ibid. 42.

and immediate to incorporate wider audiences into one's sphere of moral concern. This implies a certain type of character growth *within* a historical and social framework, but such a character can still be quite unreflective and ordinary.

The fifth supposition is that the human self cannot be completely detached from conventions and traditions. The idea of a disengaged self often appears to be presupposed in the neo-Kantian injunctive argument, existing as a non-related entity, functioning apart from the relations which presuppose it. Admittedly, this more detached, calculating, rule-governed self, is none the less embedded within many of Green's injunctive (neo-Kantian-inspired) writings on moral and political philosophy. However, from another Greenian stand-point (linked more closely with the softer 'grey on grey' argument), the self has neither this fixity nor this sense of complete disengagement. Green signals another account of the human self as a process of *continuous making* within human practices—that is, a process of self-realization within the traditions of a society. The self, in this case, is shaping and shaped continuously within conventions and social institutions.

The idea of the self embodies a complex set of issues. As indicated earlier, the eternal consciousness argument clearly problematizes the whole notion of the finite human self (as Green was keenly aware in his critique of both Hegel and John Caird).[86] But we should not imagine that, in focusing on the disengaged, reasonable, and neutral self, we have moved away from metaphysics. This latter vision of the human subject also has deep metaphysical roots. Its origins, for example, have been traced frequently to Cartesianism—a philosophy which separates mind from matter, and subject-based reason from the objective material world. It is also a subject-based metaphysics which goes hand in hand with the development of empirical natural science-based methods. Descartes is thus frequently seen as one of the key foundations of twentieth-century Western rationalist philosophy and natural science. The same isolated self keeps reappearing as a crucial figure in nineteenth- and twentieth-century philosophy.[87] But Kant, with his vision of the human subject, is probably the key figure for modern philosophy and, more particularly, modern moral philosophy. As Iris Murdoch remarks, 'How recognisable, how familiar to us, is the man so beautifully portrayed in the *Grundlegung*, who confronted even with Christ turns away to consider the judgment of his own conscience and to hear

---

[86] This point later became the central philosophical bone of contention dividing Absolute from personal Idealists; see, for a full discussion of this, Vincent, 'The Individual in Hegelian Thought', or Boucher and Vincent, *Radical Hegelian*, ch. 2.

[87] In this sense I see Husserl's use of the subject in phenomenology as also implicitly metaphysical. This critical point on Husserl is also made by Derrida, Gadamer, and Habermas, amongst others.

the voice of his own reason.' This is the isolated, rational, and self-responsible agent. In many ways it is Kant, and not Hegel, who is the dominant figure in modern ethics. Green's moral philosophy also clearly reflects, at points, these Kantian themes. However, Murdoch continues presciently, 'It is not such a very long step from Kant to Nietzsche, and from Nietzsche to existentialism and the Anglo-Saxon ethical doctrines which in some way resemble it.' The heart of all this moral philosophy is the free, rational, isolated self.[88]

For Murdoch, the only difference between the neo-Kantian and twentieth-century existentialist visions of the isolated self (and will) is 'by the degree of their interest in *reasons* for action'. In the case of existentialists this interest 'diminishes to nothing'.[89] The Kantian wing thus thinks that we are free in relation to reasons, and the existentialist wing claims there are no reasons. The true self remains as the empty choosing will. In materialist doctrines, such as physicalism, sociobiology, or behaviouralism, the final thin vestiges of self and will are surrendered to empirical science. Moral judgements are then considered neither factual nor truthful. Ethics either expresses random emotions or just becomes redundant. This is the source of the doctrine of emotivism. It is important, though, to re-emphasize the point that this generic vision of the self (as a disengaged and empty will) is yet another contentious metaphysical doctrine.

My argument is therefore that in Green's accounts of the 'grey on grey' and 'injunctive' arguments on morality, we are in fact observing *two* metaphysical accounts of the human self. Of Green's 'grey on grey' argument there are, though, *harder* and *softer* renditions. The *harder* rendition relies on a stricter sense of the agency of the eternal consciousness and the doctrine of thought. This latter doctrine (as Green observed) tends to downgrade the initiating role of the individual human self in favour of the agency of the eternal consciousness. However, this does not undermine substantive morality, but rather identifies it with the agency of the eternal consciousness. This argument is something that Green, at points, felt uneasy with; yet it keeps reappearing in his writings.

In the above scenario Green had certain philosophical alternatives. One was a qualified return to neo-Kantianism. His interest in Lotze in the late 1870s (Lotze in many ways prefaced the 'back to Kant' revival in Germany, Britain, and the USA) attests to the viability of this alternative.[90] This would have allowed him to develop the injunctive dimension and avoid the problems of the *harder* rendition of the doctrine of thought and the eternal consciousness. A second alternative was the *softer* rendition of the 'grey on grey' argument,

---

[88] Murdoch, *Sovereignty of the Good*, 80–1.   [89] Ibid. 35.
[90] See also Wempe, *Beyond Equality*, 63.

which adopts a more multifaceted, anthropological view of the self—fluid and developing in the context of ordinary human conventions, social practices, and historical circumstances. This latter view sees reason as immanent within human practices and institutions, and subject to historical contingency and fallibility—although it also considerably weakens the spiritual teleology.[91] It still views reality as existing for thought, but it does not rely upon any argument concerning the eternal consciousness. It situates the self within complex conventions and traditions. This argument thus allows Green to retain his *ex post facto* view of philosophy (the *softer* 'grey on grey' argument) and much of the relational 'doctrine of thought' (in a qualified format), without invoking the agency of the eternal consciousness. It also corresponds to the 'enabling thesis' on the role of moral philosophy. This sketch is not, though, a position that Green explicitly articulates; it is rather one which, I would suggest, is none the less implicit in some of his arguments. It gives a much reduced or restricted role for moral philosophy, certainly by comparison with either the injunctive or even the strong eternal agency arguments. Yet it still strikes me as a more apt and truthful philosophical account of morality, and it salvages aspects of Green's moral argumentation.

X. Conclusion

The central issue underlying the present chapter has been the relationship between Green's metaphysics and ethics. My contention is that Green has different responses to this issue, which are potentially problematic, for reasons which I have spelt out. Part of the problem here may well be due to the undeveloped character of Green's arguments on metaphysics, rather than any outright philosophical contradiction. The two main answers he gives are, broadly, the 'grey on grey' argument and the 'moral injunctive' view. Both views contain substantive normative accounts of morality, the former *indirectly* (via the agency of the eternal consciousness, which we as finite agents can only appreciate haltingly and *ex post facto*), and the latter *directly* (via the individual moral agent). The former argument has often been associated mistakenly with a metaethical claim. However, if one looks at Green's harder 'grey on grey' argument, in its true metaphysical and epistemological context (via the eternal consciousness doctrine), then the point is patently obvious that the eternal consciousness is the core of morality—morality referring to the agency and

---

[91] In many ways this is a Gadamerian interpretation of Green.

telos of the eternal consciousness. Individual human agents then become like ciphers, who can take a long time to make sense of the force of circumstance, to which they are subject. Yet this latter argument creates a dilemma with regard to the relationship between the finite individual agent and the eternal consciousness.

There are ways round this dilemma, in terms of the softer rendition of the 'grey on grey' argument. But I do not think that in the final analysis Green resolved this issue. Despite what many sympathetic commentators have tried to argue, he did seem committed, throughout his philosophical *œuvre*, to trying to reconcile humanity with the eternal consciousness. At the same time, he hesitated on how that argument played out. I must also confess that I remain puzzled as to what precisely Green wanted to say here, and I am not convinced that there is one single consistent view in his writings. On the one hand, Green's harder rendition of the eternal consciousness and 'grey on grey' doctrines seems very close (in effect) to John Caird's metaphysical arguments. Indeed, it hardly needs saying that many of his contemporaries actually did quite explicitly and critically read Green in this manner.[92] This would make sense of Green's view that human knowledge is the 'progressive actualization in us of a self-consciousness in itself complete, and which in its completeness included the world as its object'.[93] In our thinking, at its best, the eternal consciousness, as it were, thinks through us.[94] This also gives substance to his harder rendition of the 'grey on grey' argument. On the other hand, Green was obviously, at other points, anxious about the philosophical implications of this doctrine, and saw the need for an injunctive moral and political philosophy. In this sense, the relationship between the metaphysical and ethical doctrines remains an open and troubling factor in Green scholarship.

[92] Andrew Seth, *Hegelianism and Personality* (Edinburgh: William Blackwood and Son, 1887) is the key text here.

[93] Green, *CW* i. 131.

[94] As Green comments, the 'eternal mind uses the animal organism in man as its vehicle so as to constitute a being self-conscious, yet limited by the conditions of the organism ... this [eternal] mind constitutes the "me" in each of us' (*CW* ii. 182). This appears to be saying that there is one spiritual self-conscious being which constitutes the 'me' or 'the self' (limited by the finite organism). 'Thought' in this scenario appears to be referring to the agency of the eternal consciousness.

5

Green's Criticism of the British Moralists

T. H. IRWIN

I

At the beginning of an essay on Butler, A. E. Taylor comments on the relative neglect of some of the British moralists in British philosophy in the nineteenth century.

[O]ne of the unfortunate effects of the intellectual conquest of Britain by Germany has been the curious neglect of the very rich and valuable ethical literature which begins with Cumberland and Cudworth (or perhaps, taking dates of publication into account, one should say Samuel Clarke) and culminates in Richard Price. We might indeed have expected that men like Green and Bradley would have found a kindred spirit in the author of the *Sermons on Human Nature*; but in fact Bradley, as far as I can recollect, shows no knowledge of the British rationalistic moralists, and in the *Prolegomena to Ethics* Butler receives only the barest incidental mention.[1]

Taylor does not speculate further on the causes or the results of the neglect that he mentions. In this paper I offer a few speculations in answer to the questions that he suggests.

Taylor is not the only one to notice and to regret the relative absence of the British moralists from the moral philosophy of the previous century. Martineau expresses a similar view in his review of Whewell's *Elements of Morality*. He comments on the ignorance of the history of modern philosophy among Oxford and Cambridge philosophers.

They apply Greek or mediaeval doctrine directly to the exposure of existing fallacies and the correction of existing opinion. They leap down from Aristotle to Bentham, from Plato to Coleridge, with the fewest possible resting-places between. With the

---

[1] A. E. Taylor, 'Some Features of Butler's Ethics', *Mind*, 35 (1926), 273–300, at 273 f.

exception of Hooker, Locke, Butler and Paley (an exception far from constant), the series of great writers who have formed the modes of speculative thought in Protestant Europe is but little known to them. Hence they rarely appear at home in the province of modern philosophy ... and betray how difficult is the transition, for a mind trained in the schools of Athens and Rome, to the work of the Christian moralist and the Anglican ecclesiastic.[2]

Martineau believes that this narrowness explains the inferiority of Oxford and Cambridge philosophy to Scottish philosophy.[3]

This judgement scarcely does justice to Cambridge philosophy. Whewell's lectures on the history of moral philosophy show considerable knowledge of the subject, and considerable sympathy with some of his predecessors.[4] His editions of Butler, Sanderson, and Grotius reveal his efforts to get other people to read, as well as to hear about, some major texts in modern moral philosophy. Whewell probably set an example for Sidgwick in his close and careful study of the history of moral philosophy.

But whatever we think of Martineau's judgement on Whewell in particular, and on Cambridge in general, it seems to fit Oxford; it reflects a contemporary view of the situation that Taylor describes in retrospect. And if it fits Oxford in general, it seems to fit Green especially well.

A sign of Green's attitude to his British predecessors is his remark that Hume is 'the last great English philosopher'.[5] He explains this more fully:

In the line of speculation more distinctively English, a ... *regime* of 'strenua inertia' has prevailed since the time of Hume....

As the result of the [sc. Hume's] experiment, the method, which began with professing to explain knowledge, showed knowledge to be impossible. Hume himself was perfectly cognisant of this result, but his successors in England and Scotland would seem so far to have been unable to look it in the face. (*CW* i. 2)

The second passage suggests that when Green calls Hume an 'English' philosopher, he means 'English-speaking'; his remark is intended to cover Hume's Scottish successors.

Among those whom it covers is Reid. Green's conception of Hume's position as the logical conclusion, and implicit refutation, of the empiricism of Locke is quite similar to Reid's, so that a more recent writer speaks, quite

---

[2] James Martineau, *Essays, Reviews, and Addresses*, iii (London: Longmans, 1891), 378.
[3] Ibid. 379.
[4] William Whewell, *Lectures on the History of Moral Philosophy in England* (London: Parker, 1852); cited hereinafter as *Lectures*.
[5] Green, 'Introduction to Hume', in *CW* i. p. vii.

appropriately, of the 'Reid–Green criticism' of Hume.[6] But Green never comments on this similarity between his own judgement on Hume and Reid's judgement. His general remark on Hume's successors implies that Reid is one of those who fail to respond satisfactorily to Hume, because they do not look Hume's result in the face. This does not seem a completely fair judgement of Reid; for, whatever one thinks of Reid's answer to Hume, his assessment of what Hume has shown is very close to Green's.

Green's comment on Hume and his successors applies primarily to Hume's metaphysics and epistemology. But his view of the history of ethics is quite similar. He notices that Hume's ethical arguments are directed towards Locke's successors, but still thinks it appropriate to focus on Hume's development of Locke.

This does not interfere, however, with the propriety of affiliating him, in respect of his views on morals, no less than on knowledge, directly to Locke, whose principles and method were in the main accepted by all the moralists of that age. His characteristic lies in his more consistent application of these, and the effect of current controversy upon him was chiefly to show him the line which this application must take. (*CW* i. 321–2)

Green shows most interest in Shaftesbury's confused (as he supposes) attempts to present an alternative to Locke. He discusses Butler and Hutcheson quite briefly, and Clarke still more briefly, as incomplete efforts escape from Locke. He concludes that they all fail.

In contrast with these well-meant efforts to derive that distinction between the selfish and unselfish, between the pleasant and the morally good, which the Christian conscience requires, from principles that do not admit of it, Hume's system has the merit of relative consistency. (*CW* i. 331)

He does not suggest that Hume's British successors deserve any more consideration than their predecessors.

Further evidence of Green's view of the British moralists appears in Bradley's notes from a course of lectures ascribed to Green.[7] The lectures agree with the general position of his 'Introduction to Hume'. They treat Shaftesbury as the most significant rival to Locke, and at one point describe Butler as 'Shaftesbury

---

[6] See John Passmore, *Hume's Intentions*, 2nd edn. (London: Duckworth, 1968), 84 f. Passmore refers to Norman Kemp Smith, *Philosophy of David Hume* (London: Macmillan, 1941). Kemp Smith speaks of Green as 'adhering to the interpretation of Hume's teaching which first gained general currency through the writings of Thomas Reid, Beattie, and Dugald Stewart, and which was later accepted, almost without question, by James Mill, John Stuart Mill and Bain' (p. 80).

[7] See 'Lectures on Moral and Political Philosophy', in *CW*, v. Bristol: 108–82. Nicholson (pp. 105 f.) describes the notes and the grounds for ascribing the lectures to Green.

in vile English' (167).[8] Green does not even mention anyone after Butler, but passes at once from Butler to Kant (168).

II

What explains Green's relative indifference towards the British moralists? We might suggest some partial explanations. (1) Under the influence of Kant and Hegel, he supposes that Hume exposes the limitations not only of Lockean empiricism but also of the British answers to Lockean and Humean empiricism. Green's remarks on Hume's British successors agree with Kant's judgement that they had failed to grasp the depth and force of Hume's arguments. (2) A more parochial consideration may also be relevant. Oxford had no one like Whewell, who systematically studied the British moralists and expounded them in his lectures. Whewell discusses the British tradition as a counterweight to the harmful influence of Paley.[9] From the Oxonian point of view, the right remedy against Paley is Aristotle.[10]

These reasons for relative neglect of the British moralists do not wholly explain Green's attitude to Butler. In contrast to the other British moralists, Butler was both known and valued in Oxford in the first half of the nineteenth century. Gladstone mentions Butler as one of his 'four doctors', whom he had learned to appreciate during his years in Oxford; and later in life he published both an edition of Butler's works and essays on Butler.[11] The admiration for Butler in Oxford partly rests on his *Analogy*, but it also extends to his *Sermons* on moral philosophy.[12]

---

[8] I do not know whether the liveliness of some passages in the lectures reflects Green's manner in lectures (as opposed to his published works) or Bradley's recasting of Green in his own style.

[9] In *Butler's Three Sermons on Human Nature* (Cambridge: Deighton, 1848), Whewell mentions that Butler had been added to the reading list in one Cambridge college around 1833, with the aim of providing a useful 'addition or correction to other works' (p. ix). The sort of correction that Whewell has in mind is suggested by his sharp contrast between Butler and Paley; though he is careful to qualify the contrast, he clearly takes Butler to express views about metaethics and normative ethics that expose the errors in Paley. Among other things, he contrasts Butler's arguments about nature with Paley's dismissal of such arguments as 'usual declamation' (Whewell, *Butler's Three Sermons*, p. x; cf. Paley, *Principles of Moral and Political Philosophy* (London, 1785), Book i, ch. 6). Whewell develops his views about the bad effects of Paley's moral philosophy, and about why Butler is better than Paley, in four sermons that recall Butler's moral sermons: *On the Foundations of Morals: Four Sermons*, 2nd edn. (London: Parker, 1837).

[10] I have said a little more on this in 'Mill and the Classical World', in J. Skorupski (ed.), *Cambridge Companion to Mill* (Cambridge: Cambridge University Press, 1998), 441.

[11] Ibid. 440. Gladstone published his edition of Butler in 1896.

[12] Jane Garnett helpfully examines Butler's influence in 'Bishop Butler and the Zeitgeist: Butler and the Development of Christian Moral Philosophy in Victorian Britain', in C. Cunliffe (ed.), *Joseph*

We can form some idea of the importance of Butler's moral philosophy for some of his admirers in Oxford from an essay by Frederick Oakeley.[13] Oakeley was a contemporary of Gladstone's at Christ Church, and then a fellow of Balliol from 1827. In 1839 he became incumbent of the Tractarian centre in London, the Margaret Chapel, and in 1845 followed Newman in going over to Rome.[14] His essay on Platonic and Aristotelian ethics was published in 1837, towards the end of his time at Balliol. Oakeley shows his Tractarian sympathies in dedicating his essay to Keble,[15] and in its main argument.

He contrasts two extreme views of the relationship between 'heathen ethics' and 'divine revelation':

By some, revelation, as a practical system, is regarded as little more than a republication of heathen morality. By others, it is held to be altogether distinct from every other moral system; insomuch that to institute any comparison between it and the speculations of heathen philosophers, except in the way of contrast, is deemed an injury to divine truth, and almost a profanation of it. (p. 9)

Against these extremes, Oakeley defends an intermediate position:

Revelation has authoritatively published what heathen philosophers taught. And yet, as a system capable of realizing its designs, it stands entirely alone. It has filled up those gaps in the ancient systems, by reason of which, notwithstanding all their beauty, and even consistency, as theories, they were fundamentally, and, as things then were, irremediably defective. (p. 11)

He suggests that a fair comparison of Greek with Christian ethics supports Christianity. On the one hand, the writers of the Gospels, though not themselves Greek philosophers, agree with the best results of rational reflection. On the other hand, the success of rational moral philosophy confirms the Christian doctrine of creation, which leads us to expect that 'reason, the gift of God,

Butler's Moral and Religious Thought (Oxford: Clarendon Press, 1992), ch. 4. She comments on Oakeley and Pattison at p. 67.

[13] Frederick Oakeley, *Remarks upon Aristotelian and Platonic Ethics as a Branch of the Studies Pursued in the University of Oxford* (Oxford: Parker, 1837); subsequent page references are given parenthetically in the text. This essay is discussed by F. M. Turner, *The Greek Heritage in Victorian Britain* (New Haven: Yale University Press, 1981), 332–5.

[14] F. L. Cross, *The Oxford Movement and the Seventeenth Century* (London: SPCK, 1933), mentions one indication of Newman's admiration for Butler. He quotes Newman's reference to 'Anglicanism, the religion of Andrewes, Laud, Butler, and Wilson'. Cross comments: 'Butler, it is true, is of later date than the seventeenth century, but in his moralism (which Newman found very congenial to his own temperament), as well as in other respects, a large measure of seventeenth-century theology had survived in the author of The Analogy of Religion' (p. 9).

[15] He takes the motto of the essay from Keble: 'Such thoughts, the wreck of Paradise Through many a dreary age Upbore whate'er of good or wise/Yet lived in Bard or Sage.' See John Keble, *The Christian Year*, 2 vols. (Oxford: Parker, 1827), ii. 14 (entitled 'The groans of nature').

sincerely exercised in investigating moral truth, would terminate in something better than unmixed error' (p. 12). Hence the merits of heathen philosophy support Christianity, while its defects show the need for revelation (p. 30).

From this point of view, Oakeley discusses Platonic and Aristotelian ethics. He gives Plato a distinctly secondary place, and relies mainly on Aristotle.[16] Sometimes he mentions connections with Butler; but even when he does not mention them, his presentation of Aristotle suggests the connections.

Aristotle avoids Platonic extravagance about super-sensible forms as objects of moral knowledge, but he shares Plato's belief in objective moral truth that is not constituted by moral opinions (p. 32). He takes moral truths to be about human nature, as Butler understands it.

Aristotle, in his political, as in his more strictly ethical treatise, agrees with the best Christian moralists in paying respect to the constitution and instincts of our nature. Using the word Nature precisely in Bishop Butler's sense, Aristotle declares that then only when opportunity is given to man of satisfying his social instincts, is he properly in his natural state. (p. 79)

Aristotle also agrees with Butler in attributing to practical reason the outlook that Butler attributes to conscience. Aristotelian practical wisdom (*phronēsis*) includes more than the calculation of consequences; it also requires love of the 'fine' (morally good; *kalon*) (pp. 31 f.). Since Aristotle recognizes morally good action (*eupraxia*) as an end in itself, he rejects the Jesuitical calculations that allow us to do evil so that good may come, contrary to St Paul's prohibition (p. 66). On this point Aristotle differs from the consequentialist outlook of Paley, who is too sympathetic towards the Jesuitical principle.[17]

Once we grasp these Aristotelian principles, we can avoid misleading contrasts between Aristotelian and Christian virtues. Since the doctrine of the mean requires us to aim at the fine, it does not advise us to pursue moderation or mediocrity (p. 52). If we understand the focus of the Aristotelian virtues on the fine, we can see that they are not un-Christian virtues. Aristotle is right, for instance, to describe bravery as fearlessness for the sake of the *kalon*, though we might differ from him about the situations in which this fearlessness is required (p. 58). Similarly, we ought not to see any conflict between Aristotelian magnanimity, which requires a proper sense of dignity, and Christian humility, which refers one's abilities to their proper source (p. 60).

---

[16] 'The more the philosophy of Plato is studied, the less will he appear to be that mere enthusiast, and poet among philosophers, which many think him. In the midst of a diffuseness of style, and a fancifulness of theory, strikingly at variance with the close argument, and practical good sense, of Aristotle, there is a depth of thought, a boldness of conception, an intensity of feeling, in some parts of the Platonic philosophy, which is more nearly divine than anything else uninspired' (p. 37).

[17] Oakeley refers to Paley, *Principles*, Book ii, ch. 8.

Nor does Aristotle disagree with the Christian attitude to the moral limitations of humanity in its present state. His discussion of incontinence and
internal conflict shows that he recognizes the phenomena described by St Paul
(p. 39).[18] He agrees with Christianity in rejecting the exaggerated contempt
for the body that we find in Platonic dualism (pp. 41–2). He also agrees in
recognizing the mutual dependence of moral and intellectual development,
and exposes the error of anti-intellectual Christian moralists.[19]

The spirit of Aristotelian ethics animates the outlook of Oakeley's favourite
modern Aristotelians, Hooker and Butler.

> Hooker, indeed, was evidently a professed Aristotelian; but our greatest of ethical
> divines, without distinctly recognizing the authority of Aristotle, exhibits much of
> unpremeditated sympathy with his temper, and undesigned coincidence with his views
> ... The earlier part of the Ecclesiastical Polity of Hooker is to the Political Works of
> Aristotle what the Analogy and Sermons of Bishop Butler are to his ethical; a Christian
> commentary, showing how these subjects may be vindicated from profane uses. (p. 29)

Oakeley associates Butler with Hooker, a hero of some leading Tractarians.[20]
The connection between Hooker and Aristotle is clear. The connection
between Butler and Aristotle is less obvious.[21] But Oakeley's account of
Aristotle has prepared us for the claim that Butler provides a 'Christian
commentary'. Oakeley's interpretation of Aristotle's views on moral goodness
already answers the obvious objection that Butler's doctrine of conscience
introduces an element that is alien to Greek ethics.

Oakeley's version of these episodes in the history of ethics does not rest on
well-informed historical inquiry.[22] Given his concern to reconcile Aristotle
with the Christian conscience, we might be surprised that he mentions neither
the Fathers nor the Scholastics to whom Hooker is clearly indebted.[23] Even

---

[18] Oakeley (in contrast to many other interpreters) supposes that St Paul in Rom. 7 gives an account
of the unregenerate man; this 'is the true account of the conflict (stasis) of principles of which Aristotle
speaks in the ninth book of the Ethics. But such description does not (I humbly conceive) apply, in all
its force, to regenerated nature' (p. 39). He presumably refers to EN ix. 4.

[19] 'Aristotle, like the best Christian moralists, considers that there is an essential connexion between
the intellectual and the moral character' (p. 64). Oakeley cites Matt. 10: 16; 1 Cor. 14: 20.

[20] Keble published an elaborate edition of Hooker's Ecclesiastical Polity, 3 vols. (Oxford: Clarendon
Press, 1st edn., 1836, 7th edn., 1888).

[21] I have discussed Butler further in 'Stoic Naturalism in Butler', in J. Miller and B. Inwood (eds.),
Hellenistic and Modern Philosophy (Cambridge: Cambridge University Press, 2003), ch. 11.

[22] 'Mr Oakeley, without much learning, was a master of a facile and elegant pen' (R. W. Church, The
Oxford Movement (London: Macmillan, 1891, repr. Chicago: University of Chicago Press, 1970), 249).

[23] The moral philosophy of Aquinas was generally unappreciated in England at this time, if the
superficial, unsympathetic, and unjust treatments by Hampden and Whewell are at all typical. See
R. D. Hampden, The Scholastic Philosophy Considered in its Relation to Christian Theology (Oxford: Parker,
1833), Lecture 6; Whewell, Additional Lectures on the History of Moral Philosophy (Cambridge: Deighton,
Bell, 1862), 101.

if one ignores everyone between the ancients and the sixteenth century, one might gather from Butler's own references that he is indebted to the Stoics. Still, Oakeley's sketch of Aristotelian ethics in relation to Butler is plausible enough to deserve discussion.

It was brusquely dismissed by Mark Pattison in his critical survey of Oxford philosophy in the early nineteenth century.[24] In this essay, published in 1855, Pattison mentions Oakeley as an example of the 'common sense period of Aristotelian interpretation' (p. 464), which preceded any genuine historical understanding of Aristotle. Lacking such an understanding (in Pattison's view), Oakeley treats Aristotle as an 'adumbration of the Catholic system'.[25] He combines this unhistorical attitude to Aristotle with an equally unhistorical attitude to Butler as the only English moralist worth discussing, and as a Christian supplement to Aristotle.[26] While Pattison dismisses Oakeley's position with some scorn, he does not argue against it.[27]

Though Pattison attacked Oakeley's alleged misuse of Butler, rather than Butler's ethics in its own right, he also believed that his predecessors grossly overvalued Butler. His objections to Butler later provoked a reply from Gladstone.[28] The teaching of moral philosophy in Oxford developed partly, but not wholly, in the direction that Pattison advocated. Butler was no longer

---

[24] Mark Pattison, *Essays*, ed. H. Nettleship, 2 vols. (Oxford: Oxford University Press, 1889), ch. 11, 'Oxford Studies'; subsequent page references are given parenthetically in the text.

[25] Pattison quotes Oakeley, *Remarks*, 29 (quoted above). Pattison, being an ex-Tractarian himself, is perhaps especially eager to attack Oakeley on this point. But Oakeley's general attitude to Aristotle and Butler appears in R. D. Hampden, a particular target of Tractarian hostility. See Turner, *Greek Heritage*, 329–31.

[26] 'The anomalous practice, which is still not quite disused in this School, of coupling Butler's Sermons with Aristotle's Ethics, as though there was some peculiar affinity between the two, can only tend to confound the student's conception of the nature of the science he is studying. If English ethics in the eighteenth century were admitted as a legitimate subject in this School, then Butler would occupy his own proper place—an eminent one—in that series. Taken as he is now, the solitary modern philosopher who figures in the examination papers, he not only assumes an importance to which he is in no way entitled, but fosters a very erroneous notion that the Sermons and the Ethics taken together somehow make up an orthodox system of morals. The Christian bishop corrects the heathen. The particular lacuna in the Aristotelian system which Butler is (or was) supposed to supply is the doctrine of conscience; a supposition wholly illusory' (pp. 474 f.).

[27] Similarly, Turner, *Greek Heritage*, 335, concludes his unsympathetic discussion of Oakeley with the judgement: 'The parochialism of Oakeley's purview was as striking as the confusion of his thinking, and the latter was in no small measure the result of the former.' Turner does not explain where Oakeley is confused. He seems to reach his judgement on the strength of Oakeley's remarks on magnanimity, which do not strike me as especially confused.

[28] Gladstone, *Studies Subsidiary to the Works of Bishop Butler* (London: Oxford University Press, 1896), discusses Pattison among the 'censors of Butler' (pp. 76 f.). He refers especially to Pattison's remark that he was one of the 'liberal board of examiners' who removed Butler 'from the list of books to be taken up' in the mid-1850s (he says '20 years later', in the context of his reading Butler in 1834). See Mark Pattison, *Memoirs* (London: Macmillan, 1885), 135. Garnett, 'Bishop Butler and the Zeitgeist', 64 n., discusses the different attitudes of Literae Humaniores examiners to Butler.

prescribed as the solitary modern moralist. But the study of Butler was replaced, not by the study of the British moralists, but by the study of Kant's moral philosophy as the companion to Aristotle's *Ethics*.

III

Even these few remarks about the treatment of Butler's ethics in the generation before Green suggest that one's evaluation of Butler might reflect one's attitude to several issues of current or recent controversy in Oxford. If we consider the extreme positions of Oakeley and Pattison, we can grasp some of the significance of Green's discussion of Butler and, even more, of his failure to discuss him.

At first sight, it seems clear that Green takes Pattison's side against the old-fashioned view represented by Oakeley.[29] In his lectures on the history of moral philosophy, and in his 'Introduction to Hume', he discusses Butler among the British moralists—as Pattison advised—and gives him no special place. Nor does he suggest that Butler presents any viable alternative to the empiricist tradition that leads to Hume.

Green also aligns himself with the tendency to replace Butler with Kant. Turning away from British moralists both before and after Hume, he examines Kant in more detail. The obvious and acknowledged sources for his moral theory are Aristotle and Kant, whom he tries to reconcile.

None the less, Green agrees with some of Oakeley's main contentions, for he shares Oakeley's aim of demonstrating that the Aristotelian outlook does not conflict with the Christian conscience. Oakeley anticipates Green's argument to show that Aristotle's emphasis on the connection of the virtues with the fine marks the moral element in the Aristotelian virtues. Green follows him in arguing that we can accept the Aristotelian virtues while attributing a different content to them.

I do not mean to suggest that Green actually derives his views from Oakeley. It is unlikely that Oakeley's views were original; Pattison treats him simply as

---

[29] Pattison held no high opinion of Green. In his *Memoirs* Pattison associates the rise of 'metaphysical' outlooks with 'sacerdotal' and 'Tory' views. He comments on the rise of the Hegelian outlook, which followed the Kantian: 'But gradually the clerical party rallied their forces, and since the Franco-German war have been advancing upon us with rapid strides. This fresh invasion of sacerdotalism has been accompanied by a renewed attempt to accredit an a priori logic ... What is curious is that this new a priori metaphysic, whoever gave it shape in Germany, was imported into Oxford by a staunch Liberal, the late Professor Green. This anomaly can only be accounted for by a certain puzzle-headedness on the part of the Professor, who was removed from the scene before he had time to see how eagerly the Tories began to carry off his honey to their hive' (p. 166).

representative of a trend in Aristotelian interpretation. In any case (I would venture to suggest) Green's views are so plausible that they might reasonably occur to a careful and thoughtful reader of Aristotle, without any external source.[30] But Green could hardly be unaware of the harmonizing view of Aristotle and Butler; his treatment of Butler shows that he decisively rejects it. In accepting some of the conclusions of this harmonizing view, he substitutes Kant for Butler.

IV

So far I have argued that Green deliberately rejects the harmony of Aristotle and Butler. But whether or not I am right about this, the historical questions suggests a philosophical question: does Green lose anything by turning away from Butler and the British moralists? Would he have improved his position if he had absorbed more from Butler?

We may approach this question by examining some of Green's criticisms of Butler and of British moralists who hold similar views. He presents these criticisms in his 'Introduction to Hume', to indicate the questions that confronted Hume as matters of current dispute. These questions concern the distinctive feature of disinterested action and the conditions for an action's being virtuous or vicious. Green believes that Hobbes's and Locke's acceptance of a psychological hedonist theory of motivation and of rational desire, and their acceptance of a purely instrumental conception of practical reason, prevent a satisfactory answer to these questions. He agrees that other British moralists tried to improve on Hobbes's answers, but he argues that they did not get far enough away from the basic Hobbesian assumptions to give consistent or clear answers.

Green's approach to the history of philosophy is often illuminating, because it is both critical and sympathetic. While recognizing legitimate criticisms of what philosophers say, he tries to go more deeply into their arguments and assumptions, to find the permanently significant point of view that they partly articulate, whether he rejects it (as in the case of Locke and Hume) or accepts it (as in the case of Aristotle and Kant). His general approach, then, might encourage us to ask two questions: (1) Does he approach the British moralists in the same way? (2) If not, what would he have said if he had approached them in this way?

---

[30] I have discussed Green's views in 'Eminent Victorians and Greek Ethics: Sidgwick, Green, and Aristotle', in B. Schultz (ed.), *Essays on Henry Sidgwick* (Cambridge: Cambridge University Press, 1992), ch. 10. Unfortunately I had not read Oakeley's essay when I wrote that paper.

To defend this general view, Green considers Shaftesbury, Hutcheson, and Butler at some length. These are the authors from whom Selby-Bigge selects 'the three principal texts of the sentimental school'.[31] Members of Selby-Bigge's 'intellectual school', including Clarke, Balguy, Cudworth, and Price, do not appear in Green's discussion, except for a brief comment on Clarke. He assumes, then, that the sentimental rather than the intellectual school is worth examining in the hope of finding a viable alternative to Hobbes.

Green's and Selby-Bigge's treatment of Shaftesbury, Hutcheson, and Butler as constituting a sentimentalist school is not wholly implausible. Hutcheson takes himself to be defending the principles of Shaftesbury, and in particular derives his conception of a moral sense partly from Shaftesbury's remarks. We might suppose that the contrast which Butler draws between his own method and Clarke's rationalism is a good reason for treating him as a third sentimentalist.

Selby-Bigge's division into sentimental and intellectual moralists may appeal to the tidy-minded historian and teacher of philosophy, since it suggests the epistemological division between empiricists and rationalists.[32] One might reasonably infer that this epistemological division gives us the right basis for understanding disputes in moral philosophy as well as disputes in the rest of philosophy. Since Green's discussion of Hume concerns Hume's empiricism as a whole, he treats the earlier history of British moral philosophy as primarily an argument among sentimentalists.

This is not the only possible division among British moralists. A different division underlies Whewell's discussion of British moral philosophy from Hobbes to Bentham. Whewell classifies moralists as supporters of 'independent' or of 'dependent' morality (*Lectures*, 33, 74, 78, 85). Morality is independent if it carries its own authority apart from its consequences; it is good in itself and gives us a sufficient reason for observing it, whether or not it also leads to our own pleasure, or the maximum universal pleasure, or to rewards in an afterlife. The authority of 'dependent' morality, however, depends on whether it leads to these consequences (*Lectures*, 52, 57). Hence Whewell sometimes speaks of 'independent morality' versus 'the morality of consequences' (p. 84), and sometimes of 'the morality of principles' and 'the morality of consequences' (p. 79).

---

[31] L. A. Selby-Bigge (ed.), *British Moralists*, 2 vols. (Oxford: Clarendon Press, 1897), i. p. vi. I do not know whether Selby-Bigge's division reflects the influence of Green (on whom Selby-Bigge comments in his edition of Hume's *Enquiries*, 2nd edn. (Oxford: Clarendon Press, 1902), p. vii).

[32] This principle of division has also received some critical examination. See Louis Loeb, *From Descartes to Hume* (Ithaca, NY: Cornell University Press, 1981), 30–2 (commenting on Green among others).

Whewell's descriptions suggest two ways of distinguishing dependent from independent morality. (1) A metaphysical division: some people affirm, while others deny, that moral properties can be reduced to such non-moral properties as our own pleasure, universal pleasure, or a tendency to result in rewards after death; whereas others deny this reductive claim. (2) A normative division: some people reduce moral rightness to a tendency to promote some specific type of consequences (desired independently of morality), whereas others deny this reduction.

This division corresponds with the epistemological division at some points. For some supporters of independent morality—Clarke and Price, for instance—are rationalists about moral knowledge and motivation. On the other side, some believe that Lockean empiricism commits them to a hedonist account of motivation.

Whewell's treatment of the moral sense, however, cuts across Selby-Bigge's division between sentimentalists and intellectualists. On his view, some defenders of independent morality try to avoid the obscurities of the rationalist epistemology of Cudworth and Clarke, while still defending their essential metaphysical claims about the irreducibility of morality.[33] Butler is an 'unsystematic' defender of independent morality, whereas Shaftesbury and Hutcheson defend it more systematically, by appealing to a moral sense.

This description of a moral sense theory fits Shaftesbury quite well, since Shaftesbury is a moral realist. Since Hutcheson claims to defend Shaftesbury, we might follow Whewell and suppose that he also defends Cudworth's and Clarke's metaphysical positions on moral properties without their epistemology. If Whewell is right, Hutcheson rejects rationalism in order to defend realism and independent morality against Hobbesian voluntarism, not in order to defend Hobbes and Locke against the rationalists.

In support of Whewell, we might cite Reid. Reid is a realist and a defender of independent morality, but he also sympathizes with those who treat moral knowledge as the product of a moral sense. He argues that reference to a moral sense supports realism and independent morality, by explaining how we can form moral judgements and claim moral knowledge of the sorts of properties that Whewell has in mind.

---

[33] 'In general the moral realists were aware that they gave their adversaries an advantage, when they ascribed the discernment of moral relations to the reason, narrowed as the domain of that faculty had in later times been. They now found it more convenient to assert that moral distinctions were perceived by a peculiar and separate faculty. To this faculty some did not venture to give a name, but described it only by its operations and results, while others applied to it a term, *The Moral Sense*, which introduced a new set of analogies and connexions' (*Lectures*, 92).

Whewell's division might be challenged on some points, but it offers a useful correction to an assumption that we might too easily accept if we took Selby-Bigge's division for granted. We may be tempted to believe that the crucial differences between moral theories lie in their epistemological foundations, and that these foundations determine the rest of a theory. Whewell suggests that metaphysical and normative differences are crucial, and that different epistemological positions may take different routes to the same metaphysical and normative position. His division is consistent with Selby-Bigge's; both divisions identify central issues in dispute, and each division identifies points of agreement and disagreement that the other division may obscure.

I have described Whewell's division not because I think it is completely correct, but because it deserved Green's consideration. It suggests that one ought not to represent eighteenth-century moralists as primarily Lockeans[34] who include a few non-Lockean fragments in their positions; instead, one might try to grasp and expound the elements in their position that defend 'independent morality'. A review of Green's discussion of Shaftesbury and Butler will show what he misses as a result of inattention to Whewell.

V

According to Green, Shaftesbury is primarily a follower of Locke. Though his claims about moral goodness are inconsistent with Locke's hedonism, he does not reject Locke steadily enough to justify his claims about goodness.

Shaftesbury's special antipathy, indeed, is the doctrine that benevolent affections are interested in the sense of having for their object a pleasure to oneself, apart from and beyond the pleasure of the person whom they move us to please; but unless he regards them as desires for the pleasure which the subject of them experiences in the pleasure of another, there is no purpose in enlarging, as he does with much unction, on the special pleasantness of the pleasures which they produce. (*CW* i. 324)

Green argues that Shaftesbury has some intuitive anti-Lockean views, but does not consistently develop them.

Is this verdict justified by Shaftesbury's treatment of 'benevolent affections'? In Book II of the *Inquiry* he discusses our 'obligation' to virtue, which he takes to be our 'reason to embrace it'.[35] His answer to this question consists

---

[34] Green does not think that this description applies to Clarke, whom, however, he does not discuss at length.
[35] Shaftesbury, *Characteristics*, ed. L. E. Klein (Cambridge: Cambridge University Press, 1999), 192; subsequent page references are given parenthetically in the text.

in explaining why virtue promotes the agent's happiness. He does not say directly that this is the only reason we could have for embracing virtue; but since he suggests no other reason, he seems to assume that a sufficient reason for being virtuous must at least include a warranted belief that virtue promotes one's happiness.

We might be surprised and disappointed that Shaftesbury takes this to be the only reason for being virtuous, after what he has said about the disinterested character of the moral sense. Martineau voices this disappointment strongly.

> The idea of obligation, in the form of an ultimate authority, intuitively known, after being affirmed and justified, is again lost: the question being raised, 'What underlies this bottom of all?' 'where are the credentials of this power which legitimates itself?' If it is disappointing to find this question asked, it is still more so to hear the answer, viz. that what binds us to the right is the balance of personal happiness it brings us;—an answer at which the independent base of virtue suddenly caves in, and the goodly pile that seemed immovable is shifted on to the sands of hedonism.[36]

Martineau cites Shaftesbury's remarks about the moral sense, in order to show that he recognizes a basis of moral goodness that is independent of any appeal to self-interest. A virtuous person is one who regards the moral properties of actions as the sources of sufficient reasons in their own right. Why, then, should some reason based in self-interest be needed?

If we consider the structure of eudaimonist ethical theories, Shaftesbury's acceptance both of a disinterested conception of a moral sense and of a self-interested defence of morality should not surprise us as much as it surprised Martineau. If we understand the pursuit of happiness as the pursuit of rational structure and harmony in our different activities, it is quite reasonable to examine the contribution of virtue to happiness. One might have reasons for rejecting this non-hedonist conception of happiness, but Green can hardly believe that these are good reasons, since he himself accepts just this conception of the end of rational action. If self-interest is understood within a eudaimonist conception, it is not obvious that Shaftesbury's appeal to self-interest conflicts with recognition of a disinterested moral sense.

If, however, Shaftesbury were suggesting that unless virtue maximizes my own pleasure, I have no reason for choosing virtue, he would not be allowing any reason for the disinterested acceptance of virtue. When Martineau speaks of 'the sands of hedonism', he attributes this suggestion to Shaftesbury. But is this what Shaftesbury means?

---

[36] James Martineau, *Types of Ethical Theory*, 2nd edn. (Oxford: Clarendon Press, 1886), ii. 508.

In some passages, admittedly, he seems to accept Locke's moral psychology, including a hedonist conception of happiness. He seems to be an anti-rationalist about motivation and action.

It has been shown before, that no animal can be said properly to *act*, otherwise than through affections or passions, such as are proper to an animal ... Whatever, therefore is done or acted by any animal as such, is done only through some affection or passion, as of fear, love, or hatred moving him. And as it is impossible that a weaker affection should overcome a stronger, so it is impossible but that where the affections or passions are strongest in the main, and form in general the most considerable party, either by their force or number; thither the animal must incline: and according to this balance he must be governed, and led to action. (pp. 195 f.)

The choice of one end over another, in cases where instrumental reasoning cannot decide the issue, must result from the different impacts of desires of different strengths. It is not clear, however, whether Shaftesbury believes that every desire must result from some prior non-rational desire focused by instrumental reasoning. Hutcheson commits himself to this aspect of anti-rationalism, but Shaftesbury does not go so far.

His attitude to hedonism is also imprecise. He distinguishes the virtuous person from the straightforwardly calculating hedonist who considers, as Hobbes's 'fool' does, whether this or that virtuous action will promote his own interest. To reject the attitude of the fool, however, is not to reject one's own pleasure as a ground for pursuing the virtues in general. And Shaftesbury seems to rely on the hedonist assumption. In his view, happiness 'is generally computed' from pleasures or satisfactions (p. 201).

He agrees with Cumberland that virtuous people's outlook does not subordinate the common good to their own pleasure. In his view, the affection for the public interest is itself a source of pleasure.

[T]he natural affections, duly established in a rational creature, being the only means which can procure him a constant series or succession of the mental enjoyments, they are the only means which can procure him a certain and solid happiness. (p. 201)

These pleasures arise partly from sympathetic participation in the pleasures of others (p. 202), and partly from reflection on and approval of our own benevolent attitudes. Shaftesbury separates this reflective conscience from mere fear of punishment, even of divine punishment; someone who observes the requirements of morality simply from the fear of divine punishment lacks a necessary condition for conscience (p. 207).

This is a hedonist defence of virtue, if Shaftesbury means that the social and sympathetic pleasures enjoyed by a virtuous person are greater than those enjoyed by others, as estimated from a point of view that is neutral between the virtuous person and others. The virtuous person, on this view, gets more pleasure than the vicious person, just as we get more pleasure from savouring each bite of a well-cooked dish than we get from bolting it down without tasting it properly.

Shaftesbury, however, does not seem to intend his claims about pleasure to be understood in this way. He suggests that it is trifling to say that pleasure is our good, because 'will' and 'pleasure' are synonymous. To say that we do what we please, or that we aim at our pleasure, simply means that we choose what we think eligible. In asking where we should seek our pleasure, we are asking what is really eligible; we should be asking how to distinguish good from bad pleasure (pp. 250 f.). If we simply identify happiness with pleasure, we are saying that our good consists in doing what we like; but since our preferences and likings change, identification of our good with the satisfaction of our preferences makes our good variable and unstable (pp. 138 f.).

Sometimes, therefore, Shaftesbury argues that our happiness consists not simply in achieving our preferences and likings, but in achieving our good. A true conception of our interest shows that expression of concern for others is a vital part of our interest. Those who disagree simply rely on a mistakenly narrow conception of happiness.

Now if these gentlemen who delight so much in the play of words, but are cautious how they grapple closely with definitions, would tell us only what self-interest was, and determine happiness and good, there would be an end to this enigmatical wit. For in this we should all agree, that happiness was to be pursued, and in fact was always sought after; but whether found in following nature, and giving way to common affection; or in suppressing it, and turning every passion towards private advantage, a narrow self-end, or the preservation of mere life; this would be the matter in debate between us. The question would not be 'Who loved himself, or who not', but 'Who loved and served himself the rightest, and after the truest manner'. (p. 56)

In Shaftesbury's view, the dispute about virtue and interest has been confused by a falsely restricted view about interest.

In particular, he suggests that a person's good is not to be defined simply by reference to the satisfaction of desires. As Shaftesbury puts it, the good does not depend entirely on 'fancy', because 'there is that in which the nature of man is satisfied, and which alone must be his good' (p. 335). In the light of our conception of human nature, we can see which passions are suitable to us, and find an appropriate 'balance of ... passions', constituting 'beauty and decorum' in one's internal states (p. 277). Contrary to Hobbes, we find that society and the aims and affections that support it are natural to human beings.

[W]e may with justice surely place it as a principle, 'that if anything be natural in any creature or any kind, it is that which is preservative of the kind itself, and conducing to its welfare ... If any appetite or sense be natural, the sense of fellowship is the same. (p. 51)

The pleasures that belong to social sentiment are part of a human being's happiness not because they are greater than any other pleasures, but because of their role in the human good.

Once we see that the good appropriate to human nature consists in the right internal order of self-regarding and other-regarding sentiments and passions, we can see that happiness comes from within and not from outside a person (p. 335). All non-moral goods are beneficial to us only conditionally, since they benefit us only if they are used properly. The moral good, by contrast, is good in its own right; it is most agreeable in itself, and preferable to all these external goods (p. 332). The awareness of good order in one's own nature is itself the source of a higher enjoyment than we receive from other sources (p. 331).

If we emphasize these aspects of Shaftesbury's account of the human good, we have reason to discount or to reinterpret his references to pleasure. A hedonist defence of virtue claims that virtue is the best policy for an agent who takes his own pleasure as his ultimate end, because virtue, apart from any further result, is itself the source of the greatest pleasure. Since we have sympathetic feelings, and since we find pleasure both in the satisfaction of our sympathetic feelings and in the awareness of their satisfaction, the virtues that express and satisfy these sympathetic feelings are the best means to maximum pleasure. But while this argument fits some of Shaftesbury's remarks on virtue and happiness, it does not fit the passages where he subordinates the pursuit of pleasure to the pursuit of one's genuine good.

In the light of these reflections on Shaftesbury, we can evaluate Sidgwick's claims about his view of happiness.

In the greater part of his argument Shaftesbury interprets the 'good' of the individual hedonistically, as equivalent to pleasure, satisfaction, delight, enjoyment. But it is to be observed that the conception of 'Good' with which he begins is not definitely hedonistic; 'interest or good' is at first taken to mean the 'right state of a creature' that 'is by nature forwarded and by himself affectionately sought' ... Still, when the application of this term is narrowed to human beings, he slides—almost unconsciously—into a purely hedonistic interpretation of it.[37]

Sidgwick is right to say that Shaftesbury seems to incline in different passages towards both a hedonistic and a non-hedonistic conception of a person's good;

---

[37] Henry Sidgwick, *Outlines of the History of Ethics*, 4th edn. (London: Macmillan, 1902), 185 n.

but he is wrong to conclude that his predominant view is hedonistic. Sidgwick ignores the places where Shaftesbury criticizes a hedonist account of a person's good; these criticisms imply that Shaftesbury sometimes rejects hedonism, not just that he sometimes speaks in non-hedonist terms.

If Shaftesbury were a hedonist, his position would be unstable. His claim about the virtuous person's pleasure might be understood as a purely causal and psychological claim: that being virtuous actually produces a larger quantity of the same sort of feeling of pleasure that everyone seeks. If that is what he means, then his claim about the virtuous person involves the empirical claim that the virtuous person gets more pleasure on the whole than Hobbes's fool could get.

This empirical claim is questionable. The fool need not, presumably, leave his sympathetic feelings completely undeveloped, and so he need not entirely forgo the pleasures of the virtuous person; but he would be able to control them enough to take advantage of the prospect of cheating when it seemed to offer especially large rewards. This strategy might be at least as plausible as the one advocated by Shaftesbury.

Alternatively, Shaftesbury might mean that virtuous people gain most pleasure from being virtuous because that is what they value most; concern for the good of others, as such, is the object, not merely the cause, of a virtuous person's pleasure. In that case, we can value something for some other feature besides its pleasure. Shaftesbury must take a further step away from hedonism than he acknowledges explicitly.

This test does not show that the virtuous person is better off than others who gain what they value most. If he is really better off, his judgement about the value of virtue must be correct, and our account of a person's good must make the truth of this judgement relevant to well-being. In that case, we are committed to a non-hedonist account of what is actually valuable, not simply to a non-hedonist account of what an agent can value. Shaftesbury seems to recognize this point when he discusses the human good. In claiming that the human good includes the satisfaction of the social affections, he does not claim that by satisfying these affections we gain more pleasure, or that people actually care most about satisfaction of these affections; he claims that these are the affections that deserve to be satisfied.

On this issue, therefore, Shaftesbury is closer to Platonism than to Locke. Though many remarks suggest that he looks at virtue and happiness as Hobbes and Locke look at them, the main tendency of his position agrees with the Greek moralists whom he cites with approval. His account of our 'obligation' to virtue is expressed as a claim about enjoyment, but it is really an argument for the position of the Greek moralists: that virtue is a part of the human good, correctly conceived. A Lockean interpretation of Shaftesbury is easy and attractive; that is the interpretation that leads Hutcheson to his own defence of Shaftesbury. But closer inspection shows that Hutcheson's defence does not really defend Shaftesbury's actual position.

Green, therefore, is not entirely unjustified in his criticisms of Shaftesbury, since they reflect some genuine features of Shaftesbury's position. None the less, his judgement of Shaftesbury is one-sided and unfair, since it fails to recognize the extent to which Shaftesbury develops a theory that is opposed to Locke's. Green suggests that Shaftesbury's overall position is Lockean hedonism, and that the more plausible elements are isolated exceptions. A more accurate judgement would recognize that Shaftesbury makes considerable progress in presenting a significant alternative to Locke, though without exploring all its consequences for Lockean assumptions. Green's assessment of Shaftesbury is too close to Hutcheson's assessment to be an accurate assessment of Shaftesbury's whole position.

I have described some of Shaftesbury's position in some detail to bring out a feature of it that will strike a sympathetic student of Green's ethics. The claims about virtue and happiness that I have emphasized in Shaftesbury are claims that Green himself accepts; they are central elements in his own version of eudaimonism. His lack of sympathy with Shaftesbury causes him to overlook or to discount points of agreement between Shaftesbury and himself. The points of agreement are not at all surprising; for the Greek moralists are a common source for both Shaftesbury and Green.[38] Green fails to recognize the importance of the Greek moralists even for modern moralists who are influenced by Locke.

VI

The questions raised by Green's treatment of Shaftesbury arise with even more force in his treatment of Butler. He argues that Butler does not escape from Lockean assumptions that cripple any attempt to give an adequate account of morality and moral motivation. He overlooks the ways in which Butler defends the broadly Platonist views about independent morality that we have found in Shaftesbury. It is particularly striking that he does not discuss Butler's avowed attempt to defend the position of the Greek moralists, or the conception of nature that Butler formulates as a part of this defence. Butler's

---

[38] I speak of 'the Greek moralists' in general, since Shaftesbury is chiefly indebted to the Stoics, whereas Green appeals to Aristotle. Closer study of Shaftesbury and Butler might have encouraged Green to consider the relevant parts of Stoic ethics.

naturalism expresses views that one might reasonably expect Green to treat with some sympathy, since they are so close to his own views. Whereas Oakeley appropriately compares Butler's naturalism to Aristotle's claims about the social nature of human beings,[39] Green appeals to Aristotle, but not to Butler.

Green acknowledges that Butler recognizes particular passions that do not take the agent's pleasure as their object. But he notices that Butler takes happiness, understood as pleasure, to be the object of self-love. This conception of self-love raises difficulties for Butler's conception of the object of moral approval, so that the eventual account is unhelpfully circular.

An act is morally good, according to him, when it is approved by the 'reflex faculty of approbation', bad when it is disapproved, but what it is that this 'faculty' approves he never distinctly tells us. The good is what 'conscience' approves, and conscience is what approves the good—that is the circle out of which he never escapes. (*CW* i. 327)

To support this claim, Green relies on a passage from Butler's Preface.

The goodness or badness of actions does not arise from hence, that the epithet, interested or disinterested, may be applied to them ... but from their being what they are; namely, what becomes such creatures as we are, what the state of the case requires, or the contrary.[40]

Green quotes only 'becomes such creatures as we are' from Butler's explanation, and claims that this commits Butler to a circle.

[A]nd this, read in the light of the second sermon, must be understood to mean an action 'suitable to our whole nature', as containing a principle of 'reflex approbation'. In other words, the good action is so because approved by conscience. (*CW* i. 327 n.)

In the second Sermon Butler argues that a rash action is unnatural not simply because it goes against some principle in us, but because it goes against a superior principle.

And since, in the instance still before us, if passion prevails over self-love, the consequent action is unnatural; but if self-love prevails over passion, the action is natural: it is manifest that self-love is in human nature a superior principle to passion. This may be contradicted without violating that nature; but the former cannot. So that, if we will act conformably to the economy of man's nature, reasonable self-love must govern. (*Sermons*, II. 11)

Green takes Butler to mean: (1) Acting wrongly consists in acting unnaturally; (2) acting unnaturally consists in acting against a superior principle, and

---

[39] See Oakeley, *Remarks*, 79, quoted on p. 110 above.

[40] Joseph Butler, *Fifteen Sermons*, Preface, §39. The *Sermons* and the 'Dissertation on Virtue' are cited by the paragraphs of J. H. Bernard's edition (London: Macmillan, 1900).

ultimately against the supreme principle, conscience; (3) hence acting wrongly consists in being disapproved by conscience.

Does Green's appeal to the second Sermon justify the claim in (2)? Butler asks why it is unnatural to act against self-love. He answers (in summary) that since self-love is a rational principle, guided by authority rather than mere psychological strength, and since a human being is a rational agent, we act in accord with our nature by acting in accord with rational principle. This does not mean that disapproval by self-love constitutes the unnaturalness of the action. The unnaturalness of the action consists in its inappropriateness to a rational agent, and, given the nature of self-love, it is inappropriate to a rational agent to act against self-love. For similar reasons the unnaturalness of an immoral action does not consist in its being disapproved of by conscience. Hence Green's claim in (2) is not completely accurate.

We now have reason to doubt Green's claim in (3). Butler claims that what conscience approves of as right is natural, because it is suited to our nature as rational agents. But this does not mean that conscience approves actions as right because of some antecedent judgement that they are natural; still less does it mean that the rightness of actions consists in their being approved by conscience. Green treats Butler as though he agreed with Hutcheson's rejection of objectivism. Hutcheson believes that rightness consists in being approved of by the moral sense, and Butler (in Green's view) modifies this position only by saying that rightness consists in being approved of by conscience. Green is not the only one who interprets Butler in this way, but his interpretation is difficult to sustain in the face of Butler's account of conscience in the *Dissertation*.

This question about Butler's account of moral properties is answered in different ways by critics earlier than Green. Green's answer is similar to Kames's assessment of Butler. Kames criticizes Butler on the assumption that Butler offers a reductive analysis. In opposition to Butler (as he supposes), Kames takes the moral sense to be unanalysable and immediate, not susceptible to reductive analysis. In his view, Butler defines morality as what conscience approves of.

Dr. Butler, a manly and acute writer, hath gone farther than any other, to assign a just foundation for moral duty. He considers conscience or reflection 'as one principle of action, which, compared with the rest as they stand together in the nature of man, plainly bears upon it marks of authority over all the rest, and claims the absolute direction of them all, to allow or forbid their gratification.' And his proof of this proposition is, 'that a disapprobation of reflection is in itself a principle manifestly superior to a mere propension.'[41]

---

[41] For this and the next passage quoted see Selby-Bigge (ed.), *British Moralists*, §931.

Kames believes that this reductive and anti-realist account does not capture the distinctive character of the moral sense.

[T]he authority of conscience does not consist merely in an act of reflection. It arises from a direct perception, which we have upon presenting the object, without the intervention of any sort of reflection. And the authority lies in this circumstance, that we perceive the action to be our duty, and what we are indispensably bound to perform. It is in this manner that the moral sense, with regard to some actions, plainly bears upon it the marks of authority over all our appetites and passions. It is the voice of God within us which commands our strictest obedience, just as much as when his will is declared by express revelation.

Kames argues that an adequate account of the moral sense must add to Butler's claims about the authority of conscience a specific claim about the source of authority—that we perceive the action to be our duty. Since we must mention the perception of our duty in an account of authority, we cannot find a reductive account of duty by appeal to the authority of conscience.

Kames's criticism underlies Selby-Bigge's attitude to Butler:

It is in Butler that the sentimental school really reaches its climax. He is indeed careful not to commit himself to any decision between the claims of reason and sense ... but it is impossible not to treat his theory as intimately related to the speculation of Hutcheson, who indeed in his last work ... evidently has taken a good deal from Butler. Man as an organic whole consists not only of parts, but of parts interrelated under a reflective faculty, which is endued not only with power or attractiveness but with authority. ... To act according to human nature is to fall in with the system imposed by this authority. (*British Moralists*, i. p. xliv)

If Selby-Bigge regards his description of Butler as evidence of the sentimentalist school's reaching its climax, he probably takes Butler to claim that rightness consists simply in being approved by the reflective faculty of conscience. He agrees with Kames's criticism of Butler on this point (pp. xlii, xlvi).

Whewell raises reasonable objections to Kames's and Selby-Bigge's view. He rejects a constructivist account of Butler, in denying that Butler makes conscience 'the ultimate criterion of right and wrong'.[42] In Whewell's view, conscience is a faculty in the same sense as reason is one: 'a power by exercising which we come to discern truths, not a repository of truth already collected in a visible shape' (*Butler*, p. xiv).

We can defend Whewell's interpretation of Butler by considering what sorts of things conscience approves of. Butler describes them in two ways. (1) They are just, fair, and benevolent actions, which tend to promote the common good

---

[42] Whewell (ed.), *Butler's Three Sermons*, 9 p. xiii.

of society, and to maintain the appropriate relations of desert, responsibility, and equality, between individual agents. (2) These sorts of actions are those that fulfil human nature; we can see this by considering the 'social nature of man',[43] in so far as it includes both benevolence and the outlook connected with responsibility and fairness. Neither of these properties of morally right actions is imposed or constituted by the approval of conscience. Conscience is supreme only because it identifies and prescribes actions with these properties.

Green's disputable view about the relation between the rightness of an action and approval by conscience encourages him to suggest a way of making Butler's position more consistent.

If we insist on extracting from him any more satisfactory conclusion as to the object of moral approbation, it must be that it is the object which 'self-love' pursues, i.e., the greatest happiness of the individual, a conclusion which in some places he certainly adopts. (*CW* i. 327)

To show that Butler 'certainly adopts' this view of conscience, Green cites two passages.

Reasonable self-love and conscience are the chief or superior principles in the nature of man; because an action may be suitable to this nature, though all other principles be violated, but becomes unsuitable if either of those are. Conscience and self-love, if we understand our true happiness, always lead us the same way. (*Sermons*, III. 9)

Let it be allowed, though virtue or moral rectitude does indeed consist in affection to and pursuit of what is right and good, as such, yet, that when we sit down in a cool hour, we can neither justify to ourselves this or any other pursuit, till we are convinced that it will be for our happiness, or at least not contrary to it. (*Sermons*, XI. 20)

Green does not explain how he takes these two passages to support his account of Butler's view. Probably he takes the first passage to establish the coincidence between the prescriptions of self-love and those of conscience. He then takes the second passage to show that since self-love is superior to conscience, the prescriptions of self-love determine the prescriptions of conscience (and not the other way round).

These passages do not provide a strong case for it. Two distinct objections undermine his view. (1) He treats the second passage as an affirmation of the superiority of self-love to conscience. But the context shows that Butler is simply conceding this superiority, contrary to his own view, for the sake of argument, in order to show that someone who falsely believes in the superiority of self-love still has good reason to take morality seriously.[44] (2) But even if

---

[43] The title of Sermon I.

[44] This explanation of the 'cool hour' passage is widely, though not universally, accepted. See my 'Stoic Naturalism in Butler', 292.

Green were right on this point about the second passage, the two passages together would not support his interpretation of Butler. For even if self-love is superior to conscience, it does not follow that conscience approves actions by consideration of the agent's own happiness, or that promotion of one's own happiness makes the actions right. Though Butler believes that self-love and conscience on the whole agree, he need not infer that they respond to exactly the same features of actions.

For these reasons, Green's attempt to attribute a consistent doctrine of conscience and moral rightness to Butler rests on an interpretation that is open to fatal objections.

VII

Green deals rather brusquely with Shaftesbury, and even more brusquely with Butler. I have dealt rather brusquely in turn with Green's discussion; I have simply tried to indicate some reasons that might dissuade us from accepting Green's assessment without question. I have disputed his interpretation not simply to suggest that he is a less than careful historian, but to point out that he overlooks some relevant philosophical possibilities of the sort that he is eager to exploit in his discussions of Aristotle and Kant. In this case he seems to exaggerate the importance of Locke and Hume. He agrees with Hume's view (as he understands it) that his British predecessors in moral philosophy offered no reasonable alternative to his own sentimentalist and anti-rationalist position. Because he is so convinced that Hume is right, he does not see the reasonable alternatives even where they might be found.

But what might Green have learned if he had approached the British moralists with a more open-minded appreciation of what they had to offer? I will consider just one example.

On one important point that matters to Green, Kant seems to regress from the position of Butler and Reid. Butler regards both self-love and conscience as superior principles, guided by reasons rather than by strength of desires; Reid counts them both as rational principles. Kant does not recognize prudence as a source of rational principles in its own right; only morality is a source of categorical imperatives.[45]

Green does not follow Kant on this point. He disagrees with Kant because he appreciates Greek eudaimonism more accurately and sympathetically than

---

[45] I have discussed Kant's reasons in 'Kant's Criticisms of Eudaemonism', in J. Whiting and S. Engstrom (eds.), *Aristotle, Kant, and the Stoics* (Cambridge: Cambridge University Press, 1996).

Kant does. He does not mention that he agrees with Butler and Reid, because he goes back to their common source in Aristotle.

Green's neglect of Butler and Reid in favour of Kant and Aristotle carries some cost. Both Butler and Reid accept a duality of practical reason; they maintain that prudence and morality constitute distinct and ultimate rational principles, in so far as neither is derived from the other. Kant disagrees with them, since he believes that only morality is ultimately rational. Aristotle also disagrees with them, since he believes that only prudence is ultimately rational.

Green seems to agree with Aristotle. He takes the ultimate principle to be rational self-love directed at one's own good. He rejects Kant's treatment of all non-moral motives as simply desires for pleasure (PE §160). If, then, he allows non-moral practical reason, he cannot also accept Kant's view that only moral principles belong to practical reason.

If he rejects Kant's position about non-moral practical reason, why does he not take seriously the possibility of agreeing with Butler and Reid? His discussion of a duality of practical reason is not completely clear. He raises the question in the context of a discussion of hedonism. He considers the view that in pursuing my own good, I pursue my maximum pleasure, but in pursuing the good of others, I pursue something distinct from my maximum pleasure.

We shall have to take it that there are two co-ordinate principles, 'Benevolence' and 'Reasonable Self-Love', alike, according to the phraseology of the last century, in being calm or settled or deliberate principles, but wholly different as desires in respect of the objects to which they are directed, since one is, while the other is not, a desire for pleasure; and we shall have to suppose that these serve indifferently as grounds for moral approbation and disapprobation, the reason for rejecting desired pleasures as not good on the whole being sometimes that they are incompatible with the object sought by Benevolence, sometimes that they are incompatible with that sought by Reasonable Self-Love. (PE §226)

Though he does not mention Butler by name, Green's expressions and his reference to the 'phraseology of the last century' clearly recall Butler's views about self-love, benevolence, and (in the reference to moral approbation) conscience. But he does not seem to interpret Butler in exactly the same way as in the 'Introduction to Hume'. There he took Butler either to hold a constructivist view, so that the approval of conscience constitutes the rightness of an action, or to hold that conscience approves of actions favoured by self-love. Here, however, he may suggest that conscience approves either of actions favoured by self-love or of those favoured by benevolence.

Why does he interpret Butler in this way? When he speaks of 'calm or settled or deliberate principles', we might suppose that he represents both self-love and benevolence as superior principles. It is not clear that this is Butler's view. The two superior principles that Butler explicitly recognizes are self-love and conscience.

> Reasonable self-love and conscience are the chief or superior principles in the nature of man; because an action may be suitable to this nature, though all other principles be violated, but becomes unsuitable if either of those are. (*Sermons*, III. 9)

Does he also recognize benevolence as a superior principle? This is a rather complicated question of interpretation.[46] At any rate, he treats it as a rational principle distinct from the passion of benevolence.

But even if benevolence is a superior principle, Butler does not clearly endorse Green's view that (according to the position he considers) conscience follows either benevolence or self-love, and recognizes no distinct grounds of approbation. Butler recognizes some ways in which benevolence is not the whole of morality,[47] and he does not suggest that if conscience disagrees with benevolence in these cases, it must follow self-love. The demands of justice and of specific obligations may sometimes favour self-love over benevolence, but they may equally conflict with both.

Green, therefore, takes too restrictive a view of the operations of conscience, as Butler describes them. He assumes (1) that conscience can approve of an action only if some superior principle other than conscience antecedently approves of it,[48] and that (2) the only other superior principles are self-love and benevolence. While it is not obvious that Butler does not accept these two assumptions, the most plausible interpretation of his views on conscience rejects them.

But, however we resolve this issue about Butler, why does Green reject any duality in practical reason? His argument is brief.

> That our practical judgments as to the true good rest on two such different principles is a conclusion which, once clearly faced, every enquirer would gladly escape, as repugnant both to the philosophic craving for unity, and to that ideal of 'singleness of heart' which we have been accustomed to associate with the highest virtue. (*PE* §226)

We can avoid this repugnant conclusion either by treating benevolent desires as desires for pleasure or by arguing that self-love does not aim at a sum of pleasure. Green gives reasons for preferring the second way.

---

[46] See my 'Stoic Naturalism in Butler', 284.

[47] In *Sermons*, XII. 31, and in the *Dissertation*.

[48] Nicholas Sturgeon, 'Nature and Conscience in Butler's Ethics', *Philosophical Review*, 85 (1976), 316–56, defends this view of conscience.

Why is the conclusion so repugnant? To answer this question, we should notice an obscurity in Green's statement of the conclusion. He formulates the rejected view in two ways:

(1) these (sc. self-love and benevolence) serve indifferently as grounds for moral approbation and disapprobation.
(2) our practical judgements as to the true good rest on two such different principles.

We can see the difference between these two claims if we consider the difference between (a), it would be wrong to keep the money because you have promised to return it, and (b), it would be wrong to keep the money because keeping promises is treating persons as ends. Kantian moralists might accept both (a) and (b), and if they accept (a), they might say that promise keeping is a ground for moral approbation. But their basic principle is—we may suppose—(b), which explains why (a) gives a ground for moral approbation. Hence we might say that (a) gives the proximate ground, and (b) gives the basic ground.

Green's formulations in (1) and (2) are ambiguous between proximate and basic grounds. (1) might easily be taken to refer to proximate grounds. When Green speaks of moral approbation, he might mean that morality sometimes sees moral reasons to approve of action on the basis of self-love and sometimes sees moral reasons to approve of action on the basis of benevolence. In this case both benevolence and self-love are proximate grounds of approval, but the basic grounds are moral, and distinct from both self-love and benevolence. Though benevolence and self-love are, as Green says, 'co-ordinate' grounds, neither is the basic ground.

Alternatively, Green might mean that these *are* basic grounds. When we speak of 'moral approbation', we are referring not to a single point of view with its own basic grounds, but only to a disjunctive point of view that takes the basic grounds either from self-love or from benevolence, without subjecting these grounds to any further moral evaluation resting on distinct basic grounds.

When Green speaks of a repugnant conclusion that conflicts with aspirations for unity in theory and singleness of heart in practice, his case is much more plausible if he refers to basic grounds. We might sympathize with his view if we could give no satisfactory account of the point of view from which we approve of either benevolence or self-love. In that case we could say nothing about how we can make a rational decision on questions of great practical importance.

Sidgwick's dualism of practical reason leads us—in Sidgwick's own view, at least—to this conclusion. Sidgwick recognizes not only the duality that Butler and Reid recognize, but also a dualism that results from the rejection of any supreme principle. In his view, we must recognize self-love and benevolence as two principles that are not only not derived from anything else but are also equally rational, all things considered. He finds no third rational principle that gives us a rational basis for choosing between them. As Sidgwick says, if this is our conclusion, we have to abandon the idea of 'rationalizing' morality completely.[49]

If Green simply meant that it is repugnant to have to recognize self-love and benevolence as co-ordinate proximate grounds, his case would be weak. For if we recognize morality as containing basic grounds explaining why self-love and benevolence are legitimate proximate grounds, then we seem to have satisfied any legitimate 'craving for unity'—or at least, it is not clear that we have not satisfied it. If, then, his objections to the recognition of these co-ordinate grounds of moral approbation apply to Butler, he must assume that Butler treats benevolence and self-love as co-ordinate basic grounds, involving Sidgwick's dualism.

But this assumption about Butler is unwarranted, for reasons we have already indicated. Though his remarks are not always clear, he does not treat self-love and benevolence as co-ordinate basic grounds. He treats them both as subordinate to conscience, which contains a basic ground distinct from each of them. Since the point of view of conscience is the point of view of morality, morality constitutes a single point of view distinct from self-love.

Green's remarks about the repugnant conclusion suggest that he has Butler in mind. His implicit interpretation is close to Sidgwick's explicit interpretation of Butler. Sidgwick rejects the view that Butler treats conscience as supreme.

There remain, then, Conscience and 'Reasonable Self-love' as the two authorities in the polity of the soul. With regard to these it is by no means Butler's view (as is very commonly supposed) that self-love is naturally subordinate to conscience—at least if we consider the theoretical rather than the practical relation between the two. He treats them as independent principles, and so far co-ordinate in authority that it is not 'according to nature' that either should be overruled.[50] (*Outlines*, 195 f.)

This suggestion that the two principles are 'co-ordinate' matches the view that Green rejects. Sidgwick, however, does not treat benevolence as a superior principle, and so he avoids Green's suggestion that self-love and benevolence might be two proximate grounds for moral approbation.[51] His picture of Butler

---

[49] Henry Sidgwick, *The Methods of Ethics*, 7th edn. (London: Macmillan, 1907), 508.

[50] Sidgwick, *Outlines*, 195 f.

[51] At *Outlines*, 195, Sidgwick argues that Butler does not treat benevolence as a third superior principle.

is closer to his own conception of a dualism (not merely a duality) of practical reason, and so closer to the repugnant conclusion that Green rejects.

Here, then, insufficient attention to Butler has misled Green into treating Butler's claims about self-love and conscience as though they agreed with Sidgwick's claims about the dualism of practical reason. Because he fails to distinguish Butler from Sidgwick on this point, he assumes that if we reject a dualism as repugnant, we will also deny any sharp distinction between the points of view of enlightened self-love and of morality. But we need not accept this inference. If we treat self-love as a rational principle subordinate to conscience, we do not recognize two co-ordinate basic grounds. Like Green, Butler recognizes one supreme principle; but he identifies it with morality rather than self-love. Green does not explain what is wrong with this position. Since Butler's position seems neither free from difficulty nor obviously implausible, Green overlooks a position that deserves some discussion.

But even if we agree with Sidgwick's interpretation of Butler, or we suppose that Butler is too obscure to make it clear that Green overlooks something, we may still fairly criticize Green. For if we look at Butler's successors, they clearly express the supremacy of conscience. Price agrees with Butler in treating self-love as a rational principle, but he is more doubtful about the harmony of conscience and self-love.[52] He has no doubt about the supremacy of conscience: 'Now goodness in mankind ... is the power of reflexion raised to its due seat of direction and sovereignty in the mind; conscience fixed and kept in the throne, and holding under its sway all our passions' (p. 217). His comments on Butler and Hutcheson (pp. 215–17) make it clear not only that he affirms the supremacy of conscience, but also that he takes Butler to affirm it. Similarly, Reid is indebted to Butler's views on self-love and conscience, taking him to affirm the supremacy of conscience.[53] He affirms its supremacy on his own account: 'the disinterested love of virtue is undoubtedly the noblest principle in human nature, and ought never to stoop to any other'.[54] Since he also affirms Butler's view that self-love and conscience do not conflict, he does not treat the rejection of conflict as any weakening of the supremacy of conscience.

Even this glance at Price and Reid makes it clear that Green could have found in them both an interpretation of Butler that differs from his own and

---

[52] Richard Price, *A Review of the Principal Questions in Morals*, ed. D. D. Raphael, 2nd edn. (Oxford: Clarendon Press, 1974), 256–8; subsequent page references are given parenthetically in the text.

[53] Dugald Stewart remarks that Reid recommended Butler's *Dissertation* and *Sermons* 'as the most satisfactory account that has yet appeared of the fundamental principles of morals; nor could he conceal his regret that the profound philosophy which these discourses contain should of late have been so generally supplanted in England by the speculations of some other moralists' (Reid, *Works*, ed. W. Hamilton, 6th edn., 2 vols. (Edinburgh: Maclachlan and Stewart, 1863), i. 32).

[54] Reid, *Works*, ii. 598.

a clear statement of a position that he ought to have discussed. But these moralists do not appear in Green's account of those predecessors who deserve attention. He counts them among the successors of Hume who, not having read Kant, were unable to respond effectively to Hume.

One might have hoped that Green's neglect of these moralists would have had less serious effects if he had at any rate consulted Sidgwick, who certainly cannot be accused of ignorance of the British moralists. But on this particular issue Sidgwick does not help. We have already noticed that he gives the wrong account of Butler's views on the supremacy of conscience. He says nothing about Price's views on this question,[55] and he wrongly attributes to Reid the view that he wrongly attributes to Butler.

[S]uch a desire [sc. of one's good on the whole] must naturally regulate all particular appetites and passions. It cannot reasonably be subordinated even to the moral faculty; in fact, a man who believes that virtue is contrary to his happiness on the whole—which cannot really be the case in a morally governed world—is reduced to the 'miserable dilemma whether it is better to be a fool or a knave'.[56]

Sidgwick mistakenly assumes that because Reid tries to reconcile conscience and self-love, he cannot accept the supremacy of conscience; he relies on the same assumption in his account of Butler. And so, even if Green had consulted Sidgwick, he would not have found what he needed to form a just estimate of the views of Butler, Price, and Reid.

In criticizing Green's understanding of the British moralists, I do not mean to say that they adequately explain their position, or that it is free of difficulty, or that we ought to prefer it to Green's or to Sidgwick's position. I mean only that Green ought to have recognized and discussed it. His failure to discuss it is easily understood once we see that it is simply one aspect of his failure to see what he could learn from his predecessors among the British moralists. His sympathetic and critical attitude serves him well when he applies it to Aristotle and Kant. His unsympathetic but careful critique of Locke and Hume is also illuminating. Because he treats the British moralists neither sympathetically nor carefully, he leaves a serious gap in his own argument. He does not face squarely Oakeley's suggestion that Butler's doctrine of conscience supplies a lacuna (as Pattison puts it) in Aristotle's system.[57] This suggestion is not, as Pattison claims, 'wholly illusory'; it points to a possible lacuna in Green's own system.

---

[55] Sidgwick, *Outlines*, 224–6.   [56] Ibid. 228.
[57] See the passage from Pattison quoted at n. 29 above.

PART II
Metaphysics

6

Green's 'Eternal Consciousness'

PETER NICHOLSON

I. Introduction

Most readers of Green find it hard to pin down exactly what he means by the eternal consciousness. Moreover, so far as they can fix its meaning—and the meanings assigned vary considerably—they usually think that Green's account of it is unsatisfactory. It is commonly held that Green's conception of the eternal consciousness remains partly obscure, mysterious even, and that it is defended inadequately.

At the same time, there is wide, though not universal, acceptance that Green's philosophy is highly unified, and that the eternal consciousness is fundamental to the coherence of its claims in epistemology, metaphysics, and moral and political philosophy. Since a unified philosophy is only as strong as its weakest component, and in this case a key unifying idea is found wanting, there appears to be a major problem. If the eternal consciousness is foundational, yet discredited, this must undermine everything else. One way of eliminating the problem, sometimes adopted, is to argue that the eternal consciousness is not indispensable to Green's philosophy, and to sideline or ignore it; but it is far from clear that it is possible to uncouple the eternal consciousness from the rest without severely reducing the integrity and scope of that philosophy as he and his immediate audience conceived it.

In this paper I explore an alternative possibility. I accept that the eternal consciousness is fundamental to Green's philosophy, but deny that it is

This is a revised version of the paper entitled 'The Unity of Green's Philosophy' presented at the 2002 T. H. Green Conference at Harris Manchester College, Oxford. I am grateful to those at the Conference who commented on the paper, and in particular to the discussant, Jan Olof Bengtsson, for his acute remarks. In the original paper I emphasized the difficulties in Green's conception of the eternal consciousness, and I now think I overestimated them. This version is more positive about Green's achievement and his legacy. I am grateful to Colin Tyler, Maria Dimova-Cookson, W. H. Greenleaf, and the anonymous reader for Oxford University Press for their comments on it.

damagingly problematic. For the eternal consciousness can be interpreted, I suggest, in such a way that it successfully achieves the objective Green set for it and is not a crippling liability. I begin by presenting the best case I can for the eternal consciousness, using the version in the opening, metaphysical sections of the posthumously published *Prolegomena to Ethics* (section I). Green was in the course of publishing these sections in *Mind*, and was approaching a publisher about bringing out the entire manuscript as a book, when he died suddenly, so they may fairly be treated as a full and considered statement of his fundamental philosophical position.[1] I have not aimed at a detailed point-by-point and comprehensive account of Green's arguments there, and I have generally ignored the connected discussions elsewhere in his writings.[2] I am concerned only to sketch the main features of his position (section II). I then introduce what I call the minimal interpretation of the eternal consciousness, which I revive from Green's pupil D. G. Ritchie, and argue that it makes good sense of what Green says (section III). Finally, I discuss the legitimacy and the purpose of Green's occasional excursions which seem to extend beyond what the minimal interpretation allows (section IV). I pay particular attention to the bearing of his philosophical position on moral and religious convictions. My overall conclusion is that, far from the eternal consciousness being a threat to

[1] §§3–100 of the *Prolegomena to Ethics* were published by Green himself as 'Can There Be a Natural Science of Man?', *Mind*, 7 (1882), 1–29, 161–85, 321–48. The first article (January number) is printed as §§3–37 of the *Prolegomena* (with paragraph breaks added within §§5 and 7), the second article (April number, which opened with a few extra lines connecting it to the previous article) as §§38–64, and the third article (July number) as §§65–99 plus the first paragraph of §100. A. C. Bradley provided a note at the end of the third article explaining that the articles were the opening portions of the *Prolegomena to Ethics* (Green's title) and summarizing its opening pages (i.e. *PE* §§1–2). The articles have none of the divisions into sections, chapters, or books, and only one of the occasional breaks in the text (at the end of *PE* §73) which Bradley provides in the *Prolegomena*. Letters reveal that Green planned a fourth article for the October number, but do not indicate its extent. Green returned the proofs of the second article on the 1 March 1882. On 11 March he approached Longmans, Green and Company proposing publication of the book which became the *Prolegomena*; he fell ill suddenly on 15 March and died on the 26th (*Collected Works of T. H. Green, V: Additional Writings*, ed. P. Nicholson (Bristol: Thoemmes Press, 1997), 481–3). Previously, Green had declined an invitation to publish part of his manuscript in *Mind*, offering the Editor these reasons: 'From what I have so far written, I doubt whether I could extract anything which I should like to stand alone. I had rather confront any critics who may await me with a tolerably complete statement of what I have to say than with a fragment. If when I come to revise what I have written I find that there is any part which would appear separately without giving rise to misapprehensions, I shall be glad to let you see it' (undated letter to George Croom Robertson, in *Additional Writings*, 483–4). It is reasonable to infer that what we have in the *Prolegomena* is that 'tolerably complete statement' of his position by which Green was prepared to be judged.

[2] The development of Green's idea of the eternal consciousness can be tracked through many of his published writings. In addition, Ben Wempe argues persuasively that important elements of the eternal consciousness can be traced through Green's manuscripts back to his detailed study of Hegel's *Philosophische Propädeutik* in the early 1860s: *T. H. Green's Theory of Positive Freedom: From Metaphysics to Political Theory* (Exeter: Imprint Academic, 2004), ch. 1.

Green's philosophy, it is a considerable asset, because it enables one to draw on one's own specific moral and religious beliefs. Green's philosophy cannot, and recognizes that it cannot, endorse or prescribe such beliefs, but it can, so to speak, license our holding them.

II. Green's 'Metaphysics of Knowledge'

The first and most important 'prolegomenon' or preliminary matter which Green tackles is the nature of knowledge and what it implies about the nature of man. He has several sets of opponents in mind whom he wishes to refute. The most prominent, whom he confronts first, are those who argue for an empiricist or naturalistic account of man and of knowledge (later, as opportunities arise, I shall indicate how Green is also differentiating his position from those of ordinary common sense, of Kant, and of Hegel). Green begins, then, by setting out the case of those of his opponents who argue that there *can* be a 'natural science of man'. Contemporary adherents of the natural science of man (he seems to have in mind principally Herbert Spencer and G. H. Lewes) have moved forward from Hume, and claim to provide scientific theories to replace the two doctrines concerning morality which had previously resisted reduction to a physical science: namely, the doctrines of an innate moral sense and of free will. Thus the whole process by which 'the human animal has come ... to exhibit the phenomena of a moral life' can, they claim, be explained 'on the method of a natural history conducted according to the principle of evolution' (*PE* §7). Granted, the naturalists are inconsistent, in that they continue to prescribe how men should act, when obviously on their own theory 'to a being who is simply a result of natural forces an injunction to conform to their laws is unmeaning' (*PE* §7). But this inconsistency could be removed by abolishing the preceptive part of ethics, and by explaining the language and activity of moral injunction as 'a serviceable illusion' (*PE* §8). This last consequence, however, gives us pause, Green urges, and should lead us to reconsider the whole doctrine, despite its popularity. 'As the first charm of accounting for what has previously seemed the mystery of our moral nature passes away, and the spirit of criticism returns, we cannot but enquire whether a being that was merely a result of natural forces could form a theory of those forces as explaining himself' (*PE* §8). This is the main issue for Green. Explicitly referring to Kant and critical philosophy, Green asks, as his first question, whether 'the knowledge of nature [can] be itself a part or product of nature, in that sense of nature in which it is said to be an object of knowledge?' (*PE* §8). Green is right to make this question central.

It should be noticed that Green's attack is on those who seek to create a natural science of *man*, on the grounds that they are trying to carry science outside its proper province. He never disputes or impugns the idea of science and scientific knowledge. On the contrary, his rejection of a science of man presupposes that science itself is possible, legitimate, and successful. The point on which his whole position pivots is that science, the acquisition of knowledge of the natural world, itself necessarily requires a conception of the scientist (standing in for 'man') which cannot be accounted for in purely scientific terms. The very possibility of science presupposes that 'moralised man' (*PE* §5), that conception of human beings as moral and spiritual beings, which it is the whole thrust and purpose of a natural science of man to explain away. This, Green's claim about what is involved in the existence of science, is where we must start.

There are two principal features of Green's claim to distinguish and discuss: first, what scientific knowledge is and what this implies, logically, about the knower; and second, what, by logical extension, scientific knowledge could be and what that implies, logically, about the knower. I shall take the two features in turn, although, because they are very closely interconnected, this involves some artificiality in presentation.

Green contends that in scientific knowledge everything known, so far as it is known, consists in relations between it and other things (relations such as position and succession), themselves likewise related, and that the source of all these relations must be a consciousness or self which unifies the relations into a connected whole. The consciousness, working on the assumption that there is a single, uniform, and unalterable order of relations, decides which of its experiences is 'real' and 'objective' by checking that each new experience is combinable in one system with other recognized relations. That assumption is a necessary assumption of science in the sense that it must be made if there is to be knowledge of a world at all. The consciousness which is organizing experience must itself be outside time and space: as the condition of relations it cannot be a relation, and therefore no scientific explanation of it can be given (since natural science necessarily explains things in terms of relations). This last point is of course directed at Spencer and Lewes, whom Green took to be claiming precisely that everything about man can be explained scientifically in naturalistic terms. From Green's perspective, they are simply contradicting themselves because a natural explanation of man uses a theory about nature, but the very idea of such a theory itself presupposes that man is more than simply natural.

Green's first main conclusion, then, is that our consciousness, or under-standing—that is, the consciousness of each individual human being—' "makes nature" for us, in the sense of enabling us to conceive that there is such a thing' (*PE* §19). He argues further that our understanding 'makes nature' in the additional sense that 'it is the source, or at any rate a condition, of there being these relations' (*PE* §19). Our consciousness establishes 'the relations in which it conceives reality to consist' (*PE* §13). I take the difference between the two senses in which man 'makes nature' to be this. In the first sense, man 'makes nature' by himself connecting up (relating) all his experiences into one system or whole, the 'natural order of nature'. The order exists in his mind, and it is the creation of his consciousness or understanding. It is not 'in nature', because there is not, and there cannot be, a 'nature' outside or apart from him. This says nothing about the status of the relations which are the constituents of the order of nature which the mind creates. These might exist independently, and then be discovered by the mind. The second sense of 'man making nature' goes further in claiming that not only nature as an intelligible whole but also all its constituent parts, are the creations of man's consciousness—that is, not only the end-products of the mind's work are the mind's creation, but also all that the mind works on to produce them.

So far I have concentrated on Green's claim that, if we ask the key question, 'How is knowledge possible?', we are forced to posit a consciousness or self which is itself outside nature and which 'makes' nature. This consciousness is not in time, and to indicate this feature Green describes it as 'eternal'. 'Eternal' is perhaps not an entirely happy choice, since it is sometimes used to mean 'lasting throughout time', but Green's meaning is clear—the consciousness is eternal in that it is outside time. Green proceeds to draw out the logical implications of his position, and this brings us to the second principal feature of his position. We can approach this by reflecting that there are all kinds of relations in the actual world of which we are ignorant. Scientists are constantly discovering new relations, as their knowledge expands. The 'new' relations do not, however, come into existence when we discover them: they already exist. And they exist in the same way that all relations exist: namely, as imposed by a consciousness. Just as the condition of a scientist's knowledge is his consciousness holding all its constituent relations together in a single system of unalterable relations, and the condition of science generally is the idea of the sum of all the relations held by individual scientists forming a single system of unalterable relations (in human consciousness), so the condition of the actual world is a universal consciousness which thinks the totality of the unalterable relations which make up the world. Green often refers to the universal consciousness as 'the eternal consciousness', and occasionally calls it 'divine' (I shall return to its divinity later). Take as an example the scientific account of a flower. I have a limited knowledge of what it is. I am aware of only some of its numerous relations, and of the connections between those and all other relations. A biologist, depending on the extent of his or her 'experience and training', has a greater knowledge, though it is still 'by no means adequate to the real nature of the flower' (*PE* §63). The example up to this point is Green's, but now I extend it. The biologist in Green's day might have assimilated Darwin's theory of the origin of species, but could have had no knowledge of genetics, or of DNA. Again, the biologist's knowledge of chemistry, and how it bears upon biology, was smaller. And so on—for the aim of science is to connect all the relations together, and to grasp their total interrelatedness. What the biologist could know about the flower already is vast. (We should note something that Green does not mention: that the growth of science is a social process among scientists and a historical process connected to the development of the scientists' society; this is similar to the social and historical development of the moral ideal which Green does consider, in outline, later in the book.) But however far science has developed, we can reasonably assume that there is yet more to be known about the flower, and we can posit, as a logical extension, the possibility of the completion of science such that everything is known about the flower (and, necessarily, about everything else). That is what the eternal consciousness thinks. At any time, in any society, the common consciousness among scientists thinks less than the universal or eternal consciousness.

A human consciousness and the universal or eternal consciousness are the same in principle, and in particular, both are outside time, not in motion, not material, and cannot be explained in terms of relations (they are the conditions of nature, so the language of science, which is relational language about nature, is inapplicable to them).[3] But whereas the work of human consciousness is done by a mind in an animal body, and consequently is and must always be restrained and limited by the conditions of its animal existence, the eternal consciousness is without restraint or limit, and thinks all the relations that there are.

Let me pause to take stock. It might be thought that Green's metaphysics fails because it is not as comprehensive as he claims, but leaves something out. That is, it might be argued that in any experience there is also the initial sensation or stimulus which sets going the process of relating, a sensation which is presupposed by and outside the work of the human mind, and thus is not included in Green's theory but lies unaccounted for, a kind of Kantian thing-in-itself. However, this is a misunderstanding. Green does not deny that we have sensations of objects which are 'already real' (*PE* §86). For instance, the engine-driver who looks at a signal sees 'combinations of moving particles'

---

[3] This requires the qualification that human consciousnesses, the consciousnesses of particular human beings thinking at specific times and with the knowledge and other ideas of their specific societies, are in relations; but they cannot be reduced to and explained in terms of those relations.

(*PE* §12). The issue is what account we give of sensation, and Green's target is those who reduce reality merely to sensation. First, simply by singling out these particles, and making them a 'sensation' which he then interprets (or, possibly, misinterprets), the engine-driver's consciousness is already at work. Second, it can only be in thought, the work of consciousness, that reality lies. The ideal consciousness which we can postulate, which knows all that there is to know, and understands all relations and where they fit into a single harmonious and unalterable system of relations, knows what the sensation really is and all that the sensation is: there is nothing somehow beyond its consciousness of the sensation and thus unaccounted for. The obstacle to grasping this is the grip exercised on us by ordinary commonsensical thinking. Green realizes that the Idealist position, 'that only through understanding is there for us an objective world', is bound to seem perverse to common sense, because 'we have come to think of the understanding as specially an agency of our own, and of the objective world as specially that which is presented to us independently of any such agency' (*PE* §12). Green challenges both these common-sense thoughts. The objective world, reality, is not presented to us independently of our understanding (if it were, how could we know it?), but made by our understanding. Green's point is that any contact between the scientist and nature is not what it might seem to common sense, a contact between the scientist and something 'outside' him or her, that outside being what one would call 'real'. On the contrary, whenever the scientist touches, feels, sees, hears, or smells, there is no experience, no knowledge, no world, unless his or her understanding has imposed some relations. For instance, the scientist relates it to other things previously experienced, as coming later, as of broadly the same type and likely to behave in the same way, and so on. What we have, then, is not something outside the scientist, but something completely inside him or her and which the scientist connects up to everything else inside him or her. We should observe that what counts for Green is not simply the relations which the mind assigns, but also that the mind connects those relations to all others it is aware of in a system of interdependent relations. If a new experience can be fitted in, then the scientist treats it as real; if it cannot, then either the scientist rejects it as illusion or modifies his or her view of previous experience until once again everything fits—until it is all a single system of relations, which is, once again, 'unalterable'. Moreover, to move to the second feature of common-sense thinking, our understanding is not specially 'my' or 'your' understanding, but a consciousness which is a (much reduced) version of the single eternal consciousness.

This helps clarify Green's relationship to Kant, from whose position he wishes to distinguish his own. Green holds that Kant made the crucial advance beyond empiricism by grasping that 'the understanding makes nature': but Green is one of those who believe that Kant failed to push his critical thinking through to its full conclusion. Kant held that the understanding makes nature, but 'out of a material which it does not make' (PE §11): namely, the 'things-in-themselves', outside us, in the world, not in our minds, and therefore necessarily outside our knowledge. This for Green is 'unsatisfactory' (PE §11), because the consequence is that our theory of knowledge has to suppose 'some unaccountable pre-established harmony' between the order of nature which we create and the order of the things-in-themselves (PE §19). Green, by contrast, eliminates the category of things-in-themselves by saying that the understanding is the source not only of the order of nature, but also of the relations out of which that nature is constituted, so that there is nothing left outside the system to be a 'thing-in-itself'. This is seen best in the ideal case of the eternal consciousness which knows everything. There can be nothing else besides, no ultimate reality beyond its knowledge. The only reality is what can be (ideally) known. So there is, in a manner of speaking, an actual world which is wider than the order of nature which our minds make, but both that world and our world (nature) are constituted on the same principles. Accordingly, we can be confident that our world (by and large) depicts the actual world, and that we could depict it more fully. Green's position has the advantage over Kant's that Green can say that science deals with reality, and that its goal is to reach the truth about reality, not just about appearances.

III. The Minimal Interpretation of the 'Eternal Consciousness'

Nevertheless, it may be contended that by the time Green has filled out his conception of the eternal consciousness, he has said so much that is highly contentious and inadequately supported, that it is unacceptable. This is especially so when Green brings God into the argument (PE §54). God, it seems, is the eternal consciousness. This leads to notorious puzzles about the relationship of the consciousness of an individual human being to the eternal consciousness—that is, about the relationship of man to God and God to man. So far as the individual has knowledge, he or she thinks what the eternal consciousness thinks; and to that extent, we may say either that the eternal consciousness realizes itself in him or her, or that he or she manifests the eternal consciousness; and in both cases, more so as their knowledge increases (e.g. PE §8). But what role does the eternal consciousness play in this? The eternal consciousness appears in the individual, but Green is ambiguous about the nature and direction of this process—that is, about whether or to what extent the individual, so to say, actively acquires the eternal consciousness, and about whether or to what extent the eternal consciousness puts itself into the individual (who is passive). When Green writes that in knowledge the human being 'gradually becomes the vehicle of an eternally complete consciousness' (PE §67), or that the eternal consciousness 'reproduces itself' in the individual human soul (PE §71), or that the eternal consciousness uses the individual as its 'organ' (PE §82), he does not offer any fuller description of the process, and in particular he does not explain what part is played by the individual human being when it is the 'vehicle' or 'organ' of the eternal consciousness. It is obvious that since the individual consciousness is in principle the same as the eternal consciousness, it plays some part; but we are left with what Skorupski aptly terms a 'mystifying dialectical relation' between the eternal consciousness and the individual human being.[4]

At this point it is helpful to introduce a distinction made by D. G. Ritchie which makes explicit what is implicit in Green's position.[5] In the course of his own account of the Idealism that Green advocated, Ritchie distinguishes very sharply between two kinds of metaphysics. On the one hand is Critical Metaphysics, such as the analysis of the a priori element in knowledge, where we can argue with logical precision and reach conclusions which are certain. On the other hand is Speculative Metaphysics, which cannot have logical precision and certainty, and where the only test of validity is 'its adequacy to the explanation and arrangement of the whole Universe as it becomes known to us'.[6] Critical Metaphysics can precede science, logically analysing its necessary conditions; Speculative Metaphysics 'can never be independent of any of the sciences or of any branch of human knowledge or effort', but must

[4] John Skorupski, *English-Language Philosophy 1750–1945* (Oxford and New York: Oxford University Press, 1993), 87.

[5] Ritchie came to Balliol in October 1874, having just graduated in Classics at Edinburgh University. Green was one of his tutors. In 1878 Ritchie gained a first in *Literae Humaniores*, and soon after a fellowship at Jesus College (becoming tutor in 1881). He may well have heard Green's professorial lectures; anyway, he shows himself closely familiar with Green's position and expounds it in three articles (1888–92) reprinted as the opening chapters of *Darwin and Hegel with Other Philosophical Studies* (London: Swan Sonnenschein, 1893); see too 'Cogitatio Metaphysica', esp. §§1–23 (MS 1902, printed in his *Philosophical Studies*, ed. Robert Latta (London: Macmillan, 1905)). Ritchie acknowledged his debt to Green's teaching (*Darwin and Hegel*, p. vii). He was diligent in defending Green, including the idea of the eternal consciousness, against critics: see in particular his reviews of Andrew Seth's *Hegelianism and Personality*, *Mind*, 13 (1888), 256–63, and John Veitch's *Knowing and Being*, *Mind*, 14 (1889), 574–9 (both reprinted in P. Nicholson (ed.), *Collected Works of D. G. Ritchie*, vi (Bristol: Thoemmes Press, 1998)). For helpful comparisons of Green and Ritchie, see E. Neill, 'Evolutionary Theory and British Idealism: The Case of David George Ritchie', *History of European Ideas*, 29 (2003), 313–38, esp. 316–30 (though I disagree that in his account of the evolution of morality, Ritchie deviates from Green's position: see my Introduction to *Collected Works of D. G. Ritchie*, i, pp. xvii–xix).

[6] Ritchie, *Darwin and Hegel*, 14.

follow in their footsteps because they are the material it works on.[7] Ritchie argues that Critical Metaphysics demonstrates that the individual human being is 'an eternal (*i.e.*, time-less) self-consciousness', but he stresses that Critical Metaphysics

can tell us nothing further, can tell us nothing as to what this eternal self-consciousness is or how it is related to our individual selves. ... The attempt to find some expression for this relation, *i.e.*, to show how an eternal self-consciousness reveals itself in Time and Space is the business of Speculative Philosophy or Metaphysics. That there is an eternal self-consciousness we are logically compelled to believe, and that it is *in some way* present in our individual selves; but *in what way* is a matter of speculation: and it is still quite competent to any one who accepts the main result of the critical examination of knowledge to maintain that this latter problem is altogether insoluble; although it is a problem (or rather series of problems) which we cannot leave alone, because we are met by it at every step in our ordinary experience, if we once begin to reflect on the meaning and mutual relations of the conceptions we are obliged to use.[8]

This is what one might call the minimal interpretation of the eternal consciousness. That there is an eternal consciousness, in Green's sense, is logically implied in an analysis of what knowledge is; but as to anything beyond the necessary existence of the eternal consciousness, its characteristics and nature or its precise relationship to human beings, we can only speculate. Our speculations rest on our present knowledge, which, so far as it is true, thinks what the eternal consciousness thinks. Consequently, human knowledge being limited, our speculations are always incomplete and must forever be renewed as human knowledge expands.

If we now return to Green, we can see that Ritchie's distinction is implicit in the *Prolegomena to Ethics*, though I think it is not set before the reader so explicitly and clearly. Green writes, for instance, that as to what the eternal consciousness

in itself or in its completeness is, we can only make negative statements. *That* there is such a consciousness is implied in the existence of the world; but *what* it is we only know through its so far acting in us as to enable us, however partially and interruptedly, to have knowledge of a world or an intelligent experience. (*PE* §51)

Again, he specifically states that human knowledge, though 'growing', is 'incapable of completion' (*PE* §72). And he admits that a central question raised by his position, *why* the eternal consciousness 'reproduces' itself in human beings, is 'unanswerable' (*PE* §82) and must remain 'mysterious'

[7] Ritchie, *Darwin and Hegel*, 15.   [8] Ibid. 15–16.

(*PE* §100). 'We have to content ourselves with saying that, strange as it may seem, it is so' (*PE* §82).

Further confirmation that Green too has the minimal conception of the eternal consciousness comes from the caution with which he introduces God into his discussion. 'It is generally desirable to avoid' theological language, he writes, because of its 'misleading associations' (*PE* §54). He does not specify here how theological language misleads. But the essential point, I think, is that Green's argument only logically justifies his holding a formal conception of the eternal consciousness as 'the spiritual principle, neither in time nor in space, immaterial and immovable, eternally one with itself' (*PE* §54). Apart from the demonstration of those formal characteristics, and of the necessity of self-distinguishing consciousness as the condition of human knowledge, perception, and moral life, the conception of the eternal consciousness provided by philosophy is a blank: and the danger is that, if the eternal consciousness is identified with God, an unwary reader might fill in the blank with his or her own personal beliefs about God and with the doctrines of his or her church. Now, it is clear from elsewhere, and in particular from his two lay sermons, that Green had great reservations about theological dogmas and the church creeds based on them.[9] He believed they had grown up over the centuries and, whatever their use in their time, had become obstacles to learning the essential lessons of Christianity. For example, theological misconceptions both about religious faith and about science have led to religion and science being set in contradiction to one another—unnecessarily, since religion and science spring equally from the one, indivisible human spirit, and both are ways to God.[10] Later in the *Prolegomena* Green notes that even the language of ordinary religion, because it is not about matters of fact, is unavoidably couched in terms of the imagination, and consequently is subject to philosophical criticism, and may need to be corrected. 'Objection may properly be taken, for instance, to the ordinary representation of God as a source of rewards and penalties', who rewards goodness and punishes wickedness, because 'the figure is one which interferes with the true idea of goodness as its own reward, of vice as its own punishment' (*PE* §320). Even in the case of a reader whose theological beliefs were reasonable, and who had subjected his religious ideas to philosophical criticism, inevitably his beliefs would none the less be limited and incomplete, open to revision and to extension, and lacking the philosophical justification possessed by the formal conception of the eternal consciousness.

---

[9] 'The Witness of God' (1870) and 'Faith' (1878), *CW* iii. 230–76.
[10] 'Faith', *CW* iii. 262–6. On science and religion, see further sect. IV below.

Thus Green and Ritchie share the minimal view of the eternal consciousness. Hence it is no surprise that they react to Hegel in the same way. Both take him to be claiming that human beings can know the eternal consciousness simply by philosophical thinking, and both regard this as a fatal flaw in his philosophy. This is obvious from Green's review of John Caird's book on Hegel, written while he was composing the *Prolegomena*. Green sees Hegel as reaching the right Idealist conclusion but by the wrong method, because he 'seemed to arrive at his conclusion as to the spirituality of the world, not by interrogating the world, but by interrogating his own thoughts'. Green is emphatic that human thought (even when raised to its highest level, in dialectical philosophy) and the thought which is the eternal consciousness are utterly different, and must not be confused. The only way in which we can know the eternal consciousness is through 'an investigation of the objective world'; it cannot be done by means of the kind of introspective inquiry into what and how we can or cannot conceive, which he thought Hegel had pursued. Further, human investigation of the world relies on human understanding, which is unavoidably infirm, and therefore human thought is always limited and incomplete.[11] Ritchie pursues a very similar line. He argues that Hegel was right to take as his ideal 'a philosophic system stating the *whole* truth about the universe'. 'It is philosophical to hold that the universe is rational; for all the sciences presuppose it, and all serious human conduct presupposes it.' However, Hegel was wrong to suppose that his own particular construction of that philosophical system stated and interpreted the universe absolutely: rather, it was, as it was bound to be, incomplete and blinkered.[12] Hegel succumbed to the temptation to seek finality, and thereby was 'false to the spirit of his own philosophy'.[13]

---

[11] Green, 'Review of J. Caird: "Introduction to the Philosophy of Religion"' (1880), *CW* iii. 142–6. Edward Caird, in his introduction to R. B. Haldane and Andrew Seth (eds.), *Essays in Philosophical Criticism* (London: Longmans, Green, and Co., 1883), reports: 'To Hegel [Green] latterly stood in a somewhat doubtful relation; for while, in the main, he accepted Hegel's criticism of Kant, and held also that something *like* Hegel's Idealism must be the result of the development of Kantian principles rightly understood, he yet regarded the actual Hegelian system with a certain suspicion as something too ambitious, or, at least, premature. "It must all be done over again", he once said, meaning that the first development of idealistic thought in Germany had in some degree anticipated what can be the *secure* result only of wider knowledge and more complete reflexion' (p. 5). J. H. Muirhead (at Balliol 1875–9, and Green's pupil) puts it well, remarking as he provides a summary of Green's review of John Caird's book, 'Green believed that a philosophy of the Absolute was one thing, an absolute philosophy quite another' (*The Platonic Tradition in Anglo-Saxon Philosophy: Studies in the History of Idealism in England and America* (London: George Allen & Unwin, 1931), 209).

[12] Ritchie, *Darwin and Hegel*, 71–2.

[13] Ritchie, review of Seth's *Hegelianism and Personality*, 262.

IV. Where Green Justifiably Exceeds the Minimal Interpretation

On the face of it, the minimal interpretation of the eternal consciousness makes fewer claims and is correspondingly easier to accept and defend. Why, then, should Green have made his position more controversial and vulnerable by exceeding it, venturing into Speculative Metaphysics at all, and saying anything positive and substantive about the eternal consciousness, let alone identifying it with God? For subsequently in the *Prolegomena* we are told, for example, that we can see a progress in human history and in the development of moral ideas as the eternal consciousness becomes better known, and it is claimed that the eternal consciousness contains the moral ideal that should serve as the guide and inspiration of the individual moral agent seeking self-perfection and moral improvement for all. God '*is* all which the human spirit is capable of becoming' (*PE* §187).

The question of why Green commits himself to such statements becomes more pressing if we think that the step too far is a step he did not have to take, so that he has overextended his argument needlessly. It might be thought that the minimal eternal consciousness on its own is sufficient to establish the preliminary points he needs for his moral philosophy. The main prolegomenon to his ethics was to show that there cannot be a natural science of man. That task, surely, has been completed as soon as he has established that science, and all human knowledge and even perception of the most basic kind, requires us to presuppose that the human mind is self-conscious. This entails that human consciousness is 'free' in the sense that it is not itself a part or a product of nature (*PE* §82). On its own, Green's transcendental account of human consciousness suffices to clear the way for his later claim, when he turns from theoretical to practical philosophy, that man is capable of 'consciousness of a moral ideal and the determination of [his] action thereby' (*PE* §8). It is the non-natural, spiritual nature of man's consciousness and his self-consciousness that supports viewing every individual as a free and responsible moral agent, who acts imputably in pursuit of his or her own 'wanted objects' (i.e. he does not act instinctively in response to wants), and who is the only possible source for moral improvement and progress. And just as in the case of science, so with moral life, Green moves from what we already know. There is an Aristotelian emphasis on the underlying soundness of what ordinary morality requires of us. What Green's moral hero, the conscientious man, does is to practise ordinary morality to the full and then more—he strives always to see how it could be taken further, refined, extended. (It is, in Oakeshottian terms, the pursuit of intimations: the conscientious man identifies anomalies and tries to eliminate them.) That is, he builds up his picture of the perfect moral ideal from what is already present in the practices and ideals of his society. He works from the human. In other words, it seems that the eternal consciousness plays no operative part in Green's moral philosophy. Certainly it is not an external standard prescribing a set of rules for us to follow (note Green's denial that he has any 'prophetic utterance to offer in regard to conduct' (*PE* §2)).

There are two matters to consider in order to deal with the question of whether Green has overextended his argument when he had no need to. First, it should be apparent that, on the interpretation developed above, this question is misconceived. Green does not have the option of not moving on to a fuller, substantive account of the eternal consciousness. Once he has embarked on his transcendental journey, every step has to be taken: even the minimal interpretation of the eternal consciousness leads logically to *some* substantive account of the eternal consciousness. As we saw, Green's analysis of human knowledge and experience leads him inexorably to an eternal consciousness. Furthermore, the same analysis demonstrates that 'the eternally complete consciousness' gradually and in a limited form appears in the individual human consciousness as the individual's knowledge and experience grow (*PE* §67). Necessarily, what appears in our minds is a substantive version of the eternal consciousness (certain relations in nature are asserted as true, certain moral ideals are prescribed as right, and so on). That is, some substantive account of the eternal consciousness, exceeding the minimal and formal assertion that there is an eternal consciousness, cannot be avoided: the minimal interpretation of the eternal consciousness itself entails moving beyond it to an eternal consciousness which is not merely formal. However, the crucial distinction drawn in the preceding section still applies. That is, the formal characteristics of the eternal consciousness, as interpreted minimally, are revealed by logical analysis and are known with certainty; but any account of the substantive content of the eternal consciousness is based on human experience, with all its limitations, and is known only provisionally. In the latter case, the findings of science and our understanding of morality necessarily fall short, and therefore remain subject to correction and revision in the light of later experience.

The second matter to be considered is of a different order altogether, and emerges when we turn to the first two sections of the *Prolegomena*, which I have ignored so far. They attach much weight to the word 'conviction'.[14] In

---

[14] The word is not confined to the opening two sections but occurs occasionally, in the same sense, later as well. Thus in *PE* §37 Green writes that the whole aim of his kind of Idealism 'is to articulate coherently the conviction of there being a world of abiding realities other than, and determining, the

those opening sections, Green undertakes to state 'prevalent opinion' among educated and reflecting people. He writes that they hold 'deep convictions' about 'the great problems of life or the rights and wrongs of human conduct'. He distinguishes four ways of talking about these convictions: those of science, theology, poetry, and philosophy. Science is taken for granted as occupying a commanding position: it is rational; in fact, it is our touchstone of rationality. And that is the problem, because our deep convictions are not 'sensibly verified'. Hence they do not belong to 'the domain of natural science', and they cannot be supported by science. Worse still, our deep convictions cannot be reconciled with 'inferences from popularised science ... in any logical system of beliefs'. The convictions are left 'to take their chance alongside the seemingly incompatible scientific beliefs', and if they survive, they are retained 'merely on scientific sufferance'. There seems to be no independent justification for our convictions. Theology cannot help.[15] Although it has 'a truth of its own' and is entitled to our respect, it founds its dogmas on divine revelation, not reason. From the scientific point of view, it is 'an illusion'. Nor can poetry help. Although it too has 'a truth of its own', and it expresses convictions we share, it presents them only 'in the rapt unreasoned form of poetic utterance, not professing to do more than represent a mood of the individual poet'. Poetry appeals to our feelings, not to our reason. Least of all, according to the common view, can philosophy help. Philosophy, and especially moral philosophy, is suspect and redundant. From the point of view of science, it is a 'dull and pretentious' illusion, while from the points of view of theology and poetry, it offers 'no truth that we can feel', and has 'no interest for the imagination and no power over the heart'. In the face of this prevalent verdict, Green champions philosophy (and *a fortiori* moral philosophy). He asserts that philosophy stands above science, theology, and poetry, able to do what none of them is capable of—namely, to justify against science men's deepest convictions, and to systematize 'the ideas which poetry applies to life, together with those which form the basis of practical religion' and 'to ascertain the regions to which they on the one side, and the truths of science on the other, are respectively applicable'. Above all, then, Green is claiming that philosophy can provide a *rational* justification of conviction generally, and in particular where conviction conflicts with science.

Green takes these 'deepest convictions' as given, just as he accepts the existence of science as given: and of course he himself had deep moral and

---

endless flow of our feelings.' Whether Green had written these opening sections before his articles appeared in *Mind*, and for some reason omitted them, or wrote them later, is not known.

[15] 'Theology' here is obviously the traditional, 'dogmatic' theology which Green largely rejected.

religious convictions, idiosyncratic versions of those held by a large number of his contemporaries. The problem facing him was that those moral and religious convictions were under heavy attack, undermined especially by the dominant materialist and empiricist philosophies.[16] The assault threatened to suck all spiritual vitality from the convictions and destroy them as active ingredients in our lives. As Green had put it in 'Popular Philosophy in its Relation to Life' (1868), the failure adequately to theorize practice 'must cripple the practice itself' (*CW* iii. 124). Green's response to this in the *Prolegomena*—almost, one feels at times, his reason for writing the book—is to bolster the existing, threatened convictions. This he does negatively, by showing that the materialist philosophy is erroneous, with the result that the convictions are revealed to be safe and secure. The logic of the strategy seems to be that people already have reasons to hold and act on their convictions, and that the reasons will continue to be effective once the pressure to abandon them is relieved. (The same strategy can be observed elsewhere, notably in his lay sermons 'The Witness of God' (1870) and 'Faith' (1878), which Green printed privately and distributed to students and friends.) The strategy presupposes the convictions: there is no suggestion of trying to alter anyone's convictions, or of providing convictions to someone without them.[17] Rather, with the convictions presupposed, philosophy is used to preserve them by neutralizing what might otherwise dissolve them. This 'counter-work' to criticism (*PE* §319) is the 'important service' which philosophy can render to prepare us to cope with the perplexities of the moral life: 'a service, indeed, rather of the defensive and negative than of the actively inciting kind—a service which in a speculative and dialectical age needs to be rendered, lest the hold of the highest moral ideas on the mind should be weakened from apparent lack of intellectual justification' (*PE* §317). That is the most Green can do, by means of the reasoned argument of philosophy. Thereby Green, like Kant though not quite in the same way, deploys philosophy to 'make room for faith'.

[16] For a recent account of that attack, bringing out well the connections between religious doubt and uncertainty and the displacement by some philosophers of teleological explanation based on God by scientific explanation resting on chance, see Philip Davis, *The Oxford English Literary History, viii: 1830–1880: The Victorians* (Oxford: Oxford University Press, 2002), chs. 3 and 4.

[17] As he expressed it in a letter to a recipient of 'Faith', probably in 1878: 'it was not written with a view to altering the beliefs of those who accept the miraculous narration of the Gospels, but to save those who, like myself, are unable to do so from being shaken in their moral and religious convictions' (*Additional Writings*, 467). Pertinent too is Green's remark in a letter to H. S. Holland in 1872 that he 'never dreamt of philosophy doing instead of religion'. He describes philosophy as 'the reasoned intellectual expression of the effort to get to God', and writes that religion and philosophy are 'in such different planes that they cannot compete' (*Henry Scott Holland: Memoir and Letters*, ed. Stephen Paget (London: John Murray, 1921), 65–6; repr. in *Additional Writings*, 442).

In discussing convictions, we are working in the area of substantive ideas about the eternal consciousness, and as a logical consequence, there is no possibility of proof. Much depends on the believer and how he or she sees things (hence the importance of the assumption that the convictions are already 'there'). Thus Green is doing all that can be done: his philosophy supports convictions negatively by removing the source of doubt about them. Positively, all he can establish is that moral and religious ideas must come into any account of the eternal consciousness: but no conclusive grounds can be provided for preferring one particular doctrine or set of theological beliefs over the rest. His position did not convince everyone, of course, but it was welcomed widely as making space for moral endeavour, religion, and God, and not only by Anglicans but also by Nonconformists and Roman Catholics. The historical record provides extensive evidence that his contemporary influence was very considerable.[18] As commentators have observed, the language of the eternal consciousness does not solve all the religious believer's problems. The difficulties and puzzles of traditional theology about man's relation to God reappear in the ambiguous relation of the individual to the eternal consciousness. But the believer had these problems already. His gain is to be freed from the threats and doubts posed by materialist philosophy. To this extent, Green has achieved the aim he sets himself at the beginning of the *Prolegomena*, to make moral philosophy respectable, by showing that it can provide 'independent justification' of our 'deepest and truest views of life … in the shape of a philosophy which does not profess to be a branch either of dogmatic theology or of natural science' (*PE* §1).

I have argued that Green has given due prominence to moral and religious convictions. This is particularly significant in the case of religion. Although philosophy cannot justify or authenticate particular religious opinions, it can, so to speak, legitimate religion. Previously (section II), I explained that it is an implication of the argument that science too is essential. On Green's account, the very existence of scientific knowledge exemplifies the existence of the eternal consciousness, and the pursuit of science is one way in which we know the eternal consciousness. Religion and science, so commonly regarded at that time (due, according to Green, to faulty theology) as enemies locked in a war

---

[18] See e.g. Melvin Richter, *The Politics of Conscience: T. H. Green and His Age* (London: Weidenfeld & Nicolson, 1964), esp. 114–45; Matt Carter, *T. H. Green and the Development of Ethical Socialism* (Exeter: Imprint Academic, 2003), ch. 4; and Denys Leighton, *The Greenian Moment: T. H. Green, Religion and Political Argument in Victorian Britain* (Exeter: Imprint Academic, 2004). Bernard Reardon judged that 'Anglican theology in the last quarter of the century probably owed more to him than to any other thinker since Maurice' (Bernard M. G. Reardon, *From Coleridge to Gore: A Century of Religious Thought in Britain* (London: Longman, 1971), 308).

which only one could win, are in the terms of Green's argument compatible and mutually supportive: both are evidence of man's spiritual nature, and both provide (limited) access to the eternal consciousness, though by different routes. As Green put it in the lay sermon he delivered when he was professor, 'science, rightly understood, leaves to the spiritual life all the room which this on its part, when rightly understood, requires'.[19]

Scientific knowledge is always provisional, for the reasons given. Religious beliefs too are always provisional, and in addition, because they fall under Speculative Metaphysics, they are hypothetical. It is worth noting one implication. Green lived in a Christian society in which religious belief varied from one sect to another, and even varied between different wings of the same sect. (Today, some of those differences may have diminished, but others have arisen, with differences between Christianity and other religions, and between religion and secularism, coming to the fore.) Green's philosophical position is well equipped to take account of this situation. His Idealism is monistic, and entails that there is only one truth, in the realm of religion as in morality, and as in science. The eternal consciousness must be as it is, and no other way: it is a single, harmonious system of unalterable relations. It is differentiated, but contains no differences in the sense of oppositions or elements at variance. However, his Idealism also entails that such is the case only ultimately. Especially at the level of Speculative Metaphysics, human beings are in the process of striving towards a true understanding of the eternal consciousness, and some divergence of view is inevitable. Idealism takes monism as its goal, the final end. But that goal means that, in our present situation as human beings with partial and restricted experience and with limited understanding, we should adopt a pluralist approach in practice. Green could endorse most of the practical policies of J. S. Mill's *On Liberty*. Freedom of enquiry in science, freedom of religion, and liberal social and political institutions are supported and justified by Green's spiritual monism at least as soundly as they are by Mill's utilitarianism.

One last remark on Green and religious convictions. I have stressed that Green uses philosophy to make room for religious faith. But he should not be thought to license any and every religious conviction. Green, like Hegel, ranks Christianity (understood in a certain Protestant way, and with its theology purified) as the highest religion. This attachment to Christianity is not because of accident of birth; it is not because Green was the son and nephew of Anglican clergymen, living in a society broadly Christian, and working in a university still assigned by some as a prime function, the training of the clergy for the Established Church. Rather, for Green, religious convictions

---

[19] 'Faith', *CW* iii. 265; see generally 264–6, also 'The Witness of God', *CW* iii. 248.

are subject to philosophical criticism, and it is Christianity, in its essentials, which passes the philosophical test and which in particular coincides with the position concerning the eternal consciousness which philosophical analysis demonstrates we must hold.[20]

V. Conclusion

The worry which I voiced originally was that the eternal consciousness is a weakness in Green's philosophy, and that because his philosophy is so unified, any weakness at one point weakens the whole. Remove the eternal consciousness, and the rest collapses unsupported. Several commentators have argued recently, though for differing reasons and in different ways, that it is a mistake to conceive of the unity of Green's philosophy so rigidly. For example, Thomas contends in his detailed study and analysis of Green's moral philosophy that 'to support his ethical theory and moral psychology ... requires nothing like Green's full-blown metaphysics'.[21] Gaus argues that Green's metaphysics is not the foundation from which the rest of his philosophy is derived, so that to dispense with the eternal consciousness would not destroy the moral and political philosophy, though it would remove one justification for it.[22] And Tyler contends that the eternal consciousness 'is not the logical foundation of [Green's] epistemology', and that one can interpret the theory in human (non-theistic) terms 'without doing significant violence to Green's epistemology'.[23] On any of these views, Green's account of the eternal consciousness has failings, but they do not endanger the rest of his philosophy. From this perspective, Green's unsuccessful attempt to make his case for the eternal consciousness was a superfluous over-extension of his main philosophical position, superfluous because that position can stand on its own feet. Indeed, it might be hazarded that, if anything, the appeal of Green's philosophy would be increased for us if it were freed from claims about the eternal consciousness. For instance, it might be thought more plausible to view moral progress as men and women

---

[20] See esp. 'Faith', *CW* iii. 253–76.

[21] Geoffrey Thomas, *The Moral Philosophy of T. H. Green* (Oxford: Clarendon Press, 1987), 150; see too pp. 147 and 149, and ch. 3 generally.

[22] Gerald F. Gaus, 'Green, Bosanquet and the Philosophy of Coherence', in C. L. Ten (ed.), *Routledge History of Philosophy*, vii: *The Nineteenth Century* (London: Routledge, 1994), 413–14.

[23] Colin Tyler, *Thomas Hill Green and the Philosophical Foundations of Politics: An Internal Critique* (Lewiston, NY: The Edwin Mellen Press, 1997), 11–12. For details of Tyler's view of the eternal consciousness see pp. 26–33, also 'The Much-Maligned and Misunderstood Eternal Consciousness', *Bradley Studies*, 9 (2003), 126–38. For criticism of Tyler—and of Green—see Maria Dimova-Cookson, *T. H. Green's Moral and Political Philosophy: A Phenomenological Perspective* (Basingstoke: Palgrave, 2001), 27–32, and *idem*, 'The Eternal Consciousness: What Roles it Can and Cannot Play. A Reply to Colin Tyler', *Bradley Studies*, 9 (2003), 139–48.

gradually improving upon existing institutions and practices and ideals than as the eternal consciousness somehow gradually 'reproducing' itself in them.

However, any proposal to excise the eternal consciousness from Green's philosophy faces a serious objection. Omitting the eternal consciousness would change Green's system of ideas into something he would find unrecognizable and unacceptable, and something, moreover, which would never have been so influential as his own position was. Green treats the eternal consciousness as the governing part of the system, and if that part is removed, then the system is radically altered. One cannot exclude the contentious substantive parts of Green's discussion of the eternal consciousness, because they are necessarily connected to the formal conception of the eternal consciousness. The human consciousness at the beginning of the *Prolegomena*, when he analyses science, is *already* a mind which in terms of its formal features is eternal and which substantively is (somehow) part of the eternal consciousness; and so too is the free human moral agent (*PE* §99). Man and God are not separate terms, so that we can adopt and develop one and drop the other: they are correlative terms, each defined in relation to the other, and we cannot eliminate 'God' without altering the meaning of 'man'. Thus, if we decide to relinquish the eternal consciousness, we necessarily adopt a different conception of man, of individual human beings, from Green's. We would, from Green's point of view, have cut out the heart of his philosophy, which supplies the life-blood of the individual's intellectual and moral activity; and thereby we would have decisively weakened every part of his philosophy, including his moral and political philosophy.

In this paper I have explored an alternative and less radical approach, which is not vulnerable to the objection outlined in the preceding paragraph. I have argued that once the different levels of argument in Green's philosophy are distinguished, and the eternal consciousness is given its proper place, the problem dissolves. The eternal consciousness can be retained. I have not, of course, laid out a defence of the eternal consciousness against all the objections which have been made to it, from the earliest critics such as Andrew Seth, A. J. Balfour, and Henry Sidgwick to those in our own day. My claim is simply that Green's philosophy is all of a piece, and that the minimal interpretation of the eternal consciousness reveals the integrity of his approach and allows it to be presented in its most plausible version.

If we were to try to work out Green's philosophy as it applies today, using its methods, its content would be very different. The starting-point would be the same: a survey of contemporary opinion. That, one suspects, would show a dominance of, to put it crudely, secular attitudes in place of the religious convictions which surrounded Green. We live in a different intellectual world.

Precisely because what can be said of Green's eternal consciousness (beyond its mere existence) can be said only provisionally, hypothetically, and with the limitations under which all human beings must think, each generation must form its own picture of the eternal consciousness. The substantive filling out of an Idealist philosophy such as Green's must always, by its very nature, be in progress, because at every stage it must be open to revision; and the revisions might sometimes startle its earlier proponents. Nevertheless, one feature of the philosophy, however much it is reworked, must remain the same—the central role of the eternal consciousness.

7

Green's Idealism and the Metaphysics of Ethics

LESLIE ARMOUR

T. H. Green based his ethical and political theories on a metaphysics.[1] Reality, Green said, consists of an eternal consciousness and a number of finite consciousnesses which develop over time while participating in and being individuated from the eternal consciousness. These finite consciousnesses develop against the background of a natural world which consists of that aspect of the eternal consciousness that can be known objectively. Green's ethics are based on the notion that the proper end of finite selves or consciousnesses is to realize their potential in sharing in the eternal consciousness. To do so, they must co-operate with other finite selves and take responsibility for the self-development of all of them. A good society is one in which everyone is free in the sense of being able to participate optimally in this process. For it is Green's claim that at the heart of all our experience is a process which involves us in moral co-operation, and that our very natures depend on the successful understanding of that process.

The basis of much of Green's philosophy is a theory about relationships which leads him to think that relating is an activity, and that a stable nature of which there can be objective knowledge requires a consciousness which can be relied upon.

His metaphysics must seem problematic, for he concedes that 'no proof' in the 'ordinary sense' is forthcoming for the propositions he puts forth.[2] But his metaphysics provides a necessary foundation for his moral and political theories,

---

[1] It is set out in *Prolegomena to Ethics*, ed. A. C. Bradley (Oxford: Clarendon Press, 1883), §§1–153. The most common edition is the 4th, also ed. A. C. Bradley, from the same publisher, 1899. The edition of 1997 (Bristol: Thoemmes Press), uses the 1883 edition. Page numbers differ from 1883 to 1899, but the section numbers remain the same.

[2] *PE* §174.

GREEN'S IDEALISM AND METAPHYSICS OF ETHICS 161

because his notions of morality and community are rooted in his account of the role of agency in experience and in the notion that the intelligibility of experience and the force of our convictions about community depend on the reality of a shared mind. The absence of 'proof' does not entail the absence of reasonable grounds for his beliefs. They follow, he argued, from an analysis of experience, and I shall explore the logic of this analysis and of Green's procedure for drawing conclusions from it.

A large part of this paper is explanatory. But it is also critical and constructive. I shall argue that Green's notion of the 'eternal consciousness' must land him in a contradiction in the end if it is taken literally. This is not news, I think, but I shall also suggest modifications which may rescue him, for, as Green thought, there can be progress in philosophy. I will also take seriously some of Anthony Quinton's doubts about the theory of relations which is the foundation of Green's metaphysics. But again, I shall suggest that one can rework the problem to some advantage.

Essentially, the point I want to make is that the moral agents Green talks about and the natural world he talks about are both the result of a relating process. The dynamics of this process and the search for an explanation of it dominate much of his writing. The Kantian good will is admired by Green. It is what aims at this highest good. But it is not sufficient for Green's idea of the good itself or sufficient as an aim. The process by which the good is realized is one of individuation from the eternal consciousness, so that the selves to be realized are really the creations of a process, and do not exist apart from it, though they have a future, he thinks, which extends beyond the present life. If sense could be made of all this, Green's philosophy would be a fertile ground for further work, especially in our time when ideas of community are problematic and when the ways of assembling pluralities into unities which do not destroy their individuality is the question of the hour.

When Green says that no metaphysics such as his is subject to proof 'in the ordinary sense',[3] he means that one cannot simply lay down some unquestionable premises and show by a deductive process that the conclusion follows. This is because we ourselves are part of this process, and it is only by a reflection on what is going on that we can understand ourselves. The test of Green's theory is, or ought to be, that it enables us to make the best possible sense of our ordinary perceptual world and of the natural world as it is described in the sciences, to which, we now realize, we seem driven by a combination of objective analysis of the data, mathematics, and the communities that shape

---

[3] PE §174. See also Melvin Richter, *The Politics of Conscience, T. H. Green and his Age* (London: Weidenfeld & Nicolson, 1964), 181.

our inquiry. It must also make sense of our moral and political life. That is, it must show us why some decisions seem morally obligatory, others seem difficult, and still others leave us puzzled.

Green also believed that the correct understanding of this situation would show us that we can live in the hope of progress[4]—indeed, perhaps that progress is necessary—and that we need not put our hopes in superstitious religion or depend on the arrival of saints or master-minds to save us from disaster. He believed that the truth about life and politics can be understood by everyone, or at least, since much of his work was never published in his own lifetime, by the Oxford undergraduates to whom he addressed himself almost daily.

I. Green's Picture of the World

We must begin, then, with Green's picture of the world. The world we encounter as moral agents, scholars, and pleasure-seekers consists of a nature which is shaped by the relating activities of a universal and eternal consciousness. The individual consciousnesses through which the eternal consciousness is expressed are generally people like us, though no doubt conscious animals must be included. Human and other consciousnesses participate in the universal one. They would not exist apart from the individuating activity of this eternal reality. They can share in one another's experiences, and must do so in order to create a world through which the scope and solidity of the eternal consciousness can be expressed. Their creation is a process, one which is strongly shaped by their interdependence. This 'mutuality' is the basis of Green's ethics.

One must understand the particular way in which Green builds up this picture. He is frequently described as a Hegelian. The reality is that he really builds his metaphysics and his theory of knowledge on his analysis of what he takes to be the essential weaknesses in the philosophies of John Locke and David Hume, though it is certainly true that his theory of the history of philosophy derived from Hegel. He believed that philosophies achieved a certain essential perfection, and that it was at this point that one could see the next step, and it was this conviction that led him to collaborate in the production of the edition of the works of Hume that was for many years standard.[5]

Green's analysis of Locke and Hume persuaded him that the relationships we find in the world are the result of a relating activity, and nearly everything

---

[4] *PE* §§183–8.

[5] Thomas Hill Green and Thomas Hodge Grose, *David Hume, Essays, Moral, Political and Literary*, in *Philosophical Works* (London, 1882; repr. Aalen: Scientia Verlag, 1964).

he had to say about the world followed more or less directly from that. Later in the text of *Prolegomena to Ethics,* however, Green spoke of our knowledge of reality as being like 'reading a book', and this goes better with a different theory of relationships which may well be the correct one. I shall expound both of them.

To begin with the source, however, Hume had supposed that knowledge, if there were any, would have to be based on sensory experience. For such experience is our contact with the world, and the 'ideas', as Hume calls them, from which rationalist philosophers build their thought castles, are composed, in his view, from the ways in which we order our sensory impressions. Hume's scepticism had its most obvious roots in his doubts about causality. Causality, Hume believed, involves necessary connection. We have no impressions of cause; rather, we order our sensory impressions in ways—succession and contiguity play large parts—which give rise to the notion of cause. But all such inferences are shaky. Hume does speak of our experiences of contiguity and succession, and so some people—Anthony Quinton, for instance—suppose that he thought that, contrary to Locke, we have impressions of relations.[6] But Hume's impressions are atomic in the sense that a truth about any one of them does not entail anything about any others. If we had an actual impression of contiguity, then, from that impression and the impression of some object A, we could infer that there must be another object B even if we were not aware of it. But the thesis that we might actually perceive contiguity, as opposed to King's Cross and St Pancras close to one another, seems to be an extremely curious doctrine that would not have commended itself to Hume's down-to-earth mind. Hume, rather, seems to mean that we experience things in various orders. Green thinks that we supply the order. Whether he was right or not, Green supposed, as Quinton notes, that the doctrine that relations are not given in experience was shared by all the British empiricists.

What Green noticed, of course, is that causality is thus conceived as a relation. What is true of causes, he supposed to be true of relations generally. There are relations of impressions, but not impressions of relations. Relating is thus an activity, and in the most important cases that Hume talks about—the formation of ideas like those of causality—relating is an activity which we perform. Hume does not dwell on the problems of agency which this poses because, of course, he is also sceptical of the whole idea of the self. Hume's

---

[6] Anthony Quinton, 'T. H. Green's Metaphysics of Knowledge', in W. J. Mander (ed.), *Anglo-American Idealism, 1865–1927* (Westport, Conn.: Greenwood Press, 2000), 21–7. Lord Quinton notes, correctly enough, that Green got his doctrine of relations from Locke, *Essay On Human Understanding,* II. xxv. 8.

self is only a bundle of impressions and ideas whose continuity is a mystery. But Hume also noted that he was dissatisfied with his account of the self.[7]

What seems puzzling or downright wrong about Green's view to philosophers like Lord Quinton is something like this. It is not true that we confront a lot of isolated data and somehow relate them. Our experience always comes as a system which is more or less intelligible to us. We do have to create a system in order to find our way around London and learn how to get from King's Cross to Piccadilly Circus, but we don't create it out of bits and pieces, but from quite complex wholes which we relate to one another. We do know, however, that the properties of these wholes change with our relation to them. Things change colours in different lights, look larger as we get nearer to them. What is fixed in the system of relations? We even know from relativity theory that it is quite possible for differently placed observers to observe events in different orders. Furthermore, to get things in their right orders, we have to interpret them. To find your way from King's Cross to Piccadilly Circus, you need to interpret a lot of signs and symbols. But everything we observe functions in the same way. The physicist may look into a cloud chamber and observe vapour trails which he takes to be the work of fundamental particles that cannot be seen, and in such ways he builds up a picture of the world that allows us to find our way about in it. Lord Quinton is quite right that we never see things without relations, and such relations as 'darker than' and 'larger than' appear in immediate experience. But they are not fixed. What we think is more or less permanently true about the universe is the system we arrive at when we have maximized our abilities to make things and events intelligible and explain them.

Green's distinction between the 'eternal consciousness' and the immediate individual consciousness is just, in the end, the distinction between what is ultimately taken to be true in the special sense of what maximizes intelligibility and explanation and what we take to be true at a moment in our reflections. This distinction is reasonable. If there is no 'proof', as Green thinks, it may be because we do not have a fully determined notion of what is an explanation and what intelligibility is. But notice that the alternative basic picture is that there is simply a fixed nature independent of any relating consciousness. The argument against this is that all the relations are subject to changes in our relation to things and/or to changes in our systems which give the world intelligibility and produce explanations that we can accept.

---

[7] 'I neither know how to correct my former opinions nor how to render them consistent' (Hume, *Treatise of Human Nature* (London: John Noon, 1734), ed. L. A. Selby-Bigge with textual corrections and notes by Peter H. Nidditch (Oxford: Clarendon Press, 1978), Appendix, p. 633).

This might be a purely pragmatic notion (Quine's balancing of our given experience with the concepts we have available to make the best story). The reason why Green thinks that it is not just this is that he thinks that the relating activity is done by actual agents, and that if there is an underlying story, it must be done by another agent.

There is another option, too. Green's problem with Hume was that Hume did not—could not?—see how one could find one's way from impressions and ideas to a reliable account of the world beyond. But there is a suggestion in Hume that there is, indeed, such a world, and that it is at least hinted at in what we call our natural beliefs, which include the belief in causal connections. Hume was also a historian, and best known in his own time for his writings on English history. The British Library still lists him as 'Hume, David, the historian'. The moral of his philosophy is perhaps given in his history—there is really never enough evidence to overturn our natural beliefs, and it is best to continue in our customary ways which have evolved slowly to meet our common needs.[8] This, indeed, is the High Tory view of life.[9] Was Green not just confusing the natural beliefs of sensible people—beliefs that might be expanded into science—with the workings of the eternal consciousness? Hume, after all, could dispose of much of natural religion in this way.

There can be little doubt that this provoked Green. For there is a suggestion here that there is a way in which things 'really are', and that we cannot get at it. Whereas Hume had supposed that reality might be revealed in our

---

[8] See, of course, Hume, *A History of England*, 8 vols. (London: A. Millar, 1761); and see his remarks, idem, *Essays, Moral, Political and Literary*, in *Philosophical Works*, iii. 116 and 133–44.

[9] There is a debate about Hume's 'High Toryism', but it is based, I think, on a misunderstanding. In his *History of England* Hume defended James I and Charles I, and his first volume was hailed as a Tory work. Later, though, he was hard on the post-Restoration Stuarts, and some have thought that he took up a Whig position. But Hume's conviction was always that the English constitution evolved to respond to the natural beliefs of Englishmen. The regicides pushed the constitution too far out of line, and the Restoration aimed at a new balance. It failed because Charles II had absorbed too much autocracy from the French court and the later Stuarts threatened the notion of a broadly based state church. At the end of his life, Hume supported the American Revolution, but the case was that the revolting colonists were demanding and denied the ordinary and customary rights of Englishmen and Scotsmen. J. Joseph Miller has called a recent essay 'Neither Whig nor Tory: A Philosophical Examination of Hume's Views on the Stuarts', *History of Philosophy Quarterly*, 19:3 (July 2002), 275–308. But he equates Toryism with autocracy. The expression was originally a term of abuse, with associations with Irish Popery, but the Tories quickly became supporters of moderate constitutionalism. English Tories most commonly supported a balanced constitution even if they were (and are!) inclined to place public order at the top of their list of values. Both Tories and Whigs eventually became associated with various branches of the aristocracy, but what *most* distinguishes Tories from Whigs is that they resist change in the name of a constitutional balance which they think deeply traditional, whereas Whiggery tends to support the notion of progressive change in response to public opinion. The Conservative Party is still called 'Tory', but Hume might not recognize much kindred spirit there. No party is now called 'Whig', but Whiggery persists as an outlook on life and politics.

natural beliefs, and that the proper knowledge of the human condition might be given to us through the proper appreciation of history, Kant had gone on to speak of things in themselves. The truth about these could not be known in a straightforward way, because the ordering of experience was an activity of the human mind, though the deeper truths might be grasped through an understanding of the presuppositions of moral knowledge, the celebrated 'postulates of pure practical reason' which, Kant once said, were as good as knowledge.[10]

Hegel helped Green once more by noting that one could hardly get away with saying that one knew that something, x, the thing-in-itself, existed while insisting that one knew nothing about it. If that is not a contradiction, it takes a lot of skilled spin-doctoring to show that it is not. One may well think that it is quite easy to know that something exists and has the property of being 'ineffable'. The problem is that the conditions for knowing that something exists entail knowing that it has some property. Nothing simply 'exists', even if Kant was wrong in thinking that existence is not a real predicate. Those who think it is a real predicate also think, surely, that all existent things have some other property (like that of being a thing). And so to know that they exist we must know something else.

Both Hume's natural beliefs and Quine's pragmatic balance underplay the role of agents, Green would have said. I suppose that it cannot be emphasized too strongly that this is the point.

But many people are made itchy by Green's distinction between terms and relations. Notoriously, anyway, F. H. Bradley thought that the whole notion of relation was contradictory, indeed 'infected'.[11] So we must notice that we might take a quite different view of relations and arrive at the same point, or at any rate at a point that Green also makes in the *Prolegomena*. And it seems to me that this different version would avoid Bradley's problem. The alternative theory of relations is one that sees relations as relational properties. A relational property is simply a property in virtue of which one thing is connected to another without reference to something which stands between them which might, as Bradley thought, be mistaken for a third term. A 'third

---

[10] The Gabriele Rabel translation of 'What Does it Mean to Orient Oneself in Thinking?', in *Kant: A Study* (Oxford: Clarendon Press, 1963), 169, reads: 'As regards the degree of certainty, it is not inferior to any knowledge.' For the German text, see *Werke*, German Academy of Sciences, viii. 127 ff. Kant wrote this little work in 1786 between the editions of the *Critique of Pure Reason*. In *The Critique of Practical Reason* itself trans. Lewis White Beck (New York: Liberal Arts Press, 1956), Kant seems to go further still. On p. 126 he says that 'in the combination of pure speculative with pure practical reason in one cognition, the latter has primacy'.

[11] F. H. Bradley, *Appearance and Reality: An Essay in Metaphysics* (Oxford: Clarendon Press, 1893; 2nd edn. with appendix 1908; 9th impression, corrected, 1930), 21.

term' would require new relations. The notion of the world as a set of objects tied together by their own relational properties enables us to see the world as forming a whole which is made intelligible by its relational properties. Green does use some arguments that seem to go better with this very different theory of relations. I doubt that he thought of it this way, though it must be admitted that Green was sometimes generous in allowing himself more than one theory, and that they may sometimes exclude one another. But we might interpret this generosity as saying that 'Either A is true or B is true and both imply C. C is the conclusion I think to be true.' Though, indeed, he does not *say* any such thing.

We should think about the alternative theory of relations as relational properties, because in fact Green uses the argument, borrowed from Locke, that we do have knowledge, and that knowledge cannot be derived from anything else.[12] This is important to Green in making his Idealist point. This argument goes rather nicely with the second view of relations. Taking them as relational properties, relations are the sources of the intelligibility of the world.

So let us consider. I have suggested in various places that one can, after all, make a good case for replacing relations with relational properties. And Keith Campbell[13] has made an analogous point. The case can be put in various ways but, most simply, brotherhood is a relational property one simply has as the result of another property—being the offspring of a mother and father who have another male child. And if we have a lion and a tiger and the tiger is to the left of this lion, occupying space is a feature of lionhood as it is of tigerhood. If there are two lions in the same universe, they must have a spatial relation. That is, relations are not something added as if there might be some other description without the relations. They follow from the essential properties of a thing, properties without which the thing would be a different thing.

Campbell says he is a 'foundationist',[14] i.e. he holds that relations derive from or are supervenient in some way on their terms.[15] Relations are not the

---

[12] In §§134–52 of the General Introduction to Hume's *Treatise of Human Nature*, reprinted in *Works of Thomas Hill Green* (London: Longmans, Green), i. 114–31, Green examines Locke's arguments for the existence of God in detail. He is very critical of much that Locke says, but he accepts the doctrine that knowledge can be derived from something else. The *Works* were reprinted in 1999 (Bristol: Thoemmes Press.) The Lockean doctrine is specifically repeated in §70 of the *Prolegomena*.

[13] Keith Campbell, *Abstract Particulars* (Oxford: Blackwell, 1990), 97–133.

[14] Anthony Quinton (*Anglo-American Idealism*, 21–7) has noted that this expression is confusing, since we may confound it with foundationalism, the doctrine that all knowledge is founded on basic certainties such as sense-data or self-evident truths. 'Foundationism' is Campbell's term for the doctrine that relations have their basis in their terms in a way that does not make them independent entities.

[15] 'Supervenience' as a condition of properties is a term of art introduced by philosophers, related to, but not quite, the 'coming as something extraneous or additional' suggested by the *Oxford English Dictionary*. Philosophically, it usually means something that derives from its other terms without being independently real. It sometimes figures in materialist explanations of the fact that things often seem to

seemingly distinct entities that seem to give rise to the traditional problems. Certainly, Bertrand Russell and others had objected to all attempts to bypass the problem of relations as it had been put by the Idealist philosophers and others.[16] One can say that 'Sally is taller than Suzie' just follows from the fact that Sally is five feet, five inches tall and Suzie is five feet, four inches—65 inches are more than 64 inches. But Russell says that one still needs the relation of 'greater than', the relation that holds between 65 and 64. Campbell points out, however, that if one thinks that numbers are real (there are other defences, too!), one doesn't need the relation. The relational property of being taller than follows from the simple fact that one is 65 inches tall and the other 64. One need not, as Campbell says, be a realist about numbers to make this point; but one must, I think, hold that there is some real property that Suzie and Sally have from which it follows logically that one is taller than the other. Campbell thinks that this can be done simply by examining the 'natures' of the things concerned.[17] These 'natures', however, will be, like numbers, something that logically entails the required relational property or properties, not something that depends on their contingent situation. Campbell urges, also, that there can be unilateral relational properties, i.e. those that depend on only one of their terms. 'Tom knows Piccadilly' depends only on Tom, not at all on Piccadilly. Perhaps 'creaturehood' depends only on God. Nothing could be a creature if it were not created. Certainly lions occupy space because they are lions. If we think that space is determined by the relational properties dependent upon the essential properties of objects in it, and is not an empty bucket, as Isaac Newton thought, then space is the creation of these objects.

Campbell also says that 'foundationism' does not entail that all relations are internal. That is, not all relations are such that their absence would entail a change in the essential or identifying properties of things. This may be true in the case of relations between things like shoes and their dirt, for it is not necessary that shoes be dirty, and being dirty may not change them. At any rate, shoes can be clean or dirty, and may not be changed by being a little dirty. And, again, the relation 'dirtier than' simply follows from

---

have non-material properties. For this sense (and a critique of such attempted reductions) see Jennifer Hornsby, *Simple Mindedness: In Defence of Naive Naturalism in the Philosophy of Mind* (Cambridge, Mass.: Harvard University Press, 1997), 123–4. It sometimes figures, too, in discussions about the changing shapes of continuants; see e.g. E. J. Lowe, *The Possibility of Metaphysics* (Oxford: Clarendon Press, 1998), 128–98. Both examples suggest a distinction between kinds of properties which need not figure in the present discussion.

[16]   He was particularly critical, of course, of Leibniz.

[17]   This is Campbell's suggestion in an earlier discussion of numbers (*Abstract Particulars*, 89–91).

the fact that one shoe has an amount of dirt greater than that of another shoe.

What does this kind of theory entail? It entails that all relations should be understood as relational properties that are generated by the entities of which they are attributes. The reason why this does not make all relations internal is that entities have both necessary and merely possible properties. That is to say that some things remain 'the same thing' whether they possess or lack certain properties. Campbell's shoes need not be dirty, but they can be. The entities and their properties, necessary or contingent, form a kind of unity. Campbell calls such entities 'particulars', but, if this is true, they have much of the richness of traditional substances in the tradition rooted in Aristotle. Furthermore, they must all fit together. Sally and Suzie have to be considered together, the lion and the tiger both occupy space, the dirty shoes and the clean shoes are in the same universe. So in fact all these relational properties characterize a single particular—the particular is the universe or the whole of reality if that is something different—even though we can also consider them—especially when we think of their contingent properties—as in various ways distinct. The various options are possible only if one allows compound and complex particulars or substances—i.e. shoes as such can be clean or dirty, this is one of their properties. The property they always possess is the complex one, clean-or-dirty.

A world like Campbell's must, in fact, be an intelligible unity. And Campbell says that monism is to be taken seriously.[18] Furthermore, the range of internal relations, relations the presence or absence of which entails a change in the terms, is very large if we accept, as he does, that in physics things are no longer separate from the space they occupy. In an Einsteinian world, for instance, gravity is associated with the way in which space is shaped by the objects in it. The situation, then, is indeed the one I suggested in the examples about lions and tigers.[19] In a recent book, John Leslie[20] has argued that our awareness of 'qualia'—the properties whose *instances* are surely Campbell's particulars—makes sense only within a unity of consciousness. It is not our ability to identify them—as a computer might do—that counts. It is our ability to see them as intelligible wholes that matters. Their parts must hang together in a way that makes sense. Campbell's universe is necessarily full of logical properties. Relational properties do not just happen, they are entailed,

---

[18] Ibid. 130–1.   [19] See again ibid.

[20] John Leslie, *Infinite Minds* (Oxford: Clarendon Press, 2001), 77: 'Ability to know qualia depends on how one's consciousness at any given moment can have elements that are unified in a striking fashion, elements whose identities are in partial fusion.'

and it is a logical truth that if there exist a lion and tiger in the world, the tiger is to the north, west, south, or east of the lion, or one is on top of or below the other. It is the kind of unified world of which there can be knowledge.[21]

How does this bear on Green's case? He draws, as I said, on Locke's argument for the existence of God in the *Essay*. Green says that 'every effort fails to trace a genesis of knowledge out of anything that is not knowledge itself'.[22] That is, things must have some property by virtue of which they are intelligible and can be bearers of truth. This property in Green's view is that of forming a coherent system. Our minds do this for every experience we have. The data do not come organized in intelligible systems. To suppose that the data of the world come fully organized by themselves would seem absurd to Green, for he thinks that perceiving is something which requires the activity of an agent and always exhibits a natural teleology. The evidence that he is right comes from comparing our experiences with those of others. No two of us organize our experiences in quite the same way.

If we think of visual perception, we will notice that we are always looking at something or for something or trying to find our way. At the very least, everything we experience shows the complexities of perspective and intention and reflects the agent's interests, states of mind, and concerns.

If this is right, then the view of relations as relational properties leads to the same conclusion. The view that relations are distinct entities added in a relating process persuades us that there must be a source for this activity—the relating mind in Green's view. The view that relations are relational properties which imply a logical intelligible whole also persuades us that relations imply a mind, for the intelligence exhibited by such a world must be accounted for. Green goes on in the next section to speak of the fact that understanding the world is much like reading a book.[23] And this is something, surely, that contemporary science sustains. There are many readings of the world, but the world has to be readable.

Green opts to hold that the real world is ordered by a process of relating which is the work of a human agent or another agent in appropriate ways like a human agent. It is at this point that he runs into difficulties, and that the text seems to be somewhat uncertain.

---

[21] My thanks to my colleague Richard Sembera, who made helpful suggestions about this discussion of relations.

[22] *PE* §70.   [23] Ibid. §71.

II. How to Count Minds

Green insists that there is one universal consciousness, that it is expressed through our minds or, as he preferred to say, through our various consciousnesses, and that it is eternal. There is one such consciousness because reality is one in the sense of being the same for everyone, and it is eternal because the laws of nature which we are able to discover are unchanging. We can know that it is expressed through our minds because the analysis of experience shows that we do the relating, and it is, of course, through the relations of things that the laws of nature show themselves.

Green never seriously considers the possibility that there might be many realities—all equally coherent and all-embracing—and he also specifically denies what might be called the 'dual subject theory'.[24] One suggestion that might seem to be natural is that our experience, though our own and to some important degree specific to us and subject to our eccentricities, is shared by another more widely experiencing mind. For it is odd to think that experience ends with our experience, and we know that we can go on deepening our experience indefinitely. Faced with any object, as the designers of Rorschach tests know, we can discriminate indefinitely many things. Should we suppose that the newly found entities just popped into existence when we turned our attention to them? But Green insists that there is only one universal consciousness, though there are many expressions of it. Given that, if one accepts everything else, there will still be serious questions about how our minds can be related to the universal or absolute minds, this may well pose a difficulty.

It is Green's theory that this eternal consciousness is expressed through us. It is evident that he thinks we should believe this because our own thought leads to wider and coherent understanding and gradually reveals to us a world beyond our immediate self-consciousness. It is in this way that we 'participate' in this all-embracing mind. But if the mind participated in is eternal, it would seem to be unchanging. How, then, can it do anything?

If we look at it this way, then the suggestion of both Geoffrey Thomas and Maria Dimova-Cookson that the function of the eternal consciousness is after all just to shore up Green's epistemology against a collapse into subjectivism seems justified.[25] As such, it could be replaced by a Platonic idea or, indeed,

---

[24] Ibid. §68.
[25] See Geoffrey Thomas, *The Moral Philosophy of T. H. Green* (Oxford: Clarendon Press, 1987), 14, and Maria Dimova-Cookson, *T. H. Green's Moral and Political Philosophy: A Phenomenological Perspective* (Basingstoke: Palgrave, 2001), 65–7. Thomas says that the role of God in Green's philosophy is to

perhaps by a set of invariant natural laws. Platonic ideas do not come into or go out of existence. If natural laws are really invariant, the same is true for them.

This would suffice, indeed, for much of Green's account of history and progress, as I have suggested in another paper.[26] But it will not do for his general account of experience, which depends on there being individual minds capable of reaching beyond themselves. As a consequence, it will not do for Green's theory of truth. It also will not do for his moral and political theory.

III. The Dynamics of Consciousness and Truth

It is Green's contention that the individual self is constantly driven beyond itself. His account of this is less clear than I would wish, so I will try to put it in my own way, so as to bring out the issues.

Our experience is not a self-contained whole whose internal structure is self-sustaining. It has no natural boundaries. Its horizons constantly fade into the distance, and we can always discern more details within it. One may well say, as Green does, that what is happening is that elements of the universal consciousness are constantly entering into our experience. This seems to have advantages over saying that items simply pop into experience and, if it is true that relating is always an activity involving some workings of our minds, even if just below the level of consciousness, it has advantages over saying that what we perceive are simply parts of the surfaces of material objects or states of minds caused by such objects. For what makes our intellectual and practical life possible is, indeed, the tendency for such experiences to exhibit a certain unity and coherence in themselves and between our experiences and the experiences of others. The absence of such coherence is, after all, a major sign of psychological or psycho-physical disorder. But the totality of experience is also changed and added to by each of our experiences. What you see is, hopefully, consistent in some sense with what I see, but it is never identical. So there is no totality which expresses what we both see. Such a 'sum' would be incoherent.

H. H. Joachim, one of the most perceptive of the Idealists, insists that the whole must be dynamic rather than unchanging. Each of our experiences,

---

'block the slide into subjective idealism'. Dimova-Cookson thinks that in the end Green's eternal consciousness is superfluous.

[26] Leslie Amour, 'Progress and History in the Philosophy of Thomas Hill Green', paper read at the University of London Institute of Historical Studies, 7 March 2002.

he says, constitutes a 'significant whole'.[27] He says that such a whole 'is an organised individual experience, self-fulfilling and self-fulfilled. Its organization *is* the process of its self-fulfilment, and the concrete manifestation of its individuality. But this process is no mere surface-play between static parts within the whole.' The idea of a significant whole is the idea, I think, of an experience which is intelligible and meaningful—a whole which, in a human life, can be seen to have a history and a future,[28] something Green is very insistent upon. All the problems of knowledge have to be seen in this way.

But, then, what of the 'eternal' consciousness? Is it a 'significant whole'? Evidently not, if to be one is to have a development which has a history and a future. Is the 'eternal consciousness' the coherent system that the later Idealists made so much of in their discussions of truth? It would appear not, again because the truth must include all the activities of the individual selves and must in some sense, therefore, be involved in a process of growth.

Green's moral system, as we shall see, is one in which individuals become involved with one another, increasing one another's real freedom, and developing together into a community. In the *Prolegomena* Green seems to suggest that moral individuals are working toward an ideal state that is already actualized in the eternal consciousness. On such a view, novelty or genuine creation by individuals is impossible. This surely conflicts with Green's notion of freedom. But there are other passages in the text of *Prolegomena to Ethics* which suggest a different story.

In his Gifford Lectures, *The Idea of God in the Light of Recent Philosophy*, Andrew Seth Pringle-Pattison emphasizes these passages in his critique of Green.[29] He agrees that Green speaks of a single all-inclusive system of relations,[30] and insists that relations can only exist for a thinking consciousness.[31] But Pringle-Pattison says that 'Green's account is extremely vague about the sense in which he understands the spiritual principle to "sustain" and "constitute" nature'.

In fact, Green does speak of the spiritual principle as an *active* conscious principle. The universal consciousness is actually described as 'an agent'.[32] Still, eternity keeps creeping in. Pringle-Pattison notes[33] that Green says that the concrete whole may be described indifferently as an 'eternal intelligence

---

[27] H. H. Joachim, *The Nature of Truth* (Oxford: Clarendon Press, 1906), 76. The idea of a 'significant whole' is, I shall suggest, very important.

[28] Since Green insists on the immortality of the individual self, it *always* has a future.

[29] Andrew Seth Pringle-Pattison, *The Idea of God in the Light of Recent Philosophy* (Oxford: Clarendon Press, 1917; rev. edn. 1920), 195.

[30] Green, *PE* §27.   [31] Ibid. 29.   [32] Ibid. 32.

[33] Pringle-Pattison, *Idea of God*, 199.

realised in the related facts' or as 'a system of related facts rendered possible by such an intelligence'.[34]

There is, thus, a knot to be untangled. How is the universal consciousness both to be eternal, and so undergird the ultimate truth, and to be an active agent, sharing in the consciousness of individuals and unchanging? This is a traditional Christian theistic dilemma. God is supposed to be beyond all, one and unchanging, and also to be among us as one of us, and to be a providential spirit working in history. It is only a little surprising that Green entangles himself in this problem without quite recognizing it.

There are other possibilities in the Idealist tradition. One is the dual subject or consciousness theory which, as I noted, Green specifically denies. Others are to be found in the range of theses held by Pringle-Pattison, George Holmes Howison, and John Watson. It may be useful to look at them in order to disentangle this problem.

IV. The Metaphysics of Ethics

We must keep a clear focus, however. Green's central concern is always his moral and political theories. The best plan, therefore, is surely to look at those theories and then to ask which of the possible alternatives might enable us to understand his account of the eternal consciousness without landing him in contradiction.

His ethical theory is an account of what is good as an end: namely, self-realization. The self must be realized in a way that instantiates as much of the infinite consciousness as is possible in a finite being. It is also an account of what constitutes a good action: namely, one that aims at this end. Dimova-Cookson has noticed that there is a circularity in this duality.[35] Green defines the good as that at which the good will aims, and the good will as that which aims at the good. Dimova-Cookson does not find this very worrying, because she thinks it is inevitable—the notions are necessarily involved with one another. This is where the metaphysics begins to show itself. One can hold that the self can know the universal human good and its own end by 'participating' in the eternal self. This could lead to what Colin Tyler has called 'spiritual determinism',[36] though, and Dimova-Cookson thinks that the two agencies,

---

[34] Green, *PE* §36.

[35] Dimova-Cookson, *T. H. Green's Moral and Political Philosophy*, 67–70.

[36] Colin Tyler, *Thomas Hill Green (1836–1882) and the Philosophical Foundations of Politics* (Lewiston, NY: Edwin Mellen Press, 1997), 65.

that of the individual and that of the eternal consciousness, must be the same, while Tyler thinks that the eternal consciousness works through individuals. Certainly, the self must somehow exist and know the good in order to act, for it is always Green's theory that we act on the basis of ideas. Yet the self that is meant to be perfected seems even to be brought into existence as a genuinely distinct individual and as a moral agent in the course of moral actions. What is required, obviously, is some way of conceptualizing the dynamic situation. Green intends to insist on a fairly robust view of the eternal consciousness, and so we must know more both about his moral theory and about the mysterious eternal consciousness.

The problem does seem to be in the logic of the case. The good seems to consist in knowledge and freedom. Freedom, in turn, is largely a matter of self-development through self-awareness. Good actions, therefore, are those that seek knowledge or promote freedom. But freedom is valuable because, indeed, it enables us to participate in the eternal consciousness. This is not to deny or downplay Green's constant insistence on the importance of desire.[37] And the strong emphasis on the intellectual life may only be the result of the way in which the problems are posed in the *Prolegomena*. Indeed, Green is at pains to deny that desire and intellect can ever be reduced one to the other.[38] Pleasure and pain are involved in our search for the good, as Green concedes, but they are also related to completeness and incompleteness. Good actions must contribute not only to pleasure but also to the perfection of the individual. Green in fact defines the good as that which satisfies desire.[39] But the moral good is what satisfies a moral agent, and a moral agent is involved with self-realization and freedom.[40] It is clear that there must be an important and irreducible emotional element in the achievement of the good. But though the implication may be there, he does not develop a thesis about universal love, for instance, in the way that McTaggart does. Green's moral theory becomes involved with popular ideas of morality because what it is to aim at the required knowledge is not to develop oneself, but to enable all others to develop themselves, too; for the universal consciousness can be understood only through a shared activity. The necessary unity outstrips what any individual can know.[41]

Here again, the problem of the eternal consciousness emerges. We can know the eternal consciousness only as it appears through finite selves. Hence we must join forces with others. The first aim, inevitably, is to increase the freedom of all the participants, for only if they are free can they pursue the

---

[37] Green, *PE* §§115–36.   [38] Ibid. 130.   [39] Ibid. 171.
[40] Ibid.   [41] Ibid. 218.

good. It may seem that this is an odd view for Green to take, but he insists that the individual must be, like the eternal consciousness, 'a free cause'.[42] One might think that the eternal consciousness could force itself on us, as God imposed himself on the eighteenth- and nineteenth-century Methodists, filling them with enthusiasm. But Green thinks that we must actively participate in the eternal consciousness. And this participation is not the sort of thing that can be forced. We can act well only by willingly participating in its nature.

This helps us to understand the two issues that appear most often in discussions of Green's political theories: his view of the state and communal coercion and his belief that rights arise only in the community and are not discernible a priori as features of an abstract universal system.

A major theme of Melvin Richter's study of Green is that Green was a mutualist who, though he knew that the State had functions in the promotion of human freedom, wanted the emphasis to be always on individual co-operation.[43] Richter noticed that Green rejected the Hegelian doctrines that subordinated the institutions of civil society to those of the State. Green has faith in the Victorian institutions later championed by Bosanquet—friendly societies, co-operatives, and all manner of institutions through which people could work together. Green obviously thought that people with Bosanquet's views underplayed the role of the State. The State must provide the basic framework for Green's positive freedom. Yet it is only through mutualist institutions—co-operatives, friendly societies, and voluntary charities like the London settlement-houses—that individuals can develop and assert their individuality. Such institutions require a good deal of dedication, decision making, and sheer hard work. But Green's ideas were substantially taken over by the co-operative movement.[44]

Herbert Samuel argued rightly, however, that Green's intended state was needed to remove obstacles to individual action.[45] Education and many basic welfare services surely come under this heading, and this is why Richter is right to urge that Green went further than Bosanquet in supporting the State.

The community has to be created, and within it individuals have their rights. It is Green's theory that the individual does not really exist without the community. Richter insists, in an excellent summary of Green's position, that rights are not arbitrary creations of law and custom, and cannot exist without

---

[42] Green, PE §74.

[43] Richter, Politics of Conscience.

[44] See Arthur H. Dyke Acland and Benjamin Jones, Working Men Co-operators (London, 1884; rev. edn. ed. Julia P. Adams, Manchester: Co-operative Union, 1914).

[45] Herbert Samuel, Liberalism (London: Grant Richard, 1902), 349.

a community.[46] They are not arbitrary, because they must follow from what is necessary to attain the natural end of the human being. But they are not abstractions either. One must first develop a community.

Indeed, one might say that Green's theory is that we have rights because we have duties to a democratic society, and we must have the powers necessary to fulfil those duties. Duties are meaningless without the necessary powers.

There is, of course, a natural world that exists before human selves begin to emerge in the sense that Green has in mind. We were other sorts of animals before we were the political animals Aristotle spoke of and the social animals Thomas Aquinas insisted upon. On Green's theory this pre-existing world also exhibits mind. Indeed, I'm sure he would cheerfully have accepted that there are communities of many animals, and intelligent apes, and like any Englishman, he would have accepted the role of dogs and horses in our social and emotional lives.

But the possibility that we can be genuine social and political animals depends on the existence of a world in which mind and intelligence play a role. Knowledge does not come from nothing; the world is a readable book, as he insists.

So there is a function for the eternal consciousness throughout the process. It is the guarantor of truth, the necessary condition for the development of real humanity, and, whatever we might think now, the hope for the future.

The issue therefore is about how to construe that eternal mind.

V. Eternal Consciousness, the Choices

The Idealists who followed Green provided a variety of choices. Each one involved subtleties and difficulties of interpretation, surely not less than those of Green's own philosophy, and this is not the occasion to document the doctrines thinker by thinker. But there seem to be at least eight basic ideas. I will suggest in footnotes some philosophers whose views approximate to the various alternatives. The short summaries are at best approximations.

Four of the options are variants of monism. What one might call the 'supreme Absolutist' thesis is that there is one reality, the eternal consciousness. It is in some sense all-knowing and includes all awareness. One thinks of F. H. Bradley in these terms, but one must be careful.[47] Everything that we can speak

---

[46] Richter, *Politics of Conscience*, 234–53.

[47] Bradley held many elements of this view, but there are subtleties in his account of relations, in his theory of universals, in the notion of finite centres of experience, and in his remarks about God.

of is a partial approximation to this reality. Indeed, we really cannot speak of such an Absolute at all, for to ascribe any property to it is necessarily to exclude some other property, and so to falsify it. There is a sense in which, for Bradley, as much as for recent thinkers like Emmanuel Lévinas, the Absolute would be nothing if we were to eliminate all its expressions in the world. What we can do in our own lives and thought is to approximate to it as best we can. Generally, the larger and more coherent the system of thought, the closer it comes to reality. But such an Absolute is in some sense infinite, and 'closer' must mean 'in kind, in structure, and in quality' and not 'in quantity'. Individual minds like ours are expressions of the real in so far as they have the capacity to grasp the system and are internally coherent, but they do not have any ultimate reality of their own. This theory might seem to have obvious social, political, and religious implications, but on reflection it does not. Communities may or may not approximate more to the real than individuals, for individual minds can grasp any system that can be expressed through a community. It is not as if each mind adds something to the real, for there is nothing to add to the real. It seems unlikely on such a view that the distant approximations to reality we know best—people like us—are actually immortal, though there is no reason to suppose that they should not exist beyond the limits of a single life. The Absolute so conceived is certainly not the Judaeo-Christian God, though such a God might be an expression of it, himself or herself not quite perfectly real, but as perfectly real as anything describable can be. On some views, the unity of our experience and our inability to divide it into discrete parts is a clue to this unity, but on others the unity of our immediate experience is quite different in kind, and cannot even provide evidence for the existence of the Absolute.

What we might call the Cantorian infinitist view is close to the Absolutist view, but significantly different. On the Cantorian view, what is ultimately real is the infinite, an infinite which, like the Absolute of the first theory, exceeds the limits of any concept we can think of or construct. But it is not another thing, and not the ultimate reality. Indeed, its components, like Cantor's ordinals, are not a set. The class of such objects exceeds any defining property. Rather, reality consists of the *expressions* of this infinite. The expressions of it are individuals, more or less coherent and more or less capable of expressing reality through themselves. In terms of Judaeo-Christian theology such a reality is the divine love. (Emmanuel Lévinas, who insists that its basis is in ethics and that it must not be supposed to be an entity of any sort associates it with a Jewish tradition.) Such an infinite would be nothing if it were not expressed, for literally it has no property beyond its expressions. It is thus necessarily individuated, but each individuation is seen to be less than the infinite, and must find its way back to unity again. In this case the priority of the community is fairly obvious, and so perhaps is the religious interpretation of the doctrine. It can only be thought of as an 'agent' in the special and restricted sense that it is the source of activity and even the source of moral agency in the individuals of the world. Its components are infinite and unchanging only as real possibilities. All actual knowledge and all specific actions are the work of individual agents. Logic and mathematics give us a better insight into this reality than experience, but the deficiencies of experience give us clues about what is needed. Human agents may be more or less perfect, and a Christian reading of this doctrine might make the second person of the Trinity one such agent.[48] In so far as states, corporations, and colleges cannot actually love anyone, they would all be less real than the individual, and the communities involved would entail a kind of mutualism.[49]

Thirdly there is the kind of absolutism which makes of the Absolute essentially a system of knowledge. This Absolute is the logical completeness of our present attempts at knowing. This is perhaps the truth that Josiah Royce thought necessary to account for error, or the system of knowledge envisaged by the later Bosanquet. But such an Absolute seems to be real only in the sense that all the integers are real, though, if so, it would not be the Absolute as really envisaged by either Royce or Bosanquet.[50] Consciousness does not seem to form an intelligible feature of it. An Absolute like this seems to be neutral in politics and religion. It might be that knowledge is most effectively revealed by competing individuals, and that any one of many religions which claim insight into the ultimate nature of knowledge and which claim it somehow to be something which exists beyond the limits of time can be true on such a theory.

The fourth kind of monistic absolutism is the sort which makes ideas, as such, the ultimate reality. The Platonic Idea of the Good is the classic example. Everything real is to be understood as informed and ordered by this Idea.

---

[48] This would not involve the heresy of 'subordinationism', for the second person of the Trinity would be the full expression of the divine love, and the third person would be the principle of love in the world. But it wouldn't be exactly the orthodox doctrine, either.

[49] A contemporary version of this theory—one which emphasizes that the infinite is not another thing and strongly denies that the world can be 'totalized'—can be found in Emmanuel Lévinas, *Totalité et Infini* (The Hague: Martinus Nijhoff, 1961). Josiah Royce was much interested in Cantor, but he did not take this view to the radical extreme suggested here. That is, his infinite Absolute is in many ways conceptualizable, and he really held something closer to the third form of absolutism. See *The World and the Individual*, 2 vols. (London and New York: Macmillan, 1900) ii. 473–588.

[50] Bosanquet and Royce held views somewhat like this, though their accounts of both the Absolute and individuals were sometimes ambivalent, and they developed over time. If the Roycean Absolute embodies all the truths that there ever have been, are now, and ever will be, then it seems to have a very strong existence quite beyond our world.

Reaching it is a matter of going beyond the senses, sometimes of denying their efficacy in knowledge and of showing that all reality is unified. Such a good is objective and universal, and such theories tell against utilitarianism, hedonism, and all moral theories that calculate advantage. Knowledge of the Good is something available to those who can rise above the senses, put themselves at the service of an objective good, and master the intricacies of the whole universe. Though all absolutist theories presuppose or involve elements of an ability to grasp truths that are beyond the ordinary, and may be read in ways that make them to some extent vulnerable to élitist readings, this theory is most likely to be read as élitist. (The notion that reality is the divine love, and that knowledge is a matter of mutual or communal striving, is surely least élitist, and if read with care, not élitist at all.) This 'Platonic' theory leaves little room for the Christian God, though Plato could accommodate a demiurge without difficulty. Personifying the Good can change the theory into one of the others. If the personification is derivative from the Form of the Good—so that a god or whatever is simply the expression of the Good—then the theory is still basically Platonic. But if the personal 'embodiment' replaces the Form of the Good, one has a different theory.[51]

Politically, such theories are vulnerable to Sir Karl Popper's attacks—roughly everything that is good has to be ordered under a single good, and those who know most of it are most fit to rule.[52] But Iris Murdoch's version of it is more humanistic, less given to absolute certainties, as a result perhaps of reflection on the ways that such an idea can figure in human life.[53] Literally nothing can be added to such a good, though, of course, individual agents can discover heretofore hidden implications of it.

There are also at least four pluralistic 'personalist' views. The one closest to the monist view is the dual subject theory.[54] On this view there are two subjects to the experiences of each of us. One is the eternal consciousness, which shares in everyone's experiences. Such a consciousness must contain both the totality of knowable things and the plurality of perspectives on it held by the individuals who compose reality. It will undergo change in respect of what it shares, but it will have a complete knowledge of things as they are apart from the variety of perspectives, i.e. of the objectively shared

---

[51] It is easy to see how one can cease to be a Platonist and become a Thomist in this respect.

[52] See Karl Popper, *The Open Society and its Enemies*, 2 vols. (London: Routledge, 1945). But even if all this is true, it does not quite follow that such theories are totalitarian or oppressive, only that disputes are to be settled by argument rather than by ballot. The problem concerns who decides who has won the argument. Many countries have supreme courts with this function, and not all are dictatorships.

[53] See Iris Murdoch, *Metaphysics as a Guide to Morals* (Harmondsworth: Penguin, 1993).

[54] This was, I think, held by Pringle-Pattison in *The Idea of God*, and specifically denied by Green.

elements of experience. This view, though denied by Green, does seem to lead to moral and political views not so different from Green's, for it gives us a meaning for self-realization—coming to share as perfectly as possible the eternal consciousness—and it does suggest that we would have to co-operate in order to share fully in that consciousness. In religion, one can hold this view together with Christianity, and, indeed, since the eternal consciousness is shared with us, but is beyond our immediate grasp, one can develop a theory of revelation to go with it.[55]

Close to this is what Andrew Seth Pringle-Pattison called the *primus inter pares* view.[56] The eternal consciousness is a self like us, but fully developed. It is not different in kind, and it co-operates with us. The moral and political consequences seem to be much like those of the dual subject or consciousness theory, but religiously it is rather different. There is no being who can 'lord it over us'.[57] In Christian terms there can be a second and third person of the Trinity, but no first person.

What seems almost a minor adjustment to this picture brings us to the thesis that the Absolute is essentially a community. It manifests itself in and through us, and really has no other existence. This strengthens the communitarian political theory, and distances us further from Orthodox Christianity.[58]

Finally, there is, of course, the radical pluralist view: reality simply consists of individuals. They are interrelated, and they make for a real community, but the community itself has no divine status. This view is politically ambiguous. Individuals predominate, but the community is real. Religiously, it is explicitly atheist.[59]

VI. Where Green Might Stand

If Green had lived to develop his theory in the face of criticism—perhaps to write a metaphysical treatise in addition to his *Prolegomena*—which direction

---

[55] William Temple's philosophy looks rather like this, though his Absolute may in other ways be closer to Bosanquet's. See esp. perhaps *Christus Veritas* (London: Macmillan, 1924).

[56] See Pringle-Pattison, *Idea of God*.

[57] George Holmes Howison—see *The Limits of Evolution and Other Essays Illustrating the Metaphysical Theory of Personal Idealism* (New York and London: Macmillan, 1905)—held this view explicitly, but he gave it a special twist. His community of real selves approximates specifically to Kant's 'Kingdom of Ends'. But this only underlines tendencies which are anyhow in the theory.

[58] This notion can be found in the writings of John Watson, though he struggles rather to make it appear acceptable to Christians. See *Christianity and Idealism* (New York and London: Macmillan, 1897).

[59] This was certainly J. M. E. McTaggart's claim in *The Nature of Existence* (Cambridge: Cambridge University Press, 1921, 1927). Yet McTaggart's selves approximate rather closely to something like the Christian Trinity rendered democratic and all-inclusive.

would he have chosen? Green's theory is consistent with the dual subject view, but he rules it out explicitly. Evidently for the same reason—that there is only one eternal consciousness in his view—the various pluralist views are ruled out. The Absolute as the Form of the Good will not account for his views about agency, and neither will the pure monism of Bradley or the Absolute-as-knowledge which we might associate with Bernard Bosanquet. This seems to leave us with what I called the Cantorian infinitist view. Green died before Cantor's ideas were widely known, but he might have been attracted to this theory for the same reasons that attracted Josiah Royce. This is not to deny that adopting such a view would involve Green in a significant change.

It is, I think, the only account that will allow us to accept both what Green says about agency and what he says about the eternal consciousness. The infinite so conceived is immune to change in a curious way. Whatever is added to it or subtracted from it, it remains the same. The infinite is a collection at least as great as the integers, and indeed, the Cantorian definition of the infinite has it that such a collection is infinite if and only if it has a subset equal to the whole. The integers—1, 2, 3, 4, 5, 6, 7, 8, etc.—are one example. If we take only the even numbers 2, 4, 6, 8, 10, 12, we can put them in a one-to-one correspondence with the whole. One can take away half of them, and still have the same number. So if the eternal consciousness is like this, we can add the experiences of any number of finite centres of experience, and the whole will remain the same. Yet such an infinite is in a special sense an agent. It is nothing apart from its expressions in the world, and it must express itself in the world to be anything. Without expression, its description thus contains a contradiction. Its expressions therefore follow from its nature. We can grasp its nature only by the understanding co-operation of several of its members, just as we can understand the integers only by seeing them in their ordering and in their interrelations.

But such analogies will not work without adding some content. Thinking of the infinite as the traditional 'love of God' provides such a content, one which gives substance to a philosophy like Green's. And it may be that it is only by understanding this infinite as the love of God that such a theory will work as an explication of Green's philosophy. The infinite has to be individuated. Love requires more than one agent, and serves to bring these agents together again in the way that Green desires.

But here we face two difficulties: How can we justify such an introduction—either logically or as an element in Green's philosophy? And if we take infinity seriously, do we not lose all the ideas of moral purpose and progress that Green espoused?

The first question brings us back to the initial issue of this paper. Green admitted anyway that there is no proof for such theories 'in the ordinary sense'. But then what counts as good reasons short of the proof he supposed he could not find?

VII. Proof and Good Reasons

Green's argument for his metaphysics is rather Kantian. We not only have experiences which have a natural unity and intelligibility; we have plausible claims to knowledge. Neither would be possible without a continuing activity which provides a basis in the laws of nature for stability and for the possibility of moral development. It is this combination of eternality and agency which proves puzzling, but the puzzle can perhaps be resolved if there is a real infinity which expresses itself through something like the love of God that one finds in several religious traditions. Green in fact founded his moral and political theories on the fact that this order emerges only when (1) our selves develop in a coherent way and (2) our political systems develop in a way which allows this process of self-realization to take place. I am sure he assumed that the knowledge we most value emerges only in societies in which self-realization is possible. And it is true, of course, that for rather a long time science as we know it has at least gone hand in hand with the development of the Christian West. It has important roots in Arab science and metaphysics, but these roots belong to a period of flourishing Arab culture which was very far from the fundamentalism that we read about in our newspapers. That fundamentalism is far from all-enveloping, but fundamentalists have made intellectual life difficult in many Muslim countries. The Islam that bred mathematics and great philosophy flourished in times and places characterized by relatively open communities.

Green does not argue from his moral theories to his metaphysical theories, and there is nothing literally like Kant's account of the postulates of pure practical reason, though he might have urged that there is a mutual implication between morals and metaphysics. What is certain is that Green's moral theories make no sense unless one assumes that the world consists of selves undergoing development and capable of mutual understanding. And this seems reasonable enough.

His theory is curiously intellectual, and yet it seems that a missing part of it is a doctrine of love rather like the one adopted by McTaggart. To see this, we should ask one final question.

VIII. The Problem of Individuation: Can the Eternal Consciousness be Eliminated?

If we ask why, exactly, the 'eternal consciousness' figures in Green's philosophy, we may begin to turn up the missing clues. Green began with the notion that relating is an activity and that there must, therefore, be a cosmic 'Relator' to account for the observed complexities of the universe. This, as we saw, may be a doubtful thesis about relations and experience. But the alternative view that relations are really relational properties implies a universe with intelligible logical connections. It is a universe which needs to be read as well as experienced if we are to grasp its significance.

Yet for this it may be enough that its structure is such that it is open to the search for knowledge by individual minds. Locke's original knowledge may just be the intelligibility of the universe.

For Green's theory of progress, too, a kind of Platonic idea capable of shaping developing experience may well be sufficient. And what his moral theory requires is that individual agents should be able to work together in an intelligible universe.

Yet there remains one more issue: individuation.

Green's philosophy does not, of course, abolish nature as the object of the sciences. He certainly does not propose to replace such studies by a search for Mary Baker Eddy's God, who, reportedly, wants to convince us of the unreality of the natural world in the sense that, if we can see through it to the truth, we will see that we do not need a National Health Service. A Greenian train-driver needed as much knowledge of the workings of the steam-engine as anyone else. Science is the search for a 'single and unalterable system of relations'.[60] This system might, of course, show itself to us over time. Now in the order of nature, as it is studied by physics and chemistry, individuation comes about because entities have precise locations in space and time, and complex individuals are held together by physical and chemical laws. Objects can thus be identified in many ways, and their paths through space and time plotted. But in the end they are all reducible to their components, atoms and molecules. One atom of a given element must be just like the next atom of the same element. Electrons differ from one another only in terms of their positions in various systems. None is an individual in the sense that it is different from any others. When we come to living organisms, the components of DNA, for instance, can arrange themselves in patterns which, so far as we know, are

---

[60] Green, *PE* §21.

sufficiently different from one another that people can be identified in criminal proceedings and paternity suits. This is important in the development of the body's ability to identify intruders, but it is a matter of statistical likelihoods, and not of principle. Patterns can be repeated, and creatures can be cloned.

We should also notice that when it comes to distinguishing organisms from one another, we resort to teleology. Animals and their parasites are taken to be two organisms because the happiness of worms is the misery of dogs. It is true that the DNA of each is different. But each human cell is powered by mitochondria which seem once to have been distinct organisms and which have different DNA. We don't count them as distinct organisms, for they work together with the rest of our bits and pieces toward a common end.[61]

When we come to minds, a different problem confronts us. Each of us at any rate sits at the centre of a pool of experience. This centre is not a physiological point in the brain. The mid-point of the brain is the join between the two hemispheres, and it can be severed with only minimally strange results. Certainly we do not then have two centres of experience. Indeed, the brain seems to struggle to maintain unity, but this intelligible unity is not a feature of the atomic sense-data, or something which can be readily transposed into an account of underlying brain states.

It is this intelligible unity which needs to be explained, together with the strong sense that we need to reach out to others, that we are communal animals, that Kant's 'unsocial sociability' has a basis both in our individuation and in our reaching out to others. Both are surely a background feature of all social, political, and historical explanation.

But how does this come about, especially in the light of the fact that, as Green keeps insisting, all nature seems to form a single system? Perhaps Ralph Cudworth had the answer. Cudworth speculates that the doctrine that God is love might be literally true, and he says that the true sense of the divine love is given only 'if by it be meant, eternal, self-originated, intellectual Love, or essential and substantial goodness, that having an infinite, overflowing fulness and fecundity dispenses itself uninvidiously, according to the best wisdom, sweetly governs all, without any force or violence, and reconciles the whole world into harmony'. He adds that 'love in some rightly qualified sense, is God'.[62]

---

[61] The history of mitochondrial research is explored in Alexander Tzagoloff, *Mitochondria* (New York: Plenum Press, 1982).

[62] Ralph Cudworth, *The True Intellectual System of the Universe* (London: Richard Royston, 1678), 123 (the page number is misprinted 117 in the British Library copy); ed. John Harrison (London: Thomas Tegg, 1845), i. 179.

This is the infinite which is expressed through finite centres like us. It is also the eternal and unchanging reality that nevertheless is in some sense an agent. It is unchanging, in that the nature and quantity of the divine love—an infinite quantity—is never added to or subtracted from. But it is an agent in that it individuates, for love requires more than one agent, and also brings the agents together. It renders them all equal, and brings them together only if they are mutualists like Green and Bosanquet.

This is one of the root traditions of British Idealism. The argument for it, though, is like the argument which McTaggart advances for his community of timeless loving spirits: If we must have an eternal mind and it must also be an agent, if it must be a unity and yet express itself as a plurality, reality as infinite love seems the only possibility.

This is not, as Green said, a proof 'in the usual sense', and he would ask: Does it make sense of experience as we know it? McTaggart's philosophy was built with logic on a foundation of mysticism; Green's was built with reasonable arguments on a foundation of his moral experiences and of human experience generally. Such a view of the 'eternal consciousness' certainly makes sense of Green's moral theory. But Green does not quite offer this argument, and perhaps it is a kind of Kantianism that did not appeal to him.

8

In Defence of the Eternal Consciousness

W. J. MANDER

T. H. Green's moral and political doctrines are all built upon a metaphysical foundation which he terms 'the eternal consciousness'. A forerunner of that which in later Idealist thought became known as 'the Absolute', the eternal consciousness is a single and really existing principle which comprises the source and purpose, as well as the totality, of all that there is. According to Green's view, the whole of reality exists *for*—or, perhaps one might better say, exists *in*—the awareness of a mind both infinite and eternal. Gradually manifesting itself in finite minds, this 'world-consciousness' he understands as divine,[1] its progressive revelation serving as the explanatory foundation of both abstract moral principles and actual moral growth. It defines the true good for man individually, a good which it famously characterizes as common to all men collectively.[2]

The doctrine of the eternal consciousness has long been regarded as the Achilles' heel of Green's philosophy.[3] His arguments for it have been dismissed as weak, its claims rejected as incoherent or inconsistent—either with each other or with the world at large which they try to account for. For many

---

[1] 'world-consciousness' (*PE* §51). Despite Vincent's claim that Green gives no real reason why we should regard it as God (A. Vincent (ed.), *The Philosophy of T. H. Green* (Aldershot: Gower, 1986), 9), there is plenty of textual evidence for the claim that he *did* equate it with God. He speaks of 'the complete self-consciousness, or God' ('General Introduction to Collected Works of Hume', §111; *CW* i. 131) and describes God as 'the eternal spirit or self-conscious subject which communicates itself, in measure and under conditions, to beings which through that communication become spiritual' (*PE* §184). He speaks too of 'the one divine mind [which] gradually reproduces itself in the human soul' (*PE* §180).

[2] It is 'the perfection of human character—a perfection of individuals which is also that of society, and of society which is also that of individuals ... this perfection consisting in a fulfilment of man's capabilities according to the divine idea or plan of them' (*PE* §247).

[3] For a list of critics of the eternal consciousness, see C. Tyler, *Thomas Hill Green and the Philosophical Foundations of Politics* (Lewiston, NY: Edward Mellen Press, 1997), 26 n. 25.

philosophers, advocacy of such a metaphysical monster has been enough to condemn Green's system, and for much of the twentieth century his thought was ignored. In recent years commentators have emerged who are more sympathetic to his moral and political views, but even they have found themselves embarrassed by the eternal consciousness and have sought to free themselves from this doubtful association, either by reinterpreting Green's views in a metaphysically more palatable way, or by trying to detach them altogether from metaphysics. In this paper I wish to urge that neither of these responses is necessary, and that if we find ourselves attracted to Green's ethical and political doctrines, we need feel no discomfort about embracing the eternal consciousness which grounds them, for it is a hypothesis which can well defend itself, on its own metaphysical terms, against the many objections which have been raised against it.

I

The first and most fundamental problem which faces anyone trying to weigh up Green's doctrine of the eternal consciousness is simply that of finding any account of his meaning sufficiently clear and detailed to assess. For while the eternal consciousness is a creature which lurks continually in the background of all of his writings, only very rarely is it tempted out into the light.

This scarcity of detailed treatment is due in part to the fact that Green's principal interests lie elsewhere. He never wrote a purely metaphysical treatise, and the doctrine of the eternal consciousness as it occurs in the *Prolegomena* is really something of a staging post to further destinations; principally a theory of human willing and the subsequent development of an ethical doctrine based on a notion of the common good. It is not something argued, or significantly developed, for its own sake. Rather than stay to explore in more detail what he has uncovered, once the basic principle is established, Green moves smartly on to his next task.

If part of the problem stems from what Green has *failed* to say, another part is revealed when we turn to examine what he *has* said, for Green has a marked tendency to express himself, and even to argue, in vague, abstract, and metaphorical terms. For example, his main statement of the conclusion to the argument of Book I of the *Prolegomena* is that we are required to posit the existence of what he terms 'some unifying principle analogous to that of our understanding'. And this style of speaking continues throughout. The doctrine, he tells us, is that of 'a self-originating "mind" in the universe', simultaneously 'an end gradually realising itself' in the world, and the 'condition' of that world being what it is. This mind, of which finite mind is but a 'limited mode', and to which all things are 'relative', 'constitutes' the world as a whole through being the 'medium or sustainer' of relations (which are themselves the 'work of the mind').[4] None of these expressions carry their meanings on their face, yet none is really explained. We find ourselves much in sympathy with William James, who lamented, 'It is hard to tell just what this apostolic being but strenuously feeble writer means'.[5]

But before we join James and condemn Green for a failing at best indicative of a poor writing style and at worst of poor thinking, there is another very different outlook on the matter which needs to be explored. According to this perspective, far from being a *defect*, the way in which Green expresses himself is a mark of the thoroughgoing *consistency* of his thinking.

The general Kantianism which he adopts throws up a problem which is by no means lost on Green. For according to this scheme, the eternal consciousness is understood as that which supplies the categories by which we unify and structure our experience, as that which makes it possible. But these concepts and structures apply only within experience, and cannot legitimately be used outside or beyond it, not even to express the conditions which make possible that experience itself. As Green puts it, 'In speaking of this principle we can only use the terms we have got; and these, being all strictly appropriate to the relations, or objects determined by the relations, which this principle renders possible but under which it does not subsist, are strictly inappropriate to it.'[6] What makes thought possible cannot itself be thought.

Can we, then, say nothing about ultimate reality? Kant, who was at heart a metaphysical realist, could perhaps embrace this result, but the idea of a reality existing beyond the reach of our concepts is hardly something with which *Green* can sit contentedly. He wholly rejects the 'thing-in-itself'. To speak of any world beyond consciousness is, he claims, to use an essentially 'unmeaning phrase'.[7] The role of philosophy is not to try to guess what might or might not lie *behind* experience, but simply to analyse what falls *within* it.

The resulting dilemma in which Green finds himself is not, of course, unique to him, for many philosophers have wished to state the conditions or bounds of thought yet realized, as Wittgenstein put it in the *Tractatus*, that in order to draw a limit to thought, we should have to find both sides of the limit

---

[4] 'some unifying principle analogous to that of our understanding' (*PE* §29); 'a self-originating "mind" in the universe' (*PE* §77—the inverted commas are Green's own); 'an end gradually realising itself' (*PE* §68); 'condition' (*PE* §52); 'limited mode' (*PE* §51); 'relative' (*PE* §77); 'constitutes' (*PE* §50); 'medium or sustainer' (*PE* §63); 'work of the mind' (*PE* §24).

[5] William James, *The Principles of Psychology* (Cambridge, Mass.: Harvard University Press, 1981), 660.

[6] Green, *PE* §75.

[7] Green, 'Mr Herbert Spence and Mr G. H. Lewes' §21; *CW* i. 396. So opposed is he to the notion that, in his loyalty to Kant, he even doubts whether this really was Kant's view ('Review of J. Watson, *Kant and his English Critics*', *Works*, iii. 151).

thinkable.[8] And the history of philosophy has seen the creation of various subtle schemes to allow those in such a predicament to have their cake and eat it. For example, Wittgenstein himself introduces a distinction between what thought says and what it shows, while Green's contemporary F. H. Bradley suggests that thought, as something which must develop until it ultimately destroys itself, may point beyond its suicide to something it could never say in life.[9]

Green's own solution to the puzzle is to argue that the eternal consciousness is something *immanent* in finite life and thought. It is not something wholly *beyond* or *different* from us; rather, it is something *larger* or *wider* than us. The difficulty we experience in coming to know it is not that of one thing trying to apprehend another quite separate thing, but that of a part trying to grasp the greater whole to which it belongs. The eternal consciousness is less like something too far away for us to see than like something too large for us to see properly. The significant point here is that it is the eternal consciousness which makes us; we are its manifestations, and only in virtue of its action are we are self-conscious. To that extent we *are* acquainted with it, for we are acquainted with ourselves. But the acquaintance is only as *we* know it, with all the limitations of a partial view, not as *it* knows *itself*, in the complete totality of its being. This gives us a grasp of ultimate reality, but a limited one only. It makes talk about the eternal consciousness possible, but only of the thinnest and most metaphorical kind. If, in speaking about the eternal consciousness, Green says, we employ language which calls upon those categories and relations which exist only because of the eternal consciousness, 'it must only be on a clear understanding of its metaphorical character'.[10] Metaphor may point to what in literal terms could never be expressed. In this way it is seen that Green's (admittedly frustrating) mode of presentation, far from hindering understanding, is in truth the only one that makes it at all possible.

.

II

The first of the two principal things which Green does tell us about his great unifying principle is, of course, that it is eternal. But in what sense did Green think the eternal consciousness was eternal? The great stress which he

---

[8] Luding Wittgenstein, *Tractatus Logico-Philosophicus* (London: Routledge & Kegan Paul, 1974), Preface.

[9] F. H. Bradley, *Appearance and Reality: An Essay in Metaphysics* (Oxford: Clarendon Press, 1893), ch. 15.

[10] Green, *PE* §54.

places on the unalterability of the relations which it grounds and which make up the real world might seem to suggest that its eternity is more properly a matter of permanence than atemporal existence.[11] However, it is clear enough from the texts that what Green meant was complete timelessness. Indeed, no other interpretation can make sense of his key argument that a sequence of conscious events can never deliver consciousness of a sequence of events, for in effect what this amounts to is the claim that atomistic experience of succession is impossible. To experience the passing of time, the successive states need to be brought together in one consciousness; past, present, and future held together in one experience itself falling outside of them altogether.[12]

The eternity of Green's unifying principle is one of the greatest obstacles to a coherent understanding of it. The problem has two sides. First of all, the very notion of timeless existence is hard to grasp for beings that are through and through temporal. If all of our experience is in time, the same would seem to be true for all of the things which we experience, which can make us doubt if it is ever legitimate to bracket this condition as something inessential to existence itself. But perhaps the notion of timeless existence finds some small purchase when we think about abstract principles or mathematical objects, which seem not to exist in time.

The second aspect of the problem centres on the difficulty of relating any such timeless being to the temporal world which we know. It is one thing to posit a timeless God, ontologically separate from the temporal world, but quite another to conceive of such a God manifesting or revealing itself in that world. This second aspect of the problem becomes particularly acute with Green, for he understands the eternal consciousness as pre-eminently something which expresses itself over time through the life of the individual and the community. It is the 'essential influence' explaining, and the 'operative'

---

[11] E. B. McGilvarey, 'The Eternal Consciousness', Mind, n.s. 10 (1901), 481, 489–92. Sidgwick more modestly claims that Green equivocates between the two senses (Lectures on Philosophy of Kant (London: Macmillan & Co., 1905), 261). The notion of 'unalterability' is another of Green's metaphorical terms, for clearly I can alter many of the relations of reality (A. Quinton, 'T. H. Green's "Metaphysics of Knowledge"', in W. J. Mander (ed.), Anglo-American Idealism 1865–1927 (Westport, Conn., and London: Greenwood Press, 2000), 30).

[12] '[A] consciousness of events as a related series ... cannot properly be said to be developed out of a mere series of related events, of successive modifications of body and soul ... No one and no number of a series of related events can be the consciousness of the series as related' (PE §16). Further evidence that Green means timelessness, not permanence: 'There could be no such thing as time if there were not a self-consciousness which is not in time' (PE §52); 'Within the consciousness that they are related in the way of before and after there is no before and after' (PE §55). Reality as we experience it is even described as having a 'false appearance' in time, implying, of course, that true reality is timeless ('Fragment on Immortality', CW iii. 159).

force behind, a real history of human moral progress.[13] Yet how can that which is eternal and changeless manifest itself in that which is essentially temporal and progressive? It is worth remembering that this basic problem of reconciling eternity and change is not unique to Green, but is found in all classical religious conceptions—how can a timeless God know of, or act in, an essentially temporal world?

At least one critic has found this an insoluble tension in Green's metaphysics, calling for fundamental revision of his conception of the eternal consciousness.[14] But this response is extreme, for it may also be argued that there is a path through this most difficult of puzzles. Part of the way forward is to realize that we have here not one, but three different problems.

1. First of all, we can ask how, if reality is timeless, it can express itself in time? Would it not thereby automatically cease to be timeless? The key to solving this part of the mystery is to distinguish between *being temporal* or *having a temporal character* and *being in time* or *taking time*. Something may easily *contain* time or *express itself through* time without itself actually *enduring through* time. For example, if we take the *whole* history of the universe, then it is not itself *in* time, in the same way that *space itself*, as a whole, is not anywhere *in* space. And we can find other parallels. There are, for example, certain states or conditions which hold changelessly through time but can only be expressed through changing events. Laws of nature explain and exist through the events that obey them, but the laws of nature do not themselves take place. The case is similar with certain emotional and cognitive states. You cannot love someone without doing things for them, or believe something without it impacting on at least some of your actions, but the love or belief itself does not take time; it is simply expressed through or 'strung out over' a series of such temporal acts.

2. The second aspect of the problem is harder. In calling reality timeless, we seem to regard it as something complete or finished. Though perhaps 'strung out' across time in the manner just explained, from the timeless point of view it seems to be something whole and concluded, something which can be grasped fully in one eternal moment. Yet this character of its being seems to place it deeply at odds with the nature of time. For the very essence of time, like space, seems to be its incompleteness, its never-ending-ness, its perpetual ongoing-ness. To be temporal is to be unfinished. It is to be a 'work in progress'. Thus understood, these two ways of viewing reality seem so opposed that it is hard to grasp how they could ever come together.

---

[13] *PE* §173.   [14] See Leslie Armour, Ch. 7 in this volume.

Green himself is very sensitive to this dichotomy. Though it is 'an eternally complete consciousness', he is clear that his principle's expression in time is 'at once progressive and incapable of completion'.[15] To help elucidate this difficult relationship between the already complete and the 'work in progress', he offers us the example of reading a sentence; although we are conscious all the time that it has a meaning as a whole, only gradually or sequentially do we come to know what that meaning is. The two experiences coexist.[16] But despite Green's illustration, the tension remains throughout the *Prolegomena*. It is clearly visible, for example, among the three principal metaphors which he uses to characterize the relationship between the eternal consciousness and the individual: reproduction, participation, and realization.[17] If 'realization' makes the eternal consciousness look future, something being gradually created,

---

[15] 'an eternally complete consciousness' (*PE* §67); 'at once progressive and incapable of completion' (*PE* §72).

[16] 'In reading [a] sentence we see the words successively, we attend to them successively, we recall their meaning successively. But throughout the succession there must be present continuously the consciousness that the sentence has a meaning as a whole; otherwise the successive vision, attention and recollection would not end in a comprehension of what the meaning is' (*PE* §71). It must be confessed that Green's choice of metaphor here is not entirely a happy one, in so far as realizing that some sentence *has* a meaning and knowing what that meaning *is* are really two completely different states—you could know the first but have no idea about the second—not temporally different manifestations of the same state.

[17] *Reproduction*: 'realises or *reproduces*' (*PE* §68) 'the system of related facts, which forms the objective world, *reproduces* itself, partially and gradually, in the soul of the individual who in part knows it' (§71); 'the attainment of [the] knowledge is only explicable as a *reproduction* of itself, in the human soul, by the consciousness for which the cosmos of related facts exists—a *reproduction* of itself, in which it uses the sentient life of the soul as its organ' (§71); 'the eternal consciousness *reproduces* itself in our knowledge' (§72); the man or human self is 'a certain *reproduction* of itself on the part of the eternal self-conscious subject of the world' (§99).

It is in this context of reproduction, perhaps, that we ought to consider Green's even more obscure metaphor of a 'vehicle'—as it learns, an 'animal organism ... gradually becomes the *vehicle* of an eternally complete consciousness' (§67)—with its suggestion of distinction between the vehicle and what it conveys.

Participation: 'That there is one spiritual self-conscious being, of which all that is real is the *activity* or *expression*; that we are related to this spiritual being, not merely as parts of the world which is its *expression*, but as *partakers* in some inchoate measure of the self-consciousness through which it at once constitutes and distinguishes itself from the world; that this *participation* is the source of morality and religion; this we take to be the vital truth which Hegel had to teach' ('Review of J. Caird, *Introduction to Philosophy of Religion*', *CW* iii. 146). 'When the mind has come to see in the endless flux of outward things, not a succession of isolated phenomena, but the reflex of its own development ... then man has made nature his own, by becoming a conscious *partaker* of the reason which animates him and it' ('Value and Influence of Works of Fiction', *CW* iii. 22). There is more to, say, a flower than the relations I perceive, but this 'more' 'still lies in relations which can only exist for a conceiving mind, and which my mind is in a process of *appropriating*' (*Lectures on Logic*, §29, *CW* ii. 190). Another anomalous metaphor to note here is that we '*co-operate*' with the eternal consciousness in making the world (*PE* §10).

Realization: The animal organism is 'medium' for the '*realisation* of an eternal consciousness'; the eternal consciousness is '*realised* in or communicated to us through modifications of the animal organism' (*PE* §67). We can only understand consciousness by 'conceiving both the end, in the shape

the other two metaphors—'reproduction' and 'participation'—make it look actual, something already achieved.

One possible resolution of this uncomfortable combination which at least one commentator has tried to develop utilizes the notion of 'potential'. Green talks much about the eternal consciousness realizing itself in us, and Tyler has drawn on these statements to argue that the eternal consciousness exists within us simply as a *potential*, specifically a cognitive potential. It is 'the potential which is progressively actualised by the act of experiencing'.[18] Since I never realize my full knowing potential, we can say with Green that the eternal consciousness only ever *partially* reproduces itself in me; but since it is also true that I have an actual nature which has an actual potential, there is simultaneously a sense in which we can affirm that reality resides already complete within the eternal consciousness. For my potential is something I already have.

Though a possible reading, this interpretation has little to recommend it. Its construal of Green's numerous statements of the already completed nature of divine knowledge is hardly a natural one.[19] Nor does it sit well with the explanatory role which Green wishes to give to the eternal conscious. For in the manner of Hegel, he uses it to explain the path of history, and especially the growth of ideas, both cultural and individual, whose gradual revelation it is. But the eternal consciousness can only bear this explanatory burden if it is taken as something actual; a mere potential cannot cause or explain anything. Nor, finally, has it much to recommend it *philosophically*. We need to be able to distinguish between those things which *do* exist and might be experienced (like distant planets) and those which do not actually exist but might be experienced *if* they did (like unicorns); between saying there *is* more to the world than just our experience of it and saying there *could be* more to it than just our experience of it. In other words, the potential we seek is not just *logical* possibility—what we *might* come to know—for such possibilities are limitless and can even contradict one another; it is, rather, *counterfactual* possibility—what we *would* come to know in certain specific circumstances. The only way to make this distinction is on the basis of some actual grounding. Our capacity for growth is not some bare potential, but one grounded in some underlying reality of the human

of a completed knowledge that gradually *realises* itself in the organic process of sentient life, and that organic process itself with its history and conditions' (PE §68). '*Realises* or reproduces' (PE §68); 'the unification of the manifold of sense in our consciousness of a world implies a certain self-realization of this mind in us' (PE §82) (All italics mine.)

18 Tyler, *Thomas Hill Green and the Philosophical Foundations of Politics*, 33.

19 It is for this reason that Sidgwick, one of Green's contemporaries, who also notes the possibility of taking a 'potentialist' reading of Green, dismisses it as not capturing his true intentions here (Sidgwick, *Lectures on Philosophy of Kant*, 245 n. 1, 259).

mind. That Green would have endorsed this line of reasoning, we can be fairly confident because elsewhere we find rejected in essentially the same way a similar analysis of body as consisting simply of possible sense experiences. He argues there that the possibility needed is not mere 'chance' but 'determinate possibility', which requires an eternal law or principle already present, 'something which exists when the feelings are not being felt as much as when they are'.[20]

How, then, are we to reconcile the completeness of the eternal consciousness with the endlessness of human advance in time? Green's response to this problem is essentially Kantian in spirit. Like Kant, who insisted that the antinomies tell us nothing about reality in itself, Green insists that time is a form that *we* bring to experience, and its essential unendingness is a function of the structure which we have added, not of anything that we may be attempting to express through it. That the infinite openness of time is mere additivity and quite different from the completed infinity we wish to ascribe to God is a point Green makes quite clear in his criticism of Locke's attempt to move from the former to the latter idea.[21] At its root the contrast is, of course, that between a mathematical and a metaphysical conception of the infinite.

At this juncture it is worth observing that Green's position on this specific issue is little different from the traditional conception of God's omniscience. God knows everything, but he does so in a single, direct, and all-encompassing intuition. Were we to try to express this knowledge, however, we should have no choice but to begin to enumerate it proposition by proposition, setting out on a literally endless process. The difference is ultimately one of viewpoints. Now, it is just such a perspectival difference that Green himself appeals to in attempting to explain how an unending world may yet be complete. 'There can never be that actual wholeness of the world for us, which there must be for the mind which renders the world one,' he says.[22] These two modes of being are not opposed; rather, endless progression is the way in which a completed infinity appears to finite creatures. For finite creatures, the metaphysically infinite can only ever be expressed as the mathematically infinite.

3. The third aspect of the problem about eternity and time is close to the second, but not quite the same. It consists in the following worry. Does not the 'complete' or 'finished' nature of reality somehow rule out any genuine novelty, creation, or freedom? For part of what we understand in thinking of ourselves as existing in time is conceiving ourselves as having an open future. What we are and have been is fixed, but what we are yet to be is still undecided.

---

[20] Green, 'Lectures on the Philosophy of Kant', §20; *CW* ii. 27.
[21] Green, 'General Introduction to Collected Works of Hume', §§ 140–2; *CW* i. 119–22.
[22] Green, *PE* §72.

Yet, if one is simply unpacking what is 'there already'—even if that process were endless—everything seems 'already settled'. If the Absolute is complete, it cannot at the same time be open-futured. There seems no room for any freedom or creativity. This argument is as straightforward as it is hard to resist.

However, to see this as a problem for Green betrays a misunderstanding of his conception of freedom. Green's reason for writing Book I of the *Prolegomena*, his reason for enquiring if there can be a natural science of man, was to secure a place for human freedom, yet there is nothing in Green's notion of freedom which requires novelty. Freedom consists, not in showing that certain actions are spontaneous or ungenerated, rather than the result of causal law, but in finding a class of actions calling for explanation rationally or teleologically, rather than with reference to prior states, be that their presence or absence.[23] Nothing about teleology requires an open or undetermined future. Indeed, it might even be suggested that the very opposite holds, for how can something be explained by its goal unless that goal is in some sense already real? In this aspect of the problem, some of Green's contemporaries saw more clearly than he himself seems to have done. Edward Caird, for example, certainly thought that although the Absolute undergoes evolution, this process can introduce no genuine novelty into the universe; time does not *add* anything, but only unpacks or unfolds what is there already.[24] While he does not express himself so clearly on this point, Green can and should be read as following the same path.

III

Of course, as well as being eternal, Green holds that his unifying principle is *conscious*. And, since its being comprises the entire world, that claim amounts to a thesis of Idealism. He terms it 'a principle which is not natural', yet—lest this suggest it has being in some fashion co-ordinate and contrasting with what *is* natural—holds it better thought of as 'spiritual' or a 'self-distinguishing consciousness'.[25] Besides these few phrases, we are given little more by way of explanation of its nature as mental, so the best way to fathom his meaning is to examine the argument he develops for this being the case. The basic argument

---

[23] Human activity for Green is free; it is 'activity which is not in time, not a link in the natural chain of becoming, which has no antecedents other than itself but is self-originated' (*PE* §82). But this is not acausal; 'far from free action being *unmotivated*, it is rather determination by motives, properly understood, that constitutes freedom' ('Lectures on the Philosophy of Kant', §83; *CW* ii. 95).

[24] Edward Caird, *The Evolution of Religion*, 2 Vols. (Glasgow: James Maclehose & Sons, 1893), i. 164–5, 182, 201–2.

[25] Green, *PE* §54.

for the eternal consciousness which occurs in Book I of the *Prolegomena* is easy enough. Reality is constituted by relations. The world is a single and eternal system of related elements. But relations are the work of the mind. So, Green infers, reality too must be something essentially mind-dependent. But, he continues, quite clearly none of us individually make the world—there is more to it than just we know—so our knowledge is best taken as but one moment in the wider experience of an all-encompassing eternal consciousness whose experience *does* make up the whole world.

1. This argument has given rise to three main challenges. The first and probably the most common has been to challenge Green's thesis that relations are the work of the mind. Dimova-Cookson, for example, argues that 'Green's mistake was to believe that all sensations come from "outside", all relations from the "inside" '.[26] For Green, sensations are separate, and only thought connects, but why not say instead that relations are simply given in experience like everything else? An atomistic empiricism, such as that of Locke, Berkeley, or Hume, where all we are given is simple sensations, might well render relations the work of the mind, but why accept such an empiricism? Why not attempt a non-atomic empiricism, an empiricism where what are given in experience are relational wholes? Thus it has been objected that all Green has offered us here is an argument against an outdated and defunct psychology of atomic and unrelated sensations, and that were we to adopt some more holistic analysis of experience, then the entire argument would collapse.[27]

It is probably fair to say that Green never fully thought this through, leaving it for his successors to follow up. Pre-eminent among them was F. H. Bradley, whose position demonstrates that, even if we were to adopt such an alternative empiricism, the logical outcome would remain the same; for if we take related wholes rather than disconnected atoms as that which is given to us—this is the import of Bradley's notion of 'immediate experience' or 'feeling'—it will still turn out that relations are the 'work of the mind'. Thought will be required, not to stitch things together, but to pull them apart. For only in thought can we grasp the diversity-in-unity of such given wholes.[28]

---

[26] Maria Dimova-Cookson, *T. H. Green's Moral and Political Philosophy* (Basingstoke: Palgrave, 2001), 30.

[27] A. S. Pringle-Pattison, *The Idea of God in Recent Philosophy* (Oxford: Clarendon Press, 1917; Nov. edn. 1920), 196. In a similar vein, H. V. Knox argues that William James's radical empiricism, in which we enjoy a direct experience of change, constitutes a way of refuting Green's argument for Idealism ('Has Green Answered Locke?', *Mind*, 23 (1914), 334–48).

[28] For a more detailed comparison, see W. J. Mander, 'Bradley and Green on Relations', in W. Sweet (ed.), *Idealism, Metaphysics and Community* (Aldershot: Ashgate, 2001), 55–67.

2. Our troubles do not end here. For even if we concede to Green that relation or synthesis is properly the work of mind, there remain further difficulties
with his conception of relations. A second problem emerges if we ask ourselves
the apparently simple question: what is it that these reality-constituting relations relate? The answer we find in the text is what Green variously calls
feelings, sensations or experiences.[29] But if mind is understood in terms of its
relating or synthesizing activity, this is to bring in something irreducibly *other*
than mind—whatever it is the mental relations bind together—introducing
into the eternal consciousness system a kind of dualism wholly contrary to its
professed idealistic character.[30] On the other hand, rigorously to exclude any
such apparently non-mental element from the scheme as his Idealism appears
to require, would seem to leave him with the absurdity of relations lacking any
terms.[31] Either way, he appears to be in trouble.

Green himself was sensitive to this challenge, and goes to considerable effort
to evade it.[32] The main point of his reply is that, while we may characterize the
difference between relations and the sensations they connect as one between
the 'form' and the 'matter' of our experience, it is vital to recognize that this is
only a *logical* or *conceptual distinction*, one we make in our intellect, but which
does not correspond to any similar division in reality itself. He insists again and
again that there is, ultimately, neither pure feeling nor pure thought. '[I]t is
as impossible to divide knowledge into elements, one contributed by feeling,
the other by thought, as to analyse the life of an animal into so much resulting
from the action of the lungs, so much from the action of the heart.'[33] Their

---

[29] Some illustrative quotations: 'in order that successive *feelings* may be related objects of experience
… there must be in consciousness an agent which distinguishes itself from the feelings, uniting them
in their severality, making them equally present in their succession' (PE 32); 'a sensation apart from
a thought—not determined or acted on by a thought—would be an unrelated sensation; and an
unrelated sensation cannot amount to a fact' (PE 48); 'the terms "real" and "objective" … have no
meaning except for a consciousness which presents its experiences to itself as determined by relations'
(PE 13); 'Without relation any *simple idea* would be indistinguishable from other simple ideas' (PE 20,
Italics added).

[30] It will not do to respond that feelings or sensations are mental too, for Green builds his Idealism on
a distinction between thought and feeling, rather than on one between the mental and the non-mental.
For Green, reality is something thought, not felt, and that is how he distinguishes his own objective
Absolute Idealism from any more subjective Berkeleian Idealism. '[W]e object intuitively to any
idealism which is understood to imply an identification of the realities of the world with the feelings
of men' (PE §37).

[31] For a list of earlier instances of this objection, see Tyler, *Thomas Hill Green and the Philosophical
Foundations of Politics*, 16 n. 12. Curiously enough, Green does refer at one point to his own position as
that of 'the reduction of facts to relations' (PE §37).

[32] Green tackles the point at length in PE §§ 42–51. See also 'Lectures on Logic', §19; CW
ii. 181–2.

[33] Green, 'Lectures on the Philosophy of Kant', §4; CW ii. 6.

only reality is as a pair of reciprocal abstractions which we make from a more primitive whole. They emerge together, and their very meaning comes from opposition to each other. Together, as it were, they make up a picture, but neither is really capable of being considered in its own right for, says Green, 'it must not be supposed that the manifold has a nature of its own apart from the unifying principle, or this principle another nature of its own apart from what it does in relation to the manifold world'.[34] It is his sense that neither is really possible on its own that lies behind Green's opposition to Kant's distinction between intuition and conception, which can easily be read as putting forward two independent sources which together combine to make up experience.

Yet this response is itself deeply puzzling, for it seems to cut right across Green's original argument for Idealism. That argument used the pervasiveness of relations to argue for the ideality of all existence. But, as Hylton has argued, if thought is just one side of a distinction abstracted from experience, it cannot then constitute the whole of experience. For how can one side of a distinction drawn *within* the world then be used to ground the *whole* of that same world?[35]

The solution to this puzzle is to see that, although terms and relations emerge together as a reciprocal pair, they are very far from being elements of the same type or species. Although the distinction between thought and feeling can be made *within* consciousness, it is not a distinction into two *parts*: a thinking part and a non-thinking part. Thought is found at work in all aspects of our experience and does, indeed, the lion's share of the work, such that it is quite wrong to imagine that in experience we are given two sorts of element—nothing would be *given at all* were it not for our thinking. That experience is an encounter with existing reality is a function of the relations under which it is placed, that it is an encounter with qualitative similarity and diversity is similarly a result of relational judgement; even its individuality is added by our thinking. The Kantian model tempts us to think of intuition as providing us with particular objects in their individuality, while conception, by placing them in relations or under categories, gives them to us in their generality, but this temptation is to be resisted for, as Green points out, 'relations constitute individuality'.[36] Without the work of the mind they could not even be distinct individuals. Thus, although not simply equivalent or reducible to thought, it is only as thought that there is any kind of experience at all. Except as thought, there are no feelings. 'Abstract the many relations

---

[34] PE §75.

[35] P. Hylton, *Russell, Idealism, and the Emergence of Analytic Philosophy* (Oxford: Clarendon Press, 1990), 38.

[36] Green, 'Lectures on the Philosophy of Kant', §15; *CW* ii. 22. See also §8, *CW* ii. 12.

from the one thing and you are left with nothing,'[37] says Green. For this reason, suggests Green, instead of Kant's distinction between intuition and conception, 'it is better to substitute one between conception as determinant of particular feelings, and conception of laws and relations, as apart from the feelings which they determine'.[38]

In presenting his criticism, Hylton suggests that Green must be using the word 'thought' ambiguously—both as a partial aspect of experience and as applying to the whole of experience. He even suggests that this was a point that Green himself was prepared to admit, citing the following sentence from one of Green's reviews: 'If thought and reality are to be identified, if the statement that God is thought is to be more than a presumptuous paradox, thought must be other than the discursive activity exhibited in our inferences and analyses, other than a particular mode of consciousness'.[39] Yet Green's admission here is more easily accommodated than Hylton suggests, for instead of a type-contrast between thought as a part of reality and thought as constitutive of reality in its entirety, we can understand this sentence as drawing a degree-contrast between the thought which constitutes our own reality and the thought which constitutes reality as a whole. As our thought grounds our reality, so our thought perfected—that is, thought itself—may be regarded as grounding reality itself. Indeed, this is just how Green expresses himself elsewhere. Our difficulty in seeing how ego and non-ego are both abstractions from thought stems from our confusing thought in itself with the thought experienced by each of us, something 'which is related to thought in its truth as the undeveloped to the full actuality'.[40]

3. The suggestion of a contrast between our reality—the reality we know—and reality itself—reality as a whole—brings to the fore a third serious problem which has often been raised against Green's argument for Idealism. Reality only exists for mind. But it does not simply exist for my mind; things do not simply come into being as and in virtue of my knowing them. They are there already.[41] Hence, concludes Green, there must be a

---

[37] Green, *PE* §28.

[38] Green, 'Lectures on the Philosophy of Kant', §23; *CW* ii. 28.

[39] Green, 'Review of J. Caird, *Introduction to Philosophy of Religion*'; *CW* iii. 142.

[40] Green, 'Mr Spencer on the Independence of Matter', §55; *CW* i. 432.

[41] Reality is there *already*: 'we cannot suppose that those relations of facts or objects in consciousness, which constitute any piece of knowledge of which a man becomes master, first come into being when he attains that knowledge …. They must exist as part of an eternal universe … during all the changes of the individual's attitude towards them' (*PE* §69). '[T]here is a consciousness for which the relations of fact, that form the object of our gradually attained knowledge, already and eternally exist; and that the growing knowledge of the individual is a progress towards this consciousness' (ibid.). 'It is quite true

wider mind in which they exist all the time. Yet this argument simply invites the challenge: how do we know that nature covers more than just what we know? We all assume this, but by what right?

To see this as a problem for Green represents a fundamental misunderstanding of his whole approach. Green was never really troubled by such subjective scepticism; his position was never that of the egocentric enquirer beset by sceptical worries about the world outside. Like Kant, whom he follows, he simply assumes that knowledge is possible, and proceeds to analyse its nature and conditions.[42] But whether or not we think he was justified in this attitude, the point tells us something of immense importance regarding the nature of his overall argument. Perhaps because he termed it the 'metaphysics of knowledge', at least some of Green's contemporaries interpreted his argument as epistemological, and his Idealism as subjective in the manner of Berkeley.[43] Yet this is wholly incorrect. Indeed, at the end of the review which I cited above, he takes issue with precisely such epistemological arguments for Idealism. He criticizes the move from the epistemological anti-realism of reality-is-only-conceivable-by-thought to the ontological Idealism of reality-only-exists-for-thought, arguing instead that in developing the case for Idealism it is better to address the question of reality directly; to examine the very nature of what it is to be real and show that this involves ideas.[44] Such an Idealism we might denote 'conceptual', as opposed to epistemological. What Green is offering us is an analysis of the concept of 'reality', and whatever may be said about our *knowledge* of reality, our *conception* of reality is not the conception of something limited to our awareness of it.

that the relations which form the object-matter of our knowledge do not come into being with the experience which I or anyone happen to have of them, but on the other hand, except as relations of what is relative to consciousness, they are simply nothing; nor, unless we suppose consciousness with its world to come into existence over and over again as this man or that becomes conscious, is there any difficulty in reconciling these two propositions' ('Mr Herbert Spencer and Mr G. H. Lewes', §108; *CW* i. 487).

[42] Green's question is not 'Is knowledge possible?', but 'How is knowledge possible?' For the true task for philosophy 'is simply the consideration of what is implied in the fact of our knowing or coming to know a world, or, conversely, in the fact of their being a world for us to know' ('Mr Herbert Spencer and Mr G. H. Lewes', §2; *CW* i. 374). Again, 'Philosophy does not precede but follows, that actual knowledge of things, which it is its office to analyse and reduce to its primitive elements' ('The Philosophy of Aristotle'; *CW* iii. 48). 'The fact that there is a real external world of which through feeling we have direct experience … is one which no philosophy disputes' ('Mr Herbert Spencer and Mr G. H. Lewes', §4; *CW* i. 376). Instead, Green advocates a philosophy 'which trusts, not to a guess about what is beyond experience, but to analysis of what is within it' ('Mr Herbert Spencer and Mr G. H. Lewes', §73; *CW* i. 449).

[43] This is the charge of Pringle-Pattison in *Idea of God*, 195–9.

[44] Green, 'Review of J. Caird, *Introduction to Philosophy of Religion*'; *CW* iii. 144–5.

IV

If the eternal consciousness is hard to understand in its own right, it becomes even harder when we consider its relation to the finite world at large. As ever, Green offers us a number of different metaphors and phrases. The eternal consciousness 'renders' the relations of the world; nature 'results from' or 'exists through' its action; it 'constitutes' the world; understanding 'makes' nature, which is its 'product'.[45] But even at this level of metaphorical vagueness, a problem emerges. For perhaps the most obvious thing about these expressions is that they are all causal terms. Yet causal talk in this context seems very problematic.

The problem is not hard to see. Indeed, the three general difficulties considered above about language, time, and consciousness each contribute to the obstacle. First, if causation is a relation and, as such, the work of the mind, we cannot speak of it as applying to ultimate reality or between ultimate reality and experience. The restriction is a Kantian one, although we should note that Kant, like Green, had a similarly unfortunate habit of speaking as though noumena somehow caused our experiences. The second problem concerns time. How can the eternal consciousness have a causal role, if causation is temporal, and it, as we have seen, is timeless? In the third place, Green's conception of the self as a Kantian unity of apperception makes it hard to find any distinction in this case between cause and effect. Although in some form it makes sense to distinguish between the agent or unifying principle and the manifold it unifies, from another point of view they are the same—the world has no character but that given to it by the unifying action of the agent, while the agent has no character but that which comes from its unifying action. If causation at all, it is an immanent self-causation, for, as Green puts, 'there is no separate particularity in the agent, on the one side, and the determined world as a whole, on the other', but rather 'an indivisible whole which results from the activity of a single principle'.[46] Yet how can there be causation where there is no difference between cause and effect?

Green is fully aware of these problems. Indeed, he himself gives the example of 'cause' as a term which, strictly speaking, does not apply to ultimate reality but calls instead for metaphorical understanding.[47] What prevents this term from losing all meaning or appropriateness, he suggests, is the understanding we have of our own action in knowing the world. For, just as we make

---

[45] 'renders' (PE §52), 'results from' (PE §63), 'exists through' (PE §46), 'constitutes' (PE §50), understanding 'makes' nature (PE §38), 'product' (PE §29).

[46] PE §§76, 36. This criticism can be found in Sidgwick, *Lectures on the Philosophy of Kant*, 249, 262.

[47] PE §75.

possible our own experience by rationally structuring and conceptualizing it, so the eternal consciousness makes the world by thinking it through an eternal system of relations.[48]

But even this picture is liable to misunderstanding. On hearing that relations are the work of the mind, the picture most naturally conjured up is of three elements: the terms to be related, the relations, and the mind which creates them. However, with respect to Green's thinking, this picture is misleading; for there is no self 'behind' the relations. Green operates with a conception of mind as a 'unifying principle'—indeed, this is a term he very often prefers to use instead.[49] Unification is not simply what consciousness *does*, it is what it *consists in*. Mind is thoroughly immanent in experience; it is not some agent *behind* the experience which *has* it, and in consequence unifies it, but the very unity of the experience itself. This conception of mind or consciousness as merely a 'unifying principle' is a conception adopted by many of the British Idealists, and represents their understanding of what Kant meant by the transcendental unity of apperception.[50]

It might be charged that this is simply to explain the obscure by the even more obscure; but that would be unfair, for, even if not a complete and fully luminous explanation, the comparison is none the less useful. Even if we cannot explain it, the relationship we have to our own thinking is something experienced by all. And it seems hard to deny that we are the authors of our thoughts; they do not simply come to us, rather they are our responsibility. In this sense the relationship is, or is like, causation. Yet our own causality *in thought* seems hardly to be of the same kind as that which we encounter within experience; we are not exactly the *efficient causes* of our thoughts. There is no prior act which we can find on the part of the agent which brings about the thought. Indeed, we do not even seem clearly to be anything separate from our thoughts. Nor is it obvious that we stand temporally to our thoughts as more usual causes stand to their effects. Is a thought caused gradually as it is articulated in the mind, or must it be present in its entirety before we begin to express it? (Could one start a sentence

---

[48] Ibid. §77.

[49] 'unifying principle' (*PE* §§29, 32, 75), 'combining agency' (*PE* §29), 'combining intelligence' (*PE* §29), 'all-uniting consciousness' (*PE* §50).

[50] Green explicitly identifies it with Kant's synthetic unity of apperception (*PE* §33) arguing that its unity is correlative to that of the experience (*PE* §32). Although Kant was rather vague about the metaphysical significance of the 'I' of the transcendental unity of apperception, the British Idealists were far more bold. For them this was the self, and it was real and not just formal. However, there was not complete agreement. Pringle-Pattison, in his *Hegelianism and Personality* (Edinburgh and London: Blackwood, 1887), 23–30, objected to this conception precisely on the grounds of its abstract thinness, a worry echoed by Dewey in 'On Some Current Conceptions of the Term "Self"' *Mind*, 15 (1890), 73–4. But it was Bradley alone who saw that it is also—even just as much—the role of consciousness to divide as it is to unite.

without knowing how it is to finish?) To be sure, Green does not fully explain thought, but he points to a relation as undeniable in experience as it is creative in nature which *is* able to function as an effective metaphor for his meaning.

More understanding of the peculiar relation between eternal consciousness and the real world is had when we see that the former brings about the latter not just as its 'efficient cause' but equally as its 'final cause'. Green calls the eternal consciousness 'an end gradually realising itself', an already complete consciousness 'itself operative in the progress towards its attainment'.[51] In his moral philosophy it becomes the true good, or *summum bonum*, at which moral nature and human history aim. In other words, the world's development is not simply pushed from behind, but somehow drawn on from in front—it has a destiny or vocation to fulfil. The issue is complicated by the fact that due to the 'unending' nature of temporal progress, the goal of the process of development cannot be identified with any actual temporal state, only an eternal ideal. This teleological component in Green (which draws our attention to the fact that he is often as indebted to Aristotle as he is to Kant or Hegel) is as uncomfortable to modern philosophers as it is central to his system, but it is beyond the scope of this essay to offer a general defence of the notion of teleology. It suffices to point out that this is an element not simply in the metaphysics of the eternal consciousness, but in his ethical and political thought as a whole. It therefore cannot support differential attitudes towards these two parts of his philosophy.

V

Some of the greatest obstacles to accepting Green's doctrine of the eternal consciousness centre around its relation to, and significance for, finite life. Green employs a variety of metaphors in his attempts to articulate this relation, but often these unsettle our natural conception of who we are. At times he speaks as though we were *parts* of some wider mind, individual contributions to some greater whole. But can one mind be part of another, without destroying its own identity and autonomy? At other times he suggests that the eternal consciousness *reproduces* itself in us. But this too strikes me as problematic. It seems to imply that there must exist some original source prior to or distinct from any copies which reproduce it—but Green is no Platonist—at the same time as undermining our sense of own identity—our fate is to become mere copies, reproductions of something else.

---

[51] 'an end gradually realising itself' (*PE* §68), 'itself operative in the progress towards its attainment' (*PE* §70).

Less troubling ways can be found in which to read Green. Taking reproduction, for instance, it can be noted that not all copies need originals. One might think of a drama re-played, or re-produced, on many successive occasions. Although we would all admit that there is a play called Hamlet, changeless but susceptible to endless different interpretations, we would not thereby take ourselves to be speaking of some entity or essence which all the performances differently express. As far as existent beings go, there are just the interpretations. On such an understanding of reproduction one might regard the claim that the eternal consciousness reproduces itself in each one of us as committing itself to nothing more than a common human nature within each one of us which grounds our cognitive and moral growth. This is the view of Tyler already considered above,[52] according to which each human being has, or better is, an eternal consciousness which progressively manifests itself through our temporal lives. Talk of reproduction here implies not some ontological over-being of which we are parts, but rather the simple fact that all human minds share the same underlying structure.

Such readings may be possible, but they have little to recommend them. Textually the readings required are somewhat forced.[53] They require also that our attention be somewhat selective, for reproduction is not the only metaphor Green uses, and running throughout his work at the same time, we can also find a somewhat different picture in which, rather than creating copies of itself, the eternal source is understood as entering bodily into the things of this world. Here Green tends to employ an alternative set of metaphors, like participating, partaking, expressing and appropriating. The implications are very different. For whereas reproduction suggests qualitative identity among instances—many copies, all resembling, but distinct both from one another and their source—participation, on the other hand, suggests numerical identity—a one somehow spread out or located in many hosts.

Nor are such 'individualist' readings very satisfying philosophically, for they leave inadequately accounted for the fundamental unity of the world.

---

[52] Tyler, *Thomas Hill Green and the Philosophical Foundations of Politics*, 26–33. Also, 'all human minds are the same in the sense that they share the same underlying structure and self-creating principle, which Green labels "the eternal consciousness"' (p. 83).

[53] Though perhaps possible, Tyler's is hardly a natural reading of the following, for example: '"Objective nature" must indeed be something else than ourselves and our states of consciousness as we are apt to understand these ... but it does not follow that it is other than our states of consciousness in their full reality, i.e. in the fullness of those relations which presuppose relation to an eternal subject. I do not "make nature" in the sense that nature = a succession of states of consciousness, beginning with my birth and ending with my death. If so, the "objectivity" of nature would doubtless disappear; there would be as many "natures" as men' (Green, 'Lectures on the Philosophy of Kant', §26; *CW* ii. 32).

To reduce the fact that we all live in the same world to the fact that our human nature gives us all the same potential for experience is rather too like the quixotic sense in which Berkeley, substituting qualitative for numerical sameness, claims that we all see the same things (a sense he of course in the end withdrew when he introduced the doctrine of divine archetypes) and hardly seems to do justice to Green's more robust talk of 'the consciousness which constitutes reality and makes the world one'.[54]

But is not the alternative conception of the eternal consciousness as a kind of super-organism in which all finite lives somehow participate fatally destructive of finite human individuality and freedom? That it has been felt so can hardly be denied; while Green's work proved the inspiration for a generation of Absolute Idealists after him, it also stirred up a whole movement of Personal Idealists concerned to free Idealism from precisely this threat. (Although, from an interpretive point of view, it is notable that they took themselves to be arguing against Green, not expounding him.) The issues between these two schools are complex,[55] but we should not so swiftly think impossible or absurd any conception of the self as belonging to some larger super-organism. In this connection, what is most important to realize is that it is no part of Green's conception that individuality be submerged or difference eradicated; the unity which all form has is less like a sea in which all drops of water merge together to form one undifferentiated mass, than like an orchestra in which each player contributes their unique sound to the resultant whole. Indeed, Green would go further and claim that it is only as social creatures that we can ever be distinct individuals. 'Without Society, no persons'[56]—our individuality is something we have because, not in spite of, the whole to which we belong.

VI

Metaphysical conviction of any kind is hard to win in this age, and so without further defence and articulation of Green's positive argument it would be presumptuous to conclude that Green's theory of the eternal consciousness has been vindicated, but hopefully it has been demonstrated that, far from something so absurd that it must be simply put aside or at least change its clothes, it is a position able to defend itself against its critics as well as any other.

---

[54] Green, PE §51.

[55] See W. J. Mander, 'Life and Finite Individuality: The Bosanquet/Pringle-Pattison Debate', British Journal for History of Philosophy, 13:1 (2005), 111–30.

[56] Green, PE §190.

PART III
Political Philosophy

9

The Rights Recognition Thesis: Defending and Extending Green

GERALD F. GAUS

I. Introduction

In his *Lectures on the Principles of Political Obligation*, T. H. Green characterizes a right as 'a power claimed and recognized as contributory to a common good' (*LPPO* §99). Scholars such as Rex Martin have noted that Green's characterization of a right has multiple elements: it includes social recognition and the common good,[1] as well as the idea of a power. More formally, it seems that Green wants to say that R is a right if and only if R is (i) a power that is (ii) recognized by some others or by society as (iii) contributing to a common good. Much of the scholarship on Green has been devoted to explicating and defending this third feature, which grounds rights on Green's core idea of a common good.[2] In this chapter I shall stress claim (ii) — the recognition thesis — though we shall see that pursuing claim (ii) will enlighten us as to why Green links the recognition thesis to the common good claim, (iii). And claim (i), I shall argue, reinforces the plausibility of the recognition thesis. So

Versions of this chapter were delivered to the 2002 meeting of the Political Studies Association, Aberdeen, Scotland, and to the conference on T. H. Green and Contemporary Philosophy, Oxford, 2002. My thanks to all the participants; special thanks to David Brink, Rex Martin, Stamatoula Panagakou, Colin Tyler, and Andrew Vincent for their comments, objections, and suggestions. This is a greatly revised and expanded version of my paper 'Green's Rights Recognition Thesis and Moral Internalism', *British Journal of Politics and International Relations*, 7 (2005), 5–17.

[1] Rex Martin, 'T. H. Green on Individual Rights and the Common Good', in Avital Simhony and David Weinstein (eds.), *The New Liberalism: Reconciling Liberty and Community* (Cambridge: Cambridge University Press, 2001), 49–50. See also Maria Dimova-Cookson, *T. H. Green's Moral and Political Philosophy* (Basingstoke: Palgrave, 2001), ch. 5.

[2] And critics have attacked it. For a defence, see Martin, 'T. H. Green on Individual Rights and the Common Good'. For a criticism of the general form of the argument, see Loren E. Lomasky, *Persons, Rights and the Moral Community* (New York: Oxford University Press, 1987), 60.

all three of Green's elements work together to form a coherent conception of rights.

I first turn to the rights recognition thesis, claim (ii). Section II analyses the rights recognition claim and, more generally, the concept of a claim right. Section III introduces the idea of moral internalism, and sketches some general considerations in its favour. Section IV shows that Green advocates moral internalism, and that a version of the rights recognition thesis follows from it. Section V analyses the relation of rights to the common good, i.e. claim (iii) above. I shall argue that for Green grounding rights in the common good is not simply a normative claim, but a conceptual feature of rights, one that again relates to his moral internalism and theory of moral motivation. Section VI turns from ethical to political philosophy. I shall argue that, although an analysis of Green's moral internalism provides the basis for an interesting rights recognition thesis, it does not quite justify Green's strong requirement that actual social recognition is necessary for a right to be properly ascribed to a person. Section VII argues that this stronger recognition requirement can be grounded on Green's idea of a right as a recognized *power*, claim (i). Here is where my defence of the rights recognition thesis goes beyond Green: I argue that if Green had grasped better the concept of a power, he would have been led to an even stronger defence of the rights recognition thesis. In light of these discussions, section VIII reconsiders W. D. Ross's famous objection that Green's theory cannot recognize the rights of slaves.

II. The Correlativity of Rights and Duties

(a) Two Notions of Rights and Recognition: Creating versus Acknowledging a Moral Status

Green's recognition claim, then, is that 'rights are made by recognition. There is no right but thinking makes it so' (*LPPO* §136). My concern in this essay is the claim that recognition of R as a right is a *necessary condition* for R being a right. Although Green says that 'rights are made by recognition', he obviously cannot be interpreted as claiming that recognition is sufficient, as he provides two other necessary conditions: that R is a power, and that it contributes to the common good. So Green's distinctive recognition claim is that a necessary condition for Alf having right R is that R is in some way recognized as Alf's right. Green often stresses that for one to be a right-holder, he must be seen by others as an equal; rights 'depend for their existence ... on ... a society of men who recognise each other as *isoi kai homoioi* [equals]' (*LPPO* §116). To be a right-holder is to be recognized as such by another. This recognition thesis, as I call it, has not only been controversial, it has been largely dismissed.[3] The first reaction of most readers is to dismiss it as outrageous. W. D. Ross expresses a typical response:

> Now it is plainly wrong to describe either legal or moral rights as depending for their existence on recognition, for to recognize a thing (in the sense in which 'recognize' is used here) is to recognize it as existing already. The promulgation of a law is not the recognition of a legal right, but the creation of it, though it may imply the recognition of an already existing moral right. And to make the existence of a *moral* right depend on its being recognized is equally mistaken. It would imply that slaves, for instance, acquired the moral right to be free only at the moment when a majority of mankind, or of some particular community, formed the opinion that they ought to be free, i.e., when the particular person whose conversion to such a view changed a minority into a majority changed his mind. Such a view, of course, cannot consistently be maintained.[4]

As Ross indicates, for a person to recognize something (say, the house in which he was born) implies that the thing already exists, and that *then* the person recognizes it for what it is. Thus for Ross and most rights theorists, it makes perfect sense to say that an entire society is failing to recognize a person's moral[5] rights: the rights are there, but people do not recognize them, as they might fail to recognize true genius. Green's model of recognition, however, seems more akin to a chair at a meeting who, *in recognizing* a speaker *creates a status*; to recognize that someone has the floor just *is* to give him the floor. So it looks as if we have two models of recognition available to us: acknowledging a status and creating a status. So Green cannot be charged with a simple confusion about the way in which the idea of recognition works; it works in two ways. The question, though, remains why we should adopt the status creation rather than the status acknowledgement model of recognition, especially given its apparently counter-intuitive consequences. Let us first explore the case for Green's recognition thesis, and then, at the end, return to Ross's complaint.

(b) The Correlativity of Rights and Duties

It is often maintained—and, I will argue, ultimately correctly—that Green's recognition thesis is bound up with his doctrine of the correlativity of rights

---

[3] See Peter P. Nicholson, *The Political Philosophy of the British Idealists* (Cambridge: Cambridge University Press, 1990), 83 ff. For relatively rare, sympathetic treatments, see Rex Martin, *A System of Rights* (Oxford: Clarendon Press, 1993); Derrick Darby, 'Two Conceptions of Rights Possession', *Social Theory and Practice*, 27 (July 2001), 387–417.

[4] W. D. Ross, *The Right and the Good* (Oxford: Clarendon Press, 1930), 51.

[5] My concern in this chapter is moral, not legal, rights.

and duties. Green, though, offers not simply one, but at least two core claims maintaining the correlativity of rights and duties.

The first, and Green's most distinctive, correlativity claim maintains:

C1:   Alf's claim to possess a right against Betty implies Alf's recognition of Betty's right against Alf.

Green endorses (C1): 'on the part of every person ("*person*" in the moral sense ...) the claim, more or less articulate and reflected on, to rights on his own part is co-ordinate with his recognition of rights on the part of others' (*LPPO* §26). This may seem bound up with the rights recognition thesis (*LPPO* §§25–6).[6] If my claim of a right against you presupposes that I recognize that you have rights against me, it seems that the practice of rights implies that I must see you as a moral agent who also has claims against me. And this, in turn, seems to lead to Green's notion that rights depend on a society whose members recognize each other as moral agents (*LPPO* §138). Clearly, though, no such conclusion follows. Even granted that my *claiming* a right against you implies a recognition, 'more or less articulate and reflected on', that you have rights against me, nothing follows about mutual recognition as necessary for the right's *existence*. That the practice of *claiming my rights* presupposes recognition of the rights of others does not imply that my actually *having rights* presupposes this. I may be ignorant of my status as a rights-holder, and so I do not claim any rights, and so might not recognize others as rights-holders, but this by no means precludes me having rights. We are back to Ross's original point: what is possessed and what is recognized as being possessed are not equivalent.

Green, however, advances a more general sort of correlativity claim that most commentators do not distinguish from (C1):

C2:   The concept of a right implies the concept of a duty.

Green is clear that moral duties are 'correlative to rights' (*LPPO* §17). Given this, Green criticizes Spinoza and Hobbes for thinking that there can be rights in a condition in which there are no moral duties: 'The cardinal error of Spinoza's *Politics* is the admission of the possibility of a right in the individual apart from life in society, apart from the recognition by members of a society of a correlative claim upon and duty to each other' (*LPPO* §38). Green makes a similar criticism of Rousseau:

Rousseau, it will be remembered, speaks of the 'social pact' not merely as the foundation of sovereignty or civil government, but as the foundation of morality. Through it man becomes a moral agent; for slavery and appetite he substitutes freedom of subjection to

---

[6]   See Timothy Hinton, 'The Perfectionist Liberalism of T. H. Green', *Social Theory and Practice*, 27 (July 2001), 473–99, at 489.

self-imposed law. If he had seen at the same time *that rights do not begin till duties begin*, and that if there were no morality prior to the pact there could not be rights, he might have been saved the error which the notion of there being natural rights introduces into his theory. (*LPPO* §116)[7]

How are we to explicate Green's idea that 'rights do not begin till duties begin'? Ross's discussion of the correlativity of rights and duties, which explicitly has Green's theory in mind, is helpful. Ross distinguishes four correlativity claims:[8]

C3:   Alf's right against Betty implies a duty of Betty to Alf.
C4:   Betty's duty to Alf implies a right of Alf against Betty.
C5:   Alf's right against Betty implies a duty of Alf to Betty.
C6:   Alf's duty to Betty implies a right of Alf against Betty.

The first pair ((C3), (C4)) and the second pair ((C5), (C6)) are different types of correlativity claims. The latter pair look more like substantive moral principles according to which a person who has rights against others also has duties to them (C5), and a person who has duties to others also has rights against them (C6). Ross suggests that Green's main criticism of natural rights theory is that it ignores (C5);[9] given Green's insistence that a regime of rights presupposes conditions of mutual recognition of moral personality, it seems certain that Green accepts (C5), and, it would seem, also (C6).

While (C5) and (C6) are substantive moral theses, (C3) seems more like a formal claim about the logic of rights. Ross tells us that (C3) is 'unquestionably true'.[10] Ross also accepts (C4), as long as we restrict ourselves to moral agents (and so, for example, leave aside duties to animals). Together, (C3) and (C4) assert that rights are what Wesley Hohfeld called 'claim rights'. According to (C3)—which I shall call the *basic correlativity claim*—Alf has a *(claim) right R to X* against Betty only if Betty has a correlative duty *D* that requires her to perform some action *Y* (which might be, for example, non-interference with Alf's *X*-ing or providing him *X*).[11] If one also accepts that (C4)[12] entails that if I have a duty to you, then you have a (claim) right against me, then Alf has a right *R* if and only Betty has a correlative duty *D*.

[7] Emphasis added.   [8] Ross, *The Right and the Good*, 48.   [9] Ibid. 52–4.
[10] Ibid. 48.
[11] For Hohfeld's classic analysis, see his 'Some Fundamental Legal Conceptions as Applied in Judicial Reasoning', *Yale Law Review*, 23 (1913), 16–59. I am drawing here on L.W. Sumner, *The Moral Foundations of Rights* (Oxford: Oxford University Press, 1987), 27. For helpful explications of Hohfeld's analysis, see R. E. Robinson, S. C. Coval, and J. C. Smith, 'The Logic of Rights', *University of Toronto Law Review*, 33 (1983), 267–78; Michael Freeden, *Rights* (Minneapolis: University of Minnesota Press, 1991).
[12] Section VIII presents doubts that we should.

Ross and Green both accept the basic correlativity claim (C3), as do most contemporary rights theorists. It would thus appear that this basic correlativity claim cannot be at the heart of their dispute about the recognition thesis. However, I shall argue that, despite appearances, it is indeed fundamental to their disagreement. Claim (C3), when conjoined with certain views of moral judgement and moral motivation, generates Green's advocacy of the rights recognition thesis. (C3) and (C4), conjoined with certain other views about moral judgement and motivation, entail Ross's rejection of the recognition thesis. In what follows, Green's more distinctive correlativity claims ((C1), (C5), (C6)) play no role. This is not to deny either that they were important to Green, or that they support the rights recognition thesis (see e.g. *LPPO* §208). However, they are far more controversial than (C3) (the basic correlativity claim), which, it will be recalled, Ross called 'unquestionably true'. If it can be shown that the rights recognition thesis can be built on something as uncontroversial as the basic correlativity claim, we will have advanced a strong case for it.

III. Moral Internalism and Externalism

(a) Ross's Externalism

Given (C3) and (C4), and given his realist account of moral duties, we can see why Ross must reject Green's rights recognition thesis. For Ross a duty is 'an objective fact'[13] that is not observer-dependent—that is, the fact that 'D is a duty' does not depend on anyone's observing that D is a duty, or concluding that D is a duty. So, since moral duties are observer-independent facts in this way, and given (C4), it follows that rights are observer-independent facts.[14] Furthermore, on Ross's view, the fact that D is a duty does not depend on anyone's being motivated to act on D. Our objective duty is independent of actual desires or subjective understandings of our duty.[15] Ross thus advocates *an externalist* view of the relation of moral obligation (duty) and motivation. To be more precise, let us say:

Ross's externalism: That (i) 'D is Alf's moral duty' does not imply either that (ii) Alf understands (acknowledges, etc.) that D is his duty or (iii) that Alf is disposed to act on D.[16]

---

[13] Ross, *The Right and the Good*, 20.

[14] Recall that Ross accepts (C4), so long as we restrict consideration to the class of moral persons.

[15] See W. D. Ross, *The Foundations of Ethics* (Oxford: Clarendon Press, 1939), chs. 8 and 9.

[16] The classic paper on this issue is William K. Frankena, 'Obligation and Motivation in Recent Moral Philosophy', in K. E. Goodpaster (ed.), *Perspectives on Morality: Essays by William K. Frankena*

Ross's externalism, then, grounds his view that a person's rights are not conceptually dependent on what other people understand his rights to be, or what claims they are motivated to fulfil.

(b) Worries about Externalisms

Although externalist accounts of moral motivation certainly have supporters,[17] Ross's externalism denies what Michael Smith has called a 'platitude' about morality: that morality is part of practical reason in at least the weak sense that an ideally rational agent, who was aware of all the reasons for action that there are, would necessarily have motivating reasons to act on his moral obligations.[18] To better understand the problems with Ross's externalism, let us focus on a simpler form of externalism that denies this platitude:

Motivational externalism: That (i) Alf is a perfectly rational agent and (ii) Alf acknowledges that '*D* is my moral duty' do not together imply (iii) Alf is disposed to act on *D*.

Motivational externalism differs from Ross's externalism. As I have depicted it, Ross's externalism asserts that the existence of an obligation is external to *both* the recognition of the obligation by an agent and his motivation to act on the obligation. Motivational externalism is not committed to any view about the relation between the existence of an obligation and acknowledgement of it by a perfectly rational agent;[19] what it does say is that even if a fully rational agent acknowledges the duty, there is no necessary, internal tie, between this acknowledgement and motivation to act on the duty. So a motivational externalist would assert that the correct moral judgements of fully rational agents are independent of motivating reasons to do anything about them.

Motivational externalism understands moral judgements as purely theoretical claims about what one should do, rather than as inherently practical. That is, just as one might accept a theoretical claim in science but not be moved to do anything on the basis of it, so one can accept a moral judgement but not be moved to do anything about it. One might have a comprehensive catalogue of

(Notre Dame, Ind.: University of Notre Dame Press, 1976), 49–73. For a more sophisticated analysis, which makes some of the distinctions I shall use here, see Stephen Darwall's nice overview, 'Reasons, Motives, and the Demands of Morality: An Introduction', in Stephen Darwall, Allen Gibbard, and Peter Railton (eds.), *Moral Discourse and Practice* (Oxford: Oxford University Press, 1997), 305–12.

[17] J. S. Mill was an externalist. See his *Utilitarianism* (Indianapolis: Bobbs-Merrill, 1957), ch. 3. For a criticism of Mill's externalism, see Christine Korsgaard, *The Sources of Normativity* (Cambridge: Cambridge University Press, 1996), 78 ff.

[18] Michael Smith, *The Moral Problem* (Oxford: Blackwell, 1994), 7 ff.

[19] Thus one motivational externalist might hold that it is a necessary truth that a fully rational agent would acknowledge all her moral duties, while another might hold that, say, even fully rational Athenians could not have grasped all their moral duties, given the limits of their intellectual horizon. Much depends here on what one packs into 'fully rational', an issue I avoid here.

correct moral judgements and be fully rational, and yet not be disposed to act on any of these duties. Now this seems to miss the real practical crux of the moral 'ought': to truly accept that one morally ought to do something is to be moved to do it. Moral discourse has an ineliminable practical side: when someone seeks to show you that the poor in Africa have a right to assistance, she is not simply trying to get you to believe 'The poor in Africa have a right to assistance': she is trying to get you to act—to assist them—*because* you recognize their right. Getting you to recognize the right is itself a motivational lever in getting you to act. To a motivational externalist, however, that Betty shows a fully rational Alf that he has a moral duty to help her, that he accepts this, and that he is a rational agent, need not have the practical effect of even disposing Alf to help her. In addition, external inducements, some extra desire to be a moral person, and/or persuasion are necessary to actually move Alf to help.

This is a serious drawback to motivational externalism: it denies any necessary internal tie between awareness that one has a moral duty and doing anything about it. To the motivational externalist the recognition of the moral 'ought' can be motivationally inert even in a fully rational agent, because the 'ought'—the call of duty—remains external to the agent's motivational set. Knowing what is right has no inherent link to doing what is right. To many, perhaps especially in the British tradition of moral philosophy, an adequate account of morality must show how recognition of an 'ought' moves one to do something about it.[20] Those who endorse this link between recognition that one ought to do something (duty requires it) and actually doing one's duty thus advocate at least:

Motivational internalism: If (i) Alf is a perfectly rational agent and (ii) Alf acknowledges that 'D is my moral duty', then (iii) Alf is motivated to act on D.

Alf may have conflicting motivations; at least for present purposes, let us allow that Alf might be perfectly rational, sees that D is his duty, but also sees that acting in accord with D will be very costly to his values or interests, so he is not ultimately moved to so act. The important point of motivational internalism is that the recognition of moral obligation in a rational agent is itself a motivating influence, even if not the most powerful influence.

Unless we are prepared to deny the practical nature of morality, we must at least embrace motivational internalism. However, the following hybrid view is possible:

The hybrid view (existence externalism/motivational internalism): That (i) 'D is Alf's moral duty' does not imply that (ii) a fully rational Alf understands

---

[20] See Stephen Darwall, *The British Moralists and the Internal 'Ought': 1640–1740* (Cambridge: Cambridge University Press, 1995).

(acknowledges, etc) that D is his duty (existence externalism); but (iii) if Alf does come to believe 'D is my duty', a rational Alf is disposed to act in accordance with D (motivational internalism).

On the hybrid view, acknowledging a moral duty does have the practical effect of disposing to action, but whether one has a moral duty is an entirely external—let us say, an 'objective'—matter. The hybrid view is certainly more attractive than motivational externalism, since it preserves the practical core of morality. The worry, though, is that we are confronted with a mystery: although that D is one's moral duty is an entirely external fact, someone who forms a true belief about this fact also develops a motivation to act.[21] What is it about knowledge of *this* sort of fact that coming to believe it moves one to act, while coming to believe other sorts of facts does not have that effect? One can see why internalists are apt to see these external moral facts as 'queer' entities, for knowledge of them affects us in ways quite unlike other types of knowledge.[22] In contrast, what we might call existence internalism does not have any difficulty explaining why recognition of moral 'oughts' motivate: moral oughts, says such an internalist, move people to action because moral convictions are expressions of one's desires, will, or self-understanding, not simply attempts to track an external truth. Some internalists such as Hobbes held that moral convictions stem from the self because they are ways to achieve the ends of the self; others, closer to Kant (and Green), hold that moral oughts are matters of self-legislation and express the demands that the rational will imposes on itself.[23] In any event, the crux of all existence internalist accounts is that moral oughts arise from within the agent, and this explains why they have the power to determine action.

The question is: From where does power of an 'ought' to move us come? The hybrid view seems to say that although oughts are external facts, they are external facts that have a power over us: to believe them is to be induced to act. Existence internalists insist that this is no answer at all: it just asserts that some external facts are motivating without explaining how they are. In contrast, the existence internalist gives us a clear explanation of the power of moral judgements over us: a genuine moral requirement must express our (rational) will or desires. This line of thinking thus leads to:

Strong (recognition & motivational) internalism: That (i) 'D is Alf's moral duty' implies (ii) that under conditions C (iii) Alf recognizes D as his duty and (iv) Alf is motivated to act in accord with D.

---

[21] Ibid. 11.

[22] See J. L. Mackie, *Ethics: Inventing Right and Wrong* (Harmondsworth: Penguin, 1977), 39–40.

[23] See Darwall, *British Moralists and the Internal 'Ought'*, chs. 1, 3, and 4.

Strong internalism is almost the opposite of Ross's externalism: whereas Ross's externalism sees no necessary tie between the existence of moral duty and either acknowledgement or motivation, strong internalism insists on a necessary connection between the existence of Alf's duty and Alf's acknowledgement of it, and between his acknowledgement of it and his motivation to act on it. So if Alf under conditions C does not acknowledge D as his duty, then it is not his duty. It is important to add the second clause, about the conditions C under which Alf recognizes D as his duty. Any fully specified version of strong internalism will specify some conditions under which a person recognizes something as his duty. The most permissive version might suppose that actual recognition is required; more demanding is that a suitably reflective agent would recognize the duty; stronger still is that the agent, if deliberating in a rational way, would do so.[24]

IV. Green's Moral Internalism: The Basic Rights Recognition Thesis

(a) Green's Moral Internalism

Green's account of moral obligation and motivation belongs to the family of internalist theories. According to Green, morality is practical in so far as terms such as 'ought' and 'right' get their meaning only when they enter into practical guidance in people's dealings with each other (*LPPO* §116). The meanings of the terms are inherently practical in so far as they depend on people's recognition of common interests in their dealings.

In the *Prolegomena to Ethics* Green tells us that in those who have a desire for self-realization, this desire

will express itself in their imposition on themselves of rules requiring something to be done irrespective of any inclination to do it, irrespectively of any desired end to which it is a means, *other than this end, which is desired because conceived as absolutely desirable.* With the men in whom, and at times when, there is no such desire, the consciousness of there being something absolutely desirable will still be a qualifying element in life. *It will yield a recognition* of those unconditional rules of conduct to which, from the prevalence of unconformable passions, it fails to produce actual obedience. It will give meaning to the demand, without which there is no morality and in which all morality is involved, that 'something be done merely for the sake of its being done,' because it

---

[24] That Green's ethical theory specifies C in terms of rational deliberation, but his political theory does so in terms of actual recognition, is the concern of sects. VI and VIII below.

is a consciousness of the possibility of an action in which no desire shall be gratified but the desire excited by the idea of the act itself as something absolutely desirable in the sense that in it the man does the best that he has it in him to do. (*PE* §193)[25]

In this important passage Green is seeking to reconcile the notion of a categorical morality, in which one's duty does not depend on one's desire to perform it, i.e. with moral internalism.[26] We can see that Green insists here that either a desire to act, *or at least some sort of recognition of the desirability of acting on duty, is always present* in an agent who deliberates rationally.[27] On the part of those with the desire for the good (of self-realization), Green acknowledges—indeed, he stresses in italics—that this desire is actually present; for those who, because of their unruly passions, do not possess this desire, they too at least *recognize* the moral duty, because they see that the act is *desirable in expressing the best for man.* Throughout, the concern is to show that categorical moral law is meaningful and practical because it expresses the self, and that is why it is a practical demand on us. Without this practical pull, terms such as 'ought' and 'right' would have no meaning.

Notice, then, that Green does not quite advocate strong internalism, which, it will be recalled, holds that recognition of an obligation implies motivation to act on it. In these passages, then, Green seems closer to a view that we might call

Green's recognition internalism: 'D is Alf's moral duty' only if, when rationally deliberating, Alf recognizes the absolute desirability of acting on *D* (his duty). It is *generally true* that Alf is then motivated to act in accord with *D*.

For Green, then, the critical tie is between the claim that a moral duty pertains and its rational recognition; the relation between recognition and motivation is close, but not necessary. So in the *Prolegomena* Green does not quite advocate motivational internalism, but a sort of 'recognition existence internalism', which internally and necessarily ties the existence of a duty to its recognition in

---

[25] Emphasis in '*other than this end* …' original; emphasis in '*It will yield a recognition*' added.

[26] David O. Brink analyses this section (193) of the *Prolegomena* thus: 'Because the demands of self-realization depend only on those deliberative capacities that make one a responsible agent, they are categorical imperatives.' On Brink's analysis as well, the categorical imperative arises from within agency (*Perfectionism and the Common Good: Themes in the Philosophy of T. H. Green* (Oxford: Oxford University Press, 2003), 41; see also pp. 92 ff.). Whether or not Kant himself was an internalist or an externalist is a matter of debate. Christine Korsgaard has provided an important internalist reading of Kant in her *Sources of Normativity*.

[27] In order to fully explicate 'rational' here, we would need to analyse Green's concept of the rational will, something that goes beyond the scope of this chapter. See my 'Green, Bosanquet and the Philosophy of Coherence', in S. G. Shanker and G. H. R. Parkinson (general eds.), *The Routledge History of Philosophy*, vii: *The Nineteenth Century*, ed. C. L. Ten (London: Routledge, 1994), 408–36. On self-realization, rational deliberation, and recognition of an internal ought, see Brink, *Perfectionism and the Common Good*, 40–1.

a rational consciousness. So, in contrast to strong internalism, Green can allow that in some atypical circumstances rational people (with unruly passions) may not be motivated to act on what they see as their moral duty. It is robustly internalist, though, in so far as people never have obligations that are not part of their practical considerations, at least to the extent that in their rational deliberations they recognize moral action as desirable.

(b) The Basic Argument for the Rights Recognition Thesis

The extent to which Green's argument for the recognition thesis manifests a commitment to moral internalism has not generally been noticed.[28] I am not claiming that everything Green says about the rights recognition thesis follows from recognition internalism—clearly Green sees a connection between cor-relativity claims (C1) and (C5) (section IIb) and the rights recognition thesis (see also section VI). I do wish to claim, though, that a robust version of the rights recognition thesis can be derived from his internalism conjoined with a conception of rights that embraces (C3). So, the basic argument:

(1)   The first step is the correlativity of rights and duties, as expressed in (C3) (section IIb above). So, Alf has a right R against Betty only if Betty has a duty D to Alf.

(2)   So if Betty does not have D, Alf cannot have R.

(3)   To this we add recognition internalism: 'D is Betty's moral duty' implies that a rational Betty recognizes D.

(4)   Assume: rational Betty does not recognize D.

Therefore:

(5) D is not Betty's moral duty.

(6)   It follows given Alf does not have R.

Recognition internalism, along with correlativity, thus implies a rights recognition thesis of the form:

(7)   Alf has right R only if R implies some duty D on Betty that in her rational deliberation Betty acknowledges (and so is generally motivated to act on).

Rights, then, must be recognized in this sense: recognition of a correlative duty D by a rational agent subject to D is necessary for the existence of a right. If no rational agent thinks that she has a duty D or if no such agents are usually moved to act on D, there is no right. As Green puts it, 'it is not a question

---

[28] An exception is Rex Martin, both in his scholarly work on Green's philosophy and in his own account of rights, which is inspired by Green's. See his 'T. H. Green on Individual Rights and the Common Good', 55–6; idem, A System of Rights, 77 ff.

whether or not it ought to be claimed as a right; it simply can *not* be claimed on this condition' (*LPPO* §143).

It might be queried why the focus of the analysis is on the recognition of the duty correlative to *R*, rather than the recognition of *R* itself. Isn't this an argument about the recognition of obligations rather than rights? For one thing, Green himself tells us that it is the recognition of duties which underlies the rights recognition thesis: remember his claim that Rousseau failed to grasp that 'rights do not begin till duties begin'. So for Green the crux of the issue was the beginning of duties. Moreover, the real problem of moral motivation—how do oughts motivate?—applies only to duties: it is the recognition of duties that must motivate. Rights only raise the question of moral motivation on their duty side—when they instruct the person against whom the right is claimed that she ought to act. As Hohfeld famously pointed out, when we talk about a right that is not correlative to any duty, no strict 'ought' follows. In such a case, to say that 'Alf has a right to *X*' is merely to say that he has 'no duty to refrain from *X*-ing'—he is at liberty to *X*. But merely to have a liberty to *X* does not imply that Alf ought to *X* or that Betty ought to let him. The classic example is the liberty of two pedestrians to pick up a dollar bill lying on the sidewalk. Neither has a duty to refrain from picking it up, but neither has a claim on the other to stand aside and let him pick it up. Such 'naked liberties' often characterize competitions; people have the liberty to win, but no one has a claim to win. So if we are to analyse the ways in which rights make moral demands on us, we must focus on the duties involved in claim rights. Thus the implication of Green's internalism for the theory of rights must come via his account of duty.

V. Internalism, Rights, and the Common Good

As we saw at the outset (section I above), Green's statement of his rights recognition thesis refers to the common good. Throughout the *Lectures on the Principles of Political Obligation*, Green almost always ties together the recognition and common good claims (*LPPO* §§25, 26, 48, 99, 103, 106, 113, 139, 143, 144, 145, 148, 207; for exceptions see §§23, 24, 124, 116, 142). The precise relation between the recognition thesis and the claim that rights are based on the common good is a matter of dispute. Maria Dimova-Cookson sees a conflict between the recognition and common good claims,[29] while Rex

---

[29] Dimova-Cookson, *T. H. Green's Moral and Political Philosophy*, ch. 5.

Martin maintains that the recognition thesis is a conceptual claim about the nature of rights, whereas Green's insistence that rights rest on the common good is a distinct justificatory claim.[30] Given that Green repeatedly conjoins the recognition and common good claims, often in the same sentence, we might look for an interpretation in which they are intimately and consistently related.

The internalist interpretation of the rights recognition thesis, I believe, allows us to see why it is so closely bound up with the common good in Green's eyes. The crux of the matter is Green's theory of motivation as presented in the *Prolegomena to Ethics*. According to Green, a rational agent is not simply motivated by his 'desires but seeks to satisfy himself in gaining the objects of his desires; [he] presents to himself a certain possible state of himself, which in the gratification of the desire, he seeks to reach; in short, [he] wills' (*PE* §175). 'The "motive" which the act of will expresses is the desire for this self-satisfaction' (*PE* §104). 'This motive does indeed necessarily determine the act; it is the act on its inner side' (*PE* §105). In this sense, rational action is directed to what the agent considers good. And crucially, Green adds: 'It is superfluous to add, good *to himself*; for anything conceived as good in such a way that the agent acts for the sake of it, must be conceived as his own good' (*PE* §92). For Green, then, a rational will is a will that is seeking self-satisfaction, seeking its own good.

This immediately raises a problem for moral motivation: if all motivation is for one's own good, morality cannot be understood as acting contrary to one's own good and instead acting for the good of others. Interestingly—and puzzlingly for interpreters of Green[31] —Green seems to acknowledge that we have 'generous impulses' to help others in pain, 'simply as such', that do not apparently aim at self-satisfaction, but he is quick to insist that morality cannot be founded on them, though they 'co-operate' with the desire to act morally (*PE* §235). Given that the rational will aims at self-satisfaction—the good of the individual—a motivating morality must be consistent with such a will. Hence, on Green's conception of moral motivation, 'the opposition between self and others does not enter' (*PE* §§235, 232). Thus, 'the true good must be good for all men' (*PE* §218). Morality must identify a common good: rational self-seeking beings could all be guided by such a morality, as it does not ask of them the rationally impossible—to put aside their self-seeking to aid others. For one to live a moral life, it must be the case that 'His

---

[30]   Martin, 'T. H. Green on Individual Rights and the Common Good', 58–9.
[31]   See Nicholson, *The Political Philosophy of the British Idealists*, 68–71.

own permanent well-being he thus necessarily presents to himself as a social well-being' (*PE* §232).

Martin, who has done the most to show the contemporary relevance of Green's work, seeks to depict this argument as justifying morality on the grounds of mutual benefit, in a way that brings Green closer to David Gauthier's contractualism, albeit 'unlumbered with the Gauthierian baggage of atomistic individualism, non-cooperative bargaining strategies, and the maximization of rational self-interest'.[32] Martin is especially keen to avoid interpreting the notion of the common good in any way that even has a 'whiff' of Green's controversial claims that 'the good of each includes within it the good of all others (or is non-competitive with the good of others or is the same for everyone), that critics of Green have seized on time and again'.[33] Now it is important to see why Green is led to the controversial claim that 'the distinction commonly supposed to exist between considerate Benevolence and reasonable Self-Love, as co-ordinate principles on which moral approbation is founded, is a fiction of philosophers' (*PE* §248). Given his analysis of rational action, and given his internalist conception of morality in which it is linked to motivation, Green cannot allow morality to be a limit on self-satisfaction. It thus cannot be constituted by a bargain in which we compromise, both gaining but sometimes having to forgo opportunities for self-satisfaction. Unlike Gauthier, who seeks to show that non-maximizing behaviour can be rational, or Kurt Baier,[34] who seeks to show that there are dictums of social rationality that override individual self-seeking, Green equates the rational will with a will seeking its good. Thus for the rational will to abide by morality, morality must be its good. And this means that the good of others must converge with one's own good—morality must articulate a common good.

Given this, it follows that a necessary condition for rights to be rationally recognized is that they are understood as promoting a common good. Given the account of motivation, individuals could not be moved to act on rights unless they are (i) recognized as (ii) contributing to a common good, for only then would acting on the correlative duty be consistent with rational self-seeking action. Mutually recognized claims must be recognized as promoting a common good. If they were not, then the duties they imply would not generally motivate. And given that Green, in both his moral and his political theory, ties morality to a tendency to generally motivate, duties divorced from our motivational set could not be duties at all.

---

[32] Martin, 'T. H. Green on Individual Rights and the Common Good', 64. Cf. David Gauthier, *Morals by Agreement* (Oxford: Clarendon Press, 1986), esp. ch. 5.

[33] Martin, 'T. H. Green on Individual Rights and the Common Good', 62.

[34] See Kurt Baier, *The Rational and the Moral Order* (Chicago: Open Court, 1995).

VI. The Rights Recognition Thesis in Green's Political Philosophy

(a) A Partial Reconciliation of the Rational and Actual Recognition Theses

At this point I have defended a rights recognition thesis (call this the rational recognition thesis) according to which one can have a right against a person only if that person's rational deliberations lead her to recognize the correlative moral duty. This, of course, is an idealized recognition claim, as it applies to what is recognized in rational deliberation. Just because an irrational person does not recognize that D is his duty does not show that there is no correlative right R. Now the question is: how does this internalist recognition thesis relate to Green's claim in his political philosophy—call this the actual recognition thesis—that rights must *actually* be generally recognized in society (*LPPO* §§103, 142, 145). Certainly, these two recognition theses can split apart. On what we might call the *pessimistic assumption*, we might suppose that in our society few individuals rationally deliberate. On the pessimistic assumption, then, there will be a sharp split between what rights are justified under the rational recognition and the actual recognition theses: few people will actually recognize the demands of their rational selves. On the other hand, on an *optimistic assumption*, we would suppose that *generally* people approach rationality in their moral deliberations; if so, then what is generally recognized by most people should pretty well track what is justified by rational recognition. Last, we could adopt a *utopian assumption* and assume that everyone actually engages in rational reflection. In that case what is morally justified under rational recognition would converge with universal actual recognition.

Green looks to be neither a pessimist nor a utopian. In his political philosophy he argued that right must be recognized by society in general. The obligation, says Green, must be one that is recognized by the mass of people, or by society generally. To say that rights depend on '*social* recognition' is, then, to say that, within society S, D is generally recognized. On the optimistic assumption, it makes perfect sense, in an inquiry into what our rights are, to identify them as those that are generally recognized. As long as people *generally* deliberate rationally, what is actually recognized *generally* will express what is morally justified. Indeed, we can see on this interpretation why the condition of *general* actual recognition is not a mere compromise with the necessities of practice: general actual acknowledgement is all one would expect from a society in which most, but obviously nothing like all, rationally deliberate.

(b) The Limits of the Reconciliation Proposal

Our reconciliation proposal can explain, simply on the basis of Green's rational recognition thesis and the optimistic assumption, the truth of the important rights recognition thesis:

The importance of recognition: One has good grounds for ascribing Alf right R only if R's correlative duty D is generally recognized in his society.

Add to this our:

The rational recognition thesis: Alf does not have a right R against others generally if in their rational deliberations they do not recognize the correlative duty D.

Together, we have an interesting and important version of the recognition thesis. We only have rights if rational others recognize the correlative duties, and unless a right is actually generally recognized, we do not have good grounds for ascribing it to people. This, I think, is enough is make opponents of the rights recognition thesis bristle. But in two crucial ways it still falls short of Green's own, more robust claims about the necessity of social recognition.

First, and most obviously, it shows that general actual recognition is crucial evidence as to what our moral rights are only on the optimistic assumption. It remains possible that for any given right R, it would be recognized in people's rational deliberations, but has somehow failed to be actually recognized. In that case, R would indeed be an unrecognized moral right of ours; but Green clearly insists that rights *must* be generally recognized. So we have failed to justify this strong actual recognition claim.

Second, Green not only insists that R must be generally recognized; there must also be a general habit of acting on it, just as in his ethical theory Green insists on both recognition *and* a tie to motivation. This indeed looks as if the actual recognition thesis is simply an application of the rational recognition thesis. However, here we come to an important difference between Green's ethical and political theories. Although in the *Prolegomena* he holds that recognizing the moral law generally leads to action on the basis of that recognition, in the *Lectures on the Principles of Political Obligation* Green connects general recognition of an obligation with people having a general habit of acting on it, 'whether the habit be founded on an imagination of pleasures and pains or on a conception of what ought to be' (*LPPO* §208). So in his account of rights in his political theory, Green argues that for D to be an obligation in society S, while it is necessary that people generally conform to D, it is not necessary that in general people act on D for the right reason, i.e. that they have a moral duty to do so. Although, as Green argues, some may act on 'a conception of what ought to be' others may be motivated simply by projected pleasures and pains (i.e. punishments and rewards). The important point is that a normal person is motivated to act on D.

On the face of it, this seems an odd claim for an internalist like Green to make. Recall the motivational internalist's complaint about externalism: the externalist has no intrinsic tie between moral judgement and moral motivation; the externalist needs to supply some additional, 'external' motivation to act morally (section IIIb above). Green, though, allows what would seem to be an 'external' motivation—habit based on imagination of rewards and punishments—to qualify as an 'internal' tie. Still, this is a bona fide internalist view, as the existence of the obligation is tied to the obligation's ability to produce action in people (through habit or otherwise). If it is generally the case that, when people conclude that Alf has a right, they act on their supposed duty (either because of good moral reasons or simply out of habit), then the duty exists because it is internally connected with recognizing the obligation. So the internal tie between obligation and action need not be simply a desire to do the right thing, but any desire to act that is linked to the duty. The doctrine remains internalist because, in the absence of this habit, there is no moral obligation.

Even given all of this, the requirement that there be an actual habit of acting on the right does not appear in any way justified by the rational recognition thesis. Yes, it still qualifies as a sort of internalism, and it stays true to the internalist insistence that recognition of duty is a practical matter that motivates. But by bringing in rewards and punishments, Green has added a new dimension. Green's 'political internalism' is not simply an application of his moral internalism. Not only must we show *how* moral rights can motivate rational agents, we must show *that* they do motivate most people. And it does not matter that they act *on* morality, only that they act *in accord* with it. This is a new element in his account of the way rights function, adding a practical dimension that goes beyond the moral internalism.

VII. Extending Green's Recognition Thesis: Rights as De Jure Moral Authority

(a) Claim Rights Securing Abilities Distinguished from Rights as Powers

I believe that a friend of Green's can motivate his stronger claims about the necessity of social recognition by appealing to the usually overlooked third element of his conception of a right—the idea of a power. A closer analysis of this third element of his analysis of rights leads us to see that many (perhaps most) rights depend on social recognition in a sense other than the one I have been examining.

Although Green characterizes a right as 'a power claimed and recognized as contributory to a common good', by 'power' Green apparently has in mind 'ability'.[35] Indeed, it seems wrong for Green to say that a right *is* a power: what he often seems to have in mind is that a right is correlative with a duty that allows one to exercise an ability, or a duty that gives one the ability to act. Thus Green suggests that rights *secure* the 'free exercise of powers' (*LPPO* §25). But that a right is a claim implying a duty, which, in turn, secures one with a power, does not make the right a power. That is, we should not confuse '*R* is a power' with '*R* is a recognized claim that enables the right-holder to exercise a power'. This is clear if we employ a schema to describe claim rights: $Alf(R(X))$: $Betty(D(Y))$, which reads 'Alf has right R to X against Betty such that Betty has duty D to do Y'. We can see that X may be a power or ability that Betty's Y-ing secures, or it may be the case that Betty's Y-ing creates an ability X that Alf did not previously possess. But in both cases the ability is the *content* of the right: it is not itself the right. Although Green talks as if the right is a 'recognition' of 'certain powers' (*LPPO* §24), much of the time at least he seems to think that the recognition of the right implies an effective duty that *in turn* either allows or creates certain abilities.

Now *sometimes*, says Hohfeld, we mean by a right a *power*. Someone has a power if he or she can alter other people's liberties, claim rights and duties. Such rights are associated with *authority* to legislate. For example, that the United States Congress has the right to make laws shows that Congress has the legal power to alter the legal duties and claim rights of American citizens. It can create new duties and rights or abolish old ones. If Congress has the power to make such changes, citizens have a corresponding 'liability'—their claim rights and duties are subject to alteration by Congress.

Although many of our individual rights are partially claim rights, many of our rights are also powers. Because the employment of rights is generally at the discretion of the right-holder, the right-holder has the power to either invoke a duty owed by others or to give them a liberty (what Hohfeld describes as a 'no-duty'). If I have signed a contract according to which I have the right to buy property from you at a certain date, then you have a duty to sell it to me under the contract, though I have the power to abolish this duty, i.e. waive the right. Rights of property are associated with a wide range of powers; I can

---

[35] Nicholson, *Political Philosophy of the British Idealists*, 85.

228 GERALD F. GAUS

sell my property to you, which will change the duties of my tenants; instead of owing me a monthly rent, they will owe it to you. In so far as rights involve the discretion and decisions of the right-holder, they provide him with powers over others: he has the normative authority to alter the moral duties, claims, and liberties as he sees fit. Such rights thus empower each person with a local moral authority over others.[36]

I think it is clear that Green did not fully appreciate the sense in which a regime of rights is a regime of dispersed moral powers, and this despite his characterization of rights in terms of powers. Bernard Bosanquet's characterization is much closer to what Green has in mind: 'A right is a *claim* recognized by society.'[38] For Green, rights really are claims that are reflections of duties (thus (C4) seems in some ways the basic correlativity thesis for him). Once we see the extent to which rights really are moral powers, however, there is no temptation to reduce them to the reflection of duties. Rights typically, I think, involve moral authority.

The role of rights as delegators of localized moral authority is easily overlooked.[39] Many philosophers take what might be called a comprehensive planning approach: a good system of rights is a scheme of well-defined claims that secures to each what he is due under a morally optimal distribution of resources, primary goods, etc. This is manifest in Ronald Dworkin's famous account of liberalism: the core liberal principle is one of equality of resources, and justified schemes of rights secure the favoured distribution.[40] The problem with such accounts is that they blind us to the way in which rights help us to cope with deep moral disagreements about what the optimal distribution is. Given the complexity of our pluralistic society and intricacies of moral relations, we often disagree on the morality of acts—what (if any) God to worship, what images to look at, whether to preserve a coastline or build a resort, whether to abort a foetus—as well as what distributions are just—how

[36] See my 'Property, Rights, and Freedom', *Social Philosophy and Policy*, 11 (Summer 1994), 209–40.

[37] I have argued this case more fully in my *Justificatory Liberalism* (New York: Oxford University Press, 1996), 199–204.

[38] Bernard Bosanquet, 'The Philosophical Theory of the State', in Gerald F. Gaus and William Sweet (eds.), *The Philosophical Theory of the State and Related Essays* (Indianapolis: St Augustine Press, 2001), 196; emphasis original. Bosanquet adds, however, that a right is 'enforced by the State'. On Green's rights as claim rights and their relation to powers, see Geoffrey Thomas, *The Moral Philosophy of T. H. Green* (Oxford: Clarendon Press, 1978), 353 ff.

[39] For important exceptions, see Eric Mack, 'In Defense of the Jurisdiction Theory of Rights', *Journal of Ethics*, 4 (Jan.–March 2000), 71–98; Randy Barnett, *The Structure of Liberty: Justice and the Rule of Law* (New York: Oxford University Press, 1998), 138 ff.

[40] See his classic essay 'Liberalism', in Stuart Hampshire (ed.), *Public and Private Morality* (Cambridge: Cambridge University Press, 1978), 113–43, esp. 129 ff. Justifying liberty rights on this distributional account is especially difficult; see Dworkin, *Sovereign Virtue* (Cambridge, Mass.: Harvard University Press, 2000), ch. 3.

are partners to divide the benefits of their joint endeavour? A core liberal insight is that, rather than seeking a single morally sanctioned answer in each case, a better moral response is to delegate moral authority: in a wide range of cases the best thing to do is to leave the decision in the hands of the agents involved. But constant moral negotiation between the people involved would be a hopelessly inefficient system; if, as Green and almost all other rights theorists argue, a system of rights is supposed to allow for smooth social co-operation, it must try to at least minimize the matters that require negotiation. Transaction costs are significant impediments to achieving our aims. In this light, a regime of rights requires delegation of bits of moral authority to different people, allowing each a moral sphere to determine when the duties of others are to be invoked, when others are to be left at liberty, and when the duties of others might be altered. As one recent philosopher of rights has aptly put it, 'rights stake out chunks of moral turf'.[41]

(b) De Jure Moral Authority and Recognition

This brings us to a different defence of the rights recognition thesis. In the *Lectures on the Principles of Political Obligation* Green considers the distinction between *de facto* and *de jure* sovereignty. Green resists the idea that *de jure* sovereignty is simply 'rightful authority' that has no practical force, as when appeal is made simply to a 'general will, or the mere name of a fallen dynasty exercising no control over men in their dealings with each other' (*LPPO* §105). Instead, Green argues, the distinction 'has natural meaning in the mouths of those who, in resisting some coercive power that claims their obedience, can point to another determinate authority to which they not only consider obedience due, but to which obedience in some measure is actually rendered' (*LPPO* §105). Green's point, and he seems entirely right here, is that a political authority that has no practical effect is no political authority at all, as it cannot perform its main task of sorting out disagreements and harmonizing rights. To be any sort of authority at all, there must be some general recognition of it; only then can it perform its designated tasks. If it is not generally recognized as an authority, we might argue that it *ought* to be an authority, but cannot claim that it now is.

It is important to distinguish this argument for the necessity of social recognition of authority—call it the *argument from the point of view of authority*—from another Greenian case that can be made. We could argue for the necessity of social recognition of authority by simply applying moral internalism

---

[41] Lomasky, *Persons, Rights, and the Moral Community*, 5.

and a correlativity thesis to authority—that is, by employing the internalist recognition argument to the concept of authority. Assume that if Alf has authority over Betty, Betty has some obligation to obey Alf; that is, obligations are correlative to authority.[42] Given moral internalism, for Betty to have an obligation to obey an authority, there must be some internal connection (such as recognition). So there is no obligation unless there is at least a rational recognition of the obligation. Now, if there is no recognition of the authority, there cannot be rational recognition of the obligation to obey it. So, on this line of reasoning, the very pre-condition of authority—that those subject to it have some obligation to obey—presupposes rational recognition of the authority. This internalist argument for the recognition of authority is distinct from the argument from the point of view of authority: for while this argument requires rational recognition, the argument from the point of view of authority requires actual social recognition. According to the latter argument, the job of authority is to regulate and co-ordinate social interaction; if so, an authority that is not socially recognized simply is unable to perform the office of an authority, as one who is not socially recognized as a leader is unable to fulfil the position of 'group leader'. We can say that a person who is not recognized—either explicitly or implicitly—as a leader ought to be the leader, but not that he is the leader. The argument from the point of view of authority, then, does not depend on moral internalism or a correlativity thesis.

   The application of Green's analysis of sovereignty—understood in terms of the point of view of authority argument—to rights *qua* dispersed moral authority is manifest. To the extent that the function of rights is to localize moral authority by dispersing moral powers, they cannot fulfil this function at all if they are not generally recognized. If there are no recognized rights, we are in a state akin to civil war, each side seeking to construct its own preferred system of authority. But, as Green observes, in situations like this, there really is no sovereignty at all (*LPPO* §105). Rights as powers (dispersed moral authority) are thus defined by social recognition. Without general social recognition, no authority exists. This is, I think, a compelling defence of Green's strong social recognition claims about rights; it more directly hinges on concept of a right *qua* power. We cannot even imagine such a non-recognized right, except as something like a mere name of a fallen dynasty, or a fantasized one, exercising no control over men in their dealings with each other.

---

[42] Compare Gerald Gaus, *Political Concepts and Political Theories* (Boulder, Colo.: Westview Press, 2000), ch. 10, and Christopher McMahon, *Collective Reasoning and Collective Rationality* (Cambridge: Cambridge University Press, 2001), ch. 3.

VIII. Ross's Slave Objection Again

Having presented two arguments in favour of rights recognition theses—from moral internalism and from the social role of rights as dispersed authority—let us return to Ross's slave objection (section IIa above).

To begin, it should be stressed that although Green advocates a robust social recognition thesis (section VIb), he does not advocate, as many appear to think, a political recognition thesis according to which D is a moral duty in society S only if the state acts to ensure that people act according to D. Although Green certainly believes that the core function of the State is to maintain a system of rights, and in so doing it will clarify the limits of various rights (*LPPO* §143), he also accepts that there can be socially recognized rights and duties that are not recognized politically. Thus Green tells us that a legal slave can have 'rights the state neither gives nor can take away' (*LPPO* §145; see also §141). This is because, Green argues, the slave is engaged in social relations in which others implicitly recognize duties and obligations. If he has a family, he has rights in that family; if he engages in co-operative activities with citizens, he has the rights implicit in those practices.

Recall Ross's complaint that Green's account of rights implies that slaves acquired the 'moral right to be free only at the moment when a majority of mankind, or of some particular community, formed the opinion that they ought to be free, i.e., when the particular person whose conversion to such a view changed a minority into a majority changed his mind. Such a view, of course, cannot consistently be maintained.'[43] On the interpretation I have given, we need to be a bit more careful. Three points need to be kept in mind.

First, we must admit that if no rational agents acknowledge a duty to the slave, then the slave would have no correlative rights; that certainly follows from Green's moral internalism.

Second, however, we must be clear that even if the slave has no right in such a case, it still would not follow that the slave-owner's actions are justified. Recall that recognition is a necessary, not a sufficient, condition for a justified moral right. Thus, even though the slave-owner's right, and the correlative duties of a slave, are socially recognized, since such rights do promote a common good, they are not justified. So while the slave cannot, say, invoke a right *qua* equal, neither can the slave-owner invoke a right *qua* slave-owner, for no such right exists. So the slave does no wrong in running away or refusing to co-operate.

---

[43] Ross, *The Right and the Good*, 51. See p. 211.

Third, and most important, we must distinguish between the actual and the rational recognition theses. If a slave-owner rationally recognizes that the common good requires that he acknowledge a duty to the slave, then the slave has a moral claim right on him. Green, I think, failed to appreciate this, and so moved far too quickly from rational to actual recognition.[44] Given all claim rights for which both C3 and C4 (section IIb) hold (rights imply duties, and duties imply rights), if a rational moral agent would acknowledge a moral duty to the slave, then the slave has a corresponding right in relation to *that* person. So, even if the slave does not have a generally *socially* recognized right to be free, he still can have a rationally recognized right *vis-à-vis* those rational agents who have the requisite internal connection. So if our concern is the recognition thesis implied by moral internalism—the rational recognition thesis—then, when rational slave-owners reflecting on the common good recognize that they have a duty to the slave, they *ipso facto* create the correlative right, and the right is recognized. The only rights that are not recognized by the rational recognition requirement are those that imply duties that rational slave-owners could not recognize. We must distinguish, then, the thesis that rights depend on recognition by *others* from the claim that they depend on *general social* recognition.

However, if we focus on rights as recognized powers, then the recognition that is required is general actual recognition. These sorts of moral powers—delegated moral authority—do indeed require that the authority is actually recognized. Such rights are not the mere reflection of rationally recognized moral duties. To see this better, consider the rights of parents over their children. Parental authority might be distributed in a variety of reasonable ways, many of which can make out a reasonable claim to be advancing the common good. The parents may have sole authority over their children's education, or the more extended family, or the community, may have a say; mother and father may have exactly the same authority, or it may differ in some ways; the authority may wane in children's early adolescence, or not. Now suppose that in a society teenage parents are not recognized as having parental rights; since teenagers are themselves seen as children, they are not accorded this authority, and all parental rights are vested in the grandparents. Suppose that there is a good moral argument that teenage parents in late adolescence should be accorded full parental authority—that the best arrangement from the perspective of the common good is that they have these rights. The question is: can we infer from the premiss 'morally speaking, these teenage parents ought to have full parental rights' the conclusion that 'morally speaking, these teenage

---

[44] As I did in 'Green's Rights Recognition Thesis and Moral Internalism'.

parents do have full parental rights'? Ross would seem committed to the inference. Proponents of the actual recognition thesis plausibly disagree. They would point out that if one accepts the inference, it follows in this case that an enlightened babysitter has a moral duty to ask the teenage parents rather than the grandparents for permission for the child to watch reality television, even if no one—including the parents—recognizes that teenage parents have such rights. Suppose the babysitter asks the teenage parent, and the parent agrees; are they morally required to follow the instructions of the teenage parent even in the face of disagreement by the grandparents? Proponents of the recognition thesis insist that it would be morally wrong to do this; while flawed, the current system allows us to agree on who has moral authority over what decisions. It would be morally bad for each person to call on their own understanding of the common good, and accord authority to whom they believe it ought to be vested in; some might seek the permission of teenage parents, some consult grandparents, while some might believe that in this case aunts or uncles have the moral right to decide. This would undermine the great moral good of a consensus on who has authority over the decision; so long as the actual system can reasonably be understood as based on a notion of the common good, the rights actually recognized can do a morally required job that no idealized set of rights could possible do. They provide actual moral consensus. This great moral good of a system of recognized authority is undermined by each person deciding for himself what is the best distribution of moral authority, and acting on that ideal.

In defence of their position, strong externalists might still hold that the enlightened babysitter, insisting that the parental moral rights reside solely in the teenage parents, is morally 'progressive'. However, in saying this, strong externalists—and this probably includes most contemporary advocates of human and natural rights—seem caught in something of a paradox. On the one hand, strong externalists such as Ross think that it is a definitive criticism in a case like this that the proponent of the recognition thesis cannot say that teenage parents have the moral right even though society does not recognize it. Why is it thought to be so important to say this? It cannot be simply the value of a catalogue of true moral beliefs. No doubt the force of the criticism is that the strong externalist thinks it important that the moral rights of the teenage parents actually be respected. But strong externalism is based on the claim that true moral judgements have no inherent tie to motivation, so the strong externalist is himself unable to show that what he thinks is so important to accept as true—'Teenage parents now have rights'—matters for practice, as his entire account has been based on denying the inherent link between the truth of 'ought statements' and motivation. The strong externalist looks as if he is giving a practical criticism of the actual recognition thesis: it does not allow 'progressive' claims about unrecognized rights, but the foundation of strong externalism undermines the practical effect of holding these progressive views, as it insists on a gulf between true moral belief and action. Indeed, on the strong externalist account, even if everyone comes to acknowledge that teenage parents have parental rights, this still would not itself account for people *acting* on this recognition. *That* is truly counter-intuitive.

Any moral philosophy according to which moral rights are partially justified because they co-ordinate our activities must accept some version of an actual recognition thesis because unrecognized co-ordinators do not co-ordinate. This does not mean that proponents of such views must be morally conservative, accepting whatever rights are recognized socially. As we have seen, socially recognized rights such as those of slave-owners may be immoral. And some rights not presently recognized morally ought to be. 'To say that he [the slave] is capable of rights, is to say that he ought to have them, in the sense of "ought" in which it expresses the relation of man to an end conceived as absolutely good, to an end which, whether desired or no, is conceived as intrinsically desired' (*LPPO* §25).

IX. Conclusion

Green's rights recognition thesis is widely rejected. I have argued in this chapter that, so far from being an idiosyncratic doctrine of nineteenth-century British Idealism, a rights recognition thesis is compelling. Although an externalist such as Ross is perfectly justified in insisting that the existence of rights is independent of anyone's recognizing them or being moved to act on them, this common view is at odds with moral internalism and the practical nature of morality. I have tried to show how internalism conjoined with a generally embraced analysis of rights leads to some version of the rights recognition thesis. In doing so, I have maintained that Green's moral theory can be described as a form of moral internalism, and that his defence of the rights recognition thesis derives at least partially from his internalist commitments.

Green scholars may resist interpreting Green as a moral internalist. He is not especially clear about just what version of the thesis he endorses, though the *Prolegomena* is clear in linking up the argument for the common good with an analysis of the rational will as self-satisfying, and the *Lectures* are clear that the existence of rights requires a habit of obedience. Understanding Green's account of rights in terms of his commitment to what is nowadays called internalism explains the connection between the recognition thesis and the common good components of Green's theory of rights, and why he almost invariably links them in his characterizations of rights. I have argued that, for Green, rather than being a justificatory concern independent of the conceptual analysis of rights, appeal to the common good is part of his internalist analysis of the concepts of duties and rights.

Green's characterization of rights refers not simply to the recognition thesis and the common good, but to the claim that rights are powers. I have argued that if Green had taken more seriously the conception of rights as powers, rather than only as claims, he would have been led to compelling justification for his strong social recognition claims about rights that go beyond those justified by his moral internalism. A crucial function of rights is to disperse moral authority; taking up Green's own analysis of the necessity of social recognition of *de jure* authority, we see that rights cannot perform their function unless they achieve a degree of social recognition. Green's moral and political theory thus points to two powerful arguments supporting versions of the rights recognition thesis.

10

Rights that Bind: T. H. Green on Rights and Community

AVITAL SIMHONY

I. Introduction

It is a common communitarian criticism of liberalism that its preoccupation with rights is incompatible with, and even hostile to, the possibility of community. For rights erode the bonds of community. T. H. Green's liberalism gives the lie to that criticism. His argument that rights bind and promote an effective and inclusive vision of community is a thoroughly liberal argument. It merits the attention of both students and critics of liberalism.

Two considerations propel my claim. First, I agree with Walzer's claim that the communitarian criticism of liberalism is like 'certain fashions that seem regularly to reappear'. The communitarian criticism is 'transient but certain to return. It is a consistently intermittent feature of liberal politics and social organization'.[1] I should only add that this claim applies nicely to other critiques of liberalism, such as certain kinds of feminism and republicanism.

The second consideration lies with my belief that our appreciation of the complexity and richness of the liberal tradition will greatly benefit from giving full recognition to Green's new liberalism as a distinctive, though no less legitimate, strand in modern liberalism. Freeden has argued that political ideologies consist of core concepts, the particular arrangement and configuration of which account for different strands of liberalism.[2] We misunderstand liberalism if we view it as a fixed label of a fixed set of concepts, or a label of an ideology made of one cloth. Rather, we should appreciate that there is not *a* liberalism,

I should like to thank Abisi Sharakiya for making this essay better. My thanks to Michael Freeden for helpful comments on an earlier version of this essay published in *The Journal of Political Ideologies*.

[1] Michael Walzer, 'The Communitarian Critique of Liberalism', *Political Theory*, 18: 1 (Feb. 1990), 6.

[2] Michael Freeden, *Ideologies and Political Theory: A Conceptual Approach* (Oxford: Clarendon Press, 1996).

but liberalisms, all members of 'the family of liberalism'.[3] Adopting Freeden's conceptual framework allows us, negatively, to see that standard liberal anxiety about Green's liberal credentials is misplaced, and indeed tells us more about the nature of liberal individualism than about Green's own liberalism. Positively, we may assess Green's contribution to modern liberalism by exploring his re-conceptualization and re-configuration of rights and community.

Green has been called a philosopher of rights,[4] and it is claimed that his importance lies in his input into modern liberal thinking about rights.[5] At the same time he may be described as the most distinctive philosopher of common good and community in modern liberalism.[6] There is, however, no tension in Green's liberalism; nor does his liberalism present us with a puzzle. Rather, his argument weaves rights and community into a single liberal fabric. This results from Green's deliberate effort to reconstruct liberalism by ridding it of its earlier association with self-centred individualism. Not even Mill, widely viewed as the modernizer of liberalism, has undertaken such a transformative project.

Green's reconstruction of liberalism consisted in shifting the idea of community (and the common good) to the conceptual heart of liberalism. This primary shift was, in turn, accompanied by a re-conceptualization not only of the idea of freedom, for which he is famous, but also of the idea of rights, which is less known, notwithstanding Rex Martin's distinguished contribution in that direction.[7] Green's argument that rights bind is the focus of my essay. To appreciate this argument, however, it is first necessary to understand the communitarian charge that liberal rights are hostile to the idea of community.

II. Liberalism and the Confrontational View of Rights and Community

It is a common communitarian and feminist criticism of liberalism that its preoccupation with rights is incompatible with, and even hostile to, the possibility of community. According to this confrontational view—that rights and community stand in stark opposition—the primacy of rights, invariably

---

[3] Michael Freeden, 'The Family of Liberalisms: A Morphological Analysis', in James Meadowcroft (ed.), *The Liberal Tradition: Contemporary Reappraisals* (Cheltenham: Edward Elgar, 1996), 14–39.

[4] Ann R. Cacoullos, *Thomas Hill Green: Philosopher of Rights* (New York: Twayne Publishers, 1974).

[5] Michael Freeden, *Rights* (Milton Keynes: Open University Press, 1991), 20–1.

[6] Gerald F. Gaus, *The Modern Liberal Theory of Man* (London: Croom Helm, 1983).

[7] Rex Martin, 'T. H. Green on Individual Rights and the Common Good', in Avital Simhony and David Weinstein (eds.), *The New Liberalism: Reconciling Liberty and Community* (Cambridge: Cambridge University Press, 2001), 49–68.

referred to as the 'language of rights' and 'rights talk', entails that liberalism lacks the conceptual resources to recognize the primary value of community. Community is interpreted in terms of co-operation and fellow-feeling, shared social goals and mutual concern for the common good, social obligations and virtues. The liberal language of rights, by contrast, generates and justifies human separateness in terms of competitive and adversarial relations between narrowly self-interested individuals.

A contemporary thinker thus claims: 'Thinking in terms of rights ... does more than reflect on an egoistic, atomistic situation; it creates such a situation ... Because thinking in terms of rights rests on an atomistic picture of us as separate, thinking in terms of rights systematically denies the unity.'[8] This is a strong claim, but not atypical of a line of criticism which can be traced back to Marx. 'The so called rights of man', he claimed, are actually rights of 'egoistic man, man separated from other men and the community.'[9] For example, 'liberty as a right of man is not founded upon the relations between man and man, but rather upon the separation of man from man. *It is the right of such separation.*'[10] Moreover, 'The separation of man from man' further entails 'an individual separated from the community, withdrawn into himself, wholly preoccupied with his private interest and acting in accordance with his private caprice.' As a result, 'society ... appears as a system which is external to the individual and as a limitation of his original independence'.[11]

Though not Marxists, some leading contemporary communitarians, joined by some feminists, similarly advance the confrontational view of rights and community. That view famously informs Sandel's distinction between the 'politics of rights' with the 'politics of the common good'. The two capture, according to Sandel, rival alternative approaches to political life.[12] Some even argue that rights talk as such is dispensable, and that it is more beneficial to focus on the language of the good.[13]

The confrontational view of rights and community may be stated in three claims, bearing in mind that, for explanatory reasons, some simplification is inevitable. First, critics of liberalism forge an analytic-conceptual link between the concept of rights and the view of an atomist and egoistic individual. The liberal language of rights *is* the language of competitive self-centred

---

[8] John Hardwig, 'Should Women Think in Terms of Rights?', *Ethics*, 94 (1984), 448.

[9] Karl Marx, 'On the Jewish Question', in Robert C. Tucker (ed.), *The Marx–Engels Reader*, 2nd edn. (New York: Norton, 1978), 32.

[10] Ibid. 42; my italics.   [11] Ibid. 43.

[12] Michael Sandel (ed.), *Liberalism and its Critics* (Oxford: Basil Blackwell, 1984), 1–7. Though twenty years old, his claim still has much currency.

[13] Ronald Beiner, *What's the Matter with Liberalism?* (Berkeley: University of California Press, 1992), 80–97.

individualism. For one thing, the individual right-bearer is viewed as self-seeking and self-interested, since to claim rights is to assert one's own interests against those of others. For another, to be a right-bearer is to be a 'lone right-bearer'.[14] Atomism and egoism, according to the confrontational view, constitute not a mere historical or ideological background picture of rights, but are essentially part and parcel of the language of rights. An irreconcilable non-contingent tension between the divisive motivation of rights-holders and relations of mutual concern is conceptually bound up with the language of rights—hence the claim above that 'thinking in terms of rights' not only reflects 'an egoistic, atomistic situation; it creates such a situation'. The same conceptual connection between rights and selfish self-interest informs Sandel's claim that rights-oriented justice comes into play when the rich communal relationship of care and solidarity is diminished. Rights, then, replace virtues such as 'benevolence or fraternity'.[15]

The second claim of the confrontational view of rights and community is that the liberal vision of politics rests on the acceptance of antithetical relations between individuals and society. Recalling Sandel's rival visions of 'politics of rights' and 'politics of the common good', Taylor distinguishes, respectively, between 'a rights model society' and 'a participatory model society', contrasting the latter with the former:

> [T]he first, rights, model goes very well with a more *atomistic consciousness*, where I understand my dignity as that of an *individual bearer of rights*. Indeed—and here the tension surfaces between the two—I cannot be to willing to *trump* the collective decision in the name of individual rights if I haven't already moved some *distance from the community* which makes these decisions.[16]

Not unlike Marx, Taylor connects the 'individual bearer of rights' with 'distance from the community'. He aims his criticism at rights conceived (by Dworkin) as 'trumps'. The trump image of rights captures traditional liberal anxieties about normatively subordinating rights, and therefore individual liberty, to the calculation of an overall maximizing social purpose, or to a collective common good. For Taylor, by contrast, the trump image of rights is conceptually inseparable from an atomistic self-understanding of political life. Inescapably, not only do rights distance us from our community, but they are

---

[14] Mary Ann Glandon, *Rights Talk* (New York: The Free Press, 1991), ch. 3.

[15] Michael Sandel, *Liberalism and the Limits of Justice* (Cambridge: Cambridge University Press, 1982), 28–35.

[16] Charles Taylor, 'Alternative Futures: Legitimacy, Identity and Alienation in Late Twentieth-Century Canada', in Alan Cairns and Cynthia Williams (eds.), *Constitutionalism, Citizenship, and Society in Canada* (Toronto: University of Toronto Press, 1985), 211, my italics, and 209–10.

likely to weaken its bonds. Deployed as trumps, Taylor argues, appeals to rights entail overriding collective decision making of society, majority will—indeed the 'general will' established by the process of majority decision making or the prevailing consensus.[17]

In the same vein, critics of liberal rights focus exclusively on negative rights. This is the third premiss of the confrontational view of rights and community. Since they require non-interference, negative rights invoke the image of human separateness as a central liberal tenet. Notwithstanding Dworkin's powerful image of rights as trumps, the separating force of negative rights is more frequently captured by the spatial territorial image of boundaries. Indeed, some contemporary thinkers refer to the 'territorial conception of rights',[18] in order to highlight the very idea of non-interference in terms of an inviolable area—territory in which individuals are secured in their personal freedom understood as negative freedom. What Marx says about the right to liberty still captures the point of the third claim best: the right to liberty 'leads every man to see in other men, not the *realization*, but rather the *limitation* of his own liberty'.[19] In the same vein, Glandon, criticizing the exclusive supremacy of rights talk in the United States, holds that 'Buried deep in our rights dialect is an unexpressed premise that we roam at large in a land of strangers, where we presumptively have no obligations toward others except to avoid the active infliction of harm'.[20]

To sum up: some communitarians and feminists argue that the confrontational view of rights and community lies at the conceptual heart of liberalism. The confrontational view embraces three claims. Rights are conceptually atomistic and egoistic; rights trump societal goals and decision making, and thereby capture and enhance opposition between individuals and community; and liberal rights are essentially negative, in that they encourage each individual to see in others the limitation of her own liberty.

Is liberalism vulnerable to the confrontational view of rights and community? Are liberal rights, indeed rights as such, inimical to the value of community? My answer is this: the confrontational view of rights and community is, by no means, an essential part of liberal thinking, though certain types of liberal argument may lend it support.

---

[17] Charles Taylor, 209.

[18] The idea of boundaries captures Berlin's insistence on marking off an area of privacy as the core of negative freedom, though he uses the term 'frontiers' (*Four Essays on Liberty* (New York: Oxford University Press, 1969), 161). George Klosko employs a 'territorial' conception of rights, which I follow to highlight the same concern (*History of Political Theory: An Introductory*, ii: *Modern Political Theory* (New York: Harcourt Brace College Publishers, 1995), 101).

[19] Marx, 'On the Jewish Question', 42; italics original.

[20] Glandon, *Rights Talk*, 77; see also the entire ch. 4.

The confrontational view of rights and community may be associated with certain historical strands of liberalism as well as certain types of liberal arguments. I can touch on these arguments only briefly. One such argument emerges from Flathman's analysis of the practice of rights as essentially conflictual and self-centred. Flathman holds that the practice of rights conceptually involves conflicts of interests between individuals.[21] He argues that there cannot be a right to an x unless having or doing x is in general, and in A's (the right-holder's) judgement, advantageous for A and in some way disadvantageous for B (the obligation-holder), so that B will typically wish to avoid fulfilling his obligation to A. For to say that x is a right is to say that some A is justified in doing x despite the fact that doing it will be thought to have an adverse effect on the interests of some B. This analysis of the practice of rights as essentially embracing a conflict of interests is typical of the liberal theories on which old and new communitarians draw to prove the alleged uncommunal nature of all rights. Indeed, Flathman himself admits that his analysis of rights is at odds with the ideal of community, for 'rights involve a certain holding back, a reserve ... a competitive as well as sharing attitude ... limits to sharing'.[22]

Similarly, to the extent that rights are understood in terms of self-centred claiming, they may lead to adversarial contentious social relations. Feinberg's analysis of rights gives priority to self-centred claiming, since he holds that the practice of making claims against other people is essential to self-respect.[23] This suggests that my self-respect depends on my ability to make adversarial claims against others which sets limits on yours.

Dworkin's claim that 'the concept of rights ... has its most natural use when political society is divided, and appeals to co-operation or a common good are pointless'[24] points in the direction of Flathman and Feinberg. Dworkin's rights argument may, however, open another door to the confrontational view of rights and community. I refer to his connecting liberalism with a right-based theory. (He distinguishes between right-based, duty-based, and goal-based theories.) To the extent that liberalism is understood as a right-based theory, to the extent that liberalism is grounded on right-based morality, and is constitutively bound up with right-based individualism, to that extent the criticism that rights are hostile to community has purchase. This is because, as Raz has established, right-based morality is essentially individualist, in that it pits one's own interest against one's concern for others, such that

[21] R. Flathman, *The Practice of Rights* (Cambridge: Cambridge University Press, 1976), 1–280, 190.

[22] Ibid. 190.

[23] I follow here Jeremy Waldron, 'Nonsense upon Stilts—A Reply', in Jeremy Waldron (ed.), *'Nonsense Upon Stilts': Bentham, Burke, and Marx on the Rights of Man* (London: Methuen, 1967), 196.

[24] Ronald Dworkin, *Taking Rights Seriously* (Cambridge, Mass.: Harvard University Press, 1977), 184.

they are not only occasionally in conflict, but essentially so. Further, right-based morality is reductive, so it cannot account adequately for important community building-blocks such as the value of virtues, character, and social obligations.[25]

Now, liberals are not without a response to the confrontational view of rights and community. As I have said, some liberal arguments may be vulnerable to the confrontational view of rights and community, but that view is not, as such, an indispensable part of liberal thinking. Waldron, Gewirth, and Raz deserve mentioning here.[26] Whereas Waldron restricts himself to direct refutation of specific communitarian criticisms of liberal rights, Gewirth sets out to develop a theory of community of rights, claiming that rights create community. Divorcing liberalism from rights-based individualism, Raz refashions liberalism on communitarian-like foundations, while preserving the normative force of rights in securing individual autonomy.

Green's argument that rights are constitutive of, and are essential to, the realization of liberal community merits full inclusion in the liberal repertoire side by side with the liberal arguments of Raz, Gewirth, and Waldron's response. It is not my claim here that Green's liberal argument is better than theirs, though I believe in some respects it is. Rather, Green's liberal argument is capable of enriching contemporary liberal self-understanding of its own tradition. For the richest historical liberal source for thinking of the positive relationship between rights and community (and the common good) is the (British) new liberalism of the late nineteenth century, of which the liberalism of T. H. Green provides the first formulation.

Refuting the confrontational view of rights and community depends ultimately on the capacity of liberalism to reject the three premises which forged it. Green's fusion of rights and community possesses just that capability. First, critics of liberalism wrongly render the link between rights and competitive, selfish individualism conceptual. Green's argument reveals that the link is essentially ideological. The proper target of critics is not the institution of rights, but what they take to be its prior assumption of selfish, competitive human nature and social relations. Green's institution of rights is indeed bound up with the individual who, though a 'subject of interests',[27] is not a self-centred but a self-developing person nested in social relations of mutual interdependence and concern.

[25] Joseph Raz, *The Morality of Freedom* (Oxford: Clarendon Press, 1986), ch. 8.

[26] Waldron, 'Nonsense upon Stilts'; Alan Gewirth, *Community of Rights* (Chicago: University of Chicago Press, 1996); Raz, *Morality of Freedom*.

[27] T. H. Green, 'Introduction to the Moral Part of Hume's "Treatise"', in *Works of T. H. Green*, ed. R. L. Nettleship (London: Longmans, 1885), i: sect. 4. Hereafter 'Hume'.

Second, the confrontational view that rights are inimical to community holds that liberal thinking subscribes to a dichotomous view of the relationship between the 'individual' and 'society'. This view, in turn, justifies a 'territorial' conception of rights. It aims to carve out a certain territory in which the individual can act freely, since rights protect the territory against encroachments of consequentialist calculations, tyranny of the majority, or an overarching community. Like Marx and Taylor, Green's liberalism depends on a reluctance to postulate antithetical relations between individuals and society, for he insists on the social nature of the individual. Green does not subscribe to the view that society is primarily an external force constraining individual freedom. For Green, as for Raz, however, and contrary to Marx and Rousseau, the recognition of 'society' as a positive force does not diminish the important role of rights, but rather transforms it for liberal purposes.

The third claim of the confrontational view connects liberalism exclusively with negative rights (and negative freedom). Though he does not employ the language of positive rights, they are essential to the creation of Green's ideal of community. Unlike negative rights, positive rights are expressive of the way in which each of Green's individuals views the well-being of other individuals as essential to his own self-realization. Accordingly, positive rights play a special role in binding individuals into a community of mutually depending and realizing persons.

These three claims—the ideological connection between atomism and egoism and liberal rights, the essential communal nature of the liberal individual, and the significant role of positive rights—reveal that the inseparability of rights and community lies at the heart of Green's liberalism. Put differently, Green, like Raz, divorces liberalism from rights-based individualism.

Although exploring Green's fusion of rights and community is my explicit aim, my implicit goal is to reveal the complex nature of liberalism, which the above three claims of the inseparability thesis capture. Two issues in particular deserve attention. First, Green's reconstruction of liberal rights is bound up with re-conceiving some other liberal ideas: 'individual', 'interest' and (state) 'interference'. Second, the complexity of liberalism resists a discourse of dichotomies. Green rejects both a mere territorial and a trump conception of rights in favour of a teleological conception of rights. To endorse the latter, however, does not entail rendering rights merely 'derivative', and hence normatively less significant, a common liberal claim.

I proceed as follows. I first look at Green's re-conceptualization of rights, which he carries through by rejecting natural rights with the aid of Aristotelian teleology (section II). Then I explore the ways in which re-conceptualized rights assist in creating communal relations of mutual concern (section III).

Third, I focus on positive rights, exploring their special affinity with community (section IV). Finally, and briefly, I suggest that Green's rights argument reveals both the complexity of liberalism and important liberal continuity (section V).

III. Aristotelian, not Contractarian, Conception of Rights: A Teleological, not Territorial, Conception of Rights

The confrontational view of rights and community depends on rendering the connection between rights and self-centred individualism conceptual or analytic; but the connection between the two is really ideological. Green's rights argument is uniquely relevant here. He gives reasons both for divorcing narrow individualism from liberal rights and for marrying liberal rights with community and the common good. At the same time as he rejects self-centred competitive individualism on communitarian grounds, he importantly does not marginalize the normative significance of rights; rather, he provides a communitarian defence of liberal rights (and justice). Re-conceptualized, rights regain a central role in creating and realizing community. His double argument (a communitarian rejection of narrow individualism and a communitarian defence of liberal rights) reveals that the communitarian criticism which propels the confrontational view rests on confusing the ideological connection of rights and narrow individualism with the conceptual connection of the two.

Green believes that, though historically false, the social contract which lays the foundation for natural rights 'may be a way of conveying an essentially true conception of some moral relation of man'.[28] It is, however, precisely because the social contract is expressive of an inadequate 'moral relation of man' that 'it conveys a false notion of rights'. What is wrong with the contractarian picture of social relation? It is a relation of 'pure individualism, of simple detachment of man from man'.[29] As well, individuals are viewed as acting irrespectively of, and without concern for, each other.

This image of self-centred individualism is well captured by the idea of a social contract as a device for securing rights modelled in terms of a bargain that might be expected to emerge if a group of rational individuals, each concerned to promote his own interests (good), came together to settle the terms on which they were prepared to live in a political society. Political society (the

---

[28] T. H. Green, 'Lectures on the Principles of Political Obligation', in *LPPO* §49.
[29] Ibid. §37.

state), therefore, was viewed as instrumental in the protection of self-centred concerns.

I am not saying that Green applies this image to all social contract theories that he discusses. Hobbes fits the bill better than Locke and Rousseau. Indeed, Green finds some truth in the contractarian argument, though it is expressed in a confused way.[30] Rather, it is the type of argument that is generally associated with the social contract which he seeks to challenge: namely, the territorial conception of rights that is bound up with background assumptions about atomist and egoist individuals. At the same time that Green rejects the egoism and atomism of rights, he does not divorce the institution of rights either from the individual or from 'interest'. Rather, as we shall see below, he defends the mutuality of rights: a system of rights that both presupposes and give effect to social life of mutually dependent and mutually interested individuals.

Green does not deny that rights belong to individuals. His communitarian criticism of natural rights does not extend to making the political community or partial communities the subject of rights (though his sense of community is thicker, I believe, than the weak sense suggested by Freeden[31]).

There is no harm in saying that they [rights] belong to individuals as such, if we understand what we mean by "individual," and if we mean by it a self-determining subject, conscious of itself as one among other such subjects, and of its relation to them as making it what it is; ... they [rights] attach to the individual, but only as a member of a society of free agents, as recognising himself and recognised by others to be such a member, as doing and done by accordingly.[32]

Put differently, embedded in Green's discussion of rights is an argument that the idea of rights itself is neither egoist nor atomist. Whether it is so or not depends on the nature of the individual or social relation to which rights are attached. It is at this point that Aristotle enters Green's re-conceptualizing of rights.

Aristotle, to be sure, is not normally connected with the language of rights. Green fully acknowledges this. 'It is true that they [Plato and Aristotle] have not even a word for "rights"'. But they had a proper conception of social relation and the relationship between the individual and the state which 'laid the foundation for all true theory of rights',[33] and that is acutely absent from the contractarian account of natural rights thinkers.

---

[30] Ibid. §16.

[31] Michael Freeden, 'Human Rights and Welfare: A Communitarian View', *Ethics*, 100 (1990, 489–502). See e.g. *LPPO* §200.

[32] Green, *LPPO* §138.   [33] Ibid. §39.

Thus, 'they [natural rights thinkers] make no inquiry into the development of ... man through society'.[34] (For Aristotle, of course, individuals are social through and through.) Further, '[t]hey take no account of other forms of community than those regulated by a supreme coercive power'. (For Aristotle, the State presupposes other forms of community. Hence, Green holds that political society is a society of societies, or a community of communities.) Accordingly, the social contract account 'leave[s] out of sight the process by which men have been clothed with rights and duties'. Ultimately, whereas natural rights thinkers set individuals, 'invested with all the moral attributes and rights of humanity', over against the State, Aristotle's ' "teleological" view of man and society'[35] transcends antithetical social relations.

The Aristotelian-based teleological conception of rights exposes the 'entire misconception of the nature of a right', as held by 'writers of the seventeenth and the eighteenth centuries'.[36] The misconception embraces three flaws, one of which is fundamental and grounds the other two. The fundamental flaw is best captured in Green's notion of social recognition, which I shall discuss below. Essentially, it denies that individuals bring with them to society rights that did not derive from society; for rights conceptually depend on social relations. This flaw gives rise to two further misconceptions.

One misconception is that the contractarian account of rights divorces rights from social duty. Green holds that rights and social duty in the form of citizenship are inseparable. His argument is twofold. Mutual recognition, as we shall see shortly, constitutes rights, to be sure. But it also gives rise to the practice of duty towards others.[37] The claim that 'a capacity for rights, some claim on his fellow-men, has come to be ascribed to every man' entails 'readiness to recognize a duty and to act upon the recognition'.[38] Further, securing equal rights to all enables individuals to exercise 'obligation of support' towards their society. In Aristotelian fashion, Green believes that the state is 'a society of which the life is maintained by what its members do for the sake of maintaining it',[39] a claim which is acutely absent from the contractarian account. However, he importantly warns against the counter fallacy: that is, viewing 'the state apart from its vocation to enable the individual to fulfil ... [his] vocation'—that is self-development in mutual dependence with others. A just system of rights and citizenship are mutually supportive.

The other misconception is that the contractarian account of natural rights allows individuals to have rights against the state. Green notoriously argues

---

[34] Green, *LPPO* §113. The following two quotations are from the same section.
[35] Ibid. §39.   [36] Ibid. §178.   [37] *PE* §218.
[38] Ibid. §211. See also §§218, 239.
[39] *LPPO* §40. The following quotation is from the same section.

that there are no rights against society and the state—which raises liberal ire, though unjustifiably. Essentially, Green's claim is that there are no rights against society *as such*, and the state *as such*. There are certainly rights against an *unjust* society and an *unjust* state. In other words, Green claims that natural rights theorists ask the wrong question regarding the issue of rights against the state because of their antithetical view of individuals and the state: 'the question was never put [by them] on its proper footing. It asked not, When for the sake of the common good the citizen ought to resist the sovereign? but, What sort of injury to person and property gave him a natural right to resist?'.[40] Aristotelian teleology comes to the rescue. 'Here again the Greek theory, deriving the authority of government not from consent but from the end it serves, is sounder than the modern.'[41] Green's criticism, then, is not premissed on denying that individuals may have rights against the state; rather, he frames rights and political obligation on teleological grounds: 'For the problem of the social contract can be removed if the authority of government is held to be derived ... from the function which it serves ... If it ceases to serve its function, it loses its claim on our obedience.'

Two types of claims underpin the contrast between the contractarian and the Aristotelian accounts of rights: that is, respectively, the claim regarding the antithetical relations between the 'individual' and 'society', which is bound up with a territorial account of rights, and the claim that the 'individual' and 'society' are positively connected, which is associated with a teleological conception of rights. Essentially, the contractarian account of natural rights is premissed on a view of society (social relation) which involves an antithesis between individuals and society. Boundaries, in the shape of rights, are necessary to protect individuals' private territory, in which they can act freely, against invasion by society. Invasions may take the form of tyranny of the majority, welfarism, or overarching common good.

Some kind of social contract (between individuals who possess rights separately) is, therefore, necessary to overcome that antithesis, which, nevertheless, perpetuates a relation of tension between individuals and the state. Rights establish boundaries to shield individual spheres of voluntary action against invasion by other individuals and the state. Such is the grip of the territorial conception of rights on liberals' self-understanding that it extends to non-contractarian liberalism. Even Mill views rights as fences that encircle the individual private sphere of voluntary action, and similarly Berlin describes rights as frontiers securing individuals a zone of non-interference against public

---

[40] Ibid. §107.
[41] Ibid. §62. The next quotation is from the same section.

authority. The image of rights as 'trumps' fits the territorial bill nicely too. And so do Flathman's and Feinberg's adversarial interpretations of the practice of rights, as we have seen above. Little surprise, then, that old and new communitarians link conceptually the liberal language of rights with the image of boundaries against which they put forward a rival view of strong sociability, 'the social thesis', as Taylor calls it.

The Aristotelian account, in contrast to the boundaries account, rests on 'the social thesis'. That is, it transcends the opposition between individuals and society, since Aristotle views individuals as essentially social. The social thesis account, however, is best revealed in Marx's refusal to set up society in opposition to its individual members, since the individual is essentially social. His conception of society transcends the presumed antithetical social relation which, he believes, underpins the liberal view of rights. 'The so called rights of man', Marx maintains, are actually rights of 'egoistic man, man separated from ... the community ... Man is far from being considered, in the rights of man as a species-being; on the contrary, species-life itself—society—appears as a system which is external to the individual and as a limitation of his original independence'.[42] Whatever else 'species-life itself' is, it is quite clear that here it is the same as 'society'. Hence, the absence of 'species-life' entails that society is viewed as a source of restrictions on individual independence. This relationship of opposition between the 'individual' and 'society', argues Marx and some contemporary critics of liberalism, generates a negative conception of freedom. Negative freedom focuses on an area of non-interference which, in turn, relies on clear boundaries between an inviolable private sphere, which protects individual voluntary action, and a public or political authority, that poses a potential threat to voluntary action.

Since the communitarian claim that rights are subversive of community rests on rendering conceptual the connection between the boundaries account of social relations (presupposing competitive individualism) and rights, then the communitarians' own defence of co-operative social life as expressed in the social thesis inevitably entails that rights greatly lose their normative significance, as with Marx, and at any rate become problematic in a communitarian vision of society, as they are in Rousseau.

This is my claim. At the same time that Green, like Marx, relies on the social thesis account in order to discredit self-interested competitive individualism, which, he holds, grounds a 'false notion of rights', he, unlike Marx, does not rule out the significant role of rights, divorced from egoism and atomism, in creating co-operative social life. Rather, divorced from selfish individualism,

---

[42] Marx, 'On the Jewish Question', 43.

rights gain a special significance in the realization of co-operative social life. As Hobhouse holds, rights are conditions constitutive of community. Hence, we should properly regard Green's system of rights as a community of rights without which the liberal value of community remains unrealized. But this is to anticipate. Green, like Marx, employs the same social thesis argument which communitarians employ in their criticism of the liberal language of rights as community-subverting, but he employs that argument for the purpose of re-conceptualizing rights as essential to the realization of community. It is communitarian justification of liberal rights that communitarians seem too eager to neglect.

Nor is Green an exception to the liberal tradition. His argument is remarkably similar, notwithstanding many important differences, to Raz's re-conceptualization of rights as part and parcel of his project to rid liberalism of its association with self-centred individualism.[43] A consistent strand of communitarian liberalism launched by Green, developed by Hobhouse (and Hobson) and Dewey, propels Raz's liberalism, as well as Rawls's *Theory of Justice*. That it is, as yet, not fully recognized owes much to the staying power of the confrontational view to which liberals' own understanding sometimes contributes.

IV. Mutuality of Rights, not Egoism of Rights

Green's re-conceptualization of rights as community-creating is bound up with the idea of social recognition which encapsulates the social thesis argument, though it embraces much more. That social recognition is the conceptual core of Green's rights is not news.[44] Nor is it news to insist that social recognition is not the same as, though not abstracted from, conventional or customary recognition. My concern here is to emphasize that social recognition lies at the heart of Green's re-conceptualization of rights, with a special bearing on the relationship between rights and community in liberal tradition, and more generally between liberalism and individualism.

There are two familiar ways of overcoming antithetical social relations. One is by assuming a contract; the other, by regarding society as a supra-individual phenomenon. The social recognition thesis (to borrow from Taylor) offers

---

[43] Joseph Raz, *The Morality of Freedom* (Oxford: Clarendon Press, 1986), chs. 7, 8, 12.

[44] Martin, 'T. H. Green on Individual Rights and the Common Good'. Gerald F. Gaus, 'Green's Rights Recognition Thesis and Moral Internalism', *British Journal of Politics and International Relations*, 7:1 (2005), 5–17.

a third way. While it is critical of the one-sided individualism of the social contract, it is equally critical of the alternative one-sidedness of collectivism, which views the state as a supra-individual phenomenon. Green's third way gains clarity once we appreciate that 'social' in 'social recognition' is interchangeable with 'mutual', and that 'recognition' is bound up with non-instrumental interest.

Mutual recognition constitutes rights.[45] Hence, as mutually recognized moral claims for self-development, rights equally emphasize the development of others. Claiming rights is not, and cannot be, egoistic or self-centred, because claiming rights is mutual. That Green replaces egoism of rights with mutuality of rights owes much to the Kantian idea that reason, because universalizing, rules out egoism and justifies mutuality, which, in turn, lies at the heart of his realm of ends. Though abstract, the realm of ends is not simply individualistic, but is a community of mutually respecting individuals bound together by common reason and humanity. De-abstracted, Kantian community of mutuality lies at the core of Green's ideal community of mutual recognition.

To recognize someone is to acknowledge his or her equal status as being an end to oneself as one is, to view others on a moral par with oneself; to be able to relate to them as 'I' and 'Thou', and vice versa. It is a form of communication between self-conscious persons who are aware of others as themselves, and of their relation to them as a part and parcel of their own awareness of themselves as persons with their own ends.[46] Therefore, Green's basic right, 'the right to free life rests on the common will of the society, in the sense that each member of the society within which the right subsists in seeking to satisfy himself contributes to satisfy others, and that *each is aware* that the other does so'.[47] Mutual awareness, however, has to result in 'practical recognition'—that is, in the actual practice of 'acting and being treated'[48] as equal members of society. Embedded in social norms and arrangements, the actual practice of mutuality of rights de-abstracts the Kantian community of ends. Importantly, such practice is at the same time practice of mutual concern.

Mutual concern lies at the heart of Green's contrasting 'purely social interest' with 'egoistic interest'.[49] I said that Green's re-conceptualization of rights as community-creating involves divorcing the institution of rights from the picture of the atomistic-egoistic individual, though neither from the individual nor from the language of interest as such. Green's relational and developmental

---

[45] Green, *LPPO* §138.   [46] *PE* §§190, 200, 209, 216.
[47] *LPPO* §216; emphasis added.   [48] Ibid. §140.   [49] Ibid. §182.

individual is, at the same time, a 'subject of interests'.[50] This should come as no surprise, since the language of interest is essential to liberalism. Entirely unessential to the liberal language of interest is the connection critics make between interest and self-interest, which is, in turn, equated with selfishness. Mill took an important step towards disconnecting 'interest' from selfishness. Not only did he criticize selfishness as an obstacle to self-development, but he further, and famously, insisted on understanding utility in the wider sense. The interests that individuals pursue are 'permanent' and attach to them as 'progressive beings'.[51] Indeed, Mill holds that we have a fundamental interest in developing our individuality. Green expands this argument and carries it beyond Mill.

We can discern two senses of 'interest' in Green: 'to have an interest in' and 'pursuing "dominant interests"'.[52] The Greenian individual has a fundamental interest in self-development. Self-development, in turn, depends on the pursuit of worthy 'dominant interests'—that is, worthy life projects, which the individual chooses from the available stock of existing social practices. Neither of these two senses of 'interest' is conceptually bound up with selfish or market self-interest—hence the contrast between 'egoistic interest' and 'purely social interest'.[53]

Social interest does not have its primary ground in a kind of 'rational', strategic, self-centred calculation of how one's assistance to others may probably help one to receive such help oneself when one needs it or may otherwise benefit oneself. It is not a contingent matter of *quid pro quo*, but rather a necessary matter of persons' common humanity as purposive agents and hence of common membership in a community of ends. The reason rights give to the individual for acting in other than purely self-interested way is not the Hobbesian prudential or contingent one that if he violates others persons' rights, he may expect them to violate his own rights, but rather the logically necessary reason that the rights he necessarily claims for himself rest on grounds that apply to all other members of the community of ends.

The association of rights with 'interest' situates Green's theory with the 'interest' account of rights which is central to Raz's liberal argument. To have a right, according to this account, is to have an interest protected or furthered.

---

[50] Green, 'Hume', §4.

[51] J. S. Mill, *On Liberty and Other Essays*, ed. with an introduction by John Gray (Oxford: Oxford University Press, 1991), 15.

[52] For 'having an interest in', see e.g. Green, *PE* §§160, 190, 202, 233, 239–40, 242, 244, 254, 262. For 'dominant interests', see T. H. Green, 'Lectures on the Philosophy of Kant', in *Works of T. H. Green*, ii. §§118, 122; *PE* §§148, 234, 252, 299, 377.

[53] Green, *LPPO* §182.

At the same time as Green's rights aim to protect and promote individuals' basic interest in self-development, they importantly institutionalize a sense of shared interest in joint self-development. While the continuity of Hobhouse's rights argument with Green's is obvious, that with Raz's needs stating—which is all I can do here; I need not claim that Raz's re-conceptualization of collective rights and collective good is the same as Green's.[54] Suffice it is to draw attention to their similar project of reconstructing rights away from an essentially individualist doctrine. For both, a community of rights based on an interest account of rights does not, and cannot, institutionalize adversarial social relations of merely competing interests.

Ultimately, then, invoking rights, for Green, reveals the communal ties of individuals as always equal members in a co-operative social life which rests on appropriate notions of mutuality and reciprocity. Hence, '[The] relation of rights [is the] basis of moral relationships ... [The relationship of individuals as right bearers is the] the basis of moral relationships.'[55] Positive rights, in particular, carry the task of creating community, to which I now turn.

V. Negative and Positive Rights

The confrontational view—rights are hostile to community—focuses narrowly on negative rights, which it identifies with certain negative freedoms that are protected against coercion or interference by others. Rights seen this way are immunities, defences against the intrusions that other persons or the government might try to make into the individual's sphere of freedom.[56] To be sure, one might argue that negative rights do not simply separate, since they empower individuals to participate in the life of their society.[57] And so they do. Indeed, they have a positive dimension, since they enable individuals who exercise them to be moral agents. But if they are the sole focus of attention, they may lend some support to the confrontational thesis, because they are consistent with a lack of positive concern for the well-being of others, especially in societies where great inequalities of wealth and power exclude many from effective membership. As Green claims, in so far as 'negative rights ... rights to be let alone' are concerned, 'the less favoured members' of

[54] Raz, *Morality of Freedom*, 198–9, 202–10.

[55] T. H. Green, 'Fragments on Moral and Political Philosophy', in *LPPO* §2.

[56] e.g. Charles Taylor, 'Atomism', in his *Philosophical Papers* (Cambridge: Cambridge University Press, 1985), ii. 195.

[57] Alan Gewirth, *Human Rights: Essays on Justification and Application* (Chicago: University of Chicago Press, 1982), 3.

society indeed 'are admitted to membership of civil society',[58] but not fully and positively.

Why so? Because negative rights are correlative with duties that require only non-interference with the rights-holders. Persons can fulfil their duties by simply not interfering with one another's actions or projects. Negative rights are thus associated with the moral requirement not to harm others, but do not require one to assist others. Further, negative rights, such as the right to freedom from bodily injury, require one-to-one correlation between the right-holders and the obligation-holders; they are rights which all members of society have against all other members, and do not require societal effort to meet the needs of the weakest members of society.

Positive rights, by contrast, have a special affinity with community because, in contrast to negative rights, they are correlative not merely with non-interference, but require interference in the actions of obligation-bearers. For positive rights are correlative with others taking positive steps. They require, as Hobhouse puts it, not only mutual forbearance but also mutual aid (Green speaks of 'mutual helpfulness' and 'positive help'[59]). Mutual aid requires co-operative action, since positive rights are not simply one-to-one relationships; rather, they require the mediation of social structures and processes. Positive rights, then, justify a positive conception of the state as an enabling agency.

It is sometimes held that Green defends life, liberty, and property as fundamental rights, and that in doing so, though he is critical of natural rights, he preserves most of their content.[60] Green, however, not only revises the form of rights (by connecting them with mutual recognition), he also changes the content of rights to include positive rights. Short of employing the term 'positive rights', his consistent contrast of 'negative' (and 'abstract') and 'positive' (and 'real') in the context of talking about rights reveals their significance.[61]

He defends one fundamental right: the right to free life. 'If there are such things as rights at all, then there must be a right to life and liberty, or, to put it more properly, to free life'.[62] All other rights depend on this right. What is the foundation of the right to free life? 'The answer is, capacity ... for the determination ... by the conception of well-being as common to self

[58] Green, PE §245.

[59] L. T. Hobhouse, 'Liberalism', in Hobhouse, *Liberalism and Other Writings*, ed. James Meadowcroft (Cambridge: Cambridge University Press, 1994), 59–60. For Green, see *LPPO* §§248 and 270, respectively.

[60] Freeden, *Rights*, 20. Geoffrey Thomas, *The Moral Philosophy of T. H. Green* (Oxford: Clarendon Press, 1987), 290.

[61] Green, e.g. *LPPO* §§18, 154–5, 194, 207, and *PE* §§245, 267, 270.

[62] *LPPO* §150.

with others.'[63] It would, therefore, be more proper for Green to speak of the fundamental right to self-development. Indeed, the right to free life is grounded in the capacity for self-development.

Terminology aside, however, the substance of the fundamental right remains the same as that of the problem which reveals it. The problem is that though this capacity is 'constantly gaining on its negative side general recognition', very little is done for it 'to be enabled positively'.[64] To positively enable the capacity for joint realizability is to realize Green's idea of a 'community of good for all',[65] or, as Hobhouse relevantly, and following Green, put it, 'the good of all who stand in mutual relations',[66] that is a common good. The ideal of community in relation to the worse-off members of society remains, however, 'in effect unrealised' in so far as the state secures only 'negative rights ... rights to be left alone'.[67] To realize it requires that the state do 'more than secure individuals from violent interference by other individuals'.[68] Rather, as an enabling agency (not merely a necessary evil), the state has to provide 'positive equality of conditions'.[69] For the state to do that is to secure the worse-off members of society with 'real opportunity of self-development' which positive rights institutionalize.

An excellent example is the right not to starve (which Green discusses in connection with punishment), which is grounded in the following basic principle of just punishment:

The justice of punishment depends on the justice of the general system of rights—not merely on the propriety with reference to social well-being of maintaining this or that particular right which the crime punished violates, but on the question whether *the social organisation in which a criminal has lived and acted is one that has given him a fair chance of not being a criminal.*[70]

Note that the justice of punishment depends on the justice of the general system of rights, which is assessed according to whether society provides a fair chance or 'real opportunity of self-development' to all members, with emphasis on the worse-off and which positive rights institutionalize.

The right not to starve is a concrete application of that principle. 'Suppose a theft by a starving man ... the right violated is primary and essential one; one which, where there are many starving people, is in fact pretty sure to be

---

[63] *LPPO* §151. See also §§154–5, 207–8.

[64] Ibid. §207. See also §248.   [65] *PE* §§244–5.

[66] L. T. Hobhouse, *The Elements of Social Justice* (London: George Allen & Unwin, 1965 [1922]), 108.

[67] Green, *LPPO* §245.   [68] Ibid. §18.   [69] *PE* §267. See also §332.

[70] *LPPO* §189; *mine.*

protected by the most stringent penalties'.[71] It might be argued that, far from giving reason for a lighter punishment, the hunger of the thief should require heavier punishment in order that the temptation to steal will be neutralized.

Bentham made such an argument. He recognizes that 'the fact of extreme hunger suggests "the depravity of a man's disposition is less conclusive" than if the act had been committed by someone in different circumstances, where the temptation was weaker'. He, nevertheless—and this is the crucial point—'goes on to argue that the strength of the temptation does not excuse punishment because to do so would provide encouragement to those who may be tempted'.[72] Green could not disagree more. For,

this would be a one-sided application of the principle. [What principle? The principle that] It is not the business of the state to protect one order of rights specially, but all rights equally. [This requires that 'none gains at the expense of another (no one has any power guaranteed to him through another's being deprived of that power)'.[73]] It [the State] ought not, therefore, to protect a certain order of rights by associating special terror with the violation of them when the special temptation to their violation itself implies a violation of right in the persons of those who are so tempted, as is the case when a general danger to property arises from the fact that many people are on the edge of starvation. The attempt to do so is at once ineffectual and diverts attention from the true way of protecting the endangered right, which is to prevent people from falling into a state of starvation.[74]

The emphasis here is on the state protecting all rights equally, with special attention to the social and economic rights (positive rights) of the poor. Failing to do so would entail that the state does not protect all rights equally, but 'one special order of right specially': that is, the right to private property to the neglect of the right of the poor not to starve. Green does not quite argue that the right not to be stolen from is overridden by the right not to starve if the latter can be fulfilled only by infringing the former. He should have, though, given that the justice of punishment depends 'on the question whether the social organisation in which a criminal has lived and acted is one that has given him a fair chance of not being a criminal'.[75] But he comes close.

Providing a fair chance is securing positive rights for basic needs of life. To illustrate: Green supports legislation which interferes with freedom of contract between workers and employers, since the 'starving labourer' who is 'scarcely ... free ... to bargain for good wages with a master who offers him work'.[76]

<hr />

[71] Ibid. §194.

[72] Both are quoted by Harris and Morrow, ibid. p. 337 n. 12.

[73] Green, *LPPO* §132.   [74] Ibid. §194.   [75] Ibid. §189.

[76] T. H. Green, 'Lecture on "Liberal Legislation and Freedom of Contract"', in *LPPO*, p. 208. See also *LPPO* §§220–1, 224.

'Good wages', a decent level of income, is a positive right. As well are 'healthy houses and food, sound elementary education'.[77] A fully paid-up version of this argument which is implicit in Green is central to Hobhouse's positive liberalism. Green, not Mill, as Hobhouse acknowledges,[78] charts the course. Mill has never quite abandoned the principle of *laissez-faire*, notwithstanding his long list of exceptions. The new liberal course, however, introduced into modern liberalism a positive conception of the State as an enabling agency. It was necessary for securing not only mutual non-interference but also mutual aid in the shape of positive rights.

Mutual aid, secured by positive rights, is bound up with Green ridding 'interference' of its pejorative associations. We saw that fulfilling negative rights requires simply non-interference with others, but does not require assisting others. From the vantage-point of the confrontational view and the boundaries account of social relations, interference is essentially opposed to individual freedom, which 'territorial' rights aim to protect. Interference is always evil, even if necessary. Positive rights, by contrast, are bound up with the moral requirement to provide assistance to the worse-off members of society. Such assistance requires state interference with the freedom of action of the well-off—that is, their property rights or the free market.

'Interference', then, acquires a positive role in creating community. For it aims not so much to reduce the negative freedom of the obligation-bearer as to secure effective freedom to the worse-off, which benefits, Green claims, the well-off too. Interference with the well-off is, at the same time, aiding or enabling the development of the worse-off. Indeed, non-interference with the market (with the property rights of the well-off) is at the same time interference with the effective chance of the least favoured members of society to achieve their self-development. This claim is implicit in the example of 'a theft by a starving man' discussed above.[79]

To claim that 'interference' here is not a result of deliberate action by the well-off will not do for Green. For one thing, this sort of interference is a real obstacle to the self-development of the worse-off. For another, and importantly, starvation can be removed by deliberate state action. Nor does such interference use the well-off as mere means, since their chance of self-development (their higher well-being) is not significantly diminished. Indeed, not to interfere with poverty, squalid housing, and ill health would be for

---

[77] *PE* §332.   [78] Hobhouse, 'Liberalism', 55–60.

[79] The same claim is made more explicit in Green's claim that 'A man who possesses nothing but his powers of labour and who has to sell these to a capitalist for bare daily maintenance, might as well, in respect of the ethical purposes which the possession of property should serve, be denied the rights of property altogether' (*LPPO* §220. See also §§221, 223).

the State to violate its just role of protecting the rights of all equally. Green's principle of justice, which he defends as an alternative to both utilitarian liberalism (Mill) and neo-classical Liberalism (Spencer) is this: that no one is justified in receiving resources for higher well-being unless all, and especially the worse-off, are secured basic resources.[80]

How, then, do positive rights create community? By securing effective mutual dependence between all members of society. Green, we have seen, reconstructed rights both in form and in content. In form, rights are conceptually bound up with mutual recognition, which, in turn, connects them with social interest, both of which render rights inseparable from community. In content, positive rights are essential to the creation of effective community of mutually developing individuals by including the worse-off members of society.

Positive rights are not about dependence of one group of persons (worse-off) on another (well-off). Positive rights are about mutual dependence of all members. The importance of this point to Green's view of community cannot be overstated. The well-off recognize that their obligation to help the needy, as expressed in legislation securing positive rights, is grounded in effective equal rights for all, and acknowledge that society (of which the law is the organized voice) is essential to the equal rights of all, including themselves. Nor do positive rights infringe on the justifiable freedom of the well-off (who are required to perform certain actions of assistance), though they infringe on what they wish to do; neither are the well-off treated as mere means, since the interference in their actions is justifiable in terms of securing effective rights to all. Further, and importantly, not only the worse-off but the well-off, too, are the beneficiaries of positive rights.[81] And, of equal importance, securing positive rights to the worse-off enables them as well to contribute to the social well-being of society as a whole.

Ultimately, then, invoking rights, for Green, and especially positive rights, reveals the communal ties of individuals as always equal members in a co-operative social life, of which all are both beneficiaries and contributors. Hobhouse, who, it might be suggested, brought Green's positive liberalism to fruition, puts it best: 'Rights and duties ... are not conditions limiting the common good [community] from without, but conditions constituting the common good.'[82] This has been my main claim all along: we should properly regard Green's community of rights as a common good. Put differently, to claim that a community of rights is constitutive of the ideal community of mutually developing individuals is to reveal the complexity of Green's liberalism.

---

[80] *PE* §354.   [81] Ibid. §208.
[82] Hobhouse, *Elements of Social Justice*, 43. See also pp. 106–9.

VI. The Complexity of Liberalism and Liberal Continuity: Rights and Community

Though the explicit object of my article is to explore Green's community of rights, thereby to expose the complex nature of his liberalism, my implicit goal is to indicate the complexity of liberalism in general. In particular, I wish to draw attention, briefly as this must be, to the conceptual dynamics of liberalism, to the non-instrumental value of a teleological conception of rights, and to the connection between liberal common good (a system of rights) and liberal community (co-operative social life).

Green's community of rights illustrates the conceptual dynamics of liberalism by revealing the contingent relation between narrow individualism (atomist and egoist) and rights. Individualism, interest, and rights are among the essential ideas in the liberal conceptual basket. No simple connection between fixed concepts can, however, capture the richness of liberalism. Rather, different strands of liberalism result from changing configurations of concepts, which simultaneously depend on and shape the content of the relevant concepts, and are forged in response to problems that liberals seek to solve from within a liberal framework. An important implication of the conceptual dynamic of liberalism is that there is no single liberalism, but a family of liberalisms.[83]

To illustrate briefly: Mill was worried about 'the tyranny of the majority' and the impoverishment of liberalism by Benthamite utilitarianism. The result was placing the value of individuality at the centre of liberalism in conjunction with developmental democracy and the harm principle. Assimilating these into his liberalism, Green sought to address the 'social problem' of poverty and social injustice. Hence, sociability, which constitutes one aspect of Mill's individuality, gains centre stage in Green's liberalism, and consequently in the new liberalism, in the shape of a community of mutually dependent and developing individuals. This shift of community to the centre of Green's new liberalism is bound up with reconstruction of the institution of rights. (It is, of course, also and importantly bound up with rethinking the nature of freedom, but this cannot be discussed here.) Transformed both in form and in content, a system of rights is essential to the realization of Green's ideal of community. Indeed, a community of rights is itself a common good. In turn, transforming the language of rights is inseparable from reshaping 'interest' away from selfish self-interest to 'social interest', and state intervention from a mere obstacle to freedom to an enabling tool in the creation of a community in which the free development of each is dependent on and enhances the free development of others.

---

[83] Freeden, 'Family of Liberalisms'.

Liberals insist that securing the value of free individual development requires taking rights seriously. This, however—so goes the argument—is inconsistent with taking rights teleologically, as Green does. Much as Green's defence of positive freedom is not inimical to his liberal concerns which justify it, so his teleological conception of rights is not less liberal than the stringent rights strain in liberalism. This is the second aspect of the complexity of liberalism to which I should like to draw attention. Complexity is lost when we approach liberal arguments from a discourse of simple oppositions. We saw that Green's claim that there are no rights against the state raises 'standard' or 'mainstream' liberal ire for no good reason. Nor, I hold, does Green's teleological conception of rights.

What is the liberal worry? It is that a teleological justification of rights renders them derivative and not foundational, thereby subverting their primary, normative role. From Kant to Rawls, liberals view utilitarianism as a major threat to the integrity of human dignity. (Whether this is the case with Mill's utilitarian liberalism is debatable, but not so welfarism.) And with good reason. Much the same way that the concept of distributive justice as a basic ethical concept is foreign to utilitarianism, so is the concept of basic rights. Both distributive justice and the basic rights which implement it are unsafe in the face of a maximizing social good. The impetus for this worry is the belief that certain fundamental human interests demand protection (enshrined in rights) regardless of whether or not they maximize social utility.

An excessive worry invites an excessive response. The threat of maximizing social purpose is fenced off by assigning rights some sort of absolute normative status. Whether in the shape of natural or moral rights, rights as 'trumps', as 'primary goods', or as 'generic', rights are regarded as 'foundational' and not merely 'derivative'.

Green's teleological justification of rights does not, however, entail marginalizing their normative significance. Utilitarianism (or maximizing consequentialism) is not the only kind of teleology. Much as perfectionism (*contra* Rawls) is not necessarily maximizing, so is teleology. Green's Aristotelian teleology is non-maximizing. Indeed, like Rawls and for the same reasons, he rejects maximizing moral rightness.[84] Though teleologically understood, the normative role of rights for Green, as for Rawls, is to enable the pursuit of human flourishing, a conception of human good which they share, not least because of their common debt to Aristotle.[85] In Green's hands teleological rights are,

---

[84] See my 'Was T. H. Green a Utilitarian?', *Utilitas*, 7 (1995), 122–44.
[85] John Rawls, *Theory of Justice* (Cambridge, Mass.: Harvard University Press, 1971), 424–33, 523, 528–9.

then, not an instrumental tool for maximizing social purpose. Nor are Green's rights 'merely instrumental' to a non-maximizing social purpose.

Such criticism is sometimes advanced against the Idealist theory of rights. This is how the criticism goes. A common good justification of rights—from social purpose (the well-being of society) to 'functions' (corresponding to social positions), to rights as instrumental to discharging of functions—deprives rights of their primary normative status.[86]

The problem with this criticism is its abstractness. Surely, whether rights are merely instrumental, and thus morally subordinate, depends on the nature of social purpose or the common good. To criticize the claim that rights are relative to, or derivative of, some social good will not do, since the appeal to the promotion of some abstract good tells us nothing about actual obligations and actual rights of actual persons. The criticism, however, depends on some abstract social good which raises the ugly spectre of some tyranny over the individual, of subverting the value of the individual. The present essay demonstrates clearly the folly of such criticism if applied to Green.

Even on the abstract level, however, Green's teleological rights are not vulnerable to the said criticism. For while it is the case that they are derivative of and relative to the well-being of society (common good), the goal of society is to enable the development of all its members. Accordingly, it should be 'so organised that *everyone's capacities* have free scope for their development'.[87] Rights, and particularly positive rights, constitute that organization.

Here again, and contrary to first impressions, Green and Rawls share significant liberal insights, notwithstanding important differences between them. This is my point: Green's system of rights is itself a common good, much as Rawls views justice as the common good.[88] This, of course, is not news. The idea of the common good in terms of rightness is central to liberalism. The news, rather, is that for both Green and Rawls the idea of common good is bound up with an idea of community as co-operative social life. Whereas Green employs 'common good' to the ideal of community, Rawls views community as social union of social unions, and justice as the common good. Different labelling should not, however, obscure the substantive normative argument they share. It is that justice, or a system of rights, is constitutive of, and essential to, the realization of an ideal of co-operative life without which individuals cannot fulfil their human potential.

---

[86] Gewirth, *Human Rights*, 158–9. See also my 'Idealist Organicism: Beyond Holism and Individualism', *History of Political Thought*, 12 (1991), 529–33.

[87] Green, *LPPO* §171; mine.

[88] '*Commonweal* Interview with John Rawls', in *John Rawls, Collected Papers*, ed. Samuel Freeman (Cambridge, Mass.: Harvard University Press, 1999), 622.

At the heart of this ideal is the claim that no one can become a complete exemplar of humanity; for 'we are by ourselves but parts of what we might be'.[89] We need each other to complete our humanity. Hence, only in a social union, 'the members of a community participate in one another's nature ... the self is realized in the activities of many selves'[90] Green could not agree more.[91] The conception of a community of complementary human goods lies at the heart of their liberalism.

The good of a community of complementary human goods cannot, however, be realized without justice. As Rawls puts it, 'What binds a society's efforts into one social union is the mutual recognition and acceptance of the principles of justice; it is this general affirmation which extends the ties of identification over the whole community ... Individual and group accomplishments are no longer seen as just so many separate personal goods.'[92] That is very much the impetus behind Green's system of rights understood as community of mutual recognition. The essential implication of this argument is that rightness, system of rights or justice, is not simply prior to, or independent of, the good of a community of completion. Rather, liberal rightness is constitutive of, and essential to, the realization of a liberal community of completion. This is the liberal message (insight) of Green's re-conceptualization of rights, which finds a clear echo in the third, unfortunately neglected, part of Rawls's *Theory of Justice*. I suggest that Green more than any other modern liberal articulated this distinctive liberal argument. Indeed, as I suggested above, I believe that Green's liberalism provides us with the key to unlock a distinctive, though much unrecognized, communitarian (or positive) strand within modern liberalism.

---

[89] Rawls, *Theory of Justice*, 529.   [90] Ibid. 565.
[91] e.g. Green, *PE* §§269, 273–4, 279, 288, 360, 370.
[92] Rawls, *Theory of Justice*, 571.

11

Contesting the Common Good: T. H. Green and Contemporary Republicanism

COLIN TYLER

I. Introduction

Looking back to the 1850s and his undergraduate days at Balliol with T. H. Green, Edward Caird, and John Nichol, A. V. Dicey recalled that 'we considered ourselves advanced Radicals, not to say Republicans'.[1] Later in life Green identified himself explicitly with the radical wing of Advanced Liberalism, an orientation which implied republican leanings. Unfortunately, 'republicanism' was a rather vague concept during the period, 'representing', in Gregory Claeys's words, 'more an ethos than a programme'.[2] Consequently, and in spite of the apparent continuities in Green's political sympathies, I am not concerned here to decode Dicey's intriguing claim; nor am I concerned to assess the extent to which it would be meaningful (and if meaningful, then accurate) to describe the mature Green as a republican by the lights of his own time. Instead, I will look at Green's relation to contemporary republicanism.

Surprisingly little work has been done on Green's relationship to republicanism,[3] and he receives passing references only in the work of the contemporary

---

[1] Reminiscence of A. V. Dicey, in William Knight, *Memoir of John Nichol* (Glasgow, 1896), 140.

[2] Gregory Claeys, 'Republicanism', in John Balcham and Richard Price (eds.), *Dictionary of Nineteenth-Century History* (Harmondsworth: Penguin, 1994), 523.

[3] Dimensions of these issues are addressed in the literature: Peter Nicholson, 'T. H. Green and State Action: Liquor Legislation', *History of Political Thought*, 6 (1985), 517–60; Olive Anderson, 'The Feminism of T. H. Green: A Late-Victorian Success Story?', *History of Political Thought*, 12:4 (1991), 671–93; Eugenio Biagini, 'Neo-Roman Liberalism: "Republican" Values and British Liberalism, ca. 1860–1875', *History of European Ideas*, 29 (2003), 55–72; and Colin Tyler, *Idealist Political Philosophy: Pluralism and Conflict in Absolute Idealist Thought* (London and New York: Continuum, 2006), ch. 2.

members of the school.[4] Philip Pettit and John Braithwaite do describe him as one of a very few liberals who 'are best seen as covert republicans', in that he 'argued that liberty involves a socio-legal condition essentially [rather than merely contingently]'.[5] Hopefully, it will become clear in what follows that this is not the most important similarity.

Yet, there are differences as well. Contemporary republicans prioritize participation and democratic contestation as bulwarks against vested interests and élite rule (Barber); as mechanisms for avoiding arbitrary government, thereby securing the liberty of the citizens (Pettit and Sandel); as means of integrating and educating citizens into the republic and of helping to legitimize its power structures (Dagger); and as necessary facets of self-government and self-expression (Honohan).[6] This chapter argues that Green values participation and contestation—the life of the active citizen—for a rather different reason. Such interactions are indispensable facets of a dialogue between rational beings about the nature of the good life, and about which character types and social arrangements will most successfully help to instantiate that life in one's community, given its particular circumstances. Section II introduces the contemporary debate between liberals and republicans. Two strands are distinguished within contemporary republican thought: the 'classical', or 'protective', and the 'civic humanist'. Particular attention is paid to the respective positions of non-domination and civic virtue within each of these two strands. Section III contrasts Green's conception of true freedom with freedom as non-domination (also called 'independence'). True freedom is shown to contain negative and positive freedom (in Berlin's sense), as well as autonomy, and itself to be a facet of the intertwined processes of intra- and inter-subjective recognition. The Aristotelian and Kantian inheritances of Green's moral realism are recurring themes of this discussion. Section IV contrasts Green's conception of civic virtue with contemporary republican conceptions. Section V argues that, for Green, the common good is an inherently contested notion in human communities. Consequently, Green understands conflictual democratic participation to be a necessary feature of the good life, which should be valued primarily as a vehicle for the development of

---

[4] e.g. Benjamin Barber, *Strong Democracy: Participatory Politics for a New Age*, 4th printing (Cambridge: Cambridge University Press, 1990), 173; Richard Dagger, *Civic Virtues: Rights, Citizenship, and Republican Liberalism* (Oxford: Oxford University Press, 1997), 5, 20–1, 23, 83.

[5] John Braithwaite and Philip Pettit, *Not Just Deserts: A Republican Theory of Criminal Justice* (Oxford: Clarendon Press, 1990), 57.

[6] Barber, *Strong Democracy*, part II. Philip Pettit, *Republicanism: A Theory of Freedom and Government* (Oxford: Oxford University Press, 1997), chs. 7, 8. Michael Sandel, *Democracy's Discontent: America in Search of a Public Policy* (London: Belknap, Harvard, 1996), 25–8. Dagger, *Civic Virtues*, ch. 7. Iseult Honohan, *Civic Republicanism* (London: Routledge, 2002), 214–21.

the citizen-body. Section VI traces the political implications of this inherent social dynamic, once again contrasting Green's position with that defended by contemporary republicans. Section VII explores Green's associated claim that in certain cases the true patriot has a duty to engage in civil disobedience and even revolution. The chapter concludes by arguing that Green advocates a form of republicanism that is radical even by contemporary standards. His distinctive and coherent position straddles the divide between the protective and civic humanist variants, and shares the respective strengths of both.

II. The Contemporary Republican Landscape

John Rawls famously dismissed the proposition, later iterated by Pettit, that any 'fundamental opposition' existed between protective republicanism and political liberalism.[7] Ronald Dworkin describes himself as a 'liberal civic republican', pointing to his endorsement of an 'integrated' view of the good life, such that the citizen

will count his own life as diminished—a less good life than he might have had—if he lives in an unjust community, no matter how hard he has tried to make it just. … [This represents] the important way in which individual citizens should merge their interests and personality into political community.[8]

This very influential liberal ontology is also of a type with Richard Dagger's 'republican liberalism' and Michael Sandel's 'more civic-minded liberalism',[9] both of which maintain a 'fundamental right of autonomy', which primarily they tend to ground by appealing to an essentially Dworkian social ontology.[10]

Nevertheless, contemporary republicanism does place special weight on four particular values in a way that liberalism characteristically does not. These values are freedom understood as non-domination, participation, civic virtue, and recognition.[11] The relative importance of these values varies, depending on the

---

[7] John Rawls, *Political Liberalism* (New York: Columbia University Press, 1993), 205. Cf. Will Kymlicka, 'Liberal Egalitarianism and Civic Republicanism: Friends or Enemies?', in his *Politics in the Vernacular: Nationalism, Multiculturalism, and Citizenship* (Oxford: Oxford University Press, 2001), 327–46.

[8] Ronald Dworkin, *Sovereign Virtue: The Theory and Practice of Equality* (Cambridge, Mass.: Harvard University Press, 2000), 233; see ibid. 231–6.

[9] Dagger, *Civic Virtues*, ch. 3 (Dagger's book is even subtitled *Rights, Citizenship, and Republican Liberalism*); Sandel, *Democracy's Discontent*, 333. Honohan, *Civic Republicanism*, 262–3.

[10] Dagger, *Civic Virtues*, ch. 2.

[11] This list is endorsed by Dagger, Pettit, Honohan, and others.

specific conception of republicanism.[12] Classical or 'protective'[13] republicanism is best typified in the recent work of Philip Pettit.[14] Its primary concern is the individual's vulnerability to the whim of others, and its primary aspiration is to construct a 'non-dominating' public sphere, in which citizens are secure—or, as Pettit puts it, in which they enjoy 'independence'. The central point is not an absence of interference by other agents. Instead, it is to make interference as predictable and as fair as possible. The protective republican public sphere is one in which power is exercised 'non-arbitrarily', in the sense that it is founded upon collective decisions which track deliberately the interests of those over whom power is exercised, and which do so according to the citizens' own understanding of those interests. On this conceptually sparse view, civic virtue, democratic institutions and norms, and indispensable constitutional conventions such as open government and public contestation derive their value from their tendency to foster non-dominating circumstances in which the body politic can deliberate and act. For protective republicans, civic virtue should be fostered amongst all citizens, in order to achieve this type of checking. The underlying contention is that politically active and astute virtuous citizens impose more effective checks on the rulers than does a selfish or acquiescent mass.

Civic humanist republicans, such as Dagger, Sandel, and Honohan, reverse the internal structure of protective republicanism. They derive the significance and value of non-domination from the fact that the absence of perceived threats and of the exercise of arbitrary inference are conditions necessary for the flourishing of civic virtue among the citizen body.[15] This flourishing fosters the individual's sense of integration into society, his or her sense of belonging and hence the sense of security. Most importantly, it makes such an individual a certain sort of person. In short, the type of republicanism advocated by Sandel, Dagger, and Honohan takes as its foundational value not non-domination, but the citizens' possession and exercise of civic virtue. Civic humanist republicans

---

[12] Rawls, *Political Liberalism*, 205–6. Kymlicka implies that Rawls originated this distinction (Kymlicka, *Politics in the Vernacular*, 335, 337). Rawls actually acknowledges as his source (Political Liberalism, 206 n. 38) Charles Taylor, *Philosophical Papers* (Cambridge: Cambridge University Press, 1985), ii. 334 f.

[13] The influence of certain strands of Roman political thought on the first variant should not blind us to civic humanism's equally strong lineage from ancient Athens. See Eugenio Biagini, 'Liberalism and Direct Democracy: John Stuart Mill and the Model of Ancient Athens', in E. F. Biagini (ed.), *Citizenship and Community: Liberals, Radicals and Collective Identities in the British Isles 1865–1931* (Cambridge: Cambridge University Press, 1996), 21–44. Green seems to have appreciated this ('Witness of God', *CW* iii. 240). I discard 'classical republicanism' in favour of Held's label, 'protective republicanism', wherever ease of exposition permits (David Held, *Models of Democracy*, 2nd edn. (Cambridge: Polity, 1996), ch. 2).

[14] Pettit, *Republicanism*.

[15] Dagger, *Civic Virtue*; Sandel, *Democracy's Discontent*, esp. 317–51; and Honohan, *Civic Republicanism*.

see an individual's embodiment of civic virtue as being inherently valuable, whereas classical republicans see it as instrumentally so.

III. Independence and True Freedom

Whether they hold it to be a peripheral value (as in civic humanism) or a core one (as in the protective variant), by their very nature, republicans accord a crucial role in their theories to freedom understood as non-domination (or 'independence'). This section begins by comparing the internal structure of this concept with Green's concept of 'true freedom'. It then shows that while clear similarities exist between independence and true freedom, crucial differences are also present. Not least of these is the necessary dialectic within truly free agency which arises from the agent's simultaneous perception of her hermeneutic context as both given and requiring critical appraisal and, in some cases, reform. Neither side of this dialectical process is conceivable without its relation to the other. Hence, true freedom—the cardinal value in Green's political thought—is driven by both the inherently paradoxical structure of a rational agent's scheme of meanings and values and its incompleteness. Green's theory of true freedom will be shown to be far more complex than non-domination, entailing not merely a notion of critical social embeddedness, but also a conception of the common good as a locus of debate between citizens.

The literature on the republican conception of freedom is too large and (needlessly) involved to discuss in detail.[16] Fortunately, the basic ideas underlying its political dimensions are relatively straightforward. Pettit has observed that

> The republican conception of freedom invokes the notion, not just of interference, but of arbitrary interference: interference on an arbitrary basis. What makes an act of interference arbitrary? Roughly ... the fact that it is subject just to the *arbitrium*, the ['unconstrained'] decision or judgement, of the [interfering] agent. An act of interference will be non-arbitrary so far as it is suitably constrained: in particular so far as it is constrained to satisfy the interests of those who suffer the interference, according to their ideas about those interests; if it imposes alien ideas or interests, then it will represent imposition on an arbitrary basis.[17]

This form of freedom requires at least two things. First, arbitrary interference by other actors in the (broadly conceived) public lives of all citizens must

---

[16] Particularly important here is Philip Pettit, *Theory of Freedom: From the Psychology to the Politics of Agency* (Cambridge: Polity, 2001).

[17] Philip Pettit, 'Republican Theory and Criminal Punishment', *Utilitas*, 9:1 (March 1997), 61.

be 'resiliently absent'.[18] In order to fulfil this condition, it is not sufficient that arbitrary power is not actually exercised over an individual. In addition, there must be effective publicly promulgated mechanisms to prevent it being exercised. Second, this notion of freedom requires citizens to *recognize* that such interference is resiliently absent. Where both conditions obtain, Pettit writes, citizens possess freedom understood as 'non-domination', and thereby 'enjoy franchise'.[19] Notice that the tracking of interests is a method of sustaining independence, rather than being one of its defining characteristics. Finally, it is worth noting that in response to Skinner's objections, Pettit now accepts the importance of non-interference, even if he still argues that non-domination should be given lexical priority over it.[20]

Jonathan Wolff has summarized the philosophical commitments underlying Pettit's conception very effectively.

According to Pettit, freedom in the individual requires attention to three things: not just free action, but also freedom of the self and freedom of the person. The free self is someone who is not alienated from his or her actions, and the free person is someone who is not acting under coercion. Given that this last element is defined in terms of one's relations to others, there must be a social element to the analysis of freedom.[21]

It will become clear in this section that there are striking similarities between this theory of freedom and the one endorsed by Green.

It would not be misplaced to see Green as developing what is fundamentally a theory of situated freedom.[22] On that level at least, he is like contemporary republicans. However, Green's conception of freedom is noteworthy, not least because it involves neither simple non-interference nor simple non-domination. He develops his particular conception in his magnificent essay 'On the Different Senses of "Freedom" as Applied to Will and to the Moral Progress of Man'.[23] His discussion begins by distinguishing between the freedom of the

---

[18] Philip Pettit, *Common Mind* (Oxford: Oxford University Press, 1993), 319.

[19] Ibid. 333.

[20] Philip Pettit, 'Keeping Republican Freedom Simple: On a Difference with Quentin Skinner', *Political Theory*, 30:3 (June 2002), 339–56. Pettit employs a distinction between 'conditioning' freedom and 'compromising' it: non-arbitrary laws 'condition' freedom, although they do not 'compromise' it. Pettit claims that, almost by definition, liberals think that laws *do* compromise freedom, e.g. Jeremy Bentham; non-liberals sometimes agree, e.g. on one reading, Thomas Hobbes.

[21] Jonathan Wolff, 'No Domination', *Times Literary Supplement*, 7 May 2004, p. 11.

[22] Precisely as is the case for Hegel (see my *Idealist Political Philosophy*, ch. 1).

[23] Green, 'On the Different Senses of "Freedom" as Applied to Will and to the Moral Progress of Man' (hereafter DSF), in *LPPO*, esp. 1–2. My interpretation of Green's theory accords with that developed in Peter Nicholson, *Political Philosophy of the British Idealists: Selected Studies* (Cambridge: Cambridge University Press, 1990), study IV. See my *Thomas Hill Green (1836–1882) and the Philosophical Foundations of Politics: An Internal Critique* (Lampeter and Lewiston, NY: Edwin Mellen Press, 1998), ch. 2. Dimova-Cookson defends a very controversial interpretation in 'A New Scheme

will, juristic freedom, and 'positive', 'real', or 'true' freedom.[24] Regarding the first, Green argues that a rational agent as such necessarily possesses a free will, in that her nature as a self-conscious being entails that she must conceive of any object whose attainment she wills as being internally related to her own conception of her own good (no matter how misplaced or poorly thought out that conception is). Free will is distinguished from 'the primary or juristic sense' of the word, where freedom is an agent's 'exemption from control by other men and ability to do as he likes'.[25] In other words, juristic freedom is very close to Berlin's category of 'negative freedom' (although the former has additional extra-legal dimensions).[26] Finally, reflecting debts to Aristotle's concept of eudaimonia and the Pauline conception of freedom, Green defines 'true' freedom as the uncoerced pursuit of an object in the attainment of which the agent can—'given the law of his being'—'find satisfaction of himself'.[27] The attainment of such an object would bring the agent an 'abiding satisfaction of ... [his] abiding self'.[28]

'True freedom' is clearly more conceptually complex than non-domination. The additional complexity flows from Green's guiding idea: a rational being is truly free to the extent that she subjectively wills the attainment of an end or state of affairs that possesses objective worth.[29] This is significant because, for Green, the condition of subjective willing entails at least two things.[30] On the one hand, the agent's choice must be unconstrained by the will of another agent: hence, to realize her subjective will, the agent must be free in a negative sense. On the other hand, as a developed expression of the freedom of the will, willing subjectively (as opposed to simply capriciously) entails self-conscious deliberation by the agent prior to her adoption of a particular goal and a method of attaining that goal.[31] In other words, the agent must make an autonomous

---

of Positive and Negative Freedom: Reconstructing T. H. Green on Freedom', *Political Theory*, 31:4 (Aug. 2003), 508–32. See also Maria Dimova-Cookson, *T. H. Green's Moral and Political Philosophy: A Phenomenological Perspective* (Basingstoke: Palgrave, 2001), ch. 4.

[24] Green uses 'positive freedom' to denote this value. Clearly, that phrase has different connotations in contemporary debates. I use 'true freedom' in Green's sense, and 'positive freedom' in the sense popularized by Berlin.

[25] DSF 17.

[26] Juristic freedom is close to at least Berlin's initial restricted formulation of the concept: 'I am normally said to be free to the degree to which no man or body of men interferes with my activity' (Isaiah Berlin, 'Two Concepts of Liberty', in his *Four Essays on Liberty* (Oxford: Oxford University Press, 1969), 122).

[27] Green, DSF 1.

[28] PE §234. See ibid. §171, and Tyler, *Thomas Hill Green and the Philosophical Foundations of Politics*, 76–83.

[29] Green, PE §§171–9 *passim*. DSF 17.   [30] DSF 21.

[31] This is autonomy in the common liberal sense, so succinctly articulated by J. S. Mill ('On Liberty', in his *Utilitarianism, On Liberty and Considerations on Representative Government*, ed. H. B. Acton

choice to pursue the specific goal. Yet, even where the agent is as 'negatively' free and as autonomous as possible, she is truly free in Green's sense only to the extent that the object she endorses actually is one in which she can find abiding satisfaction. Hence, Green's concept of true freedom entails Berlin's notion of positive freedom, in that it requires the individual to be guided by 'reason' and a 'higher nature', to act as a 'self which calculates and aims at what will satisfy it in the long run'.[32] Nevertheless, Green's careful positioning of negative freedom and autonomy at the very heart of his theory of true freedom ensures that he is not open to the allegation—made by Berlin and many others—that he does, or at least logically should, justify authoritarian and even totalitarian methods in the name of promoting freedom.[33]

Green integrates this conception of freedom into a sophisticated and powerful theory of socially embedded, yet self-determining, individuality. A good point at which to begin to explore its intricacies is his pregnant claim that

social life is to personality what language is to thought. Language presupposes thought as a capacity, but in us the capacity of thought is only actualised in language. So human society presupposes persons in capacity—subjects capable of each conceiving himself and the betterment of his life as an end to himself—but it is only in the intercourse of men, each recognised by each as an end, not merely as a means, and thus as having reciprocal claims, that the capacity is actualised and that we really live as persons.[34]

Green conceives of the construction of one's sense of personal identity as being embedded in irreducibly social processes in a number of ways.[35] First, and most simply, a person (sc. a self-conscious rational agent who is capable of pursuing her own true improvement) can conceptualize her projects, attachments, relationships, and roles—initially at least—only by using frameworks that have been derived from the schemes of meaning and value into which she was socialized.[36] Second, a self-conscious agent can gain a sense of personal identity only via personal participation in ongoing reflective projects that aim at the furtherance of her own higher-order projects, roles, and attachments, and those of other persons about whom she cares (sc. through 'contributions to

---

(London: Dent, 1972), 126). Green may have avoided using 'autonomy' in this manner because of its rather different use in the Kantian tradition.

[32] Berlin, 'Two Concepts of Liberty', 132.

[33] Berlin, 'Introduction', in his *Four Essays on Liberty*, p. xlix n.; Melvin Richter, *Politics of Conscience: T. H. Green and his Age* (London: Weidenfeld & Nicolson, 1964), 202–5, 224–5, 255–9; Michael St John Packe, *Life of John Stuart Mill* (London: Secker & Warburg, 1954), 403, 526 n. 8; John Horton, *Political Obligation* (London: Macmillan, 1992), 75–6; W. H. Greenleaf, *British Political Tradition, ii: The Ideological Heritage* (London: Routledge, 1983), 29, 124–42.

[34] Green, *PE* §183.

[35] Green, 'Lectures on Moral and Political Philosophy', *CW* v. 173–82.

[36] *PE* §§216–17. DSF 23–4.

the common good').[37] Green draws these strands together with the claim that in order to enjoy true freedom, there must be a 'settled disposition on each man's part to make the most and best of humanity in his own person and in the persons of others'.[38] Let us examine these related claims in greater depth.

Green holds that a truly free individual pursues as his ultimate good the 'realisation of the soul's faculties in certain pursuits and achievements, and in a certain organisation of life'.[39] He characterizes these faculties as ideals of 'personal excellence, moral and intellectual',[40] and 'the full exercise or realisation of the soul's faculties in accordance with its proper excellence, which ... [is] an excellence of thought, speculative and practical'.[41] Serving each of these collective ideals fosters different virtues and talents, and so different faculties of the soul. The pursuits, achievements, and organizations manifesting these excellences are conceived and undertaken within a hermeneutic context of the concrete practices and institutions of one's society. In this way, they are historically conditioned and subject to re-evaluation and reform.

To satisfy a rational being, the determinate instantiations of these capacities must fit together harmoniously and be organized so as to form a systematic whole, and must be understood by the agent as so doing. When operationalized, this system of norms and values constitutes 'a perfection of the rational man, an unfolding of his capacities in full harmonious activity'.[42] This leads Green to conclude that there must be some point of orientation within this system of concepts if it is to bring an abiding satisfaction to a rational agent. Hence, he endorses Aristotle's assertion that an enriching association gains its identity from 'a good purpose'[43] or fundamental value. The agent should conceive of this ultimate value as being instantiated both subjectively and objectively—for example, as when it exists through the individual's recognition of the authority of a determinate 'conception of a complex organisation of life, with laws and institutions, with relationships, courtesies and charities, with arts and graces through which the perfection [of the agent] is to be attained'.[44]

Such a perception embodies a fundamental paradox, however, in that on the one hand it is constituted by the conception of these projects as 'given' (sc. externally created and validated), while also containing the conceptualization

---

[37] Green, 'Lecture on Liberal Legislation and Freedom of Contract' (hereafter LLFC), in LPPO 200. He develops this stage of his theory in PE, Book III.

[38] PE §244.   [39] Ibid. §254.   [40] Ibid. §355.

[41] Ibid. §254. His moral realism undermines Dimova-Cookson's claim that it is appropriate to read Green as a proto-phenomenologist. See her T. H. Green's Moral and Political Philosophy, esp. ch. 1. For an alternative perspective, see my T. H. Green and the Philosophical Foundations of Politics, ch. 2.

[42] Green, PE §255.   [43] Aristotle Politics 1251ᵃ1.

[44] Green, DSF 23; PE §§216–17.

of these same projects as being constantly open to reassessment, re-formation, and re-validation by the agent herself.[45] The first conception of her projects (as 'given') persists in virtue of the functions which it fulfils within the practical reason of a rational being. Green makes clear that the agent's perception of her determinate collective pursuits, achievements, and organizations of life—such as the social practice of 'parenthood'—as 'social facts' (adopting Durkheim's later terminology) brings three main benefits to a rational agent. (a) It gives practical force to her frameworks of meaning and value, thereby helping to produce a stable and predictable environment within which the agent can plan and perform purposive actions.[46] (b) It helps her to become conscious of her highest human capacities by presenting them to her as a concrete reality.[47] (c) It reinforces her sense of the ultimate reality of the moral universe.[48] This last point is important in that, not only is Green a moral realist, but he also believes that a rational, self-conscious agent can only revere an imperative that she believes possesses categorical force.[49] The endorsement and enforcement of values attendant upon their embodiment within and through social norms, laws, and the like reinforces the agent's perception of the inherent authority of her cardinal values. Hence, the agent is more likely to appreciate that these values are not validated by purely personal desire or whim alone, but are held to form features of a moral universe which exists independently of any subjective beliefs or desires.

Yet, as has been remarked already, there is paradox here, for in fact social practices, norms, and the like are not simply perceived as 'given'. Green observes in the *Lectures on the Principles of Political Obligation* that, although the 'active presence' of 'the idea of a social good' 'in their [the citizens'] consciousness is due to the institutions, the organisation of life, under which they are born and bred, the existence of institutions is in turn due to the action, under other conditions, of the same idea in the minds of men'.[50] In his manuscripts he develops this idea by invoking the notion of a person as a unique and active focal point of social influences: 'such relationships make up the reality of the man's self ... as [they are] centred in his self-consciousness'.[51] In fact, Green endorses what would now be called a 'practice view of social integration'.[52] The good will is the crucial organizing influence,[53] thereby ensuring that the individual has at least the capacity to help perfect the formal structure of her society. He holds that society is a relational organism: it

---

[45] *PE* §§180–91.   [46] *DSF* 23–5.   [47] *PE* §§181–3.
[48] Ibid. §§188–92.   [49] *DSF* 18–20.   [50] *LPPO* §131.
[51] Green's Papers, Balliol College, Oxford, MS23, quoted in my *Thomas Hill Green and the Philosophical Foundations of Politics*, 88. Green's contraction has been silently expanded.
[52] Dworkin, *Sovereign Virtue*, 222–7.   [53] Green, *PE* §247.

exists only in and through the rational, systematic interactions of self-conscious persons. Its character grows out of the life of its members, with the latter being 'a life determined by their intercourse with each other and deriving its peculiar features from the conditions of that intercourse'.[54]

It may be thought that we are moving too quickly, for a crucial part of Green's theory of true freedom has not yet been justified. This is the claim that true freedom aims at a goal that serves the common good. He observes in his famous 'Lecture on Liberal Legislation and Freedom of Contract' that

We shall probably all agree that freedom, rightly understood, is the greatest of blessings; that its attainment is the true end of all our effort as citizens. ... When we speak of freedom as something to be so highly prized, we mean a positive power or capacity of doing or enjoying something worth doing or enjoying, and that, too, something that we do or enjoy in common with others. ... That end is what I call freedom in the positive sense: in other words, the liberation of the powers of all men equally for contributions to the common good.[55]

Green argues that honouring a good purpose can produce a truly free action only to the extent that the particular good purpose requires the agent to prioritize the well-being of other members of his society.[56] Hence the good purpose of the family should be to raise well-balanced, conscientious, secure, and happy children; that of the sanitation board of a local council should be to improve public health; and that of a good society to realize the highest capacities of its members.[57] In other words, it may appear that Green has made something of a jump here, from the contention that enriching communities are orientated by reference to some good purpose, to the rather more contentious claim that this good purpose must be the service of a 'common good'.[58]

In fact, this is Green's development of the Kantian argument that such an agent is under a categorical imperative to find completion as an active citizen of a kingdom of ends.[59] He justifies his more demanding reformulation of this epochal idea by invoking a common ontological feature of contemporary republicanism: the need for recognition. He identifies the central idea in his manuscripts. '[It is q]uite true that an individual man neither is, nor conceives

---

[54]   Green, *PE* §184.   [55]   *LLFC* 199, 200.   [56]   *DSF* 24–5.

[57]   *PE* §§227–32, 299. *LPPO* §§38–9, 118.

[58]   A now standard distinction should be drawn between the 'Common Good' of the ideal community and the 'common good' of actual societies (particular common goods are imperfect expressions of the one Common Good) (Tyler, *T. H. Green and the Philosophical Foundations of Politics*, 96–7). The former is the ideal by which the worth of the latter is judged.

[59]   Green, *PE* §205. Immanuel Kant, 'Groundwork of the Metaphysics of Morals', in his *Practical Philosophy*, trans. and ed. M. J. Gregor (Cambridge: Cambridge University Press, 1996), 83–4 (Prussian Academy Edition iv. 433–4). On active citizenship, see Immanuel Kant, *The Metaphysics of Morals*, trans. Mary Gregor (Cambridge: Cambridge University Press, 1991), 125–6.

himself as, anything apart from relations to others. Such relationships make up the reality of the man's self, but it is only as centred in his self-consciousness that they are what they are.'[60] In effect, Green is positing the interaction of two types of recognition, which have come to be called the intersubjective and the intrasubjective.[61] In the first, in essence we assimilate our identity in response to our perceptions of the ways in which we are viewed by others, whereas in the second we construct our identities via critical reflection on the different and often competing values, loyalties, and beliefs that we find within ourselves. Green develops his broadly Hegelian theory of intersubjective recognition most fully in the *Prolegomena*.

Some practical recognition of personality by another—of an 'I' by a 'Thou' and 'Thou' by an 'I'—is necessary to any practical consciousness of it, to any such consciousness of it as can express itself in act. ... [W]e, who are born under an established system of family ties, and of reciprocal rights and obligations sanctioned by the state, learn to regard ourselves as persons among other persons because we are treated as such. From the dawn of intelligence we are treated, in one way or another, as entitled to have a will of our own, to make ourselves the objects of our actions, on condition of our practically recognising the same title in others. All education goes on the principle that we are, or are able to become, persons in this sense.[62]

A rational agent can gain a sense of herself as a rational agent via her critical analysis of her treatment as such by her fellows. In part this applies at the level of concrete social roles—one can understand what it is to be a university lecturer by critically analysing the expectations that others have of one in this role. Yet, certain things are presupposed by the very notion of the individual as the occupant of any active social role. Hence, the individual gains a sense of herself as a rational agent from her reflection on the presuppositions of her self-conscious activities as instances of rational action as such. It is in this way that we develop an idea of ourselves as self-conscious purposive agents, with higher capacities that can be realized through education and critical self-reflection.[63] These higher capacities are in part private—for example, musical and intellectual talents[64]—and in part altruistic—for example, playing our part in an extended collective endeavour or way of life, not as a scheme for mutual advantage, but as a context for the development of one's fellow citizens. It is through being recognized by others that we become aware of both ourselves

---

[60] Green Papers, Balliol College, MS23 (Green's contractions have been silently expanded).

[61] For this distinction, see Michael Sandel, *Liberalism and the Limits of Justice* (Cambridge: Cambridge University Press, 1982), 62–3.

[62] Green, *PE* §190. See G. W. F. Hegel, *Philosophy of Mind, Part 3 of the Encyclopaedia of the Philosophical Sciences*, trans. W. Wallace (Oxford: Clarendon Press, 1971), §§432 etc.

[63] Green, *PE* §190.   [64] Green, 'Lectures on the Philosophy of Kant', *CW* ii. 145.

and them as 'persons in capacity—subjects capable each of conceiving himself and the bettering of life as an end to himself'.[65]

Green's appeal to recognition has significant implications for his wider republican theory. Not least, it is important because it ensures that true freedom and civic virtue entail one another in such a way that it is possible to achieve one only to the extent that the other is achieved.[66] That is, the extent to which intersubjective relationships enable the individual to develop a rich and coherent sense of her potential for personality is in part a function of the types of relationships in which she engages. The range of possible relationships is, in turn, in part a function of one's character—of the virtues and beliefs that one has. Counterfactually, dysfunctional marital relationships,[67] the denial of educational opportunities on grounds of gender or class,[68] and all other imperfect intersubjective relationships fail to promote the full development of the relevant parties, the abusers and excluders as well as the victims. Much the same position is affirmed by contemporary republicans, including Pettit.

Agents will be free persons to the extent that they have the ratiocinative capacity for discourse and the relational capacity for discourse that goes with enjoying discourse-friendly linkages with others; that capacity, with its dual aspect, is what constitutes discursive control. Agents will exercise such freedom as persons so far as they are engaged in discourse with others, being authorized as someone worthy of address, and they will be reinforced in that freedom so far as they are publicly recognized as having the discursive control it involves.[69]

Honohan places particular emphasis on recognition, of which she identifies three key facets: 'acknowledgement, authorisation and entitlement (corresponding respectively to the harms of having one's identity and viewpoints overlooked, discounted a priori, and relegated to the private)'.[70] The underlying assumption of this approach is that recognition is valuable to the extent that it seeks to bolster the self-respect of 'the other'.

This section has established that Green founds his political thought on a conceptually complex notion of freedom. He integrates this conception into a theory of socially conditioned individuality in such a way as to require the individual to critically assess laws and conventional norms in light of her own conscientious assessment of the demands of the spirit of her community (its common good). Consequently, to be truly free in Green's sense, the individual

---

[65] *PE* §183.   [66] Ibid. §§240–5.   [67] *LPPO* §§233–46.
[68] *LLFC* 202–4. Most of Green's reflections on the principles of education appear in *CW* iii. 387–476 passim.
[69] Pettit, *Theory of Freedom*, 72–3.   [70] Honohan, *Civic Republicanism*, 260.

must possess a robust and virtuous character, a characteristically republican feature which will be explored in the next section.

IV. Civic Virtue

Iseult Honohan distinguishes four 'dimensions' of civic virtue: awareness, self-restraint, deliberative engagement, and solidarity.[71] By 'awareness' is meant the citizen's consciousness of the interdependencies linking her life with the lives of her fellow citizens. 'Self-restraint' refers to the citizen's willingness to bear the reasonable burdens of social co-operation. 'Deliberative engagement' is an activity in which members seek a consensus while accepting the likelihood that they themselves may favour another course even when a particular plan has been validated by authoritative decision-making mechanisms. Finally, solidarity is manifested in the citizens' displays of an active concern with the good of the community.

Most republicans recognize that civic virtue is not a free-standing quality and that a sympathetic institutional structure is also required, such as a legal system. Yet, they tend to be clear that such institutions are built on less tangible foundations. Hence, Pettit asks, 'What are ... [legitimate republican] laws going to require by way of supplementation if freedom as non-domination really is going to be advanced?'

The answer is, in a word, norms. The laws must be embedded in a network of norms that reign effectively, independently of state coercion, in the realm of civil society. Civil society is society under the aspect of an extrafamilial, infrapolitical association: it is that form of society that extends beyond the narrow confines of family loyalty but that does not strictly require the existence of a coercive state ... If the state is to be able to find a place in the hearts of the people, and if the laws of the state are to be truly effective, those laws will have to work in synergy with norms that are established, or that come to be established, in the realm of civil society. The laws must give support to the norms and the norms give support to the laws.[72]

Pettit's examples of authoritative norms include a sense of integrity amongst the holders of public office, norms which lead citizens to obey the laws, norms which lead citizens to condemn the performance of criminal acts and to report criminals to the police, and those 'norms [that cause] people to be critical and demonstrative about inadequate laws'.[73]

---

[71] Ibid. 160–2. Cf. Dagger, *Civic Virtues*, 14–15.

[72] Pettit, *Republicanism*, 241–2. Cf. Honohan, *Civic Republicanism*, 263, and Kalu N. Kalu, 'Of Citizenship, Virtue, and the Administrative Imperative: Deconstructing Aristotelian Civic Republicanism', *Public Administration Review* 63:4 (July/Aug. 2003), 418–27.

[73] Pettit, *Republicanism*, 242.

Green too emphasizes this interrelation. He argues that virtue and the common good intertwine through the mutual reliance on the forms of intersubjective recognition that bind together an enriching community (sc. a community which enables the individual to enjoy true freedom).[74] Indeed, virtue is given shape by the citizen's perception of the fundamental values of her society and the practical demands of its common good. This contention lies at the heart of the relational social ontology outlined above. He writes in the *Principles of Political Obligation*,

All virtues are really social; or, more properly, the distinction between social and self-regarding virtues is a false one. Every virtue is self-regarding in the sense that it is a disposition, or habit of will, directed to an end which the man presents to himself as his good; every virtue is social in the sense that unless the good to which the will is directed is one in which the well-being of society in some form or other is involved, the will is not virtuous at all.[75]

Aristotle's 'good purpose' provides a crucial point of orientation for practical citizenship. Indeed, Green praises the ancient Greeks for being the first people to understand that the good life was a life of civic duty, focused on the exercise of civic virtue.[76] Yet, he is also at pains to show that even though the respective principles embodied in the cardinal Greek virtues ('wisdom', 'fortitude', and 'temperance', together with the guiding virtue of a habitual concern for 'justice')[77] have remained essentially the same since the times of Plato and Aristotle, they have come to be understood in markedly different ways in contemporary societies. For example, the ideal of fortitude has been gradually extended from courage during war to encompass courage in the struggles for social improvement.[78] This is a general trend: virtues now tend to be justified in a more rational and egalitarian manner.[79] Initially, this change owed much to the rise of Christianity, and latterly to the writings of philosophers such as Kant as well as the example of conscientious social reformers.[80] Yet, Green stresses time and again that even now the practical instantiations of these virtues must be constantly reinterpreted to fit the actual circumstances in which disputes occur regarding the nature and requirements of the common good.[81] Similarly, they must be refined constantly in an effort to bring them into line with the Kantian categorical imperative to respect all individuals as persons. Reason and circumstance are the touchstones for social change. The underlying point remains true, however.

---

[74] Green, *PE* §§240–5.   [75] Green, *LPPO* §247.
[76] Green, *PE* §248.   [77] Ibid. §255.   [78] Ibid. §§257–60.
[79] Ibid. §§284–5.   [80] Ibid. §303.
[81] Ibid. 288–90, 301, 317–19. Green, 'Philosophy of Aristotle', *CW* iii. 58.

These activities will take different forms under different social conditions, but in rough outline they are those by which men in mutual helpfulness conquer and adapt nature, and overcome the influences which would make them victims of chance and accident, of brute force and animal passion.[82]

Whatever its specific nature, reflection on the existence of such a good and the virtues it justifies marks a fundamental step in the moral life of the individual.

An interest has arisen, over and above that in keeping the members of a family or tribe alive, in rendering them persons of a certain kind; in forming in them certain qualities, not as a means to anything ulterior which the possession of these qualities might bring out, but simply for the sake of that possession; in inducing in them habits of action on account of the intrinsic value of those habits, as forms of activity in which man achieves what he has it in him to achieve, and so far satisfies himself.[83]

He clarifies the internal dimension of this theory in the *Principles of Political Obligation* when he draws a distinction between two types of virtuous action: the honouring of negative obligations and the performance of positive actions.[84] The former include the obligation 'to forbear from meddling with one's neighbour', whereas the latter are those activities which tend to enable 'a society of men ... to make the most of their capabilities'. He calls virtues entailed by the performance of such activities ' "industry", "courage", [or] public spirit" '.[85] Elsewhere he refers to them as 'the will to know what is true, to make what is beautiful; to endure pain and fear, to resist the allurements of pleasure (*i.e.* to be brave and temperate)'.[86] Their public manifestations are harmonized in an ideal of the dedicated conscientious citizen: the individual who works to make the best of herself and her fellow citizens by engaging with them in relationships that recognize their status as rational agents and fellow citizens.[87]

Yet, not all forms of intersubjective recognition give direct and unequivocal affirmation. Hegel's dialectic of lordship and bondage is the most famous example of conflictual recognition.[88] Some republicans have found this to be a rather uncomfortable truth. For example, while Honohan accepts that 'Conflict is a reality to be acknowledged', she does not seem to think that it is something to be welcomed.[89] Green, on the other hand, does find a positive place for this less pacific type of recognition, as will become clear in the next section.

---

[82] Green, *LPPO* §248.   [83] Green, *PE* §243.   [84] Green, *LPPO* §248.
[85] Ibid.   [86] Green, *PE* §256. See ibid. §§240–90, esp. §253.
[87] Ibid. §§297–309. Green's ideal of the conscientious citizen is examined in Tyler, *Thomas Hill Green and the Philosophical Foundations of Politics*, ch. 4.
[88] Tyler, *Idealist Political Philosophy*, ch. 1, sect. 2 and ch. 2.   [89] Honohan, *Civic Republicanism*, 265.

V. Democratic Contestability and the Common Good

Dagger develops one possible—even if, to his mind, ultimately unsustainable—distinction between autonomy-based liberalism and civic virtue-based republicanism. 'The autonomous person adopts the principles by which he or she will live, which implies some degree of critical reflection on the principles available. With civic virtue, however, the emphasis is on acting, perhaps without reflection, to promote the common good.'[90] It is perhaps understandable then, that some liberals see republicanism—and civic humanism, in particular—as requiring citizens to acquiesce in a socially authorized, essentially static and overdetermined conception of the common good and the civic virtues with which it is necessarily bound up. Similarly, it has been objected that Green's combination of moral realism and social embeddedness pushes him towards a largely unquestioning endorsement of conventional norms, virtues, institutions, and values. The clear implication is that Green supports, in Berlin's memorable phrase, 'the metaphysical doctrine of the two selves—the individual stream versus the social river in which they should be merged'.[91] If such a claim were to be justified, then it would be only a short step to seeing Green as advocating a form of bourgeois democratic élitism. As Richter alleges, this would be a system in which the justification of state action 'was moralistic, involving the determination by upper-class persons of those moral traits to be encouraged; it excluded from consideration ... the possibility that the interests and tastes of middle-class reformers might not be those of the working classes'.[92] Indeed, even those scholars who do not read Green as an élitist in any crude sense, propagate the influence of the élitist reading by arguing that his politics shared the monistic structure of his metaethics. Hence, although Boucher and Vincent recognize that the latter entails 'an equivocal unity', the sense in which it is both equivocal and a unity has never been presented with sufficient clarity, even in the more sympathetic literature.[93]

However, such an attack neglects two crucial points. First, every leading contemporary republican has stressed that the degree and apparent resilience of cultural and ethical diversity ensures that both the common good and hence the demands of civic virtue are inherently contested.[94] Second,

---

[90] Dagger, *Civic Virtues*, 15. Dagger rejects this passive conception of the citizen.

[91] Berlin, 'Introduction', p. xlix n.; Horton, *Political Obligation*, 76. This is a common attack (for further references, see Tyler, *Thomas Hill Green and the Philosophical Foundations of Politics*, 125 n. 36).

[92] Richter, *Politics of Conscience*, 296.

[93] David Boucher and Andrew Vincent, *British Idealism and Political Theory* (Edinburgh: Edinburgh University, 2000), 51.

[94] Pettit, *Republicanism*, 183–203; Sandel, *Democracy's Discontent*, 5–6, 337–8, 349–51; Honohan, *Civic Republicanism*, 160–2, 179.

Green also denies any ultimate incompatibility between autonomy-based politics and one founded upon virtue. Hence it will be argued now not merely that Green believes citizenship can but also that it will take many different forms within a civilized nation. Yet, this staple of the secondary literature can be constructed in such a way (for example, by Vincent and Plant)[95] as to be perfectly compatible with a hierarchical conception of society, and so with an élitist reading of Green.[96] Instead, three far more controversial claims will be defended. First, Green believes that if true citizenship is realized, then the development of ideals of citizenship not only will take many divergent paths within a civilized society but that they *must* do so. (Green does not conceive of true citizenship as the essentially unilinear phenomenon implied by previous scholars.[97]) Second, Green recognizes that the unifying subject which (undoubtedly) he takes to underlie human consciousness can never justify a similarly unified political sphere. Third, he identifies competition between groups of citizens for influence within a decentralized democratic system as a powerful spur to personal self-realization.

On one level, Green is undoubtedly a realist about ultimate values, holding that some objects, goals, and states of affairs possess worth independently of our beliefs as to whether or not they possess worth.[98] He also asserts that in a perfect world these objects would form a harmonious system in which there would be no fundamental conflicts between the demands of, say, freedom, equality, and virtue. Moreover, his moral ontology requires that this harmony be expressed in the ideal human life as a condition of the latter's worth. Hence he concludes that a human life is valuable only to the extent that the agent self-consciously embodies these values in his character. However, even Green's most hostile interpreters are forced to concede that Green accepts explicitly that human life neither is nor can be perfect.[99] We are, and while on this earth must remain, manifestations in animal form of the spiritual principle. Hence, although he is a value monist at the level of metaphysics, he holds that irresolvable clashes must occur between fundamental goals and values in human lives on earth. For this reason, he sees pluralism as an endemic and permanent feature of human life on earth.[100] This ensures that every rational agent is to some degree

---

[95] Andrew Vincent and Raymond Plant, *Philosophy, Politics and Citizenship: The Life and Thought of the British Idealists* (Oxford: Basil Blackwell, 1984), 24–7.

[96] Kant presents the underlying point very well in his *Metaphysics of Morals*, Academy pagination p. 315.

[97] Boucher and Vincent, *British Idealism and Political Theory*, 50–1.

[98] Green, *PE* §§173–5.   [99] Berlin, *Four Essays*, pp. xlix n., lxi, 133 n., 150.

[100] Green, *PE* §§247, 288.

'always inadequate to himself; and as such disturbed and miserable'.[101] The value pluralist critique of the monistic elements of Green's thought fails to bite for this reason.

Yet, there is a twist. Remember that Green operates with an intersubjective, or relational, social ontology. Societies exist in the relationships which are presupposed by its members' specific acts of recognition: 'the life of the nation' takes 'its peculiar features' from the nature of the concrete interactions of its individual members.[102] The same obtains for all associations, whether sub-national (such as the working class), national (such as Britain), or supra-national (such as the British Empire).[103] The interaction of these two beliefs—that value pluralism is endemic in human life, and that societies are relational organisms—creates the fundamental dynamic of Green's social and political thought.[104] In essence it transforms social and political interaction into a series of processes whereby inherently incompatible values clash with no necessary prospect of their reformulation into a coherent system. Consequently, Green holds that the substantive values of a real society must be and must remain essentially contested.[105] In fact, the vigorous contestation of established norms, practices, and laws at all levels (the ideological, constitutional, and legislative levels, as well as at the levels of public and social policy, whether national, regional, municipal, or local) is valuable not merely as a device for checking the abuse of power by office-holders (as it is for Pettit).[106] More than this, public contestation brings to light new values and develops claims.[107] It helps citizens to articulate the spirit and principles of their association, thereby giving them the opportunity and motive to critically reflect upon and reform this spirit and these principles where necessary.[108] In this way, not only does society develop, but individual self-realization is promoted still further.

The less constrained and more multifarious these intersubjective processes of social interaction, the more profound are the insights into the nature of the 'soul's faculties', and the more extensive and penetrating the pressure for reform of oppressive institutions.

The range of faculties called into play in any work of social direction or improvement must be much wider, when the material dealt with consists no longer of supposed chattels but of persons asserting recognised rights, whose welfare forms an integral element in the social good which the directing citizen has to keep in view.[109]

---

[101] T. H. Green, 'The Value and Works of Fiction in Modern Times', *CW* iii. 29. Tyler, *Thomas Hill Green and the Philosophical Foundations of Politics*, 109–11, 139–40.

[102] Green, *PE* §184.   [103] Green, *LPPO* §152.

[104] Green, *PE* §184.   [105] Ibid. §308.

[106] Pettit, *Republicanism*, ch. 6 and pp. 292–7; also Rawls, *Political Liberalism*, 205.

[107] Green, *PE* §308.   [108] Ibid. §§301, 317–19.   [109] Ibid. §258.

Conceptions of the good change, then, with alterations in the various forms of human activity and the reflections elicited by those activities. Green infers from this that forms of citizenship should be internally differentiated as well, for by serving a number of different purposes through their various social memberships, individual citizens create the conditions for the improvement of the whole of society.[110] He stresses that it is very difficult to predict with any accuracy, for example, the ways in which individuals will act when presented with such momentous new opportunities as are created by enfranchising the poor.[111] Consequently, no one can predict how the idea of the common good either will or should change under these new conditions. This justifies Green's firmly held belief that there is, in the words of his friend James Bryce, a 'duty of approaching the people directly and getting them to form and express their own views'. Indeed, Bryce went so far as to describe this duty as 'at the root of all [Green's] political doctrines'.[112] The ideal is a community of self-respecting conscientious citizens; individuals who seek to discover the common good of their collectivity and who work for its realization in civic and political life, while their fellow citizens may just as honestly believe in and seek to realize competing conceptions of the common good.

How does Green manage to reconcile his contention that in the temporal world values must remain essentially contestable with his undeniable admiration for this ethos of virtuous citizenship? A critic may allege that his invocation of value pluralism logically precludes him from giving universal support for such actions. In reality, Green can reconcile these two elements because the capacity for socially concerned autonomous action operates at a different level of his political theory than of his value pluralism. The former is a motivational requirement of the good will, whereas the latter is a feature of the agent's substantive values and goals.[113] This translates into Green's claim that the common good is instantiated as both (1) the shared norms of civic virtue which structure the modes of articulating political demands, and (2) the shared justification underlying citizens' pursuits of these substantive political goals. Value pluralism, on the other hand, is an indelible feature of these substantive goals and political demands. Less formally, a true citizen always acts in accordance with the demands of civic virtue and in the service of what she understands to be the common good; yet not only does she disagree with many of her fellow citizens about what the common good is in a particular case, but

---

[110] Ibid. §§182–3.   [111] Tyler, *Idealist Political Philosophy*, ch. 2, *passim*.

[112] James Bryce, quoted ibid. See Vincent and Plant, *Philosophy, Politics and Citizenship*, ch. 1. Nicholson, 'T. H. Green and State Action: Liquor Legislation'; Tyler, *Thomas Hill Green and the Philosophical Foundations of Politics*, 112–22.

[113] Green, *PE* §§240–5.

consciously and conscientiously she favours policies which are incompatible with the policies of her fellow citizens.[114] As a result, policy objectives are being constantly articulated, contested, and redefined through the democratic process, with a general acceptance that there is no necessary prospect of discovering one coherent policy position which will be ideal for every conscientious citizen. I take this to be one key implication for this democratic theory of such statements as, 'The special features of the object in which the true good is sought will vary in different ages and with different persons, according to circumstances and idiosyncrasy'.[115] The common good is essentially contested, then.

Nevertheless, essential contestability is a matter of degree—the possibility of rational disagreement may always exist, but the reality can be more or less severe. In fact, it is the possibility of agreement on such matters which enables Green's republicanism to get off the ground. Without some level of agreement on basic values and epistemic perspectives, there can be no possibility of common endeavour and no common good.[116] This co-ordination is provided in large part by 'the influence of the common institutions which make a particular nation'.[117] For Green, social and political processes pull in opposite directions. On the one hand, the (always only partial) co-ordination of individual projects which some commentators ascribe to a divine will actually arises for Green from the intersubjective nature of individual action.[118] In other words, it arises through dynamic processes of both implicit and self-conscious interpersonal recognition and negotiation (in so far as agents function as active members of society). On the other hand, and in tension with the first process, the unavoidable nature of essential contestability in practice, when combined with relational organicism, implies that the overlaps between personal perspectives and norms—which are presupposed by a stable cultural life—are always open to change. The trick is to design a public sphere which can contain such contradictory forces, as we shall see in the following section.

VI. The Political Structure of Green's Republicanism

Benjamin Barber bases his form of strong republican democracy on 'a devotion to the local spirit of liberty manifested as continuous and noisy activity in and

---

[114] Green, *PE* §§307–8.   [115] Ibid. §239.

[116] Jeremy Waldron denies the philosophical point ('Cultural Identity and Civic Responsibility', in W. Kymlicka and W. Norman (eds.), *Citizenship in Diverse Societies* (Oxford: Oxford University Press, 2000), 160–5 *passim*).

[117] Green, *PE* §184.

[118] Moreover, as Green famously noted, 'Our ultimate standard of worth is an ideal of *personal* worth. All other values are relative to value for, of, or in a person' (ibid.).

on behalf of the local community'.[119] It would not be unfair to characterize this as the essence of Green's political vision as well. Green was very active in Oxford politics from the mid-1860s until his death in 1882. He was active in the local Liberal association, in temperance and educational reform; he spoke publicly for the extension of the franchise from 1865; and he was elected as a local councillor in 1876 (and again in 1879).[120] It was recognized among his admirers that his political radicalism was intimately connected to his philosophical thought, making it perfectly appropriate that, 'He went straight from the declaration of the poll, when he was elected a town councillor, to lecture on *The Critique of Pure Reason*'.[121]

Green's particular combination of Kantianism and Aristotelianism has at least four major implications for his wider political thought. First, his emphasis on building rational and enriching social relationships, which harmonize in such a way as to support the determinate expression of man's innate 'spiritual' capacities, ensures that a substantive conception of individuality and ethical politics can be developed, thereby escaping Hegel's criticism of Kant's 'empty formalism'.[122] On this view, the good will exists and possesses worth 'not in abstraction from other interests, but as an organising influence upon and among them'.[123] Second, the centrality accorded to self-conscious reason gives an analytical and critical edge to the will, personal agency, and political deliberation. The citizen should reflect critically on the spirit and status of her conventional rights, duties, and obligations. She should at least attempt to see beyond the letter of each, and should not accept them unthinkingly as authoritative. Third, the resulting emphasis on rationality leads Green to favour strongly the public articulation of the norms and rules within which agency is exercised, as well as prioritizing the practical stability of these norms and rules in a rational life. Fourth, this representation of the social and political world as a realm in which 'the soul's faculties' are gradually systematized serves to remind agents, politicians, and reformers that critical analysis entails not merely rational articulation and the construction of intricate webs of concepts, norms, and laws. The substantive expression of human capacities always has to be fostered, because the depth of one's moral sentiments is just as important in

---

[119] Barber, *Strong Democracy*, p. xiii.

[120] Peter Nicholson, 'Introduction', *CW* v. pp. xv–xxxi.

[121] David G. Ritchie, *Principles of State Interference: Four Essays on the Political Philosophy of Mr. Herbert Spencer, J. S. Mill, and T. H. Green* (London: Swann Sonnenschein, 1891), 131.

[122] G. W. F. Hegel, *Hegel's Logic*, trans. W. Wallace (Oxford: Clarendon Press, 1873), §§53–4. T. H. Green, *Lectures on Kant*, in R. L. Nettleship (ed.), *Works of T. H. Green*, iii (London: Longmans, Green, 1889), §118.

[123] Green, *PE* §247.

personal and political life as the complexity of one's intellectual articulation of the moral imperative (probably more so in most cases).

Each of these characteristics of the rational will has political implications, at least three of which resonate with contemporary republicans. Most fundamentally of course, remember that Green holds that the good life can only be willed subjectively (it must be freely chosen and followed by the agent), and willed (chosen) for its own sake. Hence it is impossible for anyone, even the State, to coerce an agent to perform a morally good act.[124] Consequently, the public sphere should be structured so as to allow all citizens to act in accordance with their subjective wills so long as those wills do not interfere with the like freedom of others. Politically, this justifies an extensive system of civil freedoms, or 'negative rights' ('rights to be let alone'),[125] which should be publicly promulgated and robustly defended by the State and the organs of civil society themselves, through both the use of negative sanctions (legal punishments and the like) and the resilience of an appropriately republican civic culture.[126]

Next, there is the claim that political deliberation should be a critical activity. One implication of this requirement is that the good citizen must actually be able to exercise her analytical and evaluative faculties. Hence, she must possess both a sense of self-respect and the courage to champion her own opinions in the public sphere. Green stresses in the *Prolegomena* that while negative rights are vital to 'will with a rational content' and so to a free society, they have to be supplemented by 'positive', or enabling, rights.[127] Only then can 'the less favoured members' of society be protected from, among other oppressive forces, 'unrelenting competition' for material goods. Only then can they actually develop and use their capacities for personal autonomy to pursue intrinsically valuable spiritual goods. It is on this basis that Green supports compulsory elementary education for their children, as well as leaving the door open for the provision of other services in the light of new circumstances. Citizens should receive at least a basic education, as well as being free from extreme poverty and economic oppression (for example, via abusive terms and conditions at work), and live in conditions which facilitate the civic and political expression of a conscientious and virtuous character. In short, the State should secure a robust system of positive rights, a system of effective opportunities for reflective action.

Precisely which negative and positive rights and virtues should be enforced depends on the social structure, culture, and threats of deprivation and

---

[124] Green, *LPPO* §§207–10.   [125] Green, *PE* §245.
[126] Green, *LPPO* §114.   [127] Green, *PE* §245; *LLFC passim*.

oppression which the citizen believes she and her fellow citizens face. In a perfect world these rights and obligations would form an unchanging system, which would be 'necessary to the end which it is the vocation of human society to realise'.[128] Yet, we have seen that Green recognizes that humans do not and never can live in such a perfect world. When combined with constantly changing circumstances, the criticism and redefinition of the system of rights and obligations must remain ongoing processes.[129] For this reason, Green stresses also the dynamic nature of our conceptions of civic virtue. In fact, our criticism and collective reformulation of our notions of civic virtue in particular are politically important, in that they help to foster and maintain the ideal of a 'free society' in which the citizen is able to develop and exercise her higher capacities.[130] Very similar positions are adopted by contemporary republicans.[131]

Next, Green places very great stress on the need for a predictable context for reflective agency.[132] In political terms this means that every citizen should be assured of operating within a world governed by publicly articulated norms, rules, and laws. In short, the State should secure a robust system of negative rights, a system of effective rights and freedoms from interference by others. Once again, this is a recurring theme in contemporary republican writings. Pettit emphasizes 'non-manipulability', 'the empire of law', 'dispersion-of-power', and 'the counter-majoritarian condition', among other things.[133] Dagger describes 'the importance of the rule of law as a settled matter' from a republican point of view, as it is 'an essential means of ensuring' non-domination.[134]

Taking stock, it has been established that Green advocates the creation of a political sphere characterized by non-domination, secured via the enforcement of a robust system of both negative rights and obligations as well as positive rights, in the context of which citizens can rationally plan and execute actions which grow out of their self-reflective and informed wills. One claim that is insisted upon by Green, although not prominent in contemporary republican writings, is that the rational articulation of moral imperatives must not unduly inhibit the development of one's moral sentiments. In many ways this is the most significant when identifying the ceaselessly dynamic nature of Green's active citizenship. The political system must provide opportunities for the expression of conceptions of morals and the good life which arise from reflection on the underlying principles (the 'spirit') of established practices.

---

[128] Green, *LPPO* §10.   [129] Green, *PE* §§307–9.   [130] Green, *LPPO* §§207–10.
[131] Honohan, *Civic Republicanism*, 198–9; Pettit, *Common Mind*, 321–38; Pettit, *Republicanism*, ch. 8 *passim* and p. 304.
[132] Green, *LPPO* §§25, 132.
[133] Pettit, *Republicanism*, 171–83.   [134] Dagger, *Civic Virtues*, 61; see ibid. ch. 6.

The question is, how to do this? The key is to design a public space in which citizens can forcefully express their disagreements about the fundamental values of their association, about the practical implications of those values, and about the institutional structures that are best suited to those values in the circumstances. Yet, Green is very aware of the structural forces at work in modern societies that make such intimate engagement increasingly difficult.

The size of modern states renders necessary the substitution of a representative system for one in which the citizens shared directly in legislation, and this so far tends to weaken the active interest of the citizens in the commonwealth, though the evil may be partly counteracted by giving increased importance to municipal or communal administration.[135]

In the face of expanding political territories, then, Green's dynamic and pluralist conception of service to the common good and the rational patriotism which that implies lead him to stress the importance of active participation in the daily life of one's community, in charitable groups, local councils, and the like.[136] This finds great resonance in the support of many contemporary republicans for various modes of local civic engagement, including Community Development Corporations, so-called sprawlbusters, New Urbanism, and the Industrial Areas Foundation.[137]

There is a final issue to be addressed in this section: the special rights and obligations that are characteristic of contemporary republican thought. As Andrew Mason has claimed, 'in its most powerful version, the republican challenge [to liberalism] maintains that a fully-fledged ideal of political community requires citizens to acknowledge and act upon special obligations to one another that are independent of justice (at least as liberalism, in its dominant form, conceives of justice)'.[138] The liberal worry is that an insistence that rights, duties, and obligations be justified solely by the service that they provide to the realization of the common good serves to preclude non-citizens from protection and recognition by the State. In other words, it seems that a person who does not share a common good with anyone else will possess few or even no rights, duties, or obligations. Similarly, citizens of one country would seem to owe no duties or obligations to citizens of any other; nor can they legitimately claim any rights against them.

---

[135] Green, *LPPO* §119.

[136] By far the best analysis of this aspect of Green's politics is found in Nicholson, 'T. H. Green and State Action: Liquor Legislation'.

[137] These examples, all taken from the context of the USA, appear in Sandel, *Democracy's Discontent*, 333–8.

[138] Andrew Mason, *Community, Solidarity and Belonging: Levels of Community and their Normative Significance* (Cambridge: Cambridge University Press, 2000), 96.

Certain republicans have attempted to justify such special rights for fellow citizens from considerations of mutual advantage: 'Their cooperation enables us to enjoy the benefits of the enterprise, and fairness demands that we reciprocate.'[139] Mason has presented an alternative republican justification of special rights for one's fellow citizens which appeals to the role played by modern citizenship in the grounding of one's feelings of self-respect.[140] However, Green takes a different tack, one that follows logically from the theory of recognition that was outlined earlier. He argues that for a claim against another rational being to become a right, that claim must be one that is itself grounded in a conception of the good which is already freely endorsed by that other rational being herself.[141] A conception of the good is freely endorsed to the extent that it is presupposed by the scheme of meanings and values that constitutes the particular hermeneutic context in which the particular agent acts. In this sense, then, Green adopts the position adopted by Hegel in his discussion of 'lordship and bondage'. Again following Hegel, Green presents this notion of endorsement as a form of recognition. Hence, he writes in the *Principles of Political Obligation*:

There can be no right without a consciousness of common interest on the part of members of a society. Without this there might be certain powers on the part of individuals, but no recognition of these powers by others as powers of which they allow the exercise, nor any claim to such recognition, and without this recognition or claim to recognition there can be no right.[142]

Such recognition is explicit when the members of the community are conscious of the particular (shared) notion of the good that grounds their individual normative systems of meaning and value. However, by including the notion of a possible 'claim to recognition', Green's (and Hegel's) theory leaves open the possibility of implicit recognition. Even a rational being may not be fully conscious of the values that ground her ethical beliefs and judgements. Indeed, it is more than likely that she will not be.

The notion of implicit recognition is also derived in this way by contemporary republicans. For example, Pettit argues, first, that someone who is accepted into a particular discursive community 'is authorized as a discursive partner and publicly recognized as a locus of discursive authority'. From this, he goes on to conclude that 'incorporation in any [discursive] group will be sufficient in principle for recognition by all'.[143] Similarly, Green argues that, 'Membership of any community is so far in principle membership of all communities as to

[139] Dagger, *Civic Virtues*, 59.   [140] Mason, *Community*, 108–11.
[141] *LPPO* §§151–3. For my fuller discussion see Tyler, *Thomas Hill Green and the Philosophical Foundations of Politics*, 169–92.
[142] Green, *LPPO* §31.   [143] Pettit, *Theory of Freedom*, 72.

constitute a right to be treated as a freeman by all other men, to be exempt from subjection to force except for prevention of force'.[144]

There has been such progress in this direction that, 'the idea of this social unity has been so far realised that the modern state, unlike the ancient, secures equality before the law to all persons living within the territory over which its jurisdiction extends, and in theory at least treats aliens as no less possessed of rights'.[145] Nevertheless, fellow citizens have special rights against each other, because the more determinate interpersonal relationships are, the more determinate will be the system of rights and duties that reflects and provides the context for those relationships.[146]

Green's contention that there exists a pluralistic dynamic within personal moral consciousness leads him to conclude that there can be as many equally legitimate conceptions of its requirements as there are conscientious active citizens.[147] Such a conclusion has radical implications for the grounds and force of political obligation, as will become clear in the following, final section.

VII. Patriotism and Civil Disobedience

We began by noting that being secure from arbitrary interference lies at the heart of the republican conception of freedom. Pettit gives definition to his notion of arbitrariness by introducing the 'proviso' that

the making, interpretation and implementation of the law is not arbitrary: provided that the legal coercion involved is constrained by the interests and judgements of those affected. The proviso is that the legal regime represents a fair rule of law and that it is imposed in such a manner—such a democratically contestable manner—that any aggrieved individual or group can gain, by their own standards, a fair hearing and judgement on whether an allegedly objectionable law represents the imposition of alien interests or ideas.[148]

Contestation is also central to Green's political thought.[149] In the notes to one of his political speeches, he distinguishes between the false patriot,

---

[144] Green, LPPO §140.

[145] Green, PE §280. On this theme, see Bernard Bosanquet, 'The Wisdom of Naaman's Servants', in his Social and International Ideals: Being Studies in Patriotism (London: Macmillan, 1917), 302–20, and James Bohman, 'Cosmopolitan Republicanism: Citizenship, Freedom and Global Political Authority', The Monist, 84:1 (2001), 3–21.

[146] Green, PE §§215–17.   [147] Ibid. §301.

[148] Pettit, 'Republican Theory', 62. Cf. idem, Republicanism, ch. 7, and idem, Theory of Freedom, esp. ch. 7.

[149] Tyler, Thomas Hill Green (1836–1882) and the Philosophical Foundations of Politics, 138–57, discusses this area in detail.

'who clamours for display of national strength' without regard for the justice of the cause, and the 'true patriot', who works conscientiously to make 'the people more virtuous and content'.[150] Furthermore, Green distinguishes conscientious obedience to one's conventional roles and their associated duties from the critical appreciation and performance of the demands of citizenship. The 'loyal subject' and 'the intelligent patriot' are both virtuous citizens,[151] because

'[n]o individual can make a conscience for himself. He always needs a society to make it for him. A conscientious 'heresy,' religious or political, always represents some gradually maturing conviction as to social good, already implicitly involved in the ideas on which the accepted rules of conduct rest, though it may conflict with the formulae in which those ideas have been hitherto authoritatively expressed, and may lead to the overthrow of institutions which have previously contributed to their realisation.[152]

It may be that often we can do little more than fulfil our established duties.[153] In this sense, the truly free citizen 'transcends the "law of opinion," of social expectation, ... by interpreting [that law] according to its higher spirit'.[154] This 'moral dynamic' works through the reflective interaction of every 'man and ... citizen' with the 'institutions and rules of life'.[155] Yet, Green's conception of the public realm remains irreducibly conflictual. Public opinion 'speaks with many voices according as men have ears to hear', and it is the citizen's task to identify the ideal that she believes it contains, and to push for its realization in the virtues and institutions of her society.[156]

Green is very clear about the grounds on which it is legitimate for a true patriot to resist an established law or convention or to claim a new right.[157]

The assertion by the citizen of any right, however, which the state does not recognise must be founded on a reference to an *acknowledged* social good. ... The condition of its being claimable is that its exercise should be contributory to some social good which the public conscience is capable of appreciating—not necessarily one which in the existing prevalence of private interests can obtain due acknowledgement, but still one of which men in their actions and language show themselves to be aware.[158]

In many circumstances, the citizen's obligation will be in doubt.[159] The first is where deep and unsolvable disagreements exist within the citizen-body as to who constitutes the sovereign authority. The second is where 'the government is so conducted that there are no legal means of obtaining the repeal of a law'.

---

[150] Notes for Green's speech at the Liberal Hall, Abingdon, 5 Dec. 1879, *CW* v. 352.
[151] Green, *LPPO* §122. [152] Green, *PE* §321.
[153] Ibid. §313. [154] Ibid. §301. [155] Ibid. §327. See §§241–3.
[156] Ibid. §301. [157] Ibid. §327. See §§241–3.
[158] Green, *LPPO* §143. [159] Green, *PE* §§310–28; *LPPO* §§101–12.

The third is where 'the whole system of law and government is so perverted by private interests hostile to the public, that there has ceased to be any common interest in maintaining it'. Finally, is where 'the authority from which the objectionable command proceeds' can be removed without undermining the authority 'on which the general maintenance of social order and the fabric of settled rights depends'.

Clearly it will not always be easy to gauge whether one or more of these conditions is fulfilled. In that case, it is the citizen's duty to consider whether her fellow citizens believe them to exist. Yet, Green is emphatic that popular beliefs are only a guide, and ultimately it is the individual's responsibility to decide whether he has duty of civil disobedience in any particular instance. The depths of Green's radicalism shine through when he observes that

> The presumption must generally be made that resistance to a government is not for the public good when made on grounds which the mass of people cannot appreciate ... On the other hand, it is under the worst governments that the public spirit is most crushed; and thus in extreme cases there may be a duty of resistance in the public interest, though there is no hope of that resistance finding efficient public support.[160]

How can Green reconcile this recourse to what is effectively a 'false consciousness' argument with his earlier statement that 'the assertion by the citizen of any right ... must be founded on a reference to an *acknowledged* social good'? The key is found in the ontological facet of his social theory, and in particular his employment of a form of relational organicism. Our actions are conceived and executed within hermeneutic frameworks. This entails that our actions may well have a logic of which the individual is not fully aware. This enables Green to theorize the notion of implicit recognition.[161] Clearly, it is unlikely that this will be an ideal basis for reform, yet it may be the only one available for a citizen whose conscientious self-reflexivity calls him to honour his duties as a patriotic rebel.

VIII. Conclusion

Hopefully, it is clear now that, even by contemporary standards, Green is a radical republican. Following Hegel, Green argues that the development of the moral ideal has two sides: the development of a virtuous personal

---

[160] *LPPO* §108.
[161] This theory is analysed in much greater depth in Tyler, *Thomas Hill Green and the Philosophical Foundations of Politics*, ch. 5.

character, and the development of civil, economic, and political institutions, practices, and norms which foster the exercise of that character by members of a self-determining collectivity. Clearly, these ontological commitments make it reasonable to align him, initially at least, with some form of republicanism. However, contrary to the leading contemporary republicans, for Green, as this chapter has also demonstrated, these two sides of the moral ideal—virtues and institutions—are mutually sustaining and promoting rather than being arranged in some stable causal relationship (where the presence of one is the pre-condition of the existence of the other, *but not vice versa*). If this particular ontological inseparability of virtues and institutions makes Green a republican, then what makes him a civic humanist is the nature of his moral individualism. He holds that institutions have worth only to the extent that they sustain and promote the possession and exercise of virtues by individual citizens. It is fundamentally mistaken to characterize civic virtue as entailing a blind adherence to any conventional account of the common good. In fact, he is emphatic that any form of dogma (whether scientific, political, ethical, or religious) acts as a dead weight upon one's moral life, in that it stifles critical engagement with the world, thereby retarding the growth and exercise of one's individuality. Quite simply, an unforced, circumspect good character is vital.

I have shown that Green accords participation in the reinterpretation and refinement of civic values and public policies an integral role in the conscientious life. The central political actor is the truly free, active citizen—an individual imbued with a conscientious appreciation of the demands of civic virtue, grounded in ongoing personal critical reflection on the ethical justification of those virtues. In this way Green understands civil society to be a responsive, developing context in which conflicts over substantive values and public policy are managed in such a manner as to sustain a vibrant public sphere. The political sphere is an internally differentiated network of civil associations, which together serve a number of particular functions. The overarching structure of this sphere is provided by a robust and publicly promulgated system of rights and obligations, which is in turn justified by reference to a publicly articulatable conception of the common good. Even though the specific nature of this common good is a matter of constant public debate, all citizens recognize that it must be justified by the service it provides to the realization of the agent's true freedom. This highest state of life derives its particular content from the agent's personal reflective and rational instantiation of 'the soul's faculties'.

12

Resolving Moral Conflicts: British Idealist and Contemporary Liberal Approaches to Value Pluralism and Moral Conduct

MARIA DIMOVA-COOKSON

I. Introduction

In an increasingly global world, the fact of pluralism has become a problem. While difference is welcome when each culture has its own space to flourish, in a world of fast communications and ever more elusive boundaries, communities are more and more exposed to other people's values. And even if we were to agree to disagree, there would still be at least two occasions on which we would have to reach an agreement: when we have to decide the basic principles of our political institutions and when we have to resolve moral conflicts. While the first problem was at the forefront of John Rawls's mind in the 1970s and 1980s, the September 11th events at the beginning of this century have made the second problem prominent. Here I will view these two issues as related, and seek a solution that applies to both of them.

In this paper I compare two strategies for resolving moral conflict: John Rawls's and Thomas Nagel's, on the one hand, and T. H. Green's, on the other. The reason why these two parties offer different solutions to moral conflict is because they offer different accounts of moral action. I argue that there are two important sides of moral action: our determination to do the right thing and our knowledge of the right thing to do. I call the first aspect 'volitional', as it reflects moral will, and the second 'epistemological', as it

I would like to thank Peter Nicholson, Andrew Vincent, Colin Tyler, William Mander, and an anonymous reader for their comments on this paper.

reflects moral knowledge. My claim is that while Green gives priority to the volitional aspect of morality over the epistemological one, Rawls and Nagel identify morality almost exclusively with its epistemological aspect. The fact that Green accounts for both aspects of moral action places him in an advantageous position. When moral conflict occurs, Rawls and Nagel can offer only 'epistemological' solutions, as they deal almost exclusively with moral knowledge. Green does this as well, but he fortifies his epistemological solution with a volitional one, and therefore, overall, he offers a better strategy for resolving moral conflicts. My purpose in comparing the contemporary liberal and Green's perspectives towards moral conflict is to show how Rawls's and Nagel's positions can be revised and improved by retrieving Green's ideas.

The paper starts with a review of the background arguments leading to the comparison between the contemporary liberals and Green, followed by an outline of the main claims that will be made (section II). There is a brief discussion, in section III, of the compatibility between the different themes and contexts of the two parties in comparison. Section IV explains the usefulness of the distinction between the volitional and epistemological aspects for the purpose of analysing moral action. A parallel is drawn between this distinction and Green's formal and substantive accounts of morality. Section V explains Rawls's and Nagel's strategies for resolving moral conflict, and identifies a pitfall in their moral theories: a pitfall that could be avoided by bringing Green's ideas into the contemporary discussion. Sections VI and VII deal with Green's theory of how a moral philosopher can help us get out of a moral crisis. Section VIII brings all the insights together by explaining (1) the amendments that could be made to contemporary liberal moral theory on the basis of the ideas drawn from Green's philosophy and (2) the reasons why Rawls and Nagel tend to undermine the volitional aspect of moral action.

II. Background

One of the problems that contemporary political philosophy tries to resolve is how in view of the existing pluralism of philosophical, moral, and religious doctrines we can find a common ground on which to build our political institutions. The problem has two parts: asserting the existence of pluralism, on the one hand, and the need of a universal standpoint, on the other. In *A Theory of Justice* John Rawls attempts to square the circle—that is, of acknowledging the fact of pluralism, but still asserting the existence of a universal standpoint—by introducing a distinction between the right and the good. There is a plurality amongst different concepts of the good, he argues, but the concept of the right is universal. Communitarian critics of Rawls argued that the concept of the good engulfs everything; therefore the right has no independent ground outside the good. In an attempt to express his position in a different way, Rawls introduced the distinction between political and metaphysical, where political conceptions of justice aim to be unanimous, whereas a conception that is part of a metaphysical doctrine is only one of many.

Thomas Nagel supports Rawls's distinction, and offers his own distinction between what is needed to justify belief and what is needed to justify employment of political power. The idea is that we may lack grounds to assert one belief as truer than another, but can find objective grounds for justifying decisions of ultimate political importance.[1] Establishing different levels of engaging with particular sets of values is an important part of the strategy whereby contemporary liberals deal with pluralism. This in itself is not a problem: if on one level of communication there is a conflict, it is reasonable to seek another level where the conflict can be either avoided or resolved. The problem occurs when the first level is identified as 'moral', and the second level as also 'moral', but of a superior nature. We then face the question about how there can be two levels of moral commitment. How can there be a two-tier moral system, where one set of moral beliefs is less important than another set? Contemporary attempts to defend liberalism offer a confusing explanation of morality.

The problem of a two-tier moral system consists in the following. If we assert morality of a second, which is also a higher, level, we implicitly undermine what remains a first, lower-level morality. Because we have moved on to a more complex moral problem, we undermine the place and function of traditional morality. This expresses a standard communitarian concern about the impossibility of setting aside our basic, community-based moral beliefs. Communitarians argue that we cannot, and also should not attempt to, transcend these commitments to the good that are part of our daily social practice. The problem is that if we move to a higher standard of morality, we make our primary, traditional moral commitments redundant, and this poses a question mark over the value of our routine good actions.

---

[1] Susan Mendus claims that we have to be able to distinguish between 'the existential condition of the agent in modernity and the justification of liberal neutrality', implying that we should not try to justify liberal neutrality on the grounds of one's existential condition: another level of justification should be found (Susan Mendus, 'Pluralism and Scepticism in a Disenchanted World', in Maria Baghramian and Attracta Ingram (eds.), *Pluralism: The Philosophy and Politics of Diversity* (London: Routledge, 2000), 115).

Despite these well-founded communitarian concerns, however, I believe that the 'plurality *versus* universality' dilemma which contemporary liberals face needs to be taken seriously. Pluralism of philosophical, religious, and moral beliefs is a fact of life nowadays, yet we need some moral common ground on the basis of which to build our political institutions. And if the way in which contemporary liberals try to reconcile plurality and universality is not good enough, we have to seek other alternatives. Here I offer a solution of this problem based on T. H. Green's philosophy. As the difficulty (the two-tier moral system) we face is based on a confusing interpretation of morality, what we can look for and find in Green is a better understanding of moral action. On the basis of Green's moral philosophy, I argue that moral behaviour has two components: the determination to do the right thing and the knowledge of the right thing to do. As I mentioned in the introduction, I call the first component 'volitional', and the second one 'epistemological'. My claim is that universality resides with the volitional component of moral behaviour, while plurality resides with the epistemological one. Rawls and Nagel undervalue the volitional component, and focus their moral philosophy almost entirely on the epistemological aspect of morality. For Green, the volitional aspect is the fundamental one, and this protects him from the theoretical crises caused by the existence of conflicting visions of the moral good. Faced with such crisis, Rawls and Nagel are pushed to redefine morality and seek a meta-moral level, while Green is in a position to offer philosophical guidance.

Both parties to this comparison attempt to find a universal dimension where moral conflicts could be resolved. Both parties pursue a meta-level: a level where plurality no longer exists. The difference is that while Rawls's and Nagel's path towards this meta-level is psychologically and practically untenable, Green's path is psychologically adequate and practically sound.

III. Bringing Two Different Traditions Together: Compatibility of Themes and Contexts

There is an overlap as well as a difference between the problems that Green and his contemporary counterparts face. Rawls and Nagel address the fact of pluralism: the fact that people who hold incompatible comprehensive doctrines of the good have to live together and share common institutions. The issue is whether we can reconcile conflicting understandings of how to lead a good life. Green discusses a problem similar in some ways: how can a philosopher help us deal with our moral 'perplexities'?[2] A good example is Antigone's moral dilemma as to whether to obey the law of the state or the dictates of her religion.[3] Again, as with Rawls and Nagel, we have conflicting moral theories of the good.

The difference is that for Green the subject of the moral conflict is a person, while for Rawls and Nagel it is a community. Green aims to give philosophical advice to a person who has to choose between two doctrines, while his contemporary counterparts take on themselves the task of reconciling the conflicting doctrines—that is, the groups of people who 'profess' these doctrines. They aim to give advice to governments on how to reach decisions, to legislators on how to make the law, to philosophers on how to adjudicate between conflicting claims to the truth. Their focus is not so much on how an individual can cope with the fact that his community is in conflict with another one, but on the theoretical possibility of finding the right solution. This will partly explain why Rawls and Nagel are less concerned with the volitional aspect of moral action. Traditionally, the moral will is associated with an individual, not with a group of people.[4] I will return to this issue in section VIII. At this stage, I would like to make two points. First, that although there are some differences in the themes they discuss, the overlap is sufficient for the purposes of a useful comparison. The question 'How do we deal with conflicting ideas about what our duties are?' is addressed by both parties to this comparison. Second, the different solutions which the two parties offer are partly explained by their different focus on the problem. My claim here is that Green's approach to the issue is to be recommended. The fact that Green is concerned with the person who experiences moral difficulties, while Rawls and Nagel take a more external philosophical perspective of finding the right answer, puts Green in a better position to assess what is at stake during a moral crisis.

The difference of historical contexts also has to be addressed. An obvious objection to a comparison between end of twentieth-century and end of nineteenth-century thinkers on the issue of value pluralism is that the latter did not have to face the fact of pluralism. The phenomenon of close coexistence of communities from different cultural backgrounds was not familiar to Green. What Green had to deal with, however, was the moral crisis of a generation that needed to find secular justification for moral norms that had until now rested on religious narratives. Melvin Richter argues that the reason for Green's

---

[2] *PE* §§313; 314; 321.   [3] Ibid. §321.

[4] It could be argued that a group of people can have a moral will, but one has to make a case for it.

great influence in late nineteenth-century Oxford was precisely his ability to resolve the crisis of the religious consciousness.[5] Richter claimed that the vitality of Green's philosophy can be understood if we appreciate the fact that Green lived in times of cultural change. So Green was addressing pluralism not in the sense of there being different communities, holding different moral values and having to live together, but in the sense of one community having to survive the move from one set of moral values to another. It can be argued that the task of the Victorian intellectual who had to reinvent his identity was harder than that of the late twentieth-century liberal who has to understand and accept ideological difference. It is not easy to be impartial towards other people's moral beliefs, but it is even harder to conceive how you can retain long-term impartiality towards your own moral commitments. In either case we can benefit from moral philosophers' practical guidance. Both parties offer us such.

IV. The Practical Value of the Distinction between Volitional and Epistemological Aspects of Moral Action

The distinction between the volitional and epistemological aspects of moral action is rather straightforward: the first is to do with moral will, the second with moral knowledge. Here I want to explain why such a distinction is useful for the analysis of moral action. In order to do so, I will draw a comparison between this distinction and another, more familiar one: that between the formal and the substantive definitions of moral action. The argument is that there is a link between the formal and the volitional aspects of moral behaviour, on the one hand, and between the substantive and the epistemological aspects, on the other. My purpose is to demonstrate that the universal elements of moral action reside predominantly on its volitional side.

Green follows Kant in giving a formal account of moral action. While for Kant it is 'the will to conform to a universal law for its own sake or because it is conceived as a universal law', Green claims that people's moral conduct consists 'in their imposition on themselves of rules requiring something to be done irrespectively of any inclination to do it'.[6] A formal definition describes the conditions, not the content of the moral action. Its formal nature allows it to

---

[5] Melvin Richter, *The Politics of Conscience: T. H. Green and his Age* (London: Weidenfeld & Nicolson, 1964).

[6] Green, *PE* §193.

be universal. Because it applies to moral conduct in general, it is not associated with any specific object. What Kant's and Green's definitions imply is that the most general feature of moral action is the way in which a person is engaged in it. It is not so important what we do, but how we do it. Green argues that the moral good is to be found in the 'good will'.[7] The good will, according to Green, is one's preparedness to pursue an object in a self-disinterested manner. The good will is about one's desire to do a good thing and one's preparedness to pay some personal cost for doing so. We are moral agents because we have an ability to pursue an ideal.[8]

As will be pointed out in the next paragraph, the formal account of morality is not the only one: Green needs a second, substantive account. My argument is that the formal account of moral action defines one side of it—the volitional side. The volitional element is about the actual engagement with moral action. It is about preparedness, commitment, and exercise of will. Rawls refers to the volitional aspect of morality when he speaks about strains of commitment: the costs that some will have to pay when they obey the principles of justice.[9] However, this is not central to his discussion. As opposed to being a key part of the discourse about what it means for a person to act justly, the strains of commitments are seen as something undesirable but of which we should be aware. To add extra emphasis on this point, I would say that the volitional aspect of morality is not represented in Rawls's vision of the formal structure of moral action.

In addition to his formal account, Green gives a substantive account of moral action. He comments that Kant's purely formal account of morality is a shortcoming of his theory. Green points out that when we try to apply such a purely formal definition to practice, we can encounter two problems: 'either a dead conformity to the code of customary morality, anywhere and at any time established, without effort to reform or expand it, or else unlimited license in departing from it at the prompting of any impulse which the individual may be pleased to consider a higher law'.[10] Green's determination to give a specific description of the moral ideal is also partly a response to the utilitarian challenge. Utilitarians answer a question which a formal theory of Kantian type does not: towards what is the good will directed? While Green does not agree with the utilitarians that the answer to this question is 'pleasure', he none the less thinks that a moral philosopher should be

---

[7] Green, PE §194.

[8] For a more detailed account of the role of the moral ideal in Green's moral philosophy, see John Skorupski, Ch. 3 above.

[9] John Rawls, A Theory of Justice (Oxford: Oxford University Press, 1999), 153–4.

[10] Green, PE §198.

able to give an answer. For Green, the object of moral behaviour is human perfection. And the only way to achieve human perfection is to create a society where everybody has chances to develop their capacities. The 'true good', which is the same as the 'moral good', can be found in activities that make the life of everyone together better. In a way, this definition is not substantive enough, because we can still ask what these activities are. Green is committed to further specifications of the moral ideal, and his political philosophy supplies some.[11]

Different moral philosophers give different substantive definitions of moral behaviour: it is exactly in the field of specifying what the moral good is, that the most serious contentions between different schools of thought reside. A lot of philosophical effort is dedicated to proving that 'this kind of good' is more important than 'that kind of good'. I argue that the substantive account of morality defines the epistemological aspect of moral action. I call it 'epistemological' because it involves serious philosophical arguments about the ultimate good. Rawls defines the ultimate good as 'justice', and specifies what the principles of justice are.

One could object to the parallel I draw between the formal/substantive accounts distinction, on the one hand, and the volitional/epistemological aspects distinction, on the other hand. It can be argued that such a formal/substantive distinction can operate within the epistemological framework itself. Within the scope of moral knowledge we can have formal and substantive approaches. There are more objective, or universalizable, ways of gaining moral knowledge, and there are more subjective, context-dependent ways, of making moral claims. For example, the Kantian categorical imperative can be seen as a procedure for making a universal moral statement. It can be argued that there are formal or universal elements within the scope of moral epistemology. Not all moral knowledge is of equal status. Rawls argues that moral claims about the good are contingent, while moral claims about the principles of justice have universal character.[12]

This observation makes my position—that the volitional aspect of morality stands for what is universal in it, while the epistemological aspect is necessarily contentious—more difficult to sustain. Allegedly, we can seek universality within moral epistemology alone. I would make two points here. First, what this leads us to see is that an absolute distinction between the volitional and the epistemological aspects of moral action is not possible. When we

---

[11] See T. H. Green, 'Lecture on "Liberal Legislation and Freedom of Contract" ', in *LPPO* §§194–212.

[12] This kind of argument implies, however, that the whole of morality is an epistemological project; that the singular purpose of ethics is to answer the question about what is the right thing to do.

try to find the formal principles of moral action, we are likely to make claims that have both volitional and epistemological implications. The formal conditions of moral action reflect both a state of will and a framework of reasoning that allows us to make non-contingent judgements. As we shall see in sections VI and VII, Green believes that the availability of a good will is a necessary pre-condition of the pursuit of right moral answers. In other words, a good will is an integral part of an epistemological procedure for objective reasoning. But the fact that an absolute distinction between the volitional and epistemological aspects of morality is not possible, is not a surprising find. A distinction can remain useful even when its elements are interconnected.

My second point is that here are different paths for pursuing universality. If we agree on the fact that most moral theories look for a way to make universal moral claims, we could observe that Rawls and Nagel recommend a procedure for impartial reasoning, while Green recommends the adoption of good will. The argument here boils down to the question of how we interpret the formal aspect of moral action. I would argue that, even if we agree with Rawls and Nagel that what we need to do in order to fight moral contingency is to adopt a framework of impartial reasoning, such a recommendation depends more on our volitional than on our epistemological capacities.

The formal/substantive distinction is not the definitive way of demonstrating the difference between the volitional and epistemological aspects of moral action: it is employed here as an aid. Amongst the two aspects, the volitional one is the more formalizable one.

The emphasis on the priority of the volitional over the epistemological aspect of morality should be made with a caution.[13] The observation that moral knowledge is likely to be contingent should not have a damning effect on the importance of moral knowledge. It should not detract from the weight of each specific epistemological solution. As all problems are specific, specific solutions are appropriate. The contingency is not always, but only sometimes, a problem. The relevance of this point will become clearer during the discussion of Green's solution to moral conflict in section VII as well as the discussion of the later Rawls's full renunciation of comprehensive moral doctrines in the following section.

---

[13] I made this point to address a concern raised by Andrew Vincent. He pointed my attention to the fact that the importance of the volitional aspect could be overemphasized. Unqualified priority of the volitional over the epistemological aspect could lead to the claim that epistemology is simply a matter of choice or volition by the agent, prior to any tradition or institution. Volition then becomes the key to understanding morality, or, to put it in Nietzsche's terms, morality becomes a will to power.

V. A Pitfall in Contemporary Liberal Moral Theory

Rawls's purpose in *A Theory of Justice* is to explain and defend his two principles of justice. The reason we need these principles of justice, in the first place, is that we hold different perceptions of the good. The principles of justice are needed to resolve the problems that may arise from the discrepancies in our understandings about what is good. Each of us should be allowed the freedom to pursue her or his rational life plan—the only constraints placed on us are those of the principles of justice. For Rawls, the right has priority over the good. The right is represented by the principles of justice, and the good is represented by our visions of what is a worthy life plan. By giving priority of the right over the good, Rawls resolves the conflict that may occur at the level of the good. Let me briefly review what this would look like if it were recast in moral terminology.

What Rawls calls 'the good' encompasses our individual 'moral, religious or philosophical interests'.[14] Such interests are related to the 'moral and religious obligations' which we share with other members in our community; these interests constitute a moral bond with those others.[15] So what we hold as good is not morally neutral—it is related to those 'moral and religious obligations' which we have towards the people we live with. These are what constitute our primary, communal moral engagements.

However, the principles of justice represent a different, a higher, set of moral obligations. Rawls points out that 'from the standpoint of justice as fairness, these obligations'—the obligations based on our moral, religious, or philosophical interests—'are self-imposed; they are not bonds laid down by the conception of justice'. The bonds of justice are above the moral bonds of our doctrines of the good. I believe that this introduction of a second layer of morality is problematic.

The problem, as I mentioned earlier, is that if we assert morality at a second, higher level, we implicitly undermine what remains as a first, lower-level morality. This consideration expresses the standard communitarian concern about the impossibility of setting aside our basic, community-based, moral beliefs. Undermining such beliefs is dangerous, because it may undermine the commitment to moral action in general. Speaking of a two-tier morality is a signal that we are not understanding or explaining morality as well as we should.

I see a connection between the introduction of a two-tier moral system and limiting morality as a whole to the sphere of moral epistemology, which is

---

[14] Rawls, *A Theory of Justice*, 180.   [15] Ibid. 180–1.

seeing morality only as the knowledge of the right thing to do. The reason why an epistemological vision of morality leads to a two-tier moral system is the following. If moral action is seen exclusively as the pursuit of moral knowledge, then as soon as we have an epistemological crisis, we have a crisis of morality altogether. This in turn leads to a definition of a new morality that needs to be different from all our existing moral practices. This is very clearly demonstrated by the later Rawls, whom I shall discuss at the end of this section. For the time being, I will make some additional observations on the epistemological nature of Rawls's and Nagel's moral theories.

The principles of justice are meant to give us guidelines about what to do when our understandings of the good come into conflict. And although they offer a procedure rather than ready answers, the procedure they offer sets out the conditions of objective thinking. It is an epistemological procedure. This exclusive identification of morality with the issue of finding the right thing to do is very well exemplified by the moral philosophy of Thomas Nagel. He supports Rawls's project in principle, and takes it even further in this epistemological direction.

Nagel distinguishes between the moral issues of personal ethics and those of political theory.[16] While in personal ethics we deal with a clash of personal interests, in political theory we are faced with a conflict between different moral conceptions. The way to resolve clashes of personal interests is to adopt a standpoint of impartiality. Political disagreements, however, involve not only conflicts of personal interest but also disagreements between different moral values. Therefore Nagel raises the question: 'Is there a higher-order impartiality that can permit us to come to some understanding about how such disagreements should be settled?' He answers positively, as he believes that 'liberalism depends on the acceptance of a higher order impartiality'.[17] So the impartiality needed to resolve the conflict between a personal commitment and the public interest is different from the impartiality needed to resolve the conflict between different moral values.

The solution, according to Nagel, can be found in one's ability to take an objective standpoint towards one's own beliefs and examine them in an impartial manner. Reaching agreement depends on one's capacity to see that one's moral beliefs may not be true. Nagel recommends not scepticism, but 'epistemological restraint' towards our beliefs. We should make 'the distinction between what is needed to justify belief and what is needed to justify employment of political power'.[18] He infers that what is needed to justify political power is

---

[16] Thomas Nagel, 'Moral Conflict and Political Legitimacy', *Philosophy and Public Affairs*, 16:3 (1987), 215–40, at 215.

[17] Ibid. 216.   [18] Ibid. 229.

more than what is needed to justify belief; therefore we have to adopt 'a higher standard of objectivity'.[19] Two points need to be made here. First, in a similar way to Rawls, who introduces a second-level morality, Nagel discusses a second degree of 'objectivity', and this could create more confusion than clarity. Second, for Nagel, the possibility of finding grounds for 'liberal legitimacy' depends on people's ability to think objectively and thus see the right outcome.

The identification of morality with the issue of finding out the right thing to do—that is, the perception of morality as a purely epistemological project—is most explicit in the later Rawls of *Political Liberalism*. What is interesting here is that Rawls makes this identification in the first place, but then rebels against it. He argues that we should abandon the pursuit of the truth if we are genuinely concerned about resolving moral conflicts. So he goes from one extreme to the other: from seeing morality as an epistemological project, he moves to rejecting the epistemological concern with the truth altogether. He sees that there is something disturbing about the fact of linking moral action in an exclusive manner with the pursuit of right answers, but instead of questioning the link between these two, he simply condemns the second. What he does is leap from one error to another. Let me briefly present his line of reasoning.

In *Political Liberalism* Rawls engages more directly with the issue of pluralism. The issue is how, in view of our diversity, we can find a shared basis for justifying political obligation. Our differences are not easy to resolve, because our ideas of the good are part of comprehensive metaphysical moral doctrines. We are unlikely to reach philosophical agreement, so when it comes to deciding what principles should govern the basic political institutions, we should leave our comprehensive moral doctrines aside and find a political conception of justice. The solution is very similar to the one offered in *A Theory of Justice*—we should prioritize the right over the good—but with some new emphases. Rawls argues that our concept of the good is part of a comprehensive metaphysical doctrine. The reason why comprehensive metaphysical doctrines cannot provide the needed universal dimension for grounding political obligation is that there is no way to demonstrate that one metaphysical doctrine is truer than another. 'Philosophy as the search for truth about an independent metaphysical and moral order cannot, I believe, provide a workable and shared basis for a political conception of justice in a democratic society.'[20] Metaphysical doctrines encompass all aspects of our life, and we are not likely to change our views wholesale even if this is necessary for the purpose of resolving a conflict. The moral wisdom of one metaphysical doctrine is of

---

[19] Ibid.

[20] John Rawls, 'Justice as Fairness: Political not Metaphysical', *Philosophy and Public Affairs*, 14:3 (1985), 230.

no use to another; therefore, Rawls suggests, we should leave metaphysics aside and seek moral solutions on a political level. What this shows us is that Rawls sees people's conceptions of the good as tied into epistemological systems. And although Rawls claims that he wants to avoid epistemological problems, and to find practical solutions based on agreement and shared intuitions, he implicitly associates moral beliefs with the epistemological issue of truth. So even though Rawls wants to go beyond the realm of the epistemological, he does this only after having confined traditional morality to the sphere of moral knowledge.

The later Rawls leads us again to a two-tier morality, and this time the reason is explicitly epistemological. Because the epistemological issue of truth cannot ever be resolved, and because our moral practices are attached to comprehensive metaphysical doctrines, we have to abandon our moral practices altogether. Rawls sees the limits of identifying morality with the pursuit of truth, but instead of widening his understanding of morality, he recommends a new morality altogether.

So the later Rawls presents us with an additional problem: the problem of condemning the moral value of the epistemological concern with truth. Raz explains why Rawls's project is not feasible. It is not possible for Rawls to dissociate his political conception of justice from the issue of truth. The idea is that even if Rawls recommends his political conception of justice as one that brings stability and unity, and not metaphysical unanimity, he still recommends it as the right solution of a particular problem. And if something is right, it is also true.[21] One cannot reach an agreement and act according to it if one does not believe that it is relevant and appropriate and, in this sense, true. Indeed, if we consent to a certain practice without being persuaded of its good qualities—without believing that it is the true solution of a specific problem—we are likely to be less committed to it. As the following two sections will reveal, Green ascribes high significance to the knowledge of the right thing to do. Although he thinks that this knowledge is not as important as a good will, he views it as an indispensable part of moral action.

---

[21] Raz's argument goes as follows: 'My argument is simple. A theory of justice can deserve that name simply because it deals with these matters, that is, matters that a true theory of justice deals with. In this sense there are many theories of justice, and they are all acceptable to the same degree as theories of justice. To recommend one as a theory of justice for our societies is to recommend it as a just theory of justice, that is, as a true, or reasonable, or valid theory of justice. If it is argued that what makes it *the* theory of justice for us is that it is built on an overlapping consensus and therefore secures stability and unity, then consensus-based stability and unity are the values that a theory of justice, for our society, is assumed to depend on. Their achievement—that is, the fact that endorsing the theory leads to their achievement—makes the theory true, sound, valid, and so forth. This at least is what such a theory is committed to. There can be no justice without truth' (Joseph Raz, 'Facing Diversity: The Case for Epistemic Abstinence', *Philosophy and Public Affairs*, 19:1 (1990), 6–46, at p. 15).

VI. T. H. Green on the Two Aspects of Moral Action

Dealing either with the fact of pluralism or with moral conflict implies two things. As a political philosopher, one should be able, on the one side, to explain the reasons for difference and, on the other side, to identify a universal perspective from which this difference can be resolved.[22] While Rawls and Nagel discuss two levels of commitment, one that allows plurality and one that does not, T. H. Green discusses two aspects of morality, one that stays the same in all moral actions and one that can vary according to personal and historical circumstances.

It is as late as Book IV of the *Prolegomena to Ethics* that Green introduces a very clear distinction between the two aspects of moral action: moral will and moral knowledge. In Book III he has already given both a formal and a substantive account of moral action. As discussed in section IV, there exists some overlap between, yet not a full coinciding of, the distinction between the formal and substantive account of moral action, on the one hand, and the distinction between the volitional and epistemological aspects of morality, on the other hand. The point I advanced there was that the formal account of morality—that is, the account that lays out the conditions of moral action—refers to factors the nature of which can be defined better as volitional than epistemological.

So it is not until Book IV that Green discusses the distinction between moral will and moral knowledge explicitly. In chapters 1 and 2 of Book IV he introduces two different but related distinctions. In chapter 1 he discusses the motives of a moral action, on the one hand, and the results of a moral action, on the other. In chapter 2 he addresses the difference between our 'conscience', on the one hand, and the rules and authorities we believe we have to obey, on the other. The first distinction is meant to prepare the way for the second one. In chapter 1 Green wants to answer the question about how we can be sure that we are doing the right thing. How do we test that we have acted in a moral way? To answer this question, Green needs the distinction between motives and results, because 'the spring of moral action' is located in the first, not the second. The question that chapter 2 addresses is slightly more difficult: if we face a moral dilemma, how do we find out the right course of action. Green's distinction from chapter 1 will prompt the answer to this question. In chapter 2, Green argues that the cause of a moral crisis is the clash

---

[22] There are political philosophers who would deny the possibility of such a universal perspective. Most, however, will attempt to find such a perspective in order to resolve the cases where the fact of pluralism makes it impossible for us to reach an agreement on principles of political obligation.

between external authorities, and the way to resolve the crisis is to look back at ourselves and examine the reasons we wanted to follow these authorities in the first place. There may be a question mark over the right course of action, but there is never a question mark over the correct moral motivation. A good moral philosopher is in a position to explain the link between our desire to pursue the good and the specific authorities we choose to obey in the pursuit of this good. By pointing out the difference between the two elements of moral action, as well as how they are linked, a philosopher can offer guidance to those who face a moral dilemma. I will now review the two elements of morality as discussed in chapter 1, and in the next section I will talk about Green's solution to moral conflict as offered in chapter 2.

At the opening of chapter 1, Green points out that the question 'What ought to be done?' can be answered in two senses. The first sense answers only the question 'What ought an action to be as determined in its nature by its *effects*?' The second sense answers the question 'What ought the action to be with reference to *the state of mind and character which it represents*?'[23] Green points out that while utilitarians give greater weight to the effects of an action, according to his theory, morality is better understood if we focus on 'the character of the agent', on 'the disposition we ought to cultivate', on 'the state of will' one has at the time of action.[24]

Green acknowledges that often we are not in a position to know the 'state of mind' of a moral agent, and then we can only judge her actions by their result. However, if, for example, two different actions happen to produce the same result, but they were performed by people with two different characters, the action of the person with the more virtuous character has a higher moral value.[25] For Green, the moral value of an action stems from one's state of will, from one's commitment to do what is right: 'it will only be in relation to a state of will, either as expressing [the good] or as tending to promote it, or as doing both, that an action can have moral value at all'.[26]

What is the practical value of this observation? Green has already pointed out that this understanding of moral action is of no use when we judge the actions of others or of people in the past. Because we are not in a position to know their state of mind and will, we should not be tempted to guess it. We can only base our judgements of their actions on the results these actions produce. Green's philosophical claim, that the state of will plays a primary role in defining the moral nature of action, can offer some practical guidance in two cases: first, in the case when we judge our own past actions,

---

[23] Green, PE §291; emphasis added.   [24] Ibid. §§292–3.
[25] Ibid. §294.   [26] Ibid. §293.

and second, in the case when we have to take a decision with respect to something we are about to do now.[27] Green's theory can help us answer the question about what we need to do in order to be sure that we are doing the right thing.

With respect to our own actions, we are in a position to examine both their results and the state of mind and will with which we undertook them. 'Having distinguished the question, What ought to be done?—a question to be answered in detail by examination of the probable effects of contemplated action—from the question, What should I be?—a question of motives and character—we pointed out that the latter question might properly be raised by a man with reference to his own actions, past or prospective.'[28] In other words, with respect to my own moral actions, I have a privileged position to make a judgement: I can analyse my motives. For example, I can ask myself whether I support a particular policy because it furthers the well-being of all concerned or because it benefits me. Was one's motive 'a pure desire to do good and teach the truth, or was [one] affected by any desire to lead a comfortable life, combining a maximum of reputation for usefulness with a minimum of wear and tear'?[29] A person is in a position to examine her motivation, and she also has some control over deciding on what kinds of motives to act. Therefore, Green's advice is that when we question our moral behaviour, we should be primarily engaged with making sure that we have adopted the right reasons for action.

Examining the likely results of what we do is also important, as we would like to avoid doing something bad with good intentions. It is imperative that we think about what we can achieve, and how this achievement will be beneficial to everybody concerned. Yet there are two difficulties to which Green points our attention. First, we do not have full control over the outcomes of our actions. We are not in a position to know with certainty whether the course of action we have chosen to follow will lead to the best possible result. Second, judgements on the effects of our actions depend on 'correct information or inference as to matters of facts, or on a correct analysis of circumstances'.[30] So we may lack either information or sharp thinking. However, even if we do not possess the 'skill in analysis' needed for the search of the best possible outcome in what we do, we still have full capacity to be moral agents. Our ability for moral behaviour is more crucially related to our preparedness to do the right thing than to our knowledge about what the right thing is. 'It is a sufficient spring for the endeavour after a higher goodness that I should be ashamed of

---

[27] Ibid. §296. [28] Ibid. §304.
[29] Ibid. §305. [30] Ibid.

my selfishness, indolence, or impatience, without being ashamed also of my ignorance and want of foresight.'[31]

To sum up Green's ideas so far, Green believes that when we analyse our moral behaviour, we are faced with two questions: one about the nature of our motives and one about our knowledge of the right thing to do. These questions account for the two elements in moral behaviour: the desire to pursue the good and the knowledge of the good. Two different sets of qualities are tested, depending on which element of moral behaviour we analyse. When the motivation for moral action is at stake, the qualities we need to display are commitment to do something good, strength of will, awareness of our own selfishness, and preparedness to overcome it. When the knowledge about the right thing is at stake, the qualities we need are shrewdness of mind and wealth of information. Green argues that both elements of moral action are important. Indeed, when we lack information about someone's motives, we can judge her behaviour only by its results. None the less, one's motivation, one's state of will, is the primary element, for at least two reasons. First we have more control over our state of will than over our sharpness of mind, and second, a good will itself keeps us on the look-out for the right answers. Even if we fail to choose the best course of action, when we carry a good will (the desire to pursue the good), we will keep on trying to find it, and will be prepared to learn from mistakes. A good will can compensate for lack of skill in reasoning, but not vice versa.[32]

VII.   Green's Solution of Moral Conflict

For Green, a moral conflict is caused when a person is faced with a difficult choice between incompatible duties or between contradictory commands of different institutions. A typical example is the dilemma one confronts when one has to decide whether to obey the rule of the Church or the rule of the State. Green's strategy for resolving the conflict is based on an analysis of the link between a person's ability and desire to pursue a moral ideal, on the one hand, and the authorities one is prepared to obey in doing what he believes is his duty, on the other hand. However, before Green imparts his philosophical wisdom in more detail, he draws our attention to two things: the necessity

---

[31] Green, PE §306.

[32] There is a third reason why the state of the will is more important than the actual good we pursue. For Green the disposition to do good represents in itself the object of good behaviour. The aim of moral action is to increase moral action. It takes good character in order to act in a moral way, but the development of good character is at the same time the purpose of moral action. See PE §293.

to ascertain that we are facing a genuine moral dilemma and the need to understand that his philosophical advice should be applied only in exceptional circumstances. Indeed, these two things are so important for Green, that they can be seen as an integral part of his overall strategy of how to resolve moral conflict.

When we are in two minds as to whether to follow this duty or that duty, the first thing we should do is think of the reason why we have come to this situation. Could it be that we are seeking an excuse to avoid a particular undesirable duty? A situation of moral uncertainty signals a possibility that we may be looking for an escape route from moral duty. If this is the case, we are faced not with a moral conflict but with a choice between avoiding or not avoiding a moral duty. Here, the solution should always be in favour of the moral duty. Although practically difficult (because we have to buckle down and do our duty), this is a theoretically easy case to resolve. The philosophical difficulty is in resolving authentic moral conflicts, which occur when there is no doubt that the person has moral motivation, but is still unsure about the right course of action. Such cases Green calls 'perplexities *of conscience*'. He distinguished real, or genuine, perplexities[33] from 'those self-sophistications, born of the pleasure-seeking impulse'.[34]

We have to distinguish between cases where we have genuine moral intentions but no clear answers ('perplexities of conscience') and cases where the difficulty is caused by failure to adopt a moral motivation. This is because the philosophical advice that can help us in the first case can serve as an excuse for avoiding moral action in the second case. The philosophical advice that Green is prepared to give is only in safe hands when it is given to a person already committed to acting morally. To a person unsure of their moral commitment such advice can serve as an excuse to disregard any moral authorities. 'It is a complaint as old as the time of Plato that, in learning to seek for the rationale of the rules which they are trained to obey ... men come to find excuses for disregarding them.'[35] So our first task in case of moral conflict is to test whether we have a genuine moral dilemma—that is, whether we are choosing between options either of which will engage our moral commitment to do the right thing. Green believes that most of the cases will be resolved at this stage: we will find out that we are not dealing with a real moral conflict; therefore we will not need to employ the philosophical expertise which he is so cautious in revealing.

---

[33] Green calls them bona fide perplexities.
[34] Green, *PE* §321.   [35] Ibid. §328.

If this is not the case, however, if we are choosing between two options both of which will engage our will to do the good, then there is still something we can do. We need to become aware that the choice we have to make is not between two different kinds of morality, but between two different interpretations about what is the right thing to do. We should see that the crisis we are experiencing is not a crisis of morality as a whole, but a crisis of the epistemological aspect of our moral action.

Then the solution suggests itself. If the epistemological aspect of morality is in crisis, we can seek help from the other, the volitional aspect of morality. And this is the crucial observation here: even though we have conflicting moral visions about what is right, there is no conflict about the nature of our disposition. So although I am not sure which is the right course of action, there is one certain thing: that I have committed myself to acting morally. And this is what will lead me through the crisis.

We still need to know, however, what to do in order to find out which of the conflicting solutions is right. Here Green makes a very cautious revelation. He says that moral imperatives derive their authority not from the institution that issues them but from the moral agents, themselves. As moral agents, we have the authority to revise moral norms. We are the bearers of the legitimacy of any specific moral imperatives. Public authorities are right only to the extent to which they give expression to people's pursuit of better life and to people's desire to do what it takes to make life better.

The reason why we face difficult moral choices, Green argues, is that we tend to perceive the authorities we obey as 'external' to us. We trust that our parents, the Church, or the State issue us with the right commands, and when these commands conflict, we do not see how we could be in a position to disregard one command in favour of another. Yet, Green points out, these authorities are only right to the extent that they promote the moral ideals which we have already adopted as moral agents. If we were not motivated to act morally—that is, to do our duties—these authorities could not function in the way they do. They could only exist on the basis of fear. Our voluntary moral action is the source of credibility of any social rule or institution. Our commitment to a moral ideal is primary to any specific interpretations of the moral ideal. And the demands that our parents, the Church, or the State place on us represent interpretations of how, practically, we can achieve our moral aspirations.

What all this means is that, as carriers of the moral energy that makes social institutions possible, we have the authority as well as the capacity to interpret for ourselves what is the right course of action. If necessary, we can question and revise certain commands. Green's philosophical analysis demonstrates that the legitimate purpose of any institution is the same as the purpose adopted by a moral agent: to make the life of everybody concerned better, to pursue a social good that is inclusive of an ever larger number of people. We can see that our duties are not imposed, but self-imposed:

It is the very essence of moral duty to be imposed by a man on himself. The moral duty to obey a positive law, whether a law of the State or of the Church, is imposed not by the author or enforcer of the positive law, but by that spirit ... which sets before him the ideal of a perfect life, and pronounces the obedience to the positive law to be necessary to its realisation.[36]

One of the messages we get from Green is that we should have the confidence to question authorities—a message with little novelty for us, who at the beginning of the twenty-first century do not need much assurance of our right to think about moral matters on our own. If we were to extract wisdom applicable to contemporary circumstances, it would be that we cannot hide behind the existing moral norms of our tradition. The argument that 'this is what my church tells me to do' cannot work. As a moral agent, I have the moral authority to make my own decisions. Authority to revise moral norms goes together with the responsibility to do so when necessary.

This revelation places Green very close to contemporary liberals, and not as close as he usually is to contemporary communitarians. It implies that, in the same way as Rawls and Nagel, he believed that it is possible for us to dissociate ourselves from our traditional moral beliefs and adopt new moral norms. Unlike them, however, he is very much aware of the dangers of such a process.

The reason why Green is so cautious about this revelation is that there is a danger of discrediting existing moral norms in general and not adopting new ones. Crucial to the success of this process is reaching some kind of decision about the right thing to do in the end. The lack of knowledge about the right thing to do can lead to 'moral anarchy',[37] scepticism, or 'paralysis of action',[38] each of which is undesirable. Because of such risks, a revision of moral norms should not happen on a daily basis. We should not exercise our authority to change moral norms too often. It is valuable to have a stable vision of what is good.

Green concludes that 'There is no such thing really as a conflict of duties. A man's duty under any particular set of circumstance is always one'.[39] I could offer two compatible interpretations of this claim. The first is along the lines that a man's duty is to follow his duty. What exactly the duty is can be found

---

[36] Green, PE §324.   [37] Ibid. §331.
[38] Ibid. §327.   [39] Ibid. §324.

in a number of ways: one can either follow the existing moral conventions or revise them in the spirit of one's moral ideal. The difficult choice is not between following this duty or that duty, but in choosing to take one's duties to heart. The other interpretation of this claim is that all moral conflicts should find a specific solution. Although in a moral conflict we are dealing only with an epistemological, and not with a volitional, crisis, the epistemological crisis needs to be resolved. There may not be a universal right answer, but there is a right answer for one's specific circumstances. Rawls's theory of justice can be commended on this account. It gives us a specific vision about what is the right thing to do (accept the two principles of justice), and this vision is adequate to the circumstances of late twentieth-century liberal democracies.

VIII. Back to Rawls and Nagel

Bringing Green's ideas into the contemporary liberal discussion of value pluralism and moral conflict can help us explain differently what makes moral doctrines incompatible, and what strategy we can adopt to resolve tensions. It can also explain why Rawls and Nagel undermine the volitional aspect of moral action.

When Rawls discusses incompatibility between moral, philosophical, or religious doctrines, or when Nagel discusses conflict between moral beliefs, the two liberals do not address the possibility of a 'fake' conflict. On Green's account, a conflict between different moral doctrines can only be genuine if the two conflicting sides carry honest moral intentions. A moral doctrine in itself is not a guarantor of moral intentions. Although it tends to express, and is a result of the pursuit of, such intentions, it can be employed by a person who has no moral concerns.

Incompatibility of moral doctrines does not imply incompatibility of moral wills. Green's argument is that the moral will is universal in nature, and as Rawls and Nagel do not address this issue, nothing in their theories suggests that this is not the case. So in cases of moral conflict we do not need to abandon our moral practices and seek a higher level of morality. If we follow Green's recommendations, we will examine whether or not the conflicting sides approach the matter with moral intentions. If they do not, the solution of the conflict will lie in adopting such motivation. If they already do, then all the pre-conditions for solution are already there. Having moral motivation means that one is prepared to act in the best interests of everybody concerned. If we are prepared to promote our good in unison with everyone else's, then we will be more open-minded to other people's ideas of the good.

There are two reasons why we should not abandon or leave aside our comprehensive moral doctrines. The first reason is that if we do so, our commitment to moral action in general will be undermined. If our routine moral experience is being undermined, our natural desire to do whatever is good will be weakened. The second reason is that if we do not have a clear idea about what we should do, we are likely to become moral nihilists and withdraw from moral action altogether. The actual knowledge of the right thing to do has its own motivating power. We cannot engage in moral action if we don't know what to do. That is why what we need is a revision, not abandonment, of moral doctrines.

The mistake which Rawls and Nagel made is to identify morality entirely with its epistemological aspect. What happens then is that if there is an epistemological problem, it throws the whole of moral practice out of kilter. One is advised to abandon one's moral commitments and engage with a different level of morality. Yet not all of morality needs to be revised in case of a moral crisis. What needs to be preserved through the process of resolving the crisis is one's desire to do what is good: this desire can make the revision of specific moral beliefs possible.

I now turn to the reasons why Rawls and Nagel undermine the volitional aspect of morality. As I mentioned in section III, there is some difference in the themes which Rawls and Nagel, on the one hand, and Green, on the other, address. While Green discusses how a person might deal with a choice between two conflicting duties, Rawls and Nagel focus on conflicts between moral doctrines—that is, between communities which hold different conceptions of the good. Green helps us answer the question 'What can I do to resolve moral conflict?', while the question Rawls and Nagel try to answer is 'What is the moral truth that all of us could accept?'

For the contemporary liberals, the urgent moral issues are 'once removed' from the individual. It is not the clash between the personal and the public interest, but the clash between different interpretations of the public interest, that is at stake. The individual is to some extent sheltered within his own group and comprehensive doctrine, as the conflict is at a 'higher level'. What happens is that, by moving towards a second level of morality, Rawls and Nagel drop out the first level of morality: the level that deals with personal conflicts. Let me recall that for Nagel, personal ethics differs from moral issues in political theory, because morality that resolves conflicts between moral beliefs is of a higher level than morality dealing with personal conflicts (see section V). So by moving to a higher moral level, Rawls and Nagel undermine the lower one—the one that deals with personal dilemmas.

Green's understanding of moral action can lead us towards the argument that the clash between personal interests as well as the clash between group interests call for the same kind of moral action as a way of resolving them. In either case one has to exercise power of will in restricting exclusively personal pursuits and choosing the course of action that is beneficial to everyone concerned. The volitional aspect of morality is always the same: in personal ethics or in political conflicts, it has the same formal structure of preparedness to do the right thing. It is true that finding out the right thing to do—that is, dealing with the epistemological aspect of morality—can be harder in the contexts of political theory than in the context of personal ethics. And for this reason Rawls and Nagel are right to call for a higher degree of objectivity, in that we are faced with a stronger intellectual challenge. My point is that the necessity for such an intellectual challenge should not overshadow the need for personal commitment to do what is right.

The rejection of moral pressures is very much in the spirit of late twentieth-century liberalism. According to it, nobody should be in a position to force anyone else to change her moral views, and by extension, it is not seen as a good thing to put pressure on others to do so. But Rawls's principles of justice can be implemented only at personal cost—there is a lot of moral pressure inherent in them. This has led Sandel to argue about the schizophrenic condition of the liberal citizen, lurching 'between detachment on the one hand' and 'entanglement on the other'—that is, between the promise of individual freedom, on the one hand, and the strict demands of justice, on the other.[40] Although bringing moral pressure back to the political theory landscape may not be popular with some liberals, the need to resolve moral conflict may justify it.

IX. Conclusion

The purpose of the comparison between contemporary liberal and Green's approaches to resolving moral conflict has been to enrich contemporary debates by bringing Green's ideas back to life. One of the conclusions reached as a result of this comparison is that moral conflict represents clashes between different interpretations of what is good, but poses no question as to one's commitment to moral action. Indeed, such commitment becomes even more pertinent in situations of moral crisis. Identifying what remains unchanged in

---

[40] Michael Sandel, 'The Procedural Republic and the Unencumbered Self', *Political Theory*, 12:1 (1984), 81–96, at 94.

moral conflict gives us the universal dimension from the standpoint of which we can resolve the difficulties caused by the fact of pluralism.

Another conclusion we have reached is that whatever the conflict—whether private or public interests are at stake—the same kind of moral action is being called for. Moral action has the same formal nature of choosing to do the right thing by being prepared to suffer some personal cost. I have argued in section IV that the volitional aspect of moral action is connected to its formal account, and that therefore it represents its universal dimension.

The fact that Rawls and Nagel focus on the epistemological aspect of morality has its explanation and justification. Nowadays we face the complicated task of bringing together different considered moral doctrines, each of which has many good reasons to fight for its autonomy. Our ability to understand and analyse different interpretations of the good is greatly needed. The challenges to our capacity to think have risen. In comparison with Victorian times, the epistemological aspect of morality has increased in importance. Yet, although the volitional aspect has lost in relative share, there is no reason why its importance should be seriously undermined.

So while Rawls and Nagel appeal to our capacity to think objectively, Green appeals to our preparedness for sacrifice. For Green, the knowledge of the right thing to do is inseparable from the agent's commitment to do the right thing: a crisis with the first can be resolved by resort to the second. By neglecting the volitional aspect of moral behaviour, Rawls and Nagel have lost a vital source of help with moral difficulties.

Index